HONG KONG ECLIPSE

G. B. ENDACOTT

Edited and with additional material by
ALAN BIRCH

1978

HONG KONG
OXFORD UNIVERSITY PRESS
OXFORD NEW YORK MELBOURNE
1978

Oxford University Press
OXFORD LONDON GLASGOW
NEW YORK TORONTO MELBOURNE WELLINGTON
IBADAN NAIROBI DAR ES SALAAM LUSAKA CAPE TOWN
KUALA LUMPUR SINGAPORE JAKARTA HONG KONG TOKYO
DELHI BOMBAY CALCUTTA MADRAS KARACHI

ISBN 0 19 580374 4

Printed by Hing Yip Printing Co., 44 Wong Chuk Hang Road, Hong Kong
Published by Oxford University Press, News Building, North Point, Hong Kong

CONTENTS

MAPS

APPENDIXES

MEMOIR OF
G. B. ENDACOTT, 1901–1971

BEER is a small fishing port in South Devon in the West of England. George Beer Endacott was born there on 28 February 1901, the son of a railway worker. Those who have heard George Endacott's reminiscences on the Radio Hong Kong programme 'Time to Remember' will recall the circumstances of his youth – not unique, but still worthy of notice – the background of extremely tight financial pressure on the family and the struggle of his own intelligence and ambition to escape from that cramping working-class existence. Nevertheless, despite Endacott's success, his West Country accent and the appreciation of the importance of money remained with him throughout his life.

A scholarship lad, he attended the Tavistock Grammar School where evidently he did well enough academically to win a further scholarship to the local university at Exeter. Again it may be necessary to remind some readers that this struggle to go to the university in the bleak days after World War I was one in which only the unusually able few secured success, as A. L. Rowse has so vividly described in his *A Cornishman at Oxford*. Incidentally, this link with Rowse of Oxford may be the reason why George let himself be known as a Cornishman. Certainly, in going to Oxford himself later on by dint of his own savings from his first teaching post at Poole Grammar School from 1926 to 1933, and in becoming a member of Balliol College of which he was always proud, G. B. Endacott set himself on the same path as A. L. Rowse. At Oxford, where he first read for the P.P.E. degree taken in 1935 and then the B. Litt., a research degree, his interest in economic and social history may well have been influenced by R. H. Tawney. The subject of his thesis was 'Enclosures in the County of Dorset in the 18th and 19th Centuries'. The Registrar of Hong Kong University remembers him as a mature student, balding and seemingly much older than Mr. Mellor's own generation, but typically wearing the longest college scarf he had seen, and somewhat dangerously riding a bicycle in the Broad.

When the Second World War came and shook Britain from its uneasy slumbers, Endacott was teaching in Shropshire, at Coalbrookdale on the Severn Gorge, the very birthplace of the Industrial Revolution – a fitting place of employment for an economic historian! There he taught history until 1942, when eventually he joined the Navy. There he found scope for his abilities as an interpreter attached to the French forces at Allied Headquarters in the Mediterranean theatre of war.

In 1946 Instructor-Lieutenant Endacott was demobbed. Should he resume his old teaching post in the industrial Midlands? The exotic lure of the Far East called, in the offer of an appointment as lecturer – the sole lecturer and member of staff – in the History Department of Hong Kong University. Hong Kong then, of course, was not the affluent, colourful place it has since become. In fact, the university, damaged during the occupation by the Japanese and desperately short of money, was only too representative of the struggle of the colony to lay new foundations in the period of reconstruction. George Endacott was to remain the only teacher of history in the university until 1952 when he was joined by Professor Brian Harrison from Raffles College, Singapore.

Although a busy teacher and Warden of May Hall, a post which he held until his retirement in 1962, as well as secretary to the University Appointments Board, George Endacott was also Hong Kong's historian. He wrote *The History of Hong Kong*, which he revised and brought up-to-date for the second edition, recently published. Based solidly on research in the Public Records Office, Hong Kong's local newspapers and some Chinese sources, it gives a detailed and informed view of the development of the colony from the time when Hong Kong, that unattractive rocky island, became almost accidentally British in 1841, as a result of the larger pre-occupation of the First Opium War in China, to the modern developments of the isolated, yet international industrial city-state of the post-revolutionary period from 1950 onwards. True, there are shortcomings – perhaps undue emphasis on the parts played by the Colonial Governors; sometimes a failure to explore the records as deeply as they deserve. But even if we put aside the historian's modest suggestion that this history was merely an introduction to the subject, we are still left with the interpretation which has largely informed the spirit of colonial government, of a humane concept, of an administration making the place physically a reasonable place of work and residence and, possibly more important, bringing the local Chinese population and their British rulers closer together in some sense of community. This approach (vision perhaps?) informs George Endacott's other authoritative studies of Hong Kong's history: *Government and the People* (Hong Kong University Press, 1964), *Fragrant Harbour* (written with A. Hinton) (1st edition, 1962; 2nd edition, Oxford University Press, 1968), 'Proposals for municipal government in early Hong Kong' (*Journal of Oriental Studies*, Vol. III, No. 1, June 1956), *The Diocese of Victoria Hong Kong; a hundred years of church history* (Kelly & Walsh, 1949) and particularly in the study of E. J. Eitel, Hong Kong's first major historian, who in his *Europe in China* (Noronha, Hong Kong, 1895) presented the colony's history in terms of a liberal civilizing mission in this Chinese outpost of empire (*Journal of Oriental Studies*, Vol. IV, Nos. 1–2, 1957–8). In these and other studies of the colony's governors the approach of the historian is unabashedly colonial and Endacott has been criticized for this so-called narrow point of view. However, this is a misunderstanding of the man and of the historian. First, George Endacott in his public and private life was not detached from the community around him – witness his active participation in the Prisoners' Aid Society in Hong Kong and in his membership of the Cathedral congregation and Masonic Lodge, and, on another level, his undiminished zeal to give W.E.A. lectures on the problems of Hong Kong. Then, as a historian, he was accurately reflecting the prevailing ethos of Englishmen like himself drawn to Hong Kong in the post-war years, seeing the colony as a place to accumulate wealth at a rate not possible in Britain. Yet there was a sense of responsibility to the inhabitants of Hong Kong as they, through events on the mainland, slowly acquired the feeling of belonging to their place of refuge and prosperity.

This transformation of Hong Kong has, of course, not taken place without some set-backs, notably the black period of defeat for the British in 1941 and the consequent years of occupation until 1945. George Endacott, in fact, stayed on in Hong Kong after his retirement. In 1968, by virtue of his experience and stature as the historian of Hong Kong, he was asked by the Hong Kong Government to write the history of the war and of the period of reconstruction. He died before his work could be published. There is no need here to describe the difficult process of giving birth to this last piece of historical research. All that is perhaps necessary is for the writer of this memoir to record that he was asked by the author to read the manuscript, then in an almost finished state, and, just before Endacott's death in Queen Mary Hospital in September 1971, to see it through the press. Since then there have been legal and other difficulties to delay publication. As a literary midwife, I have come to the realization that, despite the temptations to rewrite the book, which I have resisted, and to do further research, to which I have succumbed,[1] the book should appear as George Endacott conceived it. The subject, as I have found, is far from narrow; it covers many aspects of human experience and requires many skills to portray accurately the whole gamut of problems created by war. The author, as he writes in his preface, has written a book which stands alone, there being nothing comparable with it. If only for that reason, I feel justified in presenting this posthumous manuscript to the reading public.

Finally, a word of thanks should be added to G.B. Endacott's own acknowledgements to the people who helped with information and suggestions, and not least for their patience in awaiting the results of the historian's labours.

A.B.

[1] When the author conducted his research and wrote his earlier drafts of this book the supremely important source of archival material (viz., the U.K. Government's records for the war-time period) was not available to historians of the war. In the first three appendices, written by me, as well as in a number of footnotes, I have drawn upon these records.

I have also attempted, so far as the great limitation of not being able to research among Japanese records permits, to present some basic data about the campaigns and the administration during the occupation, from translated Japanese sources. See Appendixes 6, 7 and 8.

EDITOR'S PREFACE

For the demanding reader – and anyone who lived through that terrible era has a right to expect accuracy and objectivity of the historian – it ought to be explained that George Endacott intended this book for the general reader. Therefore he did not think it necessary to cite sources for his statements, so I have tried 'to steer a middle course' by giving some pointers to some of the sources. I recognize also that for a comprehensive account of this many-faceted history it would be necessary to cite literally thousands of fragments of evidence and testimony. For this reason I have tried to remedy the deficiency by including as comprehensive a local bibliography as possible, a far more extensive one than was Endacott's practice. Even so I am sure that it will be far from complete.

Finally, whilst the author most conscientiously sent out questionnaires and interviewed or obtained many personal statements from many survivors of those days, almost every day some new piece of evidence – some still possibly secret and sensitive, personally or politically – comes to light. It might seem ironical to some historians for such a small subject, *Hong Kong 1941–1945*, that the editor of this manuscript has come to the conclusion it is well nigh impossible to include and appraise every participant's story. In justification he would plead that war did mean (especially for Hong Kong) the disintegration of established society and therefore, for certain periods, almost every experience is unique. As a result there will be as many accounts and interpretations of these events as there are articulate survivors.

A.B.

AUTHOR'S PREFACE

THIS book, as its title implies, sets out to give an account of Hong Kong during the Second World War. While its central theme is the Japanese conquest and occupation, it also attempts to give a picture of the Colony on the eve of the catastrophe, including the effect of the administrative controls imposed on a free-enterprise society following the British entry into the war in Europe, as well as an account of the problems of rehabilitation consequent upon Japanese surrender. In fine, it is a history of Hong Kong covering the decade 1938–48. It attempts to give a straightforward narrative of events during these years for the general reader rather than for the history specialist, and footnotes have therefore been reduced to a minimum; but it is hoped that the numerous references in the text to the sources used will reassure the reader of the great amount of research that has been done to get at the facts. A bibliography is included.

There is no lack of published accounts of some aspect or other of this period, particularly of war or prison camp experiences and escapes and, while varying in value, they are important source material because they often appeared shortly after the incidents described, while they were still fresh in the mind. In addition, a great number of unpublished private records of experiences have been made available through the kind co-operation of those concerned. The various official war histories have of course been used. The Hong Kong Government official records have been fully consulted, including the proceedings of the Legislative Council, *Hong Kong Government Gazettes, Sessional Papers* and other official publications. It had been intended that this book should be sponsored by the Hong Kong Government and be, to that extent, an official history, but this was not to be.

Some 132 individuals have been contacted in the search for first-hand information on the events of this period, of whom some fifty-nine were interviewed, sixty-seven approached by letter and six volunteered statements in response to a public appeal in the Press. The number who refused to co-operate was small. Most gave statements or supplied material, and also agreed to be interviewed or to make further explanations by letter. All this has been an important source of information, and indeed, one of the reasons for undertaking this book at this time was to elicit the experiences of those who took part in these events, while they were still alive to relate them. But memory is notoriously unreliable, and while this source material is extremely valuable and indeed irreplaceable, much checking has clearly been necessary. English newspapers, including the *Hong Kong News* published by the Japanese from 1941 to 1945, have been consulted for the whole of the ten years. One weakness is the absence of references in the text to Chinese and Japanese sources, though the Chinese newspapers have on occasion been available in translation through the good offices of the Hong Kong Government.

Space would not permit the mention by name of all those who have helped with information. I wish to acknowledge with gratitude the Hong Kong Government's assistance in giving some financial assistance towards the cost of research. I am particularly grateful to Mr. Douglas Y. M. Cheung, the Librarian of the Colonial Secretariat Library, and his staff for their unvarying and unstinted co-operation over three and a half years. I am grateful to the Librarians of the Hong Kong University, the Hong Kong Supreme Court, the City Hall and of the Commonwealth Office Library in London for their assistance, as is the wont of Librarians. Finally my thanks are due to those who have read parts of the script and made valuable comments, and especially to Dr. Alan Birch of the University of Hong Kong History Department who undertook to read the whole manuscript to my great advantage.

Hong Kong G. B. ENDACOTT
1971

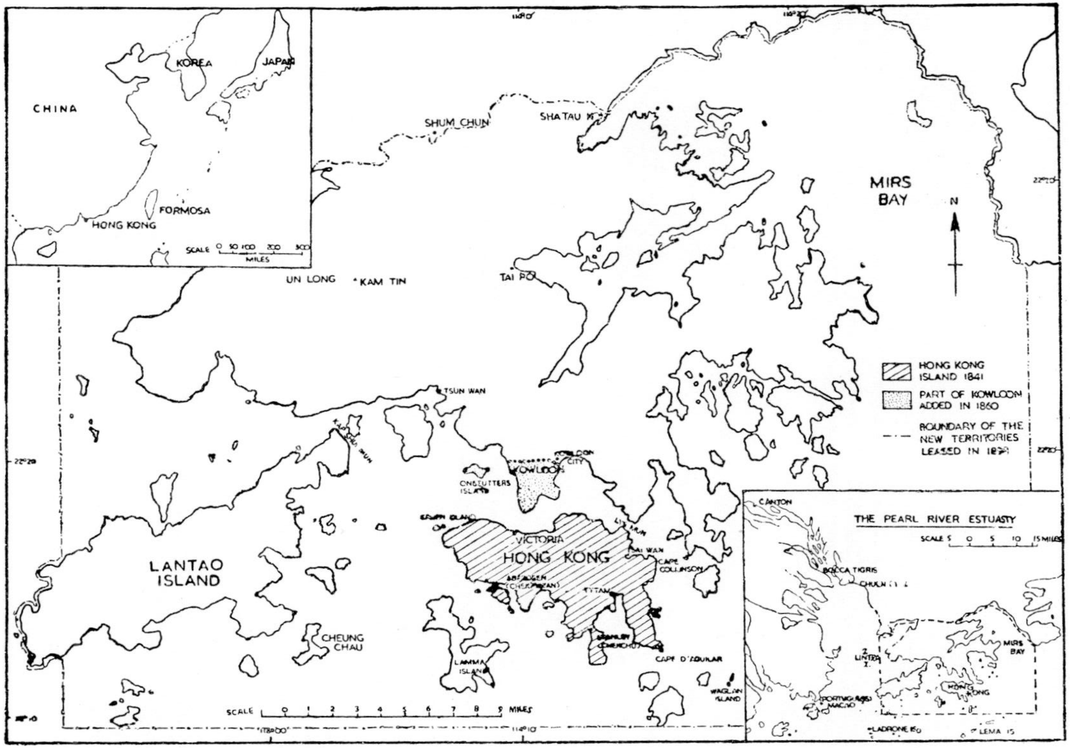

1 Map of Hong Kong and the New Territories.

PART ONE

PRE-WAR

I

THE SHADOW OF JAPAN

'The aim of the present war is the realization, first in the Far East, of His Majesty's august will and ideal that the peoples of the world should each be granted possession of their rightful homelands. To this end the countries of the Far East must plan a great coalition of East Asia . . . . Through the combined strength of such a coalition we shall liberate East Asia from white invasion and oppression.'

Tsuji, '*Why we must fight*'

THE Japanese struck Hong Kong without warning at 8.00 a.m. on the morning of 8 December 1941. Pearl Harbor, the Philippines and Malaya were simultaneously attacked in a four-pronged blitzkrieg against the Western Powers, aimed at realizing Japan's openly-avowed ambition to control East and South-East Asia. In the short space of seventeen days they forced the Governor of Hong Kong to capitulate, and imposed a military occupation which lasted effectively until 30 August 1945 when British naval units under Rear-Admiral C. H. J. Harcourt entered the harbour and re-established British authority, fifteen days after the Japanese national surrender. This catastrophic and humiliating episode in the Colony's history must be seen against a background of successive international crises which brought war to China in July 1937, to Europe in September 1939, and ultimately, in December 1941, virtually engulfed the world. It is the purpose of this chapter to give a brief résumé of this back-ground, both in Europe and the Far East, for these two theatres were closely related since it was Japan's obvious strategy to seize the opportunity to further her ambitions in the East when her rivals' hands were tied by conflict in the West.[1]

The Treaties of Versailles of 1919 narrowed Germany's

[1] *Foreign Relations of the United States*, Diplomatic Papers 1940, Vol. IV, The Far East, p. 347. Director of Naval Intelligence to Army and Naval Operations, Memorandum (in the event of Italy entering the War) 8 June 1940. See also Appendix 1, 'Prelude to War'.

frontiers, stripped her of overseas possessions, and fastened on her the war-guilt clause which was made the excuse for heavy reparations demands. The resulting feeling of victimization united the Germans and provided the sources of support for the aggressive Nazi dictatorship of Hitler, particularly when the peace-dominated Western Powers yielded to his successive demands with a pliancy which continued to yield until the attack on Poland in September 1939.

The Italians were equally disgruntled with the Versailles Treaties of 1919 and under Mussolini's rule adopted aggressive nationalist policies in East Africa and the Balkans which brought her into World War II, but not until June 1940, by which time German successes in Europe held out the prospect of valuable pickings. Both Hitler and Mussolini masked their aggressive policies under the guise of a crusade against the destructive forces of world communism in an Anti-Comintern Pact of 1936, which embraced Japan in the following year.

Japan's rise to a dominant position in the Far East had been rapid. She grasped the opportunity presented by the pre-occupation of the European Powers with the 1914–18 war to stake out those claims which were to cast an ominous shadow over the Far East for the next thirty years. At Versailles she received a mandate over the Caroline and Marshall Islands, but the disposal of the former German assets in China, claimed by both China and Japan, was not settled until three years later when the several Treaties of Washington of 1922 restored them to China.

These latter treaties also limited naval armaments, giving America, Britain and Japan respectively a 5:5:3 ratio in capital ships, and restricted British and United States fortifications in the Pacific Area; they re-affirmed the integrity of, and equality of economic opportunity in China and arranged for the four powers, Britain, United States, Japan and France, to consult each other in case of Far East disputes. Britain regarded this last agreement as making the Anglo-Japanese Treaty of 1902 redundant and it was accordingly dropped.

These arrangements left Japan very dissatisfied. She interpreted her failure to gain parity in naval armaments as a denial of great-power status, while the abrogation of the Anglo-Japanese Alliance increased her sense of isolation. Yet she gained decided advantages in that she could concentrate her fleet in the Western Pacific with the nearest fortifiable British base now at Singapore, some 3,500 miles away, and the nearest American base at Pearl Harbor, 4,500 miles away. The London Naval Treaty of 1930 continued the capital-ship 'holiday' and allotted Japan a 10:6 ratio with Britain and America in heavy cruisers and a 10:7 ratio in light cruisers. Even these concessions were accepted against the bitter opposition of the Japanese Imperial Navy, and stiffened the demand of the Ministry of Defence to be directly responsible to the Emperor. The Japanese military claimed a freedom of action which made the Kwantung Army in South Manchuria the spearhead of the movement to absorb China into the Japanese sphere.

In 1931 Japan embarked on the conquest of Manchuria and established the puppet state of Manchukuo, landing troops at Shanghai in January 1932 as an unmistakable threat to foreign rights there. The League of Nations sent out the Lytton Commission which condemned Japan but the League took no effective measures to implement the Commission's findings. In 1933 Japan quit the League and in the following year gave notice of withdrawal from the naval limitation treaties. She did attend the London Naval Conference of 1933 but her demands were unacceptable to the other Powers and the limitation of naval armaments came to an end. Japan encouraged independence movements in Inner Mongolia under her own auspices and developed the argument that there could be no stability in East Asia except under Japanese leadership and control. This long-term plan was threatened by Chiang Kai-shek's success in uniting China. In July 1937 the Japanese were involved in an incident, believed to have been engineered by them, at the Marco Polo Bridge, south of Peking, and when China rejected an ultimatum to withdraw her troops, hostilities between China and Japan began.

The Japanese occupied the coastal areas and the Yangtze River ports to block military supplies to China. Nanking fell in December 1937 and was pillaged with extreme barbarity. A quisling regime, under Wang Ching-wei, was later established there though it received little popular support. Foreign shipping was obstructed, and in December 1937 the U.S.S. *Panay* and H.M.S. *Ladybird* were bombed in separate incidents on the Yangtze. In October 1938 Hankow was occupied, forcing the Nationalist Government back to Chungking and on 12 October 1938 the Japanese landed at Bias Bay and nine days later took Canton. The Kowloon-Canton Railway was cut and food-carrying junks on the Pearl River were seized as a manifest threat to Hong Kong's trade. This had been flourishing as one of the main sources of supply to China.

Against the protests of the Treaty Powers, Japan closed the Yangtze and Pearl Rivers in March 1939 on the excuse of military operations, and treated foreigners with increasing contempt and discourtesy. She promised to re-open the rivers to normal commerce when the military situation permitted, but was really dangling the carrot of re-opening the rivers to extort concessions from the Treaty Powers. Foreign Settlements were subject to restrictions because the Japanese claimed, not without reason, that Chinese patriotic organizations took advantage of the shelter they afforded to conduct subversive anti-Japanese activities. The Munich Agreement of September 1938 which virtually handed over Czechoslovakia to Hitler, starkly revealed the weakness of the Western Powers and confirmed Japan in the view that she had little to fear from them. She had already occupied Pratas Island, close to Hong Kong, in September 1937 thereby causing some anxiety to the British and inducing the French to occupy the Paracel Islands in July 1938. She now occupied Hainan Island in February 1939 and the Spratly Islands the following month. War in Europe came in September 1939 and effectively tied the hands of Britain and her allies, while Hitler's onslaught in the summer of 1940 left France and Holland prostrate, Britain dangerously isolated, and placed European colonies in South-East Asia at Japan's mercy.

Japan rather surprisingly rejected overtures from Hitler in the Spring of 1939 for a full military alliance with the Axis Powers, preferring to remain unfettered in the timing of her own moves and wanting to avoid being used by the Axis Powers for their own ends. The subsequent non-aggression pact between Hitler and Soviet Russia produced some nervousness in Japan. Russo-Japanese relations had been strained for many years over Manchuria and Japanese claims in China, and, in marked contrast to the Western European Powers, Russia had reacted strongly, and effectively, against the Japanese. Border incidents had been common. But after 1940, and when the United States began to show her determination to oppose Japanese ambitions in East and South-East Asia, Japan at last strengthened her relations with the Rome-Berlin Axis. Up to then these had been regulated by the very limited aims of the Anti-Comintern Pact of 1936. In September 1940 Japan negotiated a military alliance with the two Fascist Powers by which each was to receive full military aid from the others, if attacked by a Power not then at war. The Japanese also wanted a non-aggression agreement with the U.S.S.R. to avoid a war on two fronts should she decide to advance southwards to South-East Asia; Stalin refused to commit himself that far, but in April 1941 agreed to a Neutrality Treaty with Japan. Each country was to remain neutral if the other were attacked by one or more Powers. However, Hitler's invasion of Russia later that summer more effectively removed Japanese fears for her security against her northern neighbour than any treaty could have done. Events then appeared to conspire to give Japan a gilt-edged opportunity to pursue her expansionist aims to the South.

As for Britain, her policy was necessarily weak in view of the threatening political situation in Europe and even weaker with the actual outbreak of the Second World War in September 1939. With her forces concentrated in Europe, she had little choice but, as far as possible, to avoid giving offence to Japan while attempting to maintain her treaty rights in China. British officials and traders in the treaty ports were insulted, British Settlements obstructed and British protests treated with contempt, all because it could be done by Japan with impunity. The attack on H.M.S. *Ladybird* elicited only perfunctory Japanese apologies in marked contrast to the large indemnity and admission of guilt in regard to the sinking of U.S.S. *Panay*. The Japanese violation of Hong Kong's frontier with China in October 1938, and in February 1939 when Lo Wu was bombed, and again in June 1940 when the border was closed for a short period, revealed Japanese disregard for British sovereignty. Japanese sources indicate[2] that they contemplated an attack on Hong Kong in June 1940 and that the battle for Hong Kong might well have taken place in that summer. Some sections of Japanese military opinion argued that Hong Kong should be taken over as part of the China War operations, without any declaration of war on Britain, leaving the question of its cession to Japan for the future. In the event, the Hanoi-Kunming Railway and the Burma Road became more important supply routes for China and the attack on Hong Kong was accordingly delayed until full-scale war in December 1941.

Earlier, Japan's blockade of the British Settlement at Tientsin had led the British to make the humiliating Craigie-Arita Agreement in July 1939 by which they agreed to take no action prejudicial to the Japanese forces in China in the pursuit of Japanese aims there, an agreement condemned by the Americans as a typical piece of British appeasement. In April 1940 the Japanese demand that the number of their nationals on the Shanghai Municipal Council should be increased to five was defeated by the electors; but the British felt that the military position there was untenable, and in August 1940 the two British battalions were withdrawn from Shanghai. Japanese pressure forced the closing of the Burma Road in July 1940 for three months. These unfortunate retreats annoyed the Chinese. American policy was to up-hold the integrity of China as guaranteed by the Nine-Power Treaty signed at Washington in 1922, to maintain her treaty rights in China, and to refuse recognition of any political changes brought about unilaterally by the use of force. Roosevelt, faced by strong American isolationist sentiment, could move but slowly; for example, the sinking of the U.S.S. *Panay* led to a demand, not for reprisals but rather for keeping Americans out of the war zone. In July 1938, following Japan's move to occupy the

[2] Editor's note: I have not been able to trace these Japanese sources, however F. C. Jones, *Japan's New Order in East Asia 1937–45* (London, 1954), p. 165, referring to the Japanese Government request to Britain to seal the Burma Road and to prevent the despatch of war materials to China *via* Hong Kong says: 'To give point to this threat 5,000 Japanese troops were concentrated along the border of the Kowloon leased Territory, and the situation became for a while so menacing that the military authorities at Hong Kong ordered the destruction of the frontier rail and road bridges over the Shumchun River. (Source: *The Times*, 25 and 27 June 1940.)

coastal areas and rivers and seize control of the Chinese Maritime Customs, the United States imposed an embargo on the export of aeronautical equipment to Japan. In January 1939, when Japan began to occupy more islands in the South China Sea, the United States' Fleet was transferred to the Pacific and in July 1939, following the British compromise with Japan in the Craigie-Arita Agreement, the Americans gave notice to abrogate their 1911 Commercial Treaty with Japan.

When war broke out in Europe in September 1939, the Japanese demanded the withdrawal of all foreign troops from China, ostensibly to avoid the war spreading to that country. The United States then announced an embargo on the export of planes, war plant, and technical information. As Holland and France were overrun by German arms in the summer of 1940, Japan raised the question of Dutch and French Colonies in South-East Asia, but was warned by the Americans against making any changes unilaterally. The Japanese made every effort, but without success, to induce the Americans to accept Japan's new position in Asia. In June 1940 Japan made a Treaty of Friendship with Thailand. At the same time after the débâcle in Europe in the summer of 1940, the Americans had to take serious defence measures, including control of the export of all goods vital to the defence of the United States; but Roosevelt allowed Japan to continue to receive American oil so as not to give Japan any excuse to seize the Dutch East Indies as an alternative source of supply.

In August 1940 the new Konoye Government in Japan forced the Vichy Authorities to agree to Japan's use of ports and airfields in French Indo-China and in the following month, to allow them to occupy Northern Indo-China up to Hanoi, to cut the important rail link with Kunming. At the same time Britain had to close the Burma Road temporarily. In September 1940 Japan joined the Axis Powers in Europe in a close military alliance. In October 1940 all American citizens were advised to leave the danger areas in the Far East.

By 1941 the situation in the Far East had become critical. In February, Nomura was sent to Washington as Japanese ambassador, and as he was a personal friend of Roosevelt it was at first believed that Japan was aiming at a détente. At the same time military conversations were begun in Singapore between British, American, Dutch and Australian and New Zealand service officers, to co-ordinate defence action in the Pacific in the event of a Japanese attack, and this co-ordination was accepted by Roosevelt and Churchill in principle at the Atlantic Conference in August 1941. Japan encouraged Thailand to demand Indo-Chinese territory, and then won Thai support by mediating to endorse the Thai claims.

On 22 June 1941 came Hitler's invasion of Russia. After some hesitation, and particularly after spectacular German successes, Japan felt free to concentrate on an advance to the South without fear of a Russian attack and the fateful decision to do so was finally taken in July 1941. In the same month, Japan imposed on the impotent Vichy authorities in Saigon an agreement by which they received Japanese forces for joint protection. In reply Roosevelt froze all Japanese assets in the United States, and this was followed by similar action by Britain and Holland. The Americans withdrew all their forces in China to the Philippines which was placed on a war footing, and the lend-lease programme was extended to China. The Japanese Government sent Kurusu to Washington in November 1941 to assist in the negotiations to end the crisis, but to no avail. Japan regarded her control of China as essential, while America insisted upon respect for treaty obligations and would recognize no change imposed by force. The American demands that Japan should withdraw from China and Indo-China, undertake to respect the integrity of China, and join America in giving up treaty rights and privileges, were regarded in Japan as renouncing everything she had won by force of arms.

The positions taken up by America and Japan allowed no compromise, and the leaders of both countries realized that war was inevitable. Japan's sudden attack was a desperate gamble to avoid a long struggle; and the plan was rather to cripple the American Pacific fleet, to occupy all South-East Asia and organize such a strong and efficient defence of her conquests as would induce Americans to accept the *fait accompli*. Thus did Japan completely miscalculate the temper of the United States.

II

HONG KONG ON THE EVE OF CATASTROPHE

'A poll, however, would disclose that the Hong Kong outlook is compounded of reaction, faith, determination, nervous anticipation, evasion and simple fatalism.'

Editorial in the *South China Morning Post*, 20 August 1941

ONE result of the extension of Japanese military operations to South China in 1938 was a massive influx of refugees into the Colony seeking safety in its traditional security. The Colonial Secretary estimated that, during the twelve months ended July 1938, a quarter of a million persons entered the Colony by railway and steamer alone and that 30,000 of them were sleeping in the streets. A census of the urban population taken by the air-raid wardens during the two nights, 14 and 15 March 1941, gave a total of 1,444,337 persons, of whom 20,000 were street-sleepers; adding 200,000 for the New Territories, this gives the total Colony civilian population at that date of about 1,650,000, compared to an estimated 997,982 in December 1937 and 988,190 in December 1936. This huge increase severely taxed available living accommodation and strained the Colony's resources in every sphere. In July 1938 Government proposed two camps for destitute refugees at North Point and Kowloon Tsai, and a third camp, for those having some means, in King's Road not far from Quarry Bay, a camp which many prisoners of war were later to know intimately. The capital cost of these camps was put at $522,500 with an annual recurrent expenditure of $367,200. In addition, the Tung Wah set up reception centres in the old Government Civil Hospital and in the Tung Wah Hospitals. These arrangements proved totally inadequate, and eventually refugee camps were established at King's Park, Ma Tau Chung, North Point, Morrison Hill, Tai Hang and Ngau Tau Kok for squatters, Kam Tin and Fanling for children, together catering for just over 11,000, and even this meagre provision was recognized as only a palliative. In March 1941 a scheme was put forward to build by private enterprise two refugee village settlements at Silvermine Bay on Lantau Island and Hebe Haven. These were to be permanent settlements and open to all, part of the object being to attract people away from the overcrowded urban area. It was primarily a social welfare scheme rather than a business proposition, though it was intended to be self-supporting. The promoters asked Government to be responsible for anti-malarial measures, but were offered only a grant of $5,000 for this purpose, and the scheme made little headway before being brought to a halt by the war.

The refugees in the urban area lived in appalling conditions. The Hong Kong Refugee and Social Welfare Council, founded in February 1940, reported, in July 1941, that 14 living units had been visited and found to be accommodating 497 residents. They were divided into anything from 2 to 7 cubicles with rents up to $8.50 per month, plus 4 to 6 bed spaces rented at from $1.70 to $6.20 per month, all sharing the same kitchen. Earlier, the demand for housing brought rent increases and evictions and Government set up a Commission of Enquiry into rents in March 1938, which reported somewhat astonishingly that there was no evidence that landlords were raising rents above the level obtaining before the recent depression in real estate. But agitation forced the Government in June 1938 to give tenants twelve months protection against eviction and to set up a committee of two official and five unofficial members of the Legislative Council, to recommend ways to give tenants more permanent security. The effect was to freeze rents on existing properties at the prevailing levels.

The visible serious effects of influx of refugees brought into question the unrestricted right of entry into Hong Kong, traditionally claimed by the Chinese. In June 1940 Government set up an Excess Population Reduction Committee and accepted its recommendations for immigration control drawn up by S. M. Middlebrook of the Malayan Civil Service, who had been seconded to the Hong Kong Government for this work. All Chinese now had to have either entry passes, frontier passes or residential certificates, and on 18 November 1940 a new Immigration Department was set up to administer the new controls, headed by R. A. D. Forrest, a cadet officer and senior

Police Magistrate. In response to Chinese protests, the fees for certificates of residence were reduced from $10 to $6 for those with 4 years' residence, and from $5 to $2 for those with 10 years' residence. The Chinese appeared to think that everyone ought to have one of these documents whether travelling or not, and the new office was immediately swamped with applications for which it was quite unprepared, so that police had to be called to control the crowds. There were complaints of administrative inefficiency and irregularity, and a Commission of Enquiry under the Chief Justice, the Hon. Sir A. D. A. MacGregor, was appointed in March 1941 to investigate the affairs of the Department, the public hearings of which attracted considerable publicity. The report issued in the middle of June 1941 condemned not only the head of the Department for not having instituted a proper financial system, but also the Treasury and the Colonial Secretariat for their unhelpful attitude. The appointment of agents to assist the general public, though sanctioned by Government, had led to irregularities, and that the agents' agreements had not been submitted to the law officers nor was any security or audit demanded. One agent, a Hungarian, had a photographic studio in the office and had been allowed to sign official cheques without countersignature by an officer of the Department. Agents had been even allowed to issue temporary residence permits though no such delegation of power had been authorized. The permit forms were unnumbered, and the general looseness of the arrangements, and lack of financial and administrative control had allowed various abuses to creep in. Conditions in the Department were described as chaotic. The report also strongly criticized the terms of the advertisement for the post of assistant director restricting applicants to those of pure European descent. The Commission's report declared Forrest unfit to be the head of a Government department. The officer was 'retired' and he left the Colony. In palliation of their abuses the Department had been hurriedly formed without adequate staff, only eight out of a staff of 290 had ever worked in a Government office before, there was no accounts officer and little help was received from other Government departments. Clearly its head had been given a most difficult assignment.

Besides the immigration difficulties, Government ran into

trouble over the evacuation of women and children, and though this mainly affected Europeans, it soon became a wider issue. Plans for the evacuation of civilians were outlined as early as August 1939 at the behest of the British authorities who properly felt responsible for the families of British servicemen and civilians employed by the Service departments. A Director of Evacuation was one of the many war-time appointments announced on 4 September 1939 with the Crown Solicitor as the first appointee. Little preparatory work had in fact been done when, on 28 June 1940, the Hong Kong Government suddenly announced plans for compulsory evacuation of European women and children. This was done on instructions from Whitehall, which feared an attack on the Colony by the Japanese. The Japanese announced that Hong Kong Chinese would be allowed to return to China on 1 and 2 July, after which the border would be closed, and some 1,800 Chinese took advantage of the two days' grace offered. The European evacuees from Hong Kong had to register with passports and health documents and be ready to embark for Manila, and thence, as shipping became available, to Australia. The families of the regular armed forces numbering 1,640 were evacuated forthwith on 1 July. Other British women and children of European descent were told to report on 2 July for registration and to be ready to sail on 5 July, with passports, travellers' cheques, a maximum of one trunk and two cases per adult, children half that baggage allowance, 'and no pets'. There were to be no exceptions, except those in the nursing or other essential services, but those without children who were willing to volunteer for the nursing service could apply to the Director of Medical Services. The Government took powers on 29 June 1940 to order any woman or child or any other person not necessary for defence purposes to leave the Colony. In fact, many women had to be exempted simply because Government and commercial offices alike faced disorganization if all the stenographers left. Many did not register because they had applied to do nursing and were waiting for the result. Eventually, on 5 July, 1,779 British women and children, out of the 2,129 who had registered three days earlier, left for Manila in two *Empress* liners. On 3 August another fifty-five persons sailed to Manila, making a total of 3,474 evacuees.

Chinese leaders advised their people to leave at their own expense. Dutch and Norwegian women were ordered by their own authorities to leave, the United States advised its women to leave, and the French were warned to prepare for evacuation. On 3 July British women and children of Portuguese origin were told to register, and they were helped in this by a Portuguese Evacuation Committee which had been formed in August 1939. The Government admitted that many women had evaded evacuation, but promised that all would be rounded up, and registration for evacuation was made compulsory. The evacuation had undoubtedly been hurried and the financial arrangements were still left undecided. Great dissatisfaction resulted and one editor charged that '. . . the evacuation was premature, clumsily carried out and entirely unaccompanied by any shock-absorbing arrangements to reduce its effect' and deplored the lack of any gesture by the Government to identify itself with the Hong Kong citizen. The Finance Committee of the Legislative Council refused to pass a token vote of $10,000 for the costs of evacuation of non-service women and children, on the ground that Europeans should not be subsidized from general taxation. The unofficial members of the Legislative Council sent a telegram to London urging that compulsory evacuation should be cancelled. The issue was debated in the Legislative Council on 25 July, when the Colonial Secretary explained that the evacuation had been ordered by London, that British women and children had been evacuated as a first step, and that the cost of transport was met from Hong Kong funds but that the responsibility for the cost of the maintenance of evacuees had not yet been decided, the natural hope being that the Home Government would meet part of the cost. The aim was stated to be the removal of women and children not normally domiciled in Hong Kong. On the charge of racial discrimination the answer was that non-domiciled women and children would be evacuated and that other women and children would probably prefer to go to China, India, Macao or Indo-China.

Eventually, on 17 October, the Government announced that maintenance for evacuees in Australia at the weekly rate of 50/– (Australian) for each women, plus 15/– for the first child, 10/– for the second child and 5/– for each additional child would be made available by the Australian Government. This would be reimbursed by the families concerned, and a Select Committee on Evacuation would be set up to deal with cases where a contribution to maintenance could not be made. Then it was announced that all maintenance from Australian official sources would cease on 25 November 1940 and that reimbursement would be demanded as arranged.

Opposition remained bitter. Evacuation was felt to be totally unnecessary; there were charges of favouritism in the case of some wives who were allowed to remain. On 13 August 1940 the number of women granted exemption was stated to be 950, of whom 500 were required by the Director of Medical Services, the Director of A.R.P., the Chief Censor and the H.K. University Nursing Detachment, 300 were running their own businesses and so were exempted under a ruling by the Secretary of State, and 150 had made their own private arrangements.

The Officer Administering the Government, General Norton, appointed an Evacuation Advisory Committee to consider applications for exemption, but few were given permission to stay. In November the men affected formed a committee under the Very Revd. J. L. Wilson, Dean of the Cathedral, to make a joint protest to the Government. The Committee did not at first question the need for evacuation but criticized the way in which it was done. It petitioned the Secretary of State, alleging that the necessary steps to prepare for this emergency measure had not been taken. Other criticisms were that there was unjust racial discrimination and unfair administration which allowed exemption to many who were not entitled to it, while refusing it to many who were entitled.

The Hong Kong Government was at fault in being unprepared when the order for evacuation came from London. The 1939 scheme was not ready; for example, the Exemption Committee under the scheme had never been constituted and the register of women and children was not up-to-date. The result was that the women were evacuated at short notice without adequate time to arrange their own affairs, and, in the absence of the proper administration, some officials granted exemption on their own authority. The Hong Kong General Chamber of Commerce protested against the evacuation on

1 July in that it caused apprehension and alarm and 'was entirely unjustified by the present situation'. The Evacuation Representation Committee, particularly after some changes in its leadership, continued, up to the Japanese attack, to conduct a virulent campaign against Government evacuation policy, but with only partial success. One woman, who had gone to Manila, returned and unsuccessfully contested the legality of the evacuation proceedings in the Supreme Court. The Manager of The Hongkong and Shanghai Banking Corporation threatened to take the case to the Judicial Committee of the Privy Council.

The Governor himself was nervous about the legality of the orders since they had been taken under the 1922 Emergency Powers Ordinance and, after discussion with the Secretary of State, he announced on 6 November 1940 that there would be no further compulsory evacuation. Some 200 persons about to be served with evacuation orders were to be allowed to stay. It was made clear at the same time, that the evacuees would not be allowed to return to Hong Kong, that restrictions on the entry of women and children would continue, that there would be no special protection for women electing to remain in Hong Kong during the emergency, and all would have to help in one of the essential or auxiliary services.

The Government promised to provide transport for those wishing to go voluntarily. The priorities were given as: first, wives and families of the combatant forces; second, those of the auxiliary services; and third, all others. The word 'British' had to be omitted because many of those serving in the Defence Services could not claim British nationality. No destinations were mentioned, though it was made known that Fiji had offered to take 500 Chinese. All women had to register by 18 November 1940. These concessions led to further demands by the husbands' Evacuation Representation Committee for the return of the wives and the Committee continued its acrimonious dispute with the Government up to the outbreak of hostilities, and at its meetings any mention of the Government was generally received with catcalls. On 5 July 1940 the families of the volunteer forces were compulsorily registered, and were promised food and housing in any emergency if unable to leave Hong Kong. All schools for British children were closed on

2 September 1940 and those staying had to make their own educational arrangements. The Under-Secretary of State, Mr. George Hall, replying in November 1940 to a parliamentary question in the House of Commons wrote that evacuation was part of the national defence policy and that it had been intended to exempt only those engaged in nursing or other essential service or whose only support was their business in Hong Kong. He explained, 'It is easy to be wise after the event . . . but at the time the order was given on the advice of the highest defence authorities, it was felt to be urgent and desirable.' Twelve months later, in November 1941, he said in reply to another question in the Commons that the political outlook in the Far East had not improved sufficiently to allow the evacuees to return.

At this distance it is difficult to see what the fuss was about and to share in the deep feeling aroused. The general opinion undoubtedly was that the evacuation had been unnecessary, that people had not been treated alike, and that it was absurd to evacuate a few thousands of European women and children while hundreds of thousands of Chinese remained. Against this, the Cabinet at home had access to information not available to individuals, which could not always be divulged. Clearly the Government had a duty to families of servicemen, and other expatriate families who had no easy refuge in China, or Macao or India; besides it was unrealistic to demand that all Hong Kong citizens should be treated equally when every third person was a recently-arrived refugee, and in any case, shipping would have been quite inadequate to evacuate all women and children without exception to Australia, assuming Australia could have received them.

Twelve months after the evacuation, the Government admitted that some 900 women still remained in the Colony. Many lived to regret having done so. Generally, the conclusion must be that the Government's treatment of the excess civilian population problem erred on the side of generosity.

The Colonial Office in London had directed that all colonies should maintain reserves of food and other essential commodities as part of the emergency preparations – a precaution in Hong Kong which the Japanese threat made as urgent as the swelling of the population made it costly.[1] The authorities were confronted with the problem of preparing for possible siege conditions. Power to control food prices was assumed on the outbreak of the European War; on 10 September 1939 the Government fixed prices at not more than 10 per cent above those ruling on 31 August, and very soon after, some of the large well-known stores were fined for charging excess prices. On 5 November 1939 a list of the chief food prices appeared in the *Gazette*. Control of prices proved to be difficult due to scarcities, high shipping and insurance charges, particularly in the summer of 1940 when the Japanese cut off supplies from the mainland and prices were temporarily trebled. In October 1939 an Essential Commodities Reserves Ordinance empowered Government to keep reserve stocks and to register and license importers. In a scheme agreed to by the trade, importers were asked to state the quantities of goods they imported and the stocks held, and supplies were allocated *pro rata*. In fact, the Government admitted, after introducing the Bill, that it had been secretly making purchases of rice during the past few months, financed by advances from The Hongkong and Shanghai Banking Corporation. The Ordinance applied only to rice at first, but it was intended to bring in other essential commodities later and its aim was to keep on hand reserves sufficient to last ninety days. This period was later extended to 130 days. It was afterwards found that much of the rice had deteriorated in store and it had to be sold to prevent further serious deterioration. In March 1941 the Controller of Rice warned that no compensation would be paid for rice which had deteriorated while in store, but only for that damaged by enemy action or by civil disturbance and only sixty days' reserve was then to be maintained. The price of rice was not at first controlled because all Hong Kong's rice was imported from Siam and the Government feared that fixing prices might discourage imports and drive the Siamese rice trade into the arms of Japan. In addition, for a time, some 50 per cent of all rice was re-exported. In October 1940 a sum of one million Hong Kong dollars was authorized for purchasing reserves of food other than rice, and in January 1941 two

[1] For a fuller treatment of the pre-1941 and post-war periods of rationing and price control see Alan Birch, 'Rationing and Price Control in War-time Hong Kong' *H.K.L.J.*, (4), 1974, pp.133–50.

million dollars were voted to purchase reserves of soy beans and peanut oil.

In February 1941 an Essential Commodities Board was set up with a well-known businessman and unofficial member of the Legislative Council as Chairman, and the Controller of Stores and Controller of Rice, as members, to assess the Colony's needs in rice, firewood, cement, coal and other important commodities. In February 1941 cement prices were controlled and on 25 February the price of firewood was fixed at $1 for forty catties; soon afterwards the export of firewood was prohibited.

Rice-control arrangements proved unsatisfactory and the Government decided to assume a monopoly of the imports and exports of rice to ensure supply and control the price. This was agreed to by the Legislative Council on 8 May 1941 and on 6 June the Government took over all reserve stocks and became the sole importer and exporter; exports in fact were now confined to the international settlement in Shanghai, which Hong Kong had undertaken to supply. The rice monopoly called for an investment of $25 million which came from surplus Government funds or bank credits.

In August 1941 the value of reserve stocks of food was given as $2,854,719 and of meat and butter as $699,576, but Government found it impossible to devise any scheme to store reserve stocks of meat and fish for the Chinese. The price of food, particularly rice, had risen so much that many were deeply concerned over the hardships to the working people and the Vicar of St. Andrew's Church, in Kowloon, the Revd. H. A. Wittenbach, headed a Social Work Committee in May 1941 to sell rice more cheaply than the normal retailers, and two depots were opened. From this Social Work Committee was formed the Equitable Rice Sales Fund Committee under the Chairmanship of the Director of Medical Services, Dr. P. S. Selwyn-Clarke. This Committee continued to function up to the Japanese attack, relying mainly on voluntary service. It not only provided rice at a reasonable price, but supplied cooked rice at three cents a bowl, and *sung*, i.e. a portion of meat or vegetable to go with the rice, at one cent per portion. The Government helped by bearing the cost of converting the basement of the Wanchai Market for this purpose and the first communal kitchen opened there on 15 September 1941. The Committee also embarked on a vegetable-marketing scheme in an attempt to cut out middlemen's profits, but without the same degree of success as in rice. It discovered that *pak choi* (white cabbage) was sold by the New Territories farmer at $3.50 per picul, by the vegetable *laan* or wholesaler at $12 per picul, and by the market stall-holder at $14 in Kowloon and $18 per picul in Hong Kong. The vegetable-wholesalers threatened retaliation and some theft from the stores occurred. Dr. Selwyn-Clarke and his Committee strongly urged the authorities to use the monopoly to subsidize the price of rice to the poor, but the Government insisted that the rice monopoly must be run on commercial lines, and that any subsidy, if decided on, must be defrayed from general funds. On 6 June 1941 the Controller of Food fixed the price of Burma rice Grade No. 1 at $14.80 per picul and Grade No. 2 at $14.00. On 13 June price control was extended to all grades of rice, *viz*, Grade A, $17.00, B, $16.20, C, $15.60, D, $15.00, E, $14.60, F, $14.00 per picul. Since these prices were above those being charged in the shops, the Equitable Rice Sales Fund Committee was strongly critical of Government policy and continued to sell its rice at the original prices. The Government also prohibited wholesale dealings in rice without the Controller's permission. On 22 August 1941 the Government reduced the prices of the various grades of rice as follows; AA $20, A $16, B $15.20, D $14, E $13.60, F $13, and cargo rice $14.

The quality of the rice slowly deteriorated and led to a demand for a reduction of prices but the Controller pointed to high freight costs and argued that of the 40 cents profit on grade A rice, 30 cents represented interest charges without taking account of storage charges and other overheads, and that selling Grade F rice costing $15 per picul, at $10 as the Committee wanted, would cost the Government $500,000 per month. He claimed that the monopoly supplied rice at the cheapest possible price and deplored any attempt to mislead people into expecting a reduction. The Food Controller also defended the monopoly in the Legislative Council and explained that the operation of feeding some 1½ million people had to be run on commercial lines but not to be profit-making;

at the same time it had to make provision for ending the scheme by writing off the value of the stocks gradually to avoid heavy final loss. In fact, when the scheme was wound up on 31 May 1941 the levies on reserve stocks, at 12 cents a picul from December 1939 to 1 June 1940, and 18 cents a picul from that date to the end of the scheme, failed to meet outstanding charges, resulting in a loss of $110,962, which had to be made up from revenue. Up to the outbreak of hostilities, the Government's policy for other foodstuffs was to lay down maximum prices for tinned food of all kinds, dairy products, tea, sugar and fresh fish and to issue comprehensive lists of such prices at frequent intervals.[2] No scheme of rationing was attempted before the outbreak of the fighting and there was little price control outside food items, except for cement and firewood.

The Equitable Rice Sales Fund Committee carried on an unsuccessful campaign to induce the poorer purchasers to eat unpolished or 'cargo' rice which was cheaper at $14 a picul and more nutritious, an important factor in view of the deterioration in the health of the community. Beriberi cases increased from 745 in 1936 to 7,229 in 1940, and there were 442 cases of pellagra in 1940 and 768 in the first six months of 1941, but the Chinese of all classes preferred polished rice regardless.

Fuel also proved a difficult problem but remained outside the scope of the Essential Commodities Reserve Ordinance of 27 October 1939. In March 1941 the export of firewood was prohibited, and Government began to organize the direct import of firewood from Sandakan, with the object of building up a reserve to help control the price and prepare for siege conditions, the first shipment being expected in March 1941. The Controller of Stores, W. J. Anderson, announced on 9 August that six ships were expected to bring some 19,000 tons of firewood during August and announced drastic action against the black market in firewood. All dealers in firewood had to be licensed and display their licence, and make a weekly return of stocks and sales, and all transactions had to be recorded in an effort to stamp out hawkers. Shortages con-

[2] The last full list appeared on 5 December 1941.

tinued, partly because of lack of shipping, and, in October 1941, 6,215 convictions for cutting wood from the hills were reported. The fuel situation was never properly under control because Chinese refugees added to the burden and import virtually ceased. Thousands were driven to comb the hills cutting trees, and when the opportunity came, damaged and unoccupied houses were stripped of all furniture and wooden fittings for fuel.

It is difficult to estimate the effect of the war in Europe and of the Japanese operations in China on Hong Kong's trade. The official figures show imports for the years 1937 to 1940 in millions of dollars as 923.4, 625.7, 599.5 and 752.7 respectively, and for the first six months of 1941 as 456.0, and exports over the same years as 844.4, 664.2, 608.8 and 621.8, and for the first six months of 1941, 353.6. These figures show a decline due to shortages of shipping, the cut-back of civilian industrial production in Britain and Europe and trade and exchange controls. They also relate only to visible trade and take no account of invisible items such as earnings from shipping, insurance, banking and managerial services. Total trade with China amounted in the years 1937 to 1940 respectively, to 796.6, 494.5, 317.8, and 411.6 millions of dollars, showing unmistakably some falling off due to the Japanese blockade of the Pearl Estuary and neighbouring coast-line, but these figures probably do not tell the whole story. The Kowloon-Canton Railway receipts dropped from $1,782,000 in 1938 to $912,900 in 1939, and $935,400 for the fifteen months to April 1941, but they show that much trade with China continued. Hong Kong's free-port status was its great asset, and much clandestine trade and blockade-running was carried on. Chinese firms moved from the mainland to the Colony, and Hong Kong began to sell more of its own manufactures. Undoubtedly there was much smuggling of war material to China by Hong Kong Chinese businessmen, but according to Professor Medlicott, Hong Kong's contribution to China's war needs dropped from 70 per cent in 1938 to 20 per cent in 1940.[3] It is, of course, impossible to state accurate figures but one competent Hong Kong observer has stated that the

[3] Cf. Footnote 12, Appendix 1.

proportion of China's total imports passing through Hong Kong doubled in 1940. There seems little doubt that, large or small, Japanese suspicions regarding Hong Kong's role in supplying China had considerable justification.

Hong Kong's industry developed during these years, partly because the war in Europe forced the colonies to rely more on their own resources, and partly because of the influx of cheap refugee labour. The old long-established industries continued to prosper. The two commercial dockyards expanded and by 1939 had built and handed over two ships of 10,000 tons each for the Glen Line. A great variety of smaller industries prospered from the flow of orders from China, the number of factories employing twenty persons or more rose from 689 in 1937 to 829 at the end of 1938 and to 1,200 by the time of the Japanese occupation in 1941, employing 90,000 workers. There was a great demand for useful ancillary war supplies such as textiles, rubber boots, electric hand-torches, dry batteries and electric light bulbs, webbing and trenching tools, most of which were exported.

Despite the calls on the public purse for the war effort, the policy of generally raising living standards and maintaining Government services was adopted in Hong Kong, on instructions from London. The loyalty shown by colonial peoples clearly demanded recognition which took the form of greater concern for their welfare, and of course it was quite impossible to call for sacrifices from those whose standard of living was already too low. The British White Paper of June 1941 on Colonial Living Standards, made public in the Hong Kong Press on 9 August 1941, stated, 'It is an imperative duty however to do all practically possible to raise the standard of large Colonial populations whose standard of living is so low . . . .' While the war effort demanded reduction of imports, the intention was also to build up reserves for post-war rehabilitation, to plan social developments in health, education and welfare, and train local personnel in these fields so that no time should be lost. In accordance with this policy, the demands of the war were not allowed to interfere with the development of resources and essential government services in Hong Kong. Fisheries and Agricultural Research stations were proposed in January 1941, also a new subsidy code for education and plans to build fifty new Chinese primary schools. In 1939 a Labour Department was set up under the Secretariat of Chinese Affairs. In April 1941 Rhodes Scholarships were made available to Hong Kong students. The Northcote Training College was opened in April 1941, and a beginning was made with the Northcote Science Block at the University, and funds for a new School of Tropical Medicine were agreed to. The Hong Kong Refugee and Social Council to assist refugees was formed in February 1940. Branches of St. John Ambulance and the British Red Cross were formed in September 1939.

To what extent were Hong Kong people prepared for the war? That much had been done cannot be gainsaid, yet much was left undone. The excessive population remained a drain on resources and a hindrance to military movement. Little restriction on the movement of aliens was possible in a free port and the Japanese were left free to move at will, and over eighty Japanese were still in the Colony on 3 December 1941; the Japanese newspaper closed on 5 December, although an English version continued. When war came, the Japanese were detained in Stanley Gaol, their treatment being in marked contrast to the treatment handed out to the British incarcerated there after the defeat.

On 25 November 1941 the Government issued a circular to the community giving advice in case of attack and warning people to avoid built-up areas; 'The Government has selected certain country areas both on the Island and mainland and has built up supplies of food in those areas. If you have no duty to perform in the district where you live, you should take your clothes, bedding and rice-bowl, and move to one of those areas as soon as you are told to do so by an official. You will be told what route to follow and once you have reached one of those areas, you will be safe, and have food, shelter and medical care.' All inhabitants were to contact the A.R.P. Warden to know what to do in a raid; if invasion came, all had to obey the military. For those who had to stay in the urban area, for example the Civil Defence Services, food would be supplied from communal kitchens if none were available from shops or restaurants. This advice was condemned in the newspapers as too vague and useless.

Hong Kong on the eve of the attack was a divided community. The Government made itself intensely disliked over the compulsory evacuation scheme and it lost respect over the scandals connected with the A.R.P. and Immigration Departments. The suspicion grew that graft was not confined to those two cases but permeated the whole Government Service, and to allay public uneasiness, the Government, in November 1941, only some three weeks before the Japanese attack, set up a Commission of Enquiry with the Chief Justice as the sole member to enquire into corruption in the Public Service. No public hearings seem to have been held, and as Sir Atholl MacGregor died on his way back to England in 1945 from the effects of internment, no further action was taken on the matter. But undoubtedly the general fears, the feeling of insecurity and the shortages were all channelled into criticism of the Government. In addition many felt that the Government did not take the people sufficiently into its confidence in regard to the war dangers and that the people were being led up the garden path, yet security considerations necessarily limited what could be publicly announced, particularly as the policy was to prepare for the emergency without seeming to challenge Japan.

The Chinese community in Hong Kong was not homogeneous. Besides Punti (*poon tei*) or people from neighbouring Kwangtung Province, there were Chiu Chow or northern Kwangtung people, and Hakka or guest families, Hok Lo or Fukinese who were mainly a fishing community, and Tanka or Egg families who lived permanently on boats, and Shanghainese and other Northerners. These Chinese communities lived side by side, having almost as little to do with each other as they had with the foreigners. The Chinese remained Chinese at heart and few were absorbed into the western community. They came to Hong Kong seeking economic opportunity and most looked forward to returning to China when they could afford to do so; in the meantime, they asked only that they should be left alone and were quite prepared to shift for themselves. Basically law-abiding, they gave little trouble to the authorities, they asked for no share in political control or for any form of State aid, and by the same token they did not expect the State to make any demands on them, beyond the normal land dues, rates and indirect taxation on luxuries.

There was but slight feeling of belonging to Hong Kong, scant loyalty to the State, and little spirit of willing sacrifice for the community. To them, Hong Kong defence was a matter for the British. Hong Kong was, therefore, an artificial society and the vast majority were there temporarily, seeking economic advantage or escape from Japanese attack, and only Eurasians, Portuguese and some local Chinese, Indians and others of long standing became westernized and regarded Hong Kong as a home worth fighting for. The refugees were an unknown quantity and the British authorities were understandably hesitant about appealing for co-operation from the resident Chinese community. So when the Hong Kong Government sought their participation in the defence preparations it had only partial success, generally confined to those educated at the University or in the Anglo-Chinese schools run by European organizations.

Summing up, no one doubted that Hong Kong would be defended. An American journalist, Harrison Forman, after an interview with General Maltby on the defence of Hong Kong, gave much offence by likening the Colony's leaders to a lot of ostriches. The more discerning could see little hope unless relief from outside came quickly.

III

HONG KONG AS PART OF AN EMPIRE AT WAR

'The Far East seems likely to play a part of increased and increasing importance both in the present war and in the future of the world.'

Duff Cooper, Cabinet Papers, 1941

HITLER's attack on Poland at dawn on 1 September 1939 in defiance of the Anglo-French guarantees to that unfortunate country, brought Europe two days later into the war that most people thought inevitable after Chamberlain's futile appeasement at Munich in September 1938. Indeed, from this latter date, Britain's defence measures were stepped up so that when the open conflict came, she was already largely on a war footing.

The Second World War soon assumed a global character from which few countries could escape. No British colony, however remote from Europe, could remain unaffected because of Britain's responsibility for colonial defence, and not unnaturally she looked for co-operation in meeting this commitment. In fact, the colonies supported Britain's war effort in what must surely be an astonishing tribute to British colonial rule. Hong Kong was no exception to this anti-Fascist solidarity, although Japanese expansionist policies in East Asia posed the more direct and immediate threat.

British administrative war measures comprised a mass of emergency legislation placing virtually the whole of national life, including human, commercial and industrial resources, under state control to ensure the optimum use of the nation's assets for essential war needs. These measures were, broadly speaking, also introduced into the colonies to mobilize colonial resources for the British war effort. Though sacrifices equal to those borne by Britain were neither imposed nor expected of Britain's colonies, nevertheless the impact of the war-time controls on colonial life was momentous. Particularly was this the case in Hong Kong with its long tradition of free enterprise and administrative *laissez-faire*.

The process of arming colonial governments with the necessarily extensive emergency powers and setting up the special war-time administrative machinery was long and complicated. In Hong Kong existing ordinances with or without amendment, were applied; for example, many of the early emergency regulations were issued under the Emergency Powers Ordinance of 1922, designed to deal with the very different problems of civil disturbance, and the Ordinance itself was amended in some respects. Some new legislation was of course inevitable which usually delegated power to the Governor in Council to make the detailed operative regulations. The important Defence Regulations of 26 August 1939 were issued by the Governor, acting alone, under the Emergency Power (Defence) Act of 24 August 1939 which was applied to all Colonies by the Emergency Powers (Colonial Defence) Order in Council and the Emergency Powers Order in Council, both dating from this time.

Such was the constitutional basis of the wide emergency powers assumed by the Hong Kong Government as a result of the imminence and outbreak of war in Europe and the crises arising from the Japanese threats. The emergency was not made the excuse to abandon the normal constitutional forms, and the substantive acts and ordinances and the regulations made pursuant to them were laid on the table of the Legislative Council and promulgated in the *Gazette*.

The Japanese attack on Canton brought the Colony's first emergency regulations of this period. These regulations, issued under the Emergency Powers Ordinance of 1922 on 28 September 1938 were designed to secure the Colony's neutrality in the Sino-Japanese hostilities. The repair and victualling of Japanese or Chinese ships engaged in hostilities was forbidden. The police were given power to require anyone not in employment to leave the Colony, to forbid meetings, processions and organizations if suspected of sedition, to impose a censorship over Chinese newspapers, placards and pamphlets; and to enrol a force of special constables. The Government also assumed power to control food prices and, shortly afterwards, to intern Chinese or Japanese combatants taking refuge in Hong Kong.

An ordinance of 25 November 1938 empowered the Government to direct the compulsory registration of British subjects, but no action was taken until March 1939 when a new Registration Ordinance required the compulsory registration of all European males aged 18 to 55 and led to the introduction of conscription in the following July.

On 4 August 1939, still acting under the 1922 Emergency Powers Ordinance and under instructions issued to all Colonies from the Colonial Office, the censorship was extended without warning to all newspapers and placards other than Chinese, and the first censors were appointed on 26 August.

On 26 August 1939, the Hong Kong Defence Regulations were published in the Gazette to take effect immediately, and in June 1940 a revised version of the regulations was issued subject to the proviso that anything done under the previous Regulations was to continue in force until revoked. Most of the emergency measures taken, until the fighting began in December 1941, were authorized by these regulations.

The Defence (Finance) Regulations were issued by the Governor on 8 September 1939, again acting under instructions from the Secretary of State under the Acts and Orders in Council, draft regulations being sent as a guide. These regulations dealt with certain economic war measures and were extended to all Colonies, the governments of which were expected to act as the Imperial Government's agents on these matters.

Immediate measures taken in Hong Kong on the outbreak of war included the closing of the East and West Lamma Channels, taking powers to control ports, ships, aircraft and transport generally, to fix the prices of essential foodstuffs, to restrict and detain suspected persons and prohibit trading with the enemy. The German community was interned in La Salle College, Kowloon, and assets of certain German firms were seized.

At the Legislative Council meeting on 12 October 1939, the Governor stated that the Secretary of State had advised that the Colony's current activities and development schemes should continue as normally as possible except for conserving foreign exchange resources, particularly as Hong Kong's currency was not linked to sterling. The intention was to reduce the demand for goods and services and to avoid taking men and materials away from essential war work. At that same session, exchange and trade controls were instituted and in November price control was instituted.

In April 1940 further wide emergency powers were taken to enforce security about the armed forces, military operations and war supplies and on any matter relating to the efficient prosecution of the war; regulations were issued dealing with sabotaging the war effort, assisting the enemy, setting up controlled and prohibited areas, and assuming power to control highways and waterways, and requisition ships and aircraft. In May, wharves, oil installations, power stations, and premises of public utilities were declared protected areas. In July, power was taken to detain all persons suspected of sympathizing with the enemy, to control assemblies, enter premises and, in October, to declare whole areas prohibited areas. From the summer of 1940 onwards, the Japanese threat became more ominous and a further profusion of emergency regulations along similar lines, implementing allied economic measures against Japan, became necessary.

How did the Hong Kong Government machine adapt itself to the new demands the emergency made upon it?

At first, responsibility for discharging special duties under the emergency regulations rested with 'competent authorities', and until the needed war-time departments could be set up, these duties were entrusted to appropriate departmental heads. In November 1939 the Secretary for Chinese Affairs became Director of Intelligence; the Finance Secretary, Stores Controller; the Harbour Master, Controller of Water Transport and Detaining Officer; the Commissioner of Police, Controller of Land Transport and Chief Security Officer; the Director of Public Works, Accommodation Officer; the Superintendent of Imports and Exports, Controller of Trade; the Chairman of the Urban Council, Controller of Food; the Crown Solicitor, Director of Evacuation; and an Army Officer, Defence Security Officer. The only new department set up in 1939 was that of the Director of Air Raid Precautions. Improvisation was the order of the day and administrative machinery was built up gradually. The compulsory Registration Ordinance was carried out by the Police, the Compulsory Service Ordinance was administered by the Military under the Defence Committee; the Director of Education became Chief Censor; the emergency camps for military internees were placed under the joint control of the Police Commissioner and the Director of Medical Services, and the Manager of the Kowloon-Canton Railway headed a War Supplies Board. As the war progressed, new Government departments became necessary. In November 1939 the Vice-Chancellor of the University became Chief Censor, and the Censorship became an independent department in the following year. An Immigration department had to be set up in November 1940 when the problems of overcrowding and security forced the Government to restrict entry into the Colony. Many of the new departments had an Advisory Committee to ensure that war emergency decisions should be discussed by those with practical knowledge. Exchange Control began in September 1939, and an Exchange Control Office was set up with an Exchange Fund Advisory Committee under the Chairmanship of the Financial Secretary and with three prominent British bankers as members. In April 1940 a War Revenue Ordinance led to the creation of a War Taxation Department under a Commissioner with a Board of War Taxation consisting of the Financial Secretary as Chairman, the Defence Secretary and three unofficial members. In addition a Board of Review of twenty prominent citizens was set up to consider cases arising from its administration.

A Labour Officer was appointed in March 1940 to complement the British Government's policy of improving living conditions in the colonies; he was responsible to the Secretary for Chinese Affairs and was advised by a Labour Advisory Board.

The Food Control Office, a vital piece of administrative machinery, became necessary after the food price control of September 1939, and the Chairman of the Urban Council became Food Controller until April 1940 when a separate appointment was made and a new Food Office set up. In December 1940 a Controller of Rice was added to the Food Control Office, and in May 1941 a Board of Directors of eight members, with the Financial Secretary as Chairman and the Controller of Food as a member, was appointed to control the Government rice monopoly. A Food and Firewood Control Board was added later, under an army brigadier as Chairman, a naval commander, the Controller of Food, the Controller of Rice, and one unofficial member. A Prices Board was set up in 1941 under the Financial Secretary, the Controller of Food, Controller of Stores, and two unofficial members.

A War Supplies Board with the head of the Kowloon-Canton Railway as Controller of Supplies appeared in 1941, and there was an Essential Commodities Board with an unofficial member of the Legislative Council as Chairman and the Controller of Food and Controller of Rice as members. The 1941 Staff List also lists a Department of Information with a cadet officer as Secretary. A Fisheries Research Station appeared in 1941, again following the Home Government's policy of raising living standards, under a member of the University staff as Director, who was also made Scientific Officer to the Controller of Food.

In addition, many civil servants had to assume additional duties. The head of the Trade and Technical Schools, a mechanical engineer, became also Controller of Land Transport, and the Harbour Master remained as Controller of Water Transport. A Metals Controller, who was a local mechanical engineer, was appointed in August 1941, and in the same month a Controller of Trade was appointed.

The civil establishment was inevitably subject to strain through the great extension of its responsibilities. There were not enough administrative officers to go round and qualified local recruits had temporarily to be brought in and all departments had to expand their assistant and clerical staffs. As will be seen, this expansion of staff with limited experience brought serious difficulties.

Economic warfare was a key battle-front of the war. British policy in regard to the colonies was to ensure the optimum use of manpower, to stimulate the production of primary resources particularly where directly contributing to the war effort, to control imports and exports so as to economize on shipping and reduce demands on British industry, thus freeing it for more essential war production, to safeguard vital foreign exchange and deny economic resources such as Malayan tin and rubber to the enemy. Unfortunately this strategy necessitated much interference with that unrestricted freedom of trade which was the basis of Hong Kong's economic prosperity as an entrepôt, and seriously affected the economic life of the Colony. The economic blockade of enemy coasts had been for centuries a British strategic weapon, but the concept of total war with the object of damaging the enemy's economic power to sustain all-out war entailed a much stricter control of trade and currency.

On 23 August 1939 all colonies were warned that war was probable, necessitating exchange control; in the meantime, gold and valuable foreign exchange had to be conserved and non-sterling imports restricted. A draft of the British Government's Defence (Finance) Regulations was sent to all colonies inviting them to act on those lines, and when war came on 3 September 1939 they were ready to play their part.

On 2 September 1939 ships entering harbour were ordered to supply one copy of the ship's manifest to the Superintendent of Imports and Exports, and, before sailing, one copy of the export manifest listing the goods loaded in Hong Kong. Under the Emergency Powers (Colonial Defence) Order in Council 1939, the Government in Hong Kong on 3 September 1939 assumed extensive powers to control the movement of all ships and aircraft, the production, storage, distribution, sale, purchase, use and price of all articles essential for defence or essential to the life of the community. On 4 September 1939 a United Kingdom Order banning the sale or transfer of British ships and aircraft without permission was applied to Hong Kong. On the same day, essential services were defined and a list published. Essential services were defined by Government Order issued on 4 September 1939 as (1) all government undertakings and (2) all undertakings, whether public or private, for the supply of water, heat light and power, communication by telegraph, radio or telephone, transport by land, sea or air, and the care of the sick. People were warned of the penalties incurred by trading with the enemy, and on 9 September the export of some forty materials of strategic value was prohibited without licence. At the same time the liquidation of German assets was begun and the old post of Custodian of Enemy Property was revived, with the Official Receiver assuming its duties. In this economic-warfare emergency legislation there was much trial and error before satisfactory arrangements were evolved.

Control of trade and control of currency went hand in hand, and both created difficulties for Hong Kong, which needed the minimum of restriction in the currency exchange markets. Hong Kong was not in the sterling area because the importance of its trade with China forced it to link its currency more closely with that country than with Britain. Hong Kong was therefore a special case for which special arrangements were necessary.

In Britain full control of imports and exports and of foreign exchange was applied. The State took over all foreign exchange privately held or subsequently acquired by British residents, made all exports subject to licence to ensure that all foreign exchange earnings should be available to the Government, and also licensed imports to ensure that foreign exchange should be made available only for essential purposes. The Hong Kong Government followed Britain's lead when, on 8 September 1939, the export from the Colony of gold, securities, foreign currency and bank notes without a permit was prohibited, and contraband articles were specified. Lists of German firms and organizations being wound up were issued from time to time and on 15 September a list of eighteen 'authorized' banks, to deal in foreign exchange, subject to government control, was issued. They included all the important British, foreign and Chinese banks, including the Japanese Yokohama Specie Bank.

In other respects Britain's lead could be followed only with difficulty. The Financial Secretary outlined the Government's economic and commercial policy in the course of his Budget speech on 12 October 1939. He said, 'The circumstances of Hong Kong and particularly the great entrepôt trade and financial business upon which the Colony lives, render impossible, or at least highly dangerous, the adoption here of the full measures of control adopted as above in the home country and elsewhere in the British Colonies.'

The steps taken instead were to ensure that foreign exchange could be purchased only from the authorized banks which were subject to Government instructions as to the purposes for which it might be used, for example, capital transfers and speculative transactions were ruled out. Because of the international character of Hong Kong, the surrender of privately-held foreign exchange was required only from British subjects residing in the Colony, but the Financial Secretary explained that foreign exchange acquired in the course of business would be excepted because this would normally be done through one of the authorized banks and would therefore be already subject to control.

In addition, the export of Chinese and Hong Kong bank notes and the dispatch of family remittances to China was made subject to nominal control, simply because the close personal ties between the people of Hong Kong and those of South China made it difficult to check the flow of funds across the border. As a result, the Home Government, fearing a leakage of sterling through Hong Kong, refused to allow unrestricted exchange dealings between London and the Colony, although it made available sufficient exchange for normal commercial needs.

The Financial Secretary also said that the Secretary of State had agreed that a full import-export licensing system was not appropriate for Hong Kong. Instead, the Hong Kong Government limited imports of luxuries by using the disincentive of increased taxation. Duties on petrol, wines and spirits were forthwith doubled, and those on Empire wines increased by 25 per cent. In addition, power was taken to prohibit the import of certain specified articles except under licence, the intention being to issue licences freely where the goods were to be re-exported, and sparingly in other cases. As the war proceeded and particularly following German victories in Europe in the summer of 1940, further measures had to be taken. In May 1940 all colonies were instructed to tighten their controls over exchange and trade, and when Italy joined in the war, trade with Switzerland, the Balkan countries, Spain, and Portugal, was forbidden. The export licence system was given added urgency because of the need to prevent strategic goods reaching the enemy or enemy-occupied countries, and the Colony's export licences were accepted by the British naval control. But no efficient system of trade control proved possible in Hong Kong despite all attempts to find one. There were no customs checks and the Colony was not in the sterling area, yet much trade was done in sterling by London companies through agents in Hong Kong, and many of the imports were destined to be re-exported.

In July 1940 when Britain tightened the control of sterling, to meet the special case of Hong Kong the Chinese continued to be allowed free sterling, but only for use in making payments to the sterling area. Britain hesitated to bring Hong Kong into the sterling area because of the entrepôt trade and the difficulty of making controls effective, owing to the large amount of its currency notes moving in and out of China where they traditionally freely circulated. Hong Kong was still allowed to retain its foreign currency earnings from commerce, though this was less serious for Britain because of the large share in the Colony's trade controlled by London firms who had to hand over to the British Government all foreign currency proceeds. Again, since much foreign trade passed through Hong Kong, Britain insisted that all exports to Britain from the Colony were to apply for United Kingdom import licences with the aim of admitting only goods of genuine empire origin.

Exports to Indo-China were subject to licence after the Japanese set up bases there. There was much smuggling via Portuguese Macao, and the British Government was seriously concerned, particularly over the sale to Japan of Chinese wolfram, antimony and tin, and in January 1941 it began to buy up to 150 tons per month of Chinese wolfram for sale to the United States. In July 1940 exports of scrap iron and oil were restricted to prevent them reaching the Japanese, a matter of defence rather than conservation of currency. The ban on the imports of foreign cars into Hong Kong had to be relaxed in July 1941 because British cars were in short supply; scarcity led to inflated values for second-hand cars, so that in August the purchase of all cars, new and second-hand, was subject to policy control. The order for the first double-decker buses for the Colony also had to be cancelled, because Britain could not supply them.

In July 1941 Japanese assets in Hong Kong were frozen,

following similar action in Britain and the United States, but trade on a barter basis was allowed to continue for some time. Blocked Japanese accounts were credited with the proceeds of commercial transactions, but no transfer of the credits to Japan was allowed. Chinese accounts in Hong Kong were also frozen at the request of the Chinese government, to prevent their use by the Japanese in occupied China.

The restriction of imports to save valuable currency was supplemented by a policy of encouraging local industries. The Allied Eastern Group Supply Council was set up in March 1941, following a conference under British chairmanship of representatives of India, Malaya, Hong Kong, Ceylon, Australia, New Zealand and the East African territories, to develop production for war needs in those areas. It recommended that naval vessels should be built in Hong Kong, and despite the threat from Japan, some steps were taken to bring materials to the Colony for this purpose. The British Ministry of Supply sent a mission to Hong Kong in 1941 to enquire into Hong Kong's potential. The Governor set up a local Board to advise on the expansion of local industries and some orders for telephone sets, woollen goods, cutlery, optical glasses, barbed wire and stirrup pumps were placed; but large-scale orders never materialized because of the fear of a Japanese attack. A plan to build an optical factory to produce 4,000 binoculars a month was strongly supported by the Government which helped to finance the scheme. The Eastern Group Supply Council wanted the factory to be in Burma but the manufacturers were anxious to have it in Hong Kong to take advantage of the supply of Chinese labour. The factory was ready in August 1941, but the Ministry of Supply refused to assume any responsibility for it or place any orders, because the factory had been moved from Shanghai to Hong Kong without its authorization.

In July 1941 the Defence (Finance) Regulations, which up to then had affected only British subjects, were made applicable to everyone; the number of banks authorized to deal with foreign exchange was reduced to eleven, and an Exchange Control Office was set up in The Hongkong and Shanghai Banking Corporation Building as from 5 August 1941. Hong Kong was thus forced into the sterling area. The Chinese were allowed to carry sums to and from Hong Kong in dollars or yuan not exceeding HK$1,000 in amount, small personal remittances to and from China also continued, and in September 1941 Chinese in Free China could draw sums up to this permitted maximum.

The Colony's coinage needed some control too, for different reasons. On 29 May 1941 paper 1-cent notes had to be issued to replace the 1-cent copper coins which were disappearing because they were more valuable as metal. In October 1941 the Press reported that the coins were to be supplemented by notes because so many coins were being smuggled to Shanghai. The Financial Secretary on 11 October 1941 laid down a premium of one per cent for the nickel 5-cent and 10-cent pieces and a half per cent for 1-cent pieces. The 5- and 10-cent pieces were pure nickel for which there was a big demand; the Government claimed it had evidence that coins were being exported in large amounts and were being sold to enemy agents. The public was admonished not to hoard nickel coins and a Bill was brought in on 16 October, replacing the 5- and 10- cent pieces by notes which began circulating a few days later. It is reasonably certain that Hong Kong coins found their way into Japanese hands via Shanghai and some no doubt found their way back again during the fighting in a more unpleasant form.

The cost of the expansion of Government services was met by the imposition of special war taxation embodied in a war budget additional to the ordinary budget. In October 1939 the Governor announced that there would be two budgets, one for ordinary Government expenditure and the other for special war expenses to fulfil the Colony's obligations as a member of the British Empire at war. He suggested that Hong Kong might help by shouldering much more of the defence burden and with gifts. He also announced, on instructions from London, that an income tax was considered the most suitable source of additional revenue in this lightly-taxed community and hoped that machinery would be ready within six months. He softened the blow by saying that high rates of tax were not envisaged, but that it was intended to impose an excess profits tax later. The income tax was estimated to yield $10 million per year, of which $7 million would, after local defence expenditure had been met, be available as a gift to the United Kingdom. The new tax met with an immediate outcry. The General Chamber of Commerce and the Chinese Chamber of Commerce both protested and the tax was condemned by all the unofficial members of the Legislative Council. The main arguments were that it would cause a flight of capital from Hong Kong, that the Chinese would resent an inquisitorial tax, and that Chinese account books would have to be translated into English.

The Government bowed to the storm. The Financial Secretary, Sydney Caine, an uncompromising advocate of income tax, was called to London to head the economic section of the Colonial Office. The Hong Kong Government agreed to set up a representative Income Tax Committee, which was later given wider terms of reference and became known as the War Revenue Committee. Following closely the Committee's report, a War Revenue budget imposed four new taxes, a Property Tax of 5 per cent on the rateable value, a Salaries Tax at 4 per cent on the first $5,000 of annual taxable income and 10 per cent thereafter, a Corporation Profits Tax and a Business Profits Tax, at, in each case, 5 per cent on profits from $10,000 to $100,000 and 10 per cent on profits in excess of the amount. At the same time certain duties were increased, such as those on liquor, to restrict demand. The Government estimated this new taxation would yield $6 million, sufficient to cover the administrative costs of the War Revenue Department, additional war expenditure on the Volunteer Forces, the Censorship Department, the internment of enemy aliens, the Department of Information, the Shipping Control Board, and the Food Control Office, totalling nearly $2 million. This would leave $4 million to build ships for Britain, though there was some doubt whether the Colony had the capacity to build up to this amount. The Chinese unofficial members of the Legislative Council pledged their support of the British war effort and at the same time, the Legislative Council voted its first direct gift of £100,000 to the British Government, additional to the military contribution of $6 million annually for five years agreed to in 1939, and $2¼ million for special defence and war expenditure. The new taxation took effect on 1 April 1940. In June 1940 another £100,000 was voted to the British

Government. Also in June 1940 an ordinance had to be passed to prevent landlords from passing on the property tax in the form of increased rents, and in December 1941 rents were fixed as at 1 July 1941 and tenants could recover all increases since that date. The 1940 Budget referred only to war taxation and estimates because the 1939 Budget covered fifteen months to 1 April 1941, as it had been decided to move the end of the financial year from 31 January to 31 March.

While the special war revenue was close to that anticipated, war expenditure was very much in excess of the estimate, and additional war taxation became necessary. At the Budget debate in the Legislative Council in January 1941 the yield of the special war taxes was stated to be just over $6 million, but the special war expenditure came to nearly $12 million instead of the anticipated $2 million, largely due to Air Raid Precautions expenditure and purchases of reserve stocks of food. Tobacco duties had already been increased in the previous October, and increased or new duties on oils, liquor entertainment and table waters were imposed; estate duties and postage rates were raised, and a 1 per cent surcharge levied on rates. To meet the deficit on war expenditure, the War Revenue Committee was revived, and the Government again urged that income tax was the fairest method of spreading the burden but did not insist on it because 'This Bill's purpose is to finance a not inconsiderable free gift from public funds to His Majesty's Government, and in such a case it would be improper to force upon the would-be donors by the use of that official majority, a taxation method to which the unofficial members of this Council had objected strongly and unanimously.' The Committee reported in May 1941, recommending increases in existing rates of war taxation from 5 per cent to 10 per cent to 6 per cent and 12 per cent, but in fact Government increased these rates to 7 per cent and 14 per cent respectively while conceding increased allowances for families. This was accepted, subject to a Government assurance that any surplus from war revenue would be devoted to the war effort or essential local services. The Government continued to threaten a full income tax, but Hong Kong was overrun before the threat could be carried out.

Hong Kong assisted the British war effort by donating to

Britain a gift of £200,000 a year from the profits of the Exchange Fund, though the British Government discouraged the Colonies from making outright gifts to Britain, preferring that these sums should be regarded as interest-free loans, and treated as reserves available to meet the cost of post-war reconstruction.

Hong Kong was willing to make a financial contribution to the British war effort. In December 1941 the sale of 3 per cent Savings Certificates was proposed to provide war material for Britain or as a free gift, but the Japanese attack prevented their issue. There were a number of private subscriptions. The South China Morning Post 'Bomber Fund' raised $2,671,076 during 1940 and 1941; $16,135 went to the Malta Relief Fund, the Committee of the British Prisoners of War Fund raised $7,115, and the British War Organization Fund, $700,000. There were many other funds, e.g. Lord Mayor's Fund for the Relief of Air Raid Victims and Mobile Canteens Fund. The total subscribed amounted to about $10 million all told. In addition the 'Bowl of Rice' campaign organized by the China Defence League aimed at raising $40,000; by this, donors ordered a meal in any one of eleven selected restaurants but ate only a bowl of rice and donated the price of the meal to the Chinese war effort. This was additional to the $172,808, raised up to July 1941 by the Chinese Relief Association and the Hong Kong and South China Branch of the British Fund for the Relief of Distress in China.

IV

THE COLONY'S OWN DEFENCE PREPARATIONS

'The present policy of the government . . . is that all the resources of Hong Kong must be retained in Hong Kong for the defence of the colony.'

Major-General A.E. Grasett, G.O.C..
Announcement in Legislative Council, 30 May 1940

THE succession of international crises during these years clearly required the Hong Kong Government to assist the imperial regular garrison forces by hurrying on its own defence preparations. These were co-ordinated by a Defence Secretary with a Defence Committee comprising representatives from the Armed Services and government departments most concerned with defence policy. Its actual membership was never publicly divulged.

One urgent need was to strengthen the local volunteer forces. This led to the compulsory registration of men of military age and the introduction of compulsory military service, two measures that perhaps first brought home to Hong Kong people the seriousness of the threat of war. The Registration Ordinance of March 1939 required all British subjects of European birth aged 18 to 55 to register and give their qualifications, and was designed as a preliminary step to compulsory service and the efficient deployment of man-power. British subjects of Chinese extraction were allowed to register voluntarily after the Chinese members of the Legislative Council had assured the Governor of Chinese support, but it was admittedly difficult to include the Chinese, even if born here, because so few possessed birth certificates. A Compulsory Service Ordinance was duly passed on 28 July 1939 and Hong Kong was Britain's first colony to follow her lead in introducing conscription. By it, all British subjects of European origin coming under the Registration Ordinance were made liable to some form of compulsory service and, if fit, to be enrolled in a Defence Reserve. Aliens were allowed to volunteer. Citizens of the Dominions were exempt if resident in Hong Kong for less than two years, though in practice they were given three months to volunteer, after which they were made subject to the Ordinance. The Reserve was divided into three groups. Firstly, for the fit, a combatant group aged 18 to 41 who were drafted into the Hong Kong Volunteer Defence Corps (H.K.V.D.C.) or the Hong Kong Naval Volunteer Force (H.K.N.V.F.). Secondly, a key-post group similar to the schedule of reserved occupations in Britain, who were given some military training but not allowed to volunteer for the armed forces without the written consent of their employers. Finally, for the less fit, a general group for non-combatant duties such as the medical services, essential services and special constabulary. A compulsory medical examination resulted in some 62.5 per cent being found fit for general service, 14.8 per cent for guard duties and 20.1 per cent for sedentary duties, leaving only 2.6 per cent rejected as unfit for service. Appeals could be lodged against being allotted to any particular group. A Compulsory Service Tribunal to review these cases consisted of at least three members taken from a panel of five chosen by the Governor. These five members were the Puisne Judge; Sir Henry Pollock, the senior unofficial member of the Legislative Council and a distinguished lawyer; a naval commander; the Deputy Assistant Adjutant-General, China Command; and a partner of the shipping firm of Mackinnon, Mackenzie. If a man were still dissatisfied, he could take his case to an Appeals Tribunal of three members consisting of the Chief Justice, an unofficial member of the Legislative Council, and the Assistant Adjutant and Quartermaster-General, China Command. Exemption from service was granted on the grounds either that 'Imperial or Colonial interests would be served thereby' or that serious hardship to the individual would result. The first Compulsory Service Tribunal sat on 28 August 1939 and heard some 250 cases; conscientious objectors were in fact extremely few. They were not posted to a combatant unit without their consent and were normally directed into medical or ambulance units. By a Government Notice of 10 August 1939 the Commissioner of Police was made responsible for the administration of the Ordinance on its civil side.

In May 1940 the G.O.C., Major-General A. E. Grasett, D.S.O., announced in the Legislative Council that the age for the combatant group would be raised from 41 to 46, and that allocation to groups would be reviewed. He considered the key-post group too large, and proposed to move some to the combatant group unless it was clearly essential for them to remain where they were, and all were to have military training. At the same time he announced the formation of an additional volunteer group for men over military age and unable to serve in operational units but who were willing and able to 'undertake static guard duties of vulnerable points'. Organized by A. W. Hughes, Manager of the Union Insurance Society of Hong Kong, with official status as an auxiliary unit of the H.K. Volunteer Defence Corps, they were nicknamed the 'Hughesiliers' and by the more waggish, the 'Methusaliers'. When the attack came this veteran group fought with singular bravery. Chinese and local Portuguese were allowed to register and according to a press report 450 Chinese and 1,000 Portuguese so registered for service. All conscripts placed in the combatant group of the Hong Kong Defence Reserve were regarded as automatically assigned to the H.K.V.D.C., including its air section, or to the H.K.N.V.F. Hong Kong residents were not permitted to do their military service in England; in fact the British Government discouraged young men from returning home to enlist.

The Hong Kong Volunteer Defence Corps had a long history going back to 1855.[1] It had been manned mainly by British of European origin with some European nationals, but the crisis now forced it to take on a more distinctively local character, a point noted with pleasure by the Governor in his 1938 budget speech. A Portuguese Company had been formed in 1924 and created a great deal of local interest; in May 1938 a Chinese Company was recruited and at about the same time

[1] The most authoritative account of the Volunteers during the Japanese campaign is *A record of the actions of the Hongkong Volunteer Defence Corps in the battle for Hong Kong, December 1941* (Hong Kong, n.d.). John Luff's *The Hidden Years* (S.C.M.P. Hong Kong, 1967) is largely based on personal accounts of members of the Volunteers, of the battle and its aftermath, the captivity of these gallant defenders of Hong Kong.

a Pay Unit was added, and the Commanding Officer, Adjutant and the Regimental Sergeant-Major became full-time regular Army appointments; annual training camps were introduced in November 1938, and a Reserve of Officers, formed in June 1939, was attached to the Corps. The addition of the conscripted element following the Compulsory Service Ordinance does not appear to have altered its character in any way. The Colonial Secretary, in view of increasing local enlistment, gave an assurance to the Legislative Council on 27 July 1939 that there would be no racial discrimination in the Corps in any respect.

On 25 August 1939 new regulations under the 1933 Volunteer Ordinance brought some changes. The structure of the Corps now comprised the following units.

Corps Headquarters, five Batteries of Artillery, the 5th Battery being Anti-Aircraft, Field Company Engineers, Beach Light Company, Corps Signals, a Mobile, Column consisting of an Armoured Car Platoon and Motor Machine-Gun Platoon, five Machine-Gun Companies, the Second, Fourth and Fifth being described as Scottish, Chinese and Portuguese respectively, an Anti-Aircraft Company (Portuguese), Air Arm, Army Service Corps Company, Field Ambulance, Pay Section, Reserve of Officers, and Training Cadre. The following were termed Auxiliary Units: Railway Operating Detachment Cadre, Special Guard Company, i.e., the 'Hughesiliers', Fortress Signal Company, and the Stanley Platoon of Prison Officers. The Nursing Detachment, described as an Affiliated Unit, was set up in March 1939. Units also had reserve sections, generally manned by those with three years' efficient service. The Armoured Car Platoon, originally a cavalry unit, had lost its horses in the previous March. The structure of the Corps shows evidence of an intention to organize it, in part at least, on national lines and the Scottish, Portuguese and Chinese infantry companies served as such; the Scottish Company followed established traditions by having its own distinctive glengarry cap, and wore the kilt on ceremonial occasions. On the outbreak of the fighting in December 1941 the Corps had broadly the above organization with the addition of a Corps Artillery Headquarters, and a 7th Infantry Company.

The same regulations increased the minimum hours of

training to 40 per year for recruits, 25 for other members, except those with three years' efficient service for whom 20 hours was deemed sufficient, and a four-day camp was compulsory. In July 1940 all members of auxiliary units had to attend parades as ordered by the Commandant. Whole-day training was introduced but was abandoned in March 1941 because of the adverse effect on business houses, so part-time training of one half-day and two evening parades per week was introduced. In November 1941 all members of the Volunteer Defence Forces and Civil Defence Services were protected against dismissal from their job or loss of pay due to the calls on their time for training with their units. A club for Chinese members of the Corps was formed in January 1941, assisted by prominent Chinese merchants. On 7 December 1941, the day before the Japanese attacked, the Volunteers were mobilized and took up their war stations.

The Volunteer Air Arm existed only on paper, almost certainly for the reason that no equipment could be given to it owing to the demands for aircraft at home.

The Hong Kong Naval Volunteer Force was formed by members of the Yacht Club on Trafalgar Day, 1933, and incorporated by Ordinance in December of the same year. The boat boys enrolled as ratings under the boat-owners as officers. A small sloop, H.M.S. *Cornflower*, was used for training. In 1937 the Legislative Council voted that the men should be given rations in addition to their 15 cents per drill, in order to make the Force more attractive. In June 1939, with war imminent, the members of the Force were made liable to service and training outside Hong Kong because of the limited training facilities available locally. When the Hong Kong Naval Defence Force came under the control of the Admiralty it automatically acquired the status of a Royal Naval Volunteer Reserve. Despite the Governor's explanation that the men would not be required to serve with the Royal Navy in time of peace and that the main purpose of the Force remained the defence of Hong Kong, certain named officers and ratings were in fact called up for general war service by Proclamation on 30 August 1939, and further lists of members of the Force called up appeared on 4 September 1939 and 26 October 1939, each man having the right of appeal against mobilization on grounds of hardship. The remainder of the H.K.N.V.F. was mobilized in July 1941. In September 1940 the pressure on British naval operations forced the return of H.M.S. *Cornflower* to operational duties with the Royal Navy, but a prominent Hong Kong businessman, Sir Robert Hotung, came to the rescue by presenting the vessel *Tai Hing* to replace it. In July 1941 a mine-watching section was added. As will be seen, the withdrawal of a number of regular naval units from Hong Kong, leaving only a token force, gave the Japanese complete control of the seas and limited the scope of the H.K.N.V.F.

Arrangements were made in 1939 to bring medical defence up-to-date. This, according to the Medical Department's Annual Report for 1939, 'involved the planning of first-aid posts, casualty clearing and relief hospitals, the recruitment and training of personnel and the collecting of ambulances, stretchers, instruments, dressings and so on'. Preparations were made for auxiliary relief hospitals at various places including the University, St. Stephen's College, Stanley, the Jockey Club premises in Happy Valley, Repulse Bay Hotel, and St. Albert's Convent. The Auxiliary Nursing Service was formed in March 1939 and attached to the Volunteers.

The colonies were instructed to prepare schemes of air raid precautions, similar to those being adopted in Britain, to meet the threat of attack from the air and the possible use of gas. So a nominal sum of $50,000 for air raid precautions was included in the estimates for 1938, being one of the earliest of the special defence measures taken in Hong Kong. The budget for the following year, presented on 13 October 1938, included the sum of $338,065 for air raid precautions, and the Governor warned that this new office would make big demands on the public purse, a warning that was to prove a considerable understatement. In June 1939 the Colonial Secretary stated in the Legislative Council that after consultation with the Secretary of State, A.R.P. policy was to provide sandbags for the protection of public buildings, to provide supplementary fire appliances and reserve medical stores, and issue respirators to those employed in essential services and special clothing for decontamination squads. It was also decided to safeguard essential services by making cash grants to public utility companies for

A.R.P. purposes and preparing plans for digging trenches when needed. Tunnels and steel shelters were ruled out on the ground that the dense population would have insufficient warning in case of attack to leave their homes and seek shelter. Instead, householders were to be advised on making their homes more secure, and respirators made available at cost price. The budget provision was accordingly increased to $1,950,000. On 1 September 1939 Wing Commander A. H. S. Steel-Perkins arrived to assume the post of A.R.P. Officer, later renamed Director of Air Raid Precautions.

Black-out exercises began in September 1938 and continued at quarterly intervals during 1939 and thereafter with increasing frequency, the first black-out under full war-time conditions coming in August 1940. A number of fines had to be imposed for breaches of the regulations and press reports show that fines for black-out offences became increasingly common after each black-out exercise, e.g., in March 1941 an infringer of the regulations was fined 10 cents for striking a match during a black-out. Even as late as April 1941 air observers during an exercise reported that Hong Kong was 'a mass of lights', and in November Government had to threaten heavier fines. The black-outs caused much inconvenience, especially during the sultry summer of 1941, as it meant ferries being stopped and transport slowed or halted. There were cases of assault in the imposed darkness, and in November 1940 the A.R.P. Director had to issue a warning against an extortion racket in which householders were threatened with report to the authorities for showing a light during a black-out. In July 1941 the press reported anti-British posters being discovered in Yaumati after one black-out had been lifted.

The A.R.P. Headquarters and training school were opened in May 1940 in Morrison Hill Road (at the post-war Harcourt Clinic) and were designed also to serve as a first aid station in time of war. The A.R.P. organization aimed at providing one A.R.P. post for each 100 houses, with four men and two women wardens working in each post on a two-shift basis. The intention was to have 1,600 posts and therefore some 9,600 wardens. By the end of 1939 there were roughly 2,400 wardens, another 250 in decontamination squads, 500 more in rescue and demolition squads, and 500 in roads and water repair parties, and 800 warden's posts had been selected. As well as a number of Police, Fire Brigade officers and others had been given A.R.P. training. Chinese wardens were paid $1.50 per day, compared with $8 per day to their European colleagues until public criticism in September 1940 led to all wardens being paid alike. Even so, recruitment was slow, and in November 1940 applications were invited for another 5,000 wardens, additional to the 2,500 already appointed, with the object of ensuring adequate shift working.

The failure to provide air-raid shelters for the masses, on the ground of probable lack of warning time to make use of them, was strongly criticized by the Chinese unofficial members of the Legislative Council in the 1939 Budget debate, and also condemned in the Press. In September 1940 the Kowloon Residents' Association came out strongly in favour of blast and splinter-proof refuges on ground floors and trench and tunnel shelters where this was practicable. It estimated the cost of trench shelters at $5 to $6 per head, and tunnels 8 feet high and 7 feet wide, at $8–10 per head, and the total cost of shelter accommodation for 500,000 at $1½ million. These arguments, and the fear of a Japanese attack on Hong Kong in the summer of 1940, led Government to reverse its decision and embark on a colossal programme of building public shelters in the form of tunnels. By October 1940 tunnels were begun in King's Park in Kowloon, and were planned for Hong Kong Island at Beaconsfield Arcade in Queen's Road, at Ice House Street, under Belcher's Fort in Kennedy Town, under Government House in Lower Albert Road opposite the Colonial Secretariat Building, another in Wyndham Street near the Dairy Farm to link with that of Queen's Road and Ice House Street and another in Pottinger Street. Two more were in Ventris Road and Leighton Hill Road in the Happy Valley, the former being 8 feet wide with numerous side corridors and designed to shelter some 60,000 persons.

In November 1940 the Legislative Council passed a supplementary vote of $1 million for tunnels: in December it voted $3 million for A.R.P. and related defence purposes and in the 1941 Budget, a further sum of $4 million was voted towards the cost of tunnels. A tunnel at Aberdeen was included, and as late as 7 November 1941 three new tunnels were said to be under construction at Shaukeiwan to cater for up to 30,000 persons. In June 1941 the A.R.P. Director appealed for another 1,500 persons to train as tunnel wardens, additional to about 4,000 wardens then enrolled. Up to 1 October 1941 the total expenditure on A.R.P. was $8,068,293, including stores and the provision for anticipated expansion. The tunnels were not planned to be gas-proof and a gas attack would have required wet blankets to be hung at the entrance. Ventilation machinery was installed in only 3 groups of tunnels out of the 10 groups covering 21 sites.

Tunnelling caused damage to Government House. This old building, dating from 1854, was to have been replaced by a new Governor's residence at Magazine Gap which had been planned and contracted for, but the project had been halted on 8 September 1939 because of the war. The old building had to be hurriedly buttressed and the first floor verandah demolished. The press reported, incorrectly, that the Governor had taken refuge in Flagstaff House, the General's residence. Later, the Japanese found that the building needed extensive repairs and they virtually reconstructed it during their occupation.

The A.R.P. Department became the subject of grave scandal. The huge sums involved and the urgency of the work afforded fertile ground for graft and irregularities, particularly in the architectural branch of the A.R.P. Department. These were brought into the open by a Commission of Enquiry appointed in August 1941 under the Puisne Judge, P. E. F. Cressall. The enquiry came about because The Hongkong and Shanghai Banking Corporation blacked-out its building in Queen's Road for $87 instead of the $500 allocated by the A.R.P. officials. Suspecting an irregularity, the Bank claimed and received $500 and then reported the facts to Government. The architect to the A.R.P. Department was asked to give evidence on the matter and, failing to attend, he was found to have shot himself, while another British official in charge of the construction of A.R.P. tunnels was admitted to hospital with acute poisoning. It became clear that the irregularities were more serious than had been suspected.

The Commission met from 14 August to 7 November 1941 and its proceedings were reported at length in the Press. Its findings were never issued. War came a month later, and Judge Cressall took a draft report with him into internment at Stanley where he died in 1944; his draft was never found and after the war the enquiry was dropped, but sufficient evidence emerged during the hearings to reveal widespread inefficiency, irregularities and graft. The financial arrangement regarding the contracts for A.R.P. works and purchase of stores was for Government to reimburse contractors the cost plus 10 per cent as a reasonable commission or profit. It was discovered that Government was paying an extra 10 per cent on its own purchases and stores; for example, some contractors bought heavy equipment for their own use and charged this to A.R.P. construction work on Government account at 10 per cent commission. Bogus cartage companies were formed which let out contracts to others, retaining the 10 per cent for themselves. For example, a supervisor of a Chinese construction firm, who was later charged with corruption but acquitted on technical grounds, admitted that he had subcontracted cartage work to other firms, including one run by his wife, who had no lorries of any sort. Ephemeral firms appeared with different names but using the same premises and having the same man in control. Some firms were unable to produce accounts which the Commission demanded because they claimed the employees concerned had decamped. One firm was suspected of gaining contracts through the influence of a woman employee who was a very good friend of the Director of A.R.P.; that firm and two others secured the contract to make breeze blocks at 49¼ cents each, though one of the firms had no experience of concrete work, and a third firm had offered to make them at 38 cents each, a circumstance which led to the blocks being named after the lady. The Professor of Civil Engineering at the University gave evidence that only 46 of the 100 blocks tested stood up to the specified pressure of 1,500 lbs. Persons were not identified when being paid; monthly summaries for the purchase of stores were certified without supporting vouchers; the issue of explosives was not carefully checked and much was stolen for re-sale. Contracts were varied and government regulations broken by their not being published in the *Gazette*. Steel helmets were bought at excessive prices, wooden sleepers for lining the tunnels were purchased at higher prices than those originally offered; while eight million sandbags which had been bought at a cost of $900,000 were found to be of very inferior quality. Only three million bags in fact had been used. Generally, the state of affairs was summed up by the Chairman as an 'Alice-in-Wonderland situation'.

Still, there was something to be said in extenuation. The decision to give mass air raid protection, taken in the summer of 1940, not only completely reversed Government's previous policy, but was regarded as extremely urgent. The new A.R.P. organization had to be built up from scratch, and the Director claimed, in giving evidence, that he had been authorized by the Government in July 1940 to spend nearly half a million dollars without the prior approval of the Finance Committee; in mitigation he pleaded that if he broke General Orders he always secured the approval of senior Government officials afterwards. The Deputy Director of Public Works explained in evidence that General Orders had been broken on the verbal authority of General Norton, Officer Administering the Government from 6 August 1940 to 13 March 1941, because of the urgency of defence needs, and the acting Financial Secretary admitted that the rules were by-passed because of the need for urgency and secrecy; the acting auditor and acting Accountant-General also explained that under the cost plus 10 per cent system, they had to accept vouchers signed by the heads of departments. It is clear that since the work had to be pressed on with quickly, normal Government safeguards were by-passed and that not enough trained supervisory staff were available. Still, what appeared to be dishonest collusion between Government officers and contractors to divert money into their own pockets through bogus companies cannot be completely excused on these grounds.

In addition to A.R.P., a number of other auxiliary defence services had to be strengthened or improvised. A Police Reserve had been formed in 1927 comprising a Chinese Company, an Indian Company, a Flying Squad, and an Emergency Unit. It numbered 290 men in 1938, and was called out for active service in November of that year; and in the following year its strength was increased to 450, comprising the Chinese Company of 200, the Indian Company 200, and 50 each in the other two sections. It remained on active service until the Japanese took control of the Colony. A press report made in July 1941, but not mentioned in any Government publication, stating that the Chinese were invited to enrol as special constables in a Chinese Special Constabulary numbering 3,000 men to aid the Police in an emergency, probably refers to this Police Reserve. In September 1941 the Police were given military status as a militia in time of war and made liable to serve under their own officers as part of the defence forces. This presumably removed the danger of their being shot as armed civilians if they were captured by the enemy.

A number of other auxiliary services had to be organized as greater war preparedness became necessary. They were at first organized on an *ad hoc* basis, but on 4 July 1941 Civil Defence Corps regulations were issued, giving them a more definite organization, and between August and November various Auxiliary Corps came into being, all organized on similar lines. They were (1) Auxiliary Fire Service, under the Chief Officer, Fire Brigade, (2) Auxiliary Transport Service, under the Commissioner of Police, (3) Auxiliary Medical Corps, under the Director of Medical Services, (4) Auxiliary Conservancy Corps, under the Chairman of the Urban Council, (5) Auxiliary Civil Pay and Accounts Service, under the Accountant-General, (6) Auxiliary Labour Corps, under the Controller of Labour, (7) Auxiliary Supply Corps, under the Chief Manager, Kowloon-Canton Railway, (8) Auxiliary Ordinance Corps, under the Controller of Stores, dealing chiefly with firewood, (9) Auxiliary Quartering Corps, under the Rating and Valuation officer, (10) Auxiliary Public Works Corps, under the Director of Public Works, (11) Auxiliary Rescue and Demolition Corps, under the Director of Public Works, (12) the Auxiliary Communications Service, under the Postmaster-General.

The main aim of this organization of auxiliaries was to place them under some form of discipline, to provide uniforms or arm-bands and to prepare for war emergencies when normal civilian employment might cease. These auxiliary services were manned by those normally employed in these services in peace time, and by others directed under the Compulsory Service Ordinance for one reason or another into the non-combatant group of the Defence Reserve, and by Chinese volunteers.

In November 1941 Government was still appealing for recruits for the Civil Defence Services and a recruiting office was set up in Gloucester Arcade. The appeal for men and women irrespective of race was, of course, directed mainly to the Chinese to fill junior positions as administrative officers, nurses, clerks, motor engineers, doctors and various posts requiring professional qualifications. The Government approached the chief Hong Kong firms saying, 'We chiefly need responsible Chinese, preferably with a knowledge of English, to be trained for posts as junior officers in the Civil Defence Services.' It promised to look after the welfare of their dependants and the Defence Secretary announced 'members of the Civil Defence Services and their families would naturally have preference over non-members for billets, food and medical attention. A scheme of compensation for war injuries will be applied to all members'. The comment in the press was that Chinese should be offered senior jobs. But time was running out and clearly the difficulty was to induce local people to take an active part in civil and military defence and to occupy responsible posts in the rapidly expanding government departments.

One factor which probably hampered the Hong Kong defence effort was the extraordinary change-over in high-ranking government personnel just before the Japanese attack. A new Defence Secretary was appointed on 26 April 1941 and a new Commissioner of Police in the same month. The General Officer Commanding the Garrison, Major-General A. E. Grasett, a Canadian, left in August 1941 and his successor, Major-General C. M. Maltby, took over. The Governor, Sir Geoffrey Northcote, retired on medical advice and left on 6 September 1941; his successor, Sir Mark Young, arrived four days later from Barbados.[2] The Colonial Secretary, N. L. Smith, left and his successor, Mr. F. C. Gimson, arrived on Sunday, 7 December 1941, the night before the attack came.

[2] This statement, whilst borne out by G. C. Hamilton, *Government Departments in Hong Kong 1841–1966* (Hong Kong, 1967), the list of Governors on p. 17 is somewhat misleading. For the seven-month period (August 1940–March 1941) Lt.-General E. F. Norton was the Officer Administering the Government. This appointment of a 'Military Governor', to tighten up emergency precautions was seen by some influential officials in Hong Kong (e.g. the Commissioner, Chinese Maritime Customs, E. F. Pritchard) as a provocation to the Japanese.

V

THE PATTERN OF DEFENCE

'If Japan goes to war with us there is not the slightest chance of holding Hong Kong or relieving it.'

Winston Churchill to General Ismay, 7 January 1941

DISCUSSIONS on the defence of Hong Kong during the inter-war years always had a certain degree of ambivalence because, under the Washington Naval Limitation Treaty of 1922, the Colony was subject to a standstill agreement which precluded any extension of its military installations. Japan denounced the Treaty in December 1934; this termination took effect two years later, from which time Hong Kong was no longer subject to any such restriction. Even so, British service chiefs recognized that Hong Kong could not become a powerful military base since the Japanese in Taiwan could neutralize it at will, and doubted if it could be defended even if a large supporting fleet were available. It was therefore regarded as an outpost, important, but not so vital as to warrant the sending of large reinforcements to meet any possible threat. Like the British forces in Shanghai, the Hong Kong garrison was recognized to be in a tactically hopeless situation whose withdrawal would strengthen the over-all British military position, and, in fact, the two British battalions in Shanghai pulled out in August 1940. Yet withdrawal meant losing face, encouraging Japanese aggression, and discouraging the will to resist of China and other friendly Asian nations; besides, it was important to deny the Hong Kong harbour and port facilities to a potential enemy. Churchill put the argument succinctly in a letter to General Ismay given at the head of this chapter.

Clearly Hong Kong was to be defended for non-strategic reasons. The Japanese occupation of Hainan Island, the seizure of the Spratly Islands and the advance into French Indo-China left Hong Kong more dangerously isolated, and at the same time, with the concentration of British forces in Europe, the relief of Hong Kong in any emergency appeared even more problematic.

In 1937, when the defence of Hong Kong was free from any treaty restriction, a defence plan was adopted based on holding the Island and sufficient of the mainland to protect the harbour. Heavy artillery at strategic points on the Island's south coast gave protection against attack by sea, and a line of pill-boxes stretching from Gindrinkers Bay in the west to Tide Cove and thence over the hills to Port Shelter in the east, against attack by land. This line became well-known later as the Gindrinkers Line. Its pill-boxes were to be manned by the heavy machine-guns of the Middlesex Regiment, sited to give them connected arcs of fire. These were to be supplemented by light infantry patrols, and supported by mobile and medium artillery. The plan appeared to assume that sufficient troops would be made available to man these extensive Island and mainland defences.

However, a fresh look at the Colony's defence arrangements was demanded when, in May 1938, the Japanese landed troops at Amoy and Bias Bay, and appeared on the Hong Kong frontier, while at the same time the European situation grew more threatening. A new defence plan was evolved in that year, based on the realization that only limited forces would be now available in war time and that defence would have to be confined to the Island. In the New Territories, where the attack was expected, there would be delaying action sufficient to enable all military stores to be removed, and bridges and military installations to be destroyed. There was no intention to hold either Kowloon or the New Territories by military force; on the contrary it was anticipated under the new plan that the withdrawal of all forces to the Island of Hong Kong would be completed within forty-eight hours of the opening of war. The Gindrinkers Line of defence posts was discarded.

The pre-war garrison regular forces were weak. The naval forces normally comprised four destroyers, but one of these was absent from Hong Kong waters and two sailed for Singapore on the day of the Japanese attack, leaving only H.M.S. *Thracian*. There were also four gunboats *Cicala, Tern, Robin,* and *Moth*, a flotilla of eight motor torpedo-boats, and some smaller harbour vessels. The military garrison comprised four infantry battalions, the 2nd Royal Scots, the 1st Middlesex, the 2/14 Punjabis and the 5/7 Rajputs. There were just over four regiments of artillery, two Coastal Regiments of the Royal Artillery and a Medium Defence Battery manning the coastal guns; one A.A. Regiment, and the 1st Hong Kong Regiment of the Hong Kong and Singapore Royal Artillery. The latter manned mainly the mobile artillery and comprised two mountain batteries, each of two troops, one equipped with 3.7 howitzers using pack mules and the other with 4.5 howitzers on wheels, while their medium batteries used 6-inch howitzers. The H.K.S.R.A. was below strength as an attempt to recruit a number of local Chinese had been unsuccessful. The coastal defences just mentioned comprised 29 guns; there were eight 9.2-inch in batteries at Cape D'Aguilar, Stanley, and Mount Davis; fifteen 6-inch, in batteries at Pak Sha Wan, Big Wave Bay, Stanley, Chung Hom Kok, Mount Davis, and Stonecutters Island; two 4.7-inch at Belcher's Fort and four 4-inch divided between Cape D'Aguilar and Aberdeen. In the air there was a small R.A.F. flight of three Vildebeeste torpedo-bombers, quite obsolete, and two Walrus amphibians. There were local volunteer naval and military forces as detailed in a previous chapter but little civil defence until 1940.

The Island was parcelled out among the four infantry regiments, the Rajputs taking the north-east sector, the Punjabis the south-east, and the two British battalions, the rest. Beaches and other likely landing places were guarded by newly constructed pill-boxes manned by the Middlesex with their heavy machine-guns, with carefully co-ordinated arcs of fire designed to cover all vulnerable areas. The Punjabis were also to operate briefly on the mainland, before withdrawing to take up their station on the Island. A boom was placed across the Lye Mun Channel and the approaches to the harbour were mined, as were the beaches. Arrangements were made to dismantle the Gap Rock Lighthouse, thirty miles to the south.

At one point it looked as if the Hong Kong defences would be greatly strengthened to permit of more than a token resistance. In November 1940 Air Chief Marshal Sir Robert Brooke-Popham was appointed Commander-in-Chief Far East, based in Singapore. He strongly urged that the Colony should be held and that the reinforcements sufficient for this purpose should be sent, but the British Chief of Staff decided, on 7 February 1941, to leave the defence as it was. Again, in April 1941, representatives from the British, Dutch and American armed services met at Singapore to co-ordinate plans to meet a possible Japanese attack and evolved the so-called A.B.D.A. (American, British, Dutch, and Australian) Agreement by which, among other things, Hong Kong was to be given a more active role as an advanced United States naval base. This never materialized, for the British Chiefs of Staff regarded Hong Kong as too vulnerable, and, in any case, the United States did not accept the Agreement. Staff conversations regarding concerted action by the four Powers in the Far East continued during the year but hostilities commenced without any explicit agreement being reached.

Finally came the tragedy of the Canadian reinforcements. In August 1941 Major-General A. E. Grasett, commanding the garrison in Hong Kong, handed over to Major-General C. M. Maltby and returned to Britain. Being a Canadian, he travelled via Canada, and in Ottawa, he urged the Canadian Government under Mackenzie King to send two battalions to assist in the defence of Hong Kong, arguing that it would then be able to hold out for a prolonged period. This was a matter of some moment to the Canadians and Americans who were deeply concerned about the possibility of war in the Pacific for which they were militarily unprepared. The General went on to London where he represented to the Chiefs of Staff that a small reinforcement would boost the morale of the Hong Kong garrison out of all proportion to the numbers involved and might deter the Japanese by demonstrating Britain's determination to fight over Hong Kong. He suggested that Canada might be willing to send two battalions. This was agreed and the Canadians were asked to supply them.

The two Canadian battalions selected were the Royal Rifles of Canada, which had been stationed in Newfoundland, and the Winnipeg Grenadiers, which had been serving in the West Indies. They were admittedly not ready for immediate combat mainly because of shortages of newer weapons, but as Sir Lyman Duff's subsequent 'Report on the Canadian Expeditionary Force to Hong Kong'[1] pointed out, the whole of the Canadian Forces were short of equipment at that time, so that any regiments sent would have been similarly handicapped. The two regiments had to receive heavy drafts of raw recruits to bring them up to strength. The main factor in the choice was the wish to conserve the Canadian 4th and 6th Divisions, whose training was more advanced, for service in Europe. British military intelligence advised that war with Japan was not expected for some time, and that the men would have time to complete their training in Hong Kong.

They disembarked on 17 November 1941 with a small headquarters staff and other ancillary personnel. Their transport and heavy equipment never arrived, the ship carrying it being diverted by the Americans when war with Japan appeared imminent. In three weeks they found themselves locked in fierce combat, quite untrained for the role they were expected to play.

When, in October 1941, General Maltby received news of the Canadian reinforcements he revised his defence plan. Had he known that he had barely eight weeks left in which to train his men in their new positions, he would no doubt have acted differently. He decided that three battalions could now be deployed on the mainland, supported by the mobile and mountain artillery of the Hong Kong and Singapore Royal Artillery, leaving three battalions to garrison the Island as before. There was, of course, no question under the revised plan of holding the Japanese at the frontier, or of holding any part of the mainland indefinitely. The calculation was that the mainland could be held for much longer than the forty-eight hours which had been considered up to then the maximum possible. Maltby's cautious estimate was one week; the longer the troops on the mainland resisted, the longer the Island bastion would be able to hold out.

The revised defence plan was essentially a return to the pre-1938 plan based on the Gindrinkers Line. It was to stretch over eleven miles from Gindrinkers Bay, in the west, to the Shing Mun Reservoir, then to Tide Cove and over the hills via Tate's Cairn to Silverstrand Beach on Port Shelter and

[1] *Report on the Canadian Expeditionary Force to the Crown Colony of Hong Kong*, by Right Hon. Sir Lyman P. Duff, G.C.M.G., Royal Commissioner (Ottawa, 1942).

along the shore to Nam Wai in the east; its main feature was a line of pill-boxes built to take medium machine guns, supported by light-infantry patrols. The strongest point in the Line was the Shing Mun Redoubt,[2] a twelve-acre network of pill-boxes, concrete fire trenches covering attack from any direction, and underground shelters, as well as an artillery observation post; it was situated on the northern part of Smugglers' Ridge where it sloped down to the reservoir and its function was to bar the easiest and most vulnerable route to Kowloon. There were additional defensive positions along the short Ma Lau Tong Line from the north-east arm of Junk Bay to Kwun Tong, and an even shorter Hai Wan Line skirting the strongly fortified Devil's Peak which commanded the narrow Lye Mun Channel, the main entrance to the harbour, and which it was intended to hold.

Considerable progress had been made with the construction of the Line up to 1938, when the defence plan, of which it was an essential element, was abandoned. The result was that in 1941 much work was needed to make the Line fully operational, and, in the event, time ran out before the troops could be well-drilled in their positions. Still, the work was pushed on and commanding officers were briefed confidentially on their roles. The troops did not take up their positions in the Line immediately to avoid giving any hint to the Japanese that an attack on the Colony was anticipated, although, in any case, manning the line had to be delayed until the Canadians arrived.

There were weaknesses about the Gindrinkers Line. Much of it was under observation from Tai Mo Shan, and Needle Hill directly overlooked the Shing Mun Redoubt. It was a first and last line of defence since there was no space between it and Kowloon for a second line. Its length was excessive for only three battalions and it could only be thinly manned.

General Maltby attempted in October 1941 to increase his forces by recruiting a battalion of Chinese infantry under British officers, which he intended should be a machine-gun battalion, but by the time he had secured permission from the War Office and begun enlistment, it was too late. Over 600

[2] A. Muir, *The First of Foot* (Edinburgh, 1961), Ch. IV, pp. 81–128.

local Chinese young men offered themselves but because of the physical standards demanded, 5 feet 7 inches tall and a minimum of 125 lbs. weight, only 35 had actually been accepted by the first week in November. This would have been the first Chinese unit in the British army, though a number of local Chinese had been accepted into various units in such capacities as engineers, drivers, cooks, and mechanics, and of course considerable numbers had joined the Hong Kong Volunteer Defence Corps and the Hong Kong Volunteer Naval Force. Some had also joined the Hong Kong and Singapore Royal Artillery for service in Hong Kong, a regiment which celebrated its centenary in June 1941 and was recruited mainly from India, under British officers and some British N.C.Os.

As mentioned previously, in February 1940 the British Government decided that food supplies to last 130 days should be held for the Services, instead of the 90 days previously agreed as adequate, and at the same time Government agreed that reserves of essential food for the civilian population, such as rice, should be held for a similar period. In January 1941 all military stores and supplies were also increased to last for the same period. In the summer of 1940 Japanese troops moved again to the Hong Kong frontier, and also secured airfields and the right to station military forces in northern French Indo-China. This produced a scare and, under the fear of a Japanese attack, certain emergency measures were taken. The railway bridge at Lo Wu was made unusable, arrangements were made to demolish bridges and military installations in the New Territories and, as already mentioned, British women and children were evacuated to Australia.

On the arrival of the Canadians, the garrison forces moved into their new positions. One brigade of three regiments under Brigadier Wallis occupied the Gindrinkers Line on the mainland; the 2nd Royal Scots were on the left from Gindrinkers Bay to the Shing Mun Redoubt, the 2/14 Punjabis defended Shatin and Tide Cove and the 5/7 Rajputs took over the rest of the line to Port Shelter. They were supported by the Second Mountain Battery, the 3.7-inch howitzer Troop of the 1st Mountain Battery, and one medium battery, all of the H.K.S.R.A. There was a gap east of the Shing Mun Redoubt between the Royal Scots and the Punjabis which had been deliberately left to be covered by infantry patrols, so as to free one company as a reserve until the direction of the main Japanese attack should become apparent. Under earlier plans the Punjabis had been the battalion selected for mainland duty, and naturally one of its companies was deputed to cover the demolition parties. It accordingly moved to Fanling. Under these arrangements one Company of Rajputs was held in reserve.

The second, or Island Brigade, under the Canadian Brigadier J. K. Lawson, consisted of the Royal Rifles of Canada, the Winnipeg Grenadiers and the 1st Middlesex. The latter, as a heavy machine-gun unit, manned the pill-boxes mainly on the southern and western shores of the Island. The Royal Navy's role, assisted by the Hong Kong Volunteer Naval Force, was to withdraw all naval stores to Aberdeen, to man the harbour defences and to round up all junks and sampans to deny their use to the enemy on withdrawal to the Island. The R.A.F. planes were to strike only if a suitable target presented itself and only then at dawn or dusk. They were virtually destroyed in the first Japanese air-raid. The total strength of the garrison was about 12,000 men.

There were obvious weaknesses about the defence, besides those concerning the Gindrinkers Line. The absence of air support made reconnaissance virtually impossible and there was no radar to detect enemy forces approaching Hong Kong, with the result that the defence had to be prepared to meet attack from any quarter. Also ruled out were tactical air-strikes against enemy preparations and movements. Two anti-aircraft batteries were quite inadequate to meet air attack. In a lesser degree the lack of naval support was serious and though the few naval ships gave a good account of themselves, they were too few to prevent a landing.

Security over defence matters was sadly lacking and the Japanese were able to gain all the information necessary for success in their attack. It is difficult to see how it could have been otherwise. The open frontier, at least up to the imposition of immigration restrictions in July 1940, prevented any strict check being made on immigrants, and many supporters of the Japanese-sponsored puppet régime in Nanking under Wang Ching-wei entered the Colony unhindered and collaborated with the Japanese. The latter, like everyone else, were free to come and go, and Japanese agents found little difficulty in getting jobs as a cover to their activities. One named Yamaguchi was arrested on a charge of espionage and interned in La Salle College in August 1940. On the other hand, a Colonel Suzuki, who was in Hong Kong to learn English under regular interchange arrangements and who made no effort whatever to learn the language, was allowed to remain because of an unwillingness to annoy the Japanese, although his expulsion had been recommended. The lack of security could only be of advantage to the Japanese whose intelligence regarding Hong Kong was excellent. Maps were later found on Japanese officers, accurately pin-pointing every military installation. The Japanese were thus able to direct their air bombing and artillery shelling with the maximum effect.

On the other hand, by comparison, British intelligence was poor. In 1940 General Grasett felt so dissatisfied that he sent officers to Chungking to gain intelligence of Japanese troop movements. General Maltby, just before the attack, estimated Japanese forces in the Canton area at three divisions, with a brigade of artillery and a tank regiment, whereas there existed an army of four divisions. This seriously underestimated the Japanese, particularly in regard to artillery. Estimates of the fighting quality of the Japanese proved to be disastrously adrift. They were held to be wooden in their approach, inefficient at night operations, effective against the Chinese but likely to find the going very different when facing European troops. Their equipment for instance, light machine-guns, was thought to be unequal to that of the British, and their aircraft were regarded as of inferior quality, their pilots unused to night work and Japanese bombing inaccurate. The Japanese were grossly and inexcusably underestimated. More realistic estimates of the Japanese by British service attachés in Tokyo and by those with first-hand knowledge of the excellence of Japanese equipment and tactics in China and who warned of their efficiency were disregarded as defeatist.

Hong Kong on the other hand was considered by most of the garrison to be impregnable, a view presumed to be good for morale. 'Hong Kong is a fortress' was the comforting assurance given by a very senior military officer in an address to the Hong Kong Rotary Club on 21 February 1941.

Chiang Kai-shek was naturally eager to see Hong Kong defended, particularly after the British military withdrawal from North China. To assist the British, the Nationalists sent a mission to the Colony under the control of Admiral Chan Chak who was already living there while recuperating from an operation. Commander Henry Hsu, who had also lived in Hong Kong, was his chief aide. The mission's main function was to liaise with the British; to pass information from Chungking to the Hong Kong Government, using their own radio equipment; to exchange information with the Hong Kong police and to combat fifth-columnists. Major-General S. K. Yee, another Hong Kong man, was sent to the Colony after the fall of Canton in 1938, as a representative of the Chinese General Staff, to work with British Military Staff Intelligence Officers and exchange military information; he also represented the Chinese Secret Service and had contacts with the Hong Kong Police, and generally his mission was to assist the British with counter-espionage measures and help deal with enemy agents. The British gave an undertaking that these Chinese Officers should not be allowed to fall into enemy hands in case of war. The Chinese authorities pressed the Hong Kong Government to arm the local Chinese to fight the Japanese in conjunction with the Nationalist armies and the British naturally refused this facile suggestion, having regard to the mass of refugees whose reliability could not be taken for granted. In any case, in 1940 it was impossible because of the lack of arms; moreover Britain was adhering to the policy of giving no offence to Japan. Britain remained lukewarm towards China, and not without reason in view of the long years of anti-British demonstrations in the Treaty Ports.

The Japanese forces comprised the 38th Division, commanded by Lt.-General T. Sano, a well-equipped, well-organized and experienced formation with a good record in South China; made up of the 228th, 229th and 230th Infantry Regiments, each of three battalions, under Major-General Ito, supported by mountain artillery, anti-tank guns, field artillery, howitzers, mortars, heavy artillery, engineers, landing craft and overwhelming air support. Its rear was protected against Chinese attack by the 66th Regiment. The invading force did not greatly outnumber the defenders, but with three other divisions in South China to call upon in need, and with control of the sea and air, the Japanese had a decided advantage. In action, they proved to be disciplined, supremely fit, aggressive, resolute, well-led, sensibly armed and equipped, and prepared to use unorthodox tactics. They seized the initiative from the start and never lost it.

A. PRE-WAR HONG KONG

1 Japanese troops landing at Bias Bay, just outside the Colony's sea frontier with China, 1939. (*Asia Magazine*)

2 British Defences at the Chinese border: Nam Kam To Bridge, connecting the New Territories with Chinese territory near Shamchun, looking south. (*P.R.O. Hong Kong*)

3 Pedder Street, in the commercial and shopping heart of Hong Kong. (*P.R.O. Hong Kong*)

PART TWO

WAR

I

THE JAPANESE ATTACK ON THE MAINLAND[1]

'I saw no reason why the period between their crossing of the frontier and the evacuation of the mainland by my forces should not extend to a period of seven days or more. I gave no guarantee and still maintain this was a fair estimation. . . .'

Major-General C.M. Maltby,
Despatch on Military operations in Hong Kong.
Submitted 21 November 1945

JAPAN's general strategy was to cripple the United State's Pacific fleet, seize the South-East Asian colonial territories by a series of lightning campaigns and then organize its defence strongly enough to ensure the ultimate acceptance by the United States and her allies of its absorption into the Japanese sphere through a compromise peace. After much debate the plan finally adopted was for approximately simultaneous attacks on 7/8 December on Pearl Harbor, Hong Kong, the Philippines and Malaya, the omens for which appeared favourable for 1941 was the blackest period of the war for Britain and her allies. The essential factors for Japan were surprise and

[1] The major authoritative sources for the military history of the Hong Kong campaign are

1. S. W. Kirby, *The War against Japan: Official History of the Second World War* (H.M.S.O., London, 1957–61), Vol. 1, Chs. VII–IX, pp. 107–56, Appendix 6 gives the Japanese order of battle.
2. Major-General C.M. Maltby's 'Despatch': Supplement to *London Gazette*, 29 January 1948.
3. Sir Mark Young, 'Despatch': Events in Hong Kong on 25 December 1941, Special Supplement to the *Hong Kong Government Gazette*, vol. XC, 2 July 1948, pp. 1–3.
4. C. P. Stacey, *Official History of the Canadian Army in the Second World War: Six Years of War*, Ottawa, Cloutier, 1955), Ch. XIV, pp. 437–91, notes, pp. 590–4.
5. K.D. Bhargava and K.N.V. Sastri, *Official History of the Indian Armed Forces in the Second World War 1939–45: Campaigns in S.E. Asia* (Combined Inter-Services Historical Section, India and Pakistan, Orient Longman, 1960).
6. Louis Allen, 'Notes on Japanese Historiography, World War II', *Military Affairs*, 1 December 1971, pp. 133–8, in a thorough and extensive note on the Japanese official histories of the war, mentions as 'most useful': Hattori

speed. The Japanese onslaught was therefore made suddenly and without warning and not unnaturally gave them a clear initial advantage.

British military intelligence may have been poor, but persistent Chinese reports of Japanese troop movements on the other side of the border could not be ignored and, in the first week of December 1941, General Maltby felt it necessary to take the required defensive measures. By the evening of 7 December, the three battalions manning the Gindrinkers Line had taken up their positions and the Punjabis were in a forward position at Fanling at Company strength keeping the frontier under observation. The Anti-Aircraft Batteries were standing by in readiness, and the Island battalions had taken up their stations, with the 1st Middlesex occupying the pill-boxes around the Island, the Royal Rifles of Canada taking the eastern part of the Island and the Winnipeg Grenadiers, the western. The Volunteers were withdrawn from camp at Fanling and were mobilized on 7 December, and the harbour defences were manned. On that Sunday evening notices were flashed on the cinema screens recalling all service personnel to their units.

At 4.45 a.m. on 8 December intelligence officers at Army Headquarters picked up broadcasts from Tokyo warning all Japanese that war with the United States and Britain was impending. Shortly afterwards, a naval signal from Singapore confirmed that Malaya was being invaded. General Maltby and his staff then descended the three flights of steps to the 'Battlebox', the underground battle headquarters completed in 1940, fifty feet below ground and directly underneath the military headquarters building in Murray Barracks. At dawn, heavy troop movements on the other side of the frontier at

---

Takushiro, *Dai Tōa Sensōshi Tenshi* ('A Complete History of the War in Greater East Asia'), (Tokyo, Hara Shobō, 1967 reprint). Chapter II refers to the war in China, including Hong Kong.

Regimental histories have been written for the following units and appropriate sections of these give detailed accounts of local front actions:

B. Haig, *Fourteenth Punjab Regiment. A short history, 1939–45* (London, 1950).

P.K. Kemp, *The Middlesex Regiment (Duke of Cambridge's Own) 1919–52* (Aldershot, 1956).

A. Muir, *The First of Foot, the history of the Royal Scots* (Edinburgh, 1961).

Anon. *A record of the actions of the Hong Kong Volunteer Defence Corps in the battle for Hong Kong, December 1941* (Hong Kong, [1956)].

Shum Chun confirmed the worst fears of Japanese intentions. At 7.30 a.m. the frontier bridges were demolished, roads at Fanling made impassable and the Punjabis under Major Gray began their retreat to Taipo covering the demolition parties.

The first Japanese attack came at 8.0 a.m., simultaneously with that on Pearl Harbor allowing for the international date line, when a flight of twelve bombers, protected by thirty-six fighters, struck the Kai Tak airfield, and put all five R.A.F. planes out of action, as well as eight civilian planes. The Japanese bombing was accurate and skilful and the dive-bombing brought the planes down to within sixty feet of their targets, much to Maltby's surprise and grudging admiration. Shamshuipo Barracks were also attacked but without much damage.

At the same time the Japanese began to cross the Shum Chun River, placing temporary bridges in position with surprising rapidity. They used three regiments, that is, nine battalions; the 228th and 230th advanced on the western side of the New Territories, and the 229th, crossing into Laffan's Plain, advanced along the eastern side towards Tide Cove. The main assault was intended to be made on the west, using the threat of landing sea-borne forces behind the defence. The Japanese plan therefore threw the main burden of defence on the Royal Scots, holding the western section of the Gindrinkers Line. This line had no 'Maginot' solidity but it was hoped that patrols working outwards would give warning of the direction of the main Japanese attacks and alert the defence in time to organize counter-measures.

The Japanese pressed south with unexpected speed, using rough narrow paths through the hills and they were guided by spies, pro-Japanese sympathizers. Their standard of night work showed a high degree of fitness and training, and rubber-soled boots enabled them to move noiselessly on to their objective and they wore quilted uniforms into which could be inserted camouflage material which proved most effective, making their snipers particularly difficult to deal with. All three regiments made rapid progress.

After covering the demolition parties, the forward company of Punjabis retired in good order, using its Bren-gun carriers, assisted by a unit of the Hong Kong Volunteer Defence Corps in armoured cars. They fell back to Monastery Ridge just forward of the British line which they reached early next day, 9 December, and continued to hold the ridge all that day until they withdrew into the main British lines as darkness fell. They had been expected to hold their ground much longer, but the speed and weight of the Japanese thrust proved too threatening for one company to contain. Japanese forces began to cross Tide Cove during the night of the 8/9 December, and steadily continued to cross all next day, moving towards Buffalo Hill from which to threaten the eastern end of the British line. On the morning of the 9th, the reserve company of Rajputs was ordered up to fill the gap between the Royal Scots on Smugglers Ridge and the Punjabis at Shatin, and it took up its position just off the Taipo road. The Punjabi Battalion Headquarters was at Kowloon upper reservoir at the head of the Shatin Valley.

On the west the Japanese advance was equally threatening, and the 230th Regiment occupied the summit of Tai Mo Shan by 4 o'clock on the same day that they had crossed the frontier. By dusk on the 9th the Japanese were poised to attack the Royal Scots in force. That regiment was below strength because many of its troops were affected with malaria, resulting in a large number of casualties. In addition, soldiers were out of condition and had had to do a great deal of digging for defensive works, and had little respite. They had originally been earmarked for the eastern end of the line but had been switched to the west and so were less practised in their role than they might otherwise have been.

The Japanese directed their attack on the strongest single point in the line, the Shing Mun Redoubt. The Redoubt was the Royal Scots' A Company headquarters and was manned by a single platoon, which had also to supply night patrols consisting of one officer and nine men three times a night, to the east and north-east. The Japanese 228th Regiment under Colonel Doi, on the night of the 9th, which was as murky as the previous night had been brilliantly fine, carried out a bold assault on the Redoubt. Avoiding British patrols and particularly the 10 o'clock patrol, he silently infiltrated about 150 of his men along the Smugglers' Path at the foot of the eastern slope of the Ridge. These men then scaled the Ridge and at about 11 p.m. descended on the Redoubt from above as the spearhead of the assault and throwing grenades down the ventilation shafts. The surprise was complete. The main force of Japanese troops attacked from the direction of the reservoir in overwhelming strength and by 4.0 a.m. the Redoubt had fallen, after five hours of fierce fighting. One pill-box held out until 7.0 a.m. but was then damaged by a British shell in a barrage directed at the fallen bastion with the object of preventing any further Japanese advance. The attack was a complete surprise and its success, the reward of boldness, initiative and willingness to use unorthodox methods, jeopardized the whole line.

The Japanese version of this attack was that their 228th Regiment in its probing of the British positions, discovered the weakness in the manning of the Redoubt, and decided to attack immediately, though this position came within the objective allotted to the 230th Regiment; its Colonel Doi was called upon by his divisional commander to explain why he sent his men to attack an objective that was outside his own allotted sector, and his explanation was accepted.[2]

Brigadier C. Wallis, former commanding officer of the Rajputs, and in command of the Mainland Brigade, ordered the Royal Scots to counter-attack at dawn with the support of the company of Rajputs on their right and with strong artillery cover to retake the lost position, but their commanding officer felt himself in no position to do so with any chance of success, and no immediate counter-attack was made.

The fall of the Shing Mun Redoubt proved decisive. The way was now open to Kowloon, and a reserve company of the Winnipeg Grenadiers was hurried across from the Island to take up a position at the junction of the Taipo and Castle Peak roads. The right flank of the Royal Scots was dangerously exposed. The Japanese were naturally eager to exploit their success, and on the morning of the 10th their patrols attacked the Royal Scots and the Rajputs. The Punjabis in the centre of the Gindrinkers Line were also heavily shelled, and the pill-boxes along the hill slopes above Tide Cove, were system-

[2] Refer to translation of Japanese document in Appendix 6.

atically shelled and destroyed. Unfortunately, Stonecutters Island was dive-bombed and shelled and some guns, used as supporting artillery for the Punjabis, were put out of action. The two exposed companies of the Royal Scots occupying positions on the extreme left of the Line, one just south of Tsun Wan and the other in the valley leading to Pineapple Pass were brought back to form a new line on Golden Hill where they dug in on the bare, weathered granite as best they could.

During 10 December there was little fighting, the Japanese contenting themselves with patrol activity, reconnaissance, and striking at military targets with artillery and from the air. H.M.S. *Cicala* which had shelled Japanese positions during their advance, after surviving a rain of bombs and shells, eventually received a direct hit and had to return to Aberdeen; she was replaced by *Tern*.

On the morning of the 11th, the two companies of the Royal Scots, holding Golden Hill and the countryside to the west, were strongly attacked in their new positions, following a heavy mortar barrage. They had little more cover than weapon pits, and after bitter and often hand-to-hand fighting, during which they suffered heavy casualties including both company commanders killed, they withdrew towards Lai Chi Kok. There was a danger of a Japanese break-through to Kowloon, and the Winnipeg Grenadiers were ordered up the Castle Peak road, behind the Royal Scots, and armoured cars and Bren-gun carriers of the H.K. Volunteer Defence Corps were also sent along the road. The Japanese then attacked D Company of the Royal Scots which had been left in an exposed position to the north, on Golden Hill, but were repulsed with heavy losses. General Maltby now decided, after only forty-eight hours' fighting, that it was too risky to attempt to hold the mainland if the three battalions there were to be brought back intact to the Island to take their allotted part in its defence, and ordered their withdrawal. The security of the Island was always the first consideration, and there was never any intention to make an all-out stand on the mainland. The Naval Commodore protested that he was not ready to carry out the necessary demolitions, transfer naval stores and ferry the troops across to the Island and so the order to evacuate the mainland was delayed for twenty-four hours, until noon on the 11th.

The fighting on the mainland was now virtually over and thereafter all efforts were concentrated on evacuation. The withdrawal plan was explained by Brigadier Wallis to all commanders at 8.0 a.m. that same morning, purely as a precautionary measure, for he prefaced his remarks by stating he did not anticipate withdrawal for at least a week. The plan was for the Royal Scots, the Canadians and most of the artillery to retire to embarkation points at Shamshuipo Barracks, and at the Jordan Road ferry terminal. The Rajputs and supporting mobile artillery were to retire to the Ma Lau Tong Line which protected the fortified Devil's Peak peninsula opposite the north-east corner of the Island. The Punjabis were to retire along the ridge of hills behind Kowloon, pass through the Rajputs and make for Devil's Peak, for embarkation. The plan was designed to avoid bringing the troops into the Kowloon built-up area where they might be delayed by street fighting, or sniped at from houses occupied by collaborators; also an important part of the withdrawal plan was the destruction before evacuation of all installations in Kowloon likely to be of use to the enemy, and the passage of troops might have delayed the necessary measures. General Maltby intended to retain the Devil's Peak peninsula up to the Ma Lau Tong Line permanently, because it occupied a commanding position, was well fortified, and could easily be supplied from the Island across the narrow Lye Mun passage, also it would effectively keep the Japanese forces away from a too dangerous proximity to the Island. The withdrawal was, generally speaking, carried out according to plan. The Royal Scots and Canadians withdrew under the cover of the Punjabis and embarked from their pre-arranged points on the afternoon and evening of the 11th.

The Punjabis had the more arduous task of making a night trek along the range of hills behind Kowloon, especially as they could not set out before midnight since they had to cover the troops embarking at points on the west Kowloon shore. They were to pass through the Rajput lines, whose battalion headquarters was at Customs Pass, and who were to cover their retreat. The Punjabis were short of mules and during the long night march along the rough hill-paths, and loaded down with ammunition and equipment, they very naturally lost their way. The main body made their way down a steep incline to the Clearwater Bay Road, and then along Anderson Road to Devil's Peak; but the Punjabi headquarters group missed the path and came down at Kai Tak, whence they made their way to the Star Ferry at Tsim Sha Tsui, holding back Japanese forces at almost point blank range as they embarked, and assisting ferry loads of frightened Kowloon residents into the bargain. The Rajput commander, failing to make contact with the Punjabis at the agreed time, withdrew to the Ma Lau Tong Line as had been arranged. On the evening of the 12th the Ma Lau Tong Line was given up and two companies of Rajputs retired to the Hai Wan Line, closer to Devil's Peak, the more easily to cover the embarkation of the troops waiting to cross to the Island.

On the night of the 12th the embarkation at Lye Mun began, and by 4.0 a.m. on the early morning of the 13th the Punjabis were across, with the gunners of a howitzer company and one company of Rajputs. General Maltby then decided on a complete evacuation of the Devil's Peak area, instead of maintaining two companies of Rajputs there as had been intended. The evacuation therefore went on, and had to be completed after daylight on the 13th. The Navy was summoned to assist in this dangerous operation, and H.M.S. *Thracian* and the flotilla of M.T.B.'s loaded the last men in broad daylight to bring them safely across to the Island.

The success of the evacuation was partly due to a surprising absence of any Japanese interference. The decision to withdraw, and the speed at which it was done appeared to take them by surprise, and the probable explanation is that they thought a full-scale attack would be necessary to clear the mainland and were preparing to mount it. An infantry attack on the Ma Lau Tong Line without any artillery preparation had been repulsed with heavy loss, and the Japanese appeared to think that the British had more troops in strong defensive positions than was actually the case.

The British mainland forces had been preserved intact, but they lost their 170 mules because the military transports had been deserted by their Chinese crews, and even the ferries had to be manned by the naval parties. The mules were to be sadly missed in moving artillery on to the Island; they were insufficient in number in any case because battalions had had to share the mule corps, and there had never been enough to serve all regiments, batteries and corps at any one time. Ammunition and blankets had to be abandoned, but the withdrawal was made with surprisingly little loss. The defence of the mainland had lasted five days.

Conditions in Kowloon during the withdrawal became chaotic, and heart-rending scenes occurred. The residents there were left in the dark as to the gravity of the progress of the fighting and since the optimistic British communiqué gave no inkling of the true position, most Kowloon residents knew nothing of the withdrawal until the Japanese appeared. The wildest rumours spread, and on the 12th the ferries were jammed. The Government was bitterly criticized for not informing Kowloon residents of the decision to withdraw British forces from the mainland, but secrecy was of course essential, as any hint of it would have endangered the operation. People just had to be left to their fate. The police were withdrawn and looting followed; fifth-column agents were at work and gun-fire was frequently heard. The electricity generating station, the docks, and all military and other installations of vital importance to the enemy were made unserviceable before withdrawal.

Most British and allied merchant ships in harbour had made good their escape before the fighting began, and the remainder were scuttled. The installations and surviving batteries on Stonecutters Island were destroyed and stores evacuated under heavy dive-bombing and artillery fire. Just before the evacuation of the mainland, junks and sampans in the harbour were rounded up and assembled in the Yau Ma Tei typhoon shelter which was then blocked by sinking three river-steamers across the entrance. This was done to keep the harbour waters free and deny small vessels to the Japanese. But the decision to withdraw from the mainland came too suddenly to allow the planned impounding of all small vessels to be carried out, and in due course the Japanese were not short of craft to ferry their troops across the harbour to attack the Island.

The Hong Kong Volunteer Defence Corps was held in reserve on the Island, with the exception of some units who were brought across to the mainland for specific duties. No. 1 Company, under Capt. A. H. Penn, took post at Kai Tak to protect the airfield from air-borne attack and also to act as a reserve for the troops manning the Gindrinkers Line, and one of its platoons, equipped with Bren-gun carriers, patrolled the Castle Peak Road. The Field Company Engineers of the H.K.V.D.C. under Major J. H. Bottomley, with their special local knowledge, were made responsible for the railway and road demolitions from the frontier to Tide Cove while a party of this unit was attached to the Punjabi company for demolition work on the frontier itself and for laying mines. They achieved their tasks before falling back under cover of the Punjabis and the H.K.V.D.C. Armoured Car Platoon.

Operating in secrecy on the mainland was Force 'Z', a small select band of men specially trained for sabotage operations behind the enemy lines. It was an irregular unit consisting of three civilians, including F. W. Kendal, a Canadian, who was its commander, an officer of the Middlesex Regiment who was second in command, a R.A.F.V.R. officer from the Malayan Civil Service, and nine men from the Hong Kong Volunteer Defence Corps, and it operated under the command of the Secret Operations Executive (S.O.E.) in Singapore, where some of them went for special courses in explosives and sabotage equipment. In the winter of 1940–1 they began training in earnest at a secluded bungalow on the edge of the Jubilee reservoir, using equipment furnished by the S.O.E., helped by the H.K.V.D.C. which supplied food and clothing and by the Hong Kong military authorities which helped in preparing the supply dumps. These latter were in two natural caves, one 1,800 feet up on the south-east slope of Tai Mo Shan and the other on the border at Lin Ma Hang.

On the Sunday night before the fighting began, the members of the Force (except one who was away on a course in Singapore), and one who was left in Hong Kong to liaise with the Garrison forces, moved into the hills to be ready to assume their mission. On the outbreak of the fighting, two of them, including Mr. Kendal, their Commander, had to return to Hong Kong, going via the Shing Mun Redoubt from which they were able to make their escape during the Japanese attack. They were unable to return to the New Territories and remained in Hong Kong to help in the Island's defence, and eventually escaped to Free China with Admiral Chan Chak as related elsewhere. The surrender on Christmas Day came too soon for the 'Z' Force to have much success in achieving its objectives, which were to damage Japanese communications, disrupt their operations by sabotage and then to escape to Free China with as much intelligence as could be gathered. Working in secrecy and in country held by the enemy, progress was necessarily slow, but one member, Corporal D. R. Holmes of the H.K.V.D.C., made his way on Christmas night to a pipe factory in Tsuen Wan used as a transport park and single-handed blew up Japanese lorries with time-bombs. Four recent recruits were sent back to the Island with the intention of re-joining their H.K.V.D.C. units and became prisoners of war and the one Chinese civilian member was also sent back and disappeared into the community. This left in the field only three experienced members of the 'Z' Force who retired to the border at Lin Ma Hang where they remained a month to gain intelligence before making their getaway into Free China. They reached Waichow in February 1942, being helped *en route* by the villagers on whom they were forced to rely after their own supplies had been lost through looting.

General Maltby always feared having to meet an attack by sea, and on the 11th the Japanese landed on Lamma Island and attempted to cross to Aberdeen, but were driven off by gunfire. There was never any serious Japanese intention to land from Lamma and the action was purely diversionary, but the threat was one which the General could not ignore.

On the critical night of the 12th the morale of the civilian population was badly shaken by a colossal explosion. It was decided to bring several tons of dynamite from store at Green Island to the Island; all military posts and pill-boxes were informed, but the time of departure of the vessel, the P & O launch *Jeanette*, was put forward two hours, and though this change in the arrangements was notified, the lighter was fired on from a pill-box manned by men of the Middlesex Regiment, situated at the end of the vehicular ferry pier. The explosion rocked the Central District, doing extensive damage over a wide area, and gave rise to rumours of Japanese landings and sabotage, leaving people in ignorance of the cause of the disaster. The loss of the gunpowder was serious as it was intended to use it to blast fire lanes to prevent the spread of fires expected from the bombing of crowded areas.

The mainland troops after days of continuous action were in no condition to assume their island battle stations immediately, and fortunately they were given a five days' respite before they were again called upon to battle with the enemy.

Meanwhile, with the whole of the mainland in their hands and with undisputed control of sea and air, the Japanese began to prepare for the assault on Hong Kong Island. They first attempted to persuade the Governor to surrender voluntarily. No sooner had the British retreating troops been successfully ferried across to the Island on 13 December than a small launch bearing a white flag left Kowloon pier at 9.0 a.m., with a Japanese staff officer and three British women as hostages, bearing a letter from the Japanese Commander, Lt.-General Sakai, demanding the surrender of the Island and offering a five-hour truce. The Japanese ultimatum reads as follows:

> Since our troops have joined battle I have gained possession of the Kowloon Peninsula despite the good fighting qualities of your men, and my Artillery and Air Force, which are ready to crush all parts of the Island, now await my order. Your Excellency can see what will happen to the Island and I cannot keep silent about it. You have all done your duty in defending Hong Kong so far, but the result of the coming battle is plain, and further resistance will lead to the annihilation of a million good citizens and to such sadness as I can hardly bear to see. If Your Excellency would accept an offer to start negotiations for the surrender of Hong Kong under certain conditions, it will be honourable. If not, I, 'repressing my tears', am obliged to take action to overpower your forces.[3]

The Governor declined the offer and categorically stated his intention to defend Hong Kong. A later communiqué was issued in these words, 'His Excellency summarily rejects the proposal. This Colony is not only strong enough to resist all attempts at invasion but all the resources of the British Empire,

[3] F.O. 371/27752. Cypher telegraph from Governor to Secretary of State, 14 December 1941.

the United States and the Republic of China are behind us and those who have sought peace can rest assured that there will be no surrender. . . .'[4]

The Japanese then began the systematic shelling of military targets, artillery posts, troop concentrations and military and naval installations. On 13 December a 9.2-inch gun on Mount Davis was knocked out. Belcher's Fort was hit and fires started at West Point and Kennedy Town. On the 14th the shelling increased, and one A.A. 3-inch gun on Mount Davis received a direct hit with severe casualties, causing some Chinese gunners to desert. Many Chinese transport drivers deserted. On the 15th there began a systematic and accurate enemy shelling of the pill-boxes on the northern shore of the Island from gun positions alleged to have been already prepared in peace time in the Kowloon-side godowns, and certainly the Japanese were able to bring heavy artillery into action extremely quickly. On the 15th at 9.0 p.m. they attempted a landing at Pak Sha Wan after a H.K.V.D.C. battery there had been heavily shelled; this invasion force crossed the channel in small rubber boats and rafts kept afloat by empty petrol tins to carry equipment, while the men swam, pushing these improvised craft. The numbers were small, three companies was the maximum estimate, and the attackers were beaten off. Fifth columnists were active, some used lights to help direct Japanese fire, some acted as snipers, and some urged Chinese to desert or quit the civil auxiliary services. Admiral Chan Chak, General Yee, and their men, battled with some success to keep this underground threat in check. The Japanese had begun collecting small ferrying craft, and this continued up to the 18th despite shelling from the Island, and despite H.M.S. *Thracian*'s daring raid on boat concentrations on the night of the 15th/16th, when she made her way up the harbour as far as the Kowloon electric power station.

On the 16th the shelling increased in intensity, accompanied by attack from the air directed at military objectives such as artillery sites and pill-boxes, and by nightfall more than

[4] The immediate reply was in tone rather less brusque. 'He [the Governor] acknowledges the spirit in which this communication is made but he is unable in any circumstances to hold any meeting or parley on the subject of the surrender of Hong Kong.'

half of the pill-boxes between Lye Mun and Happy Valley had been destroyed.

At about 9.30 a.m. on the 17th the Japanese made a second attempt to force the Island's surrender without further fighting. Two Japanese launches bearing a white flag and again with a British woman hostage and two dachshunds and a pregnant Russian woman,[5] brought Col. Toda, Lt. Miguno, and Mr. Othsu with a letter from Lt.-General Sakai and Vice-Admiral Niimi with proposals for the surrender of the Colony, and promising a truce until 4.0 p.m. Their overtures were bluntly rejected by Sir Mark Young: 'His Excellency declines most absolutely to enter into any negotiations for the surrender of Hong Kong and he takes this opportunity of notifying Lt.-General Takashi Sakai and Vice-Admiral Masaichi Niimi that he is not prepared to receive any further communication from them on the subject.'[6] The bombardment of military objectives on the expiry of the truce continued, particulary directed at the pill-boxes along the north-east shore, and there was a short bombing raid on the Central District.

The Japanese attempted to supplement this softening up of the defence by propaganda designed to undermine morale. Leaflets were dropped appealing to the Hong Kong Chinese to help drive out the British exploiters and showing a picture of thin, poverty-stricken Chinese side by side with a fat prosperous John Bull, and comparing that with the happy and prosperous Chinese family living in the Japanese co-prosperity sphere. The same appeal of Asia for the Asians and an end to western exploitation was made to the Indians who were urged to desert and promised assistance in overthrowing British rule. The British were regaled from across the harbour with popular songs aimed at inducing a nostalgia for home and peace.

On the 18th the bombardment intensified still further, and all indications pointed to the imminence of an assault. The Central District was shelled again, the Colonial Secretariat building being damaged. The Asiatic Petroleum Company's oil storage tanks at North Point and a neighbouring paint

[5] Gwen Dew, *Prisoner of the Japs* (London, 1944), p. 34. The Japanese invited Gwen Dew to take their photographs.

[6] S. W. Kirby, *The War against Japan*, Vol. I (London, 1950), pp. 128–9.

1 Guns of Hong Kong's coastal defences. (*Asia Magazine*)

2 A British Army Patrol in the New Territories. (*Asia Magazine*)

3 Sham Shiu Po Barracks. (*P.R.O. Hong Kong*)

4 An Indian Hill Regiment in Hong Kong. (*Asia Magazine*)

5 Lyon Searchlight Unit. (*Asia Magazine*)

6 Japanese bombers dropping bombs on military targets on Hong Kong Island. (*Jt. Services Public Relations, G.H.Q., Hong Kong*)

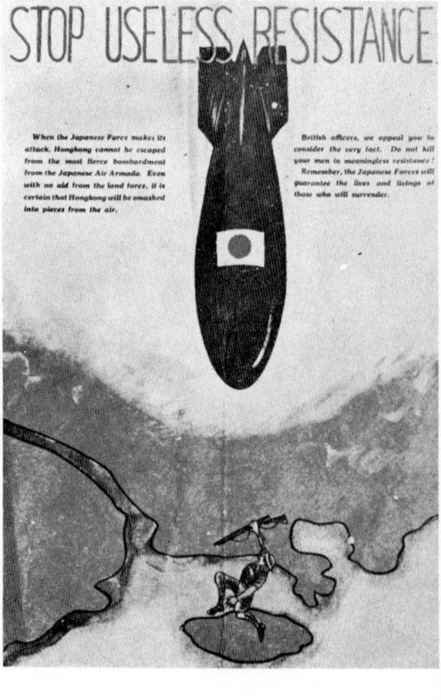
STOP USELESS RESISTANCE.
When the Japanese Force makes its attack, Hongkong cannot be escaped from the most fierce bombardment from the Japanese Air Armada. Even with no aid from the land force, it is certain that Hongkong will be smashed into pieces from the air.
British officers, we appeal you to consider the very fact. Do not kill your men in meaningless resistance!
Remember, the Japanese Forces will guarantee the lives and livings of those who will surrender.

7 Propaganda leaflets dropped by the Japanese on Allied forces. (*Mr. P. Braga*)

8 Japanese campaign medal for the South China/Hong Kong theatre of war. (*Professor C.J. Grant, H.K.U.*)

9 A battle scene: Japanese troops advancing on the Island. (*'The Fall of Hong Kong'–film made by Japanese Army, 1941-2*)

PY. MOST SECRET MESSAGE 0521Z/21st December IN

From N.O.I/C. Hong Kong. Date 21.12.41.
Recd. 0933.

NAVAL CODE (K.3. (OLD) BY W/T

Addressed Admiralty.

727

MOST IMMEDIATE.

For Secretary of State from Governor Hong Kong begins.

Military situation is now as follows:- Enemy hold key position on hills and G.O.C. advises that we are very rapidly approaching a point at which only remaining resistence open to us will be to hold for short time only a small pocket in centre of city leaving bulk of fixed population to be overrun.

I feel it will be my duty to ask terms before this position is reached.

If (?H.M.) Government feels able to give assent (?please) cable single word ABILITY repetition ABILITY. Governor Ends.

0521Z/21.

MOST SECRET.

1439A/21st December.

To Commodore, Hong Kong 449.

From: Admiralty.

IMMEDIATE.

Following for Governor.

Your message 0521 has been received. It crossed a message from the Prime Minister, who is temporarily out of reach as follows: Begins:-

To C. in C. and Governor of Hong Kong.

The eyes of the world are upon you. We expect you to resist to the end. The honour of the Empire is in your hands. Ends.

In spite of conditions you and G.O.C. are facing, the difficulties of which are clearly understood, H.M.G's desire is that you should fight it out as in Prime Minister's message.

1439A/21

10 Two war messages. (*Public Records Office, London*)

11 Japanese troops entering Hong Kong. ('*The Fall of Hong Kong*')

12 Japanese troops being welcomed on Nathan Road. (‘*The Fall of Hong Kong*’)

factory had been set on fire and for some days a pall of dense black smoke covered the north-east of the Island making a perfect cover for the attackers. The shore-line from Causeway Bay to Lye Mun was again heavily shelled until hardly a pill-box remained, and the road was blocked with debris. It came as no surprise when that night the Japanese mounted their assault, and carried the war to the Island.

II

THE ASSAULT ON THE ISLAND: THE FIRST THREE DAYS 18–21 DECEMBER 1941

'There must however be no thought of surrender. Every part of the Island must be fought and the enemy resisted with the utmost stubbornness. The enemy should be compelled to expend the utmost life and equipment. There must be vigorous fighting in the inner defences and, if need be from house to house. Every day that you are able to maintain your resistance you help the Allied cause all over the world, and by a prolonged resistance you and your men can win the lasting honour which we are sure will be your due.'

Winston Churchill to Sir Mark Young
23 December 1941[1]

By the night of 14 December the three infantry battalions and the other formations which had been evacuated from the mainland, had, after an all too short period of recuperation, taken up their new battle stations on the Island. The defence was organized in two brigades, the East Brigade under Brigadier C. Wallis with headquarters at Tai Tam Gap, and the West Brigade under the Canadian Brigadier J. K. Lawson, with headquarters at Wong Nei Chong Gap. The former included the 5/7 Rajputs which occupied the key position on the north-east perimeter where they manned the pill-boxes and beach defences from Causeway Bay to Pak Sha Wan; they also had one company in the hills above Taikoo, where the battalion headquarters was situated, and a reserve company at Tai Hang village above Causeway Bay. Two companies of the 1st Middlesex occupied the pill-boxes on the east and south coasts from Pak Sha Wan to the Chung Hom Kok peninsula. The Royal Rifles of Canada, with its battalion headquarters at Tai Tam Gap, covered the south-east sector from Pak Sha

[1] Cab. 65/20. Most secret, most immediate telegram from Admiralty to Governor, 23 December 1941.

Wan to Stanley, with a reserve company at Lye Mun Gap. Two companies of the H.K. Volunteer Defence Corps, No. 1 which had served at Kai Tak, and No. 2 (Scottish) under Major H. R. Forsyth, were in reserve at Tai Tam Valley and Pottinger Gap respectively.[2] The 'Hughesiliers' under Major the Hon. J. J. Patterson defended the North Point Power Station. There were the heavy coastal batteries, already described, also mobile artillery units of the Hong Kong and Singapore Royal Artillery, both pack and wheeled, and a battery of five A.A. guns. H.K. Volunteer Defence Corps Batteries; Numbers 1, O.C. Capt. G. F. Rees; 2, O.C. Capt. D. J. S. Crozier; and 4, O.C. Capt. K. M. A. Barnett manned guns at Pak Sha Wan, at Cape D'Aguilar and Stanley, and No. 5, A.A. Battery under Capt. L. Goldman, was at Sai Wan Hill.

The West Brigade comprised the following: The 2/14 Punjabis who took over the shore defences from Causeway Bay to Belcher's Point and were responsible for defending the north-west sector including Government House and General Maltby's Headquarters, their battalion headquarters being in MacDonnell Road. The Winnipeg Grenadiers, with headquarters at Wanchai Gap, were in defence positions covering the south-western part of the Island, except one company which was held in reserve at Wong Nei Chong Gap. The Middlesex had two companies manning the pill-boxes along the southern and western shores, from Chung Hom Kok to Belcher's Point, and an improvised 'Z' Company, consisting of the regimental band, cooks, and some of the staff, and nicknamed 'the odds and sods', was in the Leighton Hill area where the battalion commander had his headquarters. The Royal Scots, with a number of officer replacements recruited from the H.K.V.D.C., were held in reserve at Wanchai Gap, as were the H.K. Volunteer Defence Corps companies, No. 4 under Capt. R. K. Valentine, at High West; No. 5 (Portuguese) under Capt. C. A. D'Almada, at Mount Davis; No. 6 (Portuguese) under Capt. H. A. de B. Botelho, armed with Lewis guns for anti-aircraft defence, along the harbour shore-line; No. 7 under Capt. J. G. B. Dewar, at Magazine Gap and No. 3 (Eurasian Company), under Major E. G. Stewart on Jardine's

[2] For a fuller account of the actions of the Volunteers see the official history previously mentioned.

Look-out. The H.K. Volunteer Defence Corps under Col. H. B. Rose had its headquarters in Peak Mansions on the Peak. The artillery comprised, as already mentioned, heavy 9.2-inch guns and 6-inch guns at Mount Davis, and a battery of 4.7-inch guns at Belcher's Point. In addition there were the remainder of the H.K.S.R.A. mobile batteries, some anti-aircraft guns at Mount Davis, Wong Nei Chong Gap and Wanchai Gap, and a Volunteer battery, No. 3 under Capt. C. W. L. Cole, which was posted at Aberdeen to protect the newly-improvised naval base there, the Commodore and his staff being at the Aberdeen Trade School. The Middlesex Regt. was under the direct command of Garrison Headquarters, except that the companies manning the pill-boxes were under the operational control of the local battalion commanders.

The Japanese pounding undoubtedly severely reduced the defence, particularly in the area between North Point and Shaukeiwan, by disrupting communications and destroying artillery observation posts, beach lights, shore pill-boxes and a number of gun emplacements. Although General Maltby, according to his Despatch,[3] anticipated attack from across the harbour because the route was short and could be given full artillery protection, nevertheless he could not disregard a possible attack from seaward and since he had no aircraft or radar to give him early warning, he felt it necessary to position his forces so as to cover every contingency. This added immeasurably to his problems of supply, field communication and rapid concentration of forces where needed. The pill-boxes alone numbered seventy-two and caused considerable dispersal of troops, and since most of these were held by the Middlesex, this regiment with its great fighting traditions was not able to operate as a single unit. For signals communications, lines laid three feet underground connected all pill-boxes, shelters, batteries and battalion and company commanders. The Hong Kong Telephone Company placed its circuits at the disposal of the Military and its employees formed a volunteer unit, the Fortress Signals Company, which took over the care of the military lines in the built-up area. Coastal defence measures included a boom laid close inshore which had been

[3] 'Operations in Hong Kong from 8 to 25 December 1941', *Supplement to London Gazette*, 29 January 1948.

intended to protect the whole length of the northern shore of the Island, but the crews of the boom ships deserted, having completed only that part from Green Island to about the Western Market.

The crescendo of shelling on 18 December, the dive-bombing of observation posts, and the collecting of small craft of every type on the Kowloon side, all pointed to a Japanese assault that night, for which conditions were particularly favourable as moonrise was after midnight and high-tide just before that hour; and all unit commanders were alerted accordingly. In addition, the night was dark with intermittent rain. The Japanese used the same three regiments, the 228th, 229th and 230th, which had been so successful in the mainland fighting; two battalions of each made the assault in two waves, and the third battalion remained for the time in Kowloon in reserve. The assault began at 10.0 p.m. with simultaneous landings by the 230th regiment at North Point, the 228th at Taikoo and the 229th at Sai Wan, all in the sector held by the Rajputs. The second wave followed and all six battalions were landed by midnight; their divisional commander, Lt.-General Sano, came ashore at Taikoo at one o'clock in the morning. The Japanese plan was to leave isolated points of resistance for later mopping up and to press on immediately to the high ground from which the built-up areas and city of Victoria could be threatened. The Rajputs were utterly unable to prevent the landings, especially as their defence positions had already been largely neutralized by shelling, and they were overrun with very heavy casualties including virtually all their officers, though isolated bodies of men held out for some hours. General Maltby ordered a platoon of the Middlesex to link up with the reserve company of Rajputs at Tai Hang to help make a defence line, supported by artillery cover, to bar the route to the Central District, and he tried to strengthen his forces by drafting corps personnel to a more active combatant role and calling upon the Commodore for naval field-service parties; but these moves were quite inadequate to carry out the vital task of disputing the Japanese landings or preventing a bridgehead being formed. In his Despatch, General Maltby admitted that he doubted if the Japanese landing force totalled more than two battalions, and thought they were operating in small groups. It was a serious underestimate.[4]

The power station naturally came under early attack and the 'Hughesiliers', comprising four officers and sixty-six men all over the age of fifty-five, with some Free French and some Middlesex, many of them wounded, put up a heroic defence until the afternoon of the 19th when some had to leave the burning buildings and were killed or captured in house-to-house fighting, except a few who managed to gain the British lines; some, including Major Patterson, held out until their ammunition was exhausted, when they were compelled to surrender; some Middlesex men remained in the power station for some hours longer when they too were forced to lay down their arms.

During the night, the 230th Regiment advanced along the track called Sir Cecil's Ride and approached the top of Jardine's Look-out above Wong Nei Chong Gap, the 228th made for Mount Butler and Quarry Gap, and the 229th on the left, reached the summit of Mount Parker, captured the old fort on Sai Wan Hill and overran the 5th A.A. Battery of the H.K.V.D.C. there before it was even aware that the Japanese had landed, and advanced to Lye Mun Gap threatening the Brigade nerve centre at Tai Tam Gap. The Volunteer Defence Corps battery at Pak Sha Wan was surrounded and the guns put out of action, but the Volunteers astonishingly managed to hold out until the 21st. There were other similar isolated pockets of stubborn and courageous resistance; but the fact remains that the Japanese landings were not met with sufficient co-ordinated strength to offer any prospect of repulse and the Rajputs were left to bear the brunt of the assault.

During the night of the 18th/19th General Maltby, as has been said, moved forces into the Causeway Bay and Tai Hang area to bar the Japanese from an advance to the Central District through the built-up areas of Bowrington and Wanchai, and a defence line running roughly north and south between the hills and the harbour shore was accordingly formed and remained a feature of the fighting up to the surrender. The Japanese kept up the pressure against this line and forced its

[4] Maltby, op. cit. para. 68, p. 715.

gradual withdrawal westwards, but they had no intention of being bogged down by house-to-house fighting, and they made their main effort along the summit of the line of hills running east and west in the centre of the Island.

In the east, Brigadier Wallis attempted during the night to retake Sai Wan Hill using a company of the Royal Rifles; they reached the top but were unable to scale the walls of the Fort and had to withdraw under heavy fire leaving the Lye Mun Peninsula in Japanese hands, including some 6-inch howitzers at Lye Mun Gap. He also sent a unit of the Royal Rifles to occupy Mount Parker to protect his left flank, but they found the Japanese already in possession and they were not in sufficient strength to risk an attack. No. 1 Company of the Volunteers soon received its baptism of fire. It was disposed in the Tai Tam Valley with its machine-gun carriers patrolling the road from Stanley to Tai Tam Gap and with one platoon at Quarry Gap. The Japanese gained the Gap in a pre-dawn attack in great strength but only after casualties forced the defenders to withdraw; the Royal Rifles had agreed to assist them but lost their way in the dark and the strategic Gap could not be held by only one platoon. Further east, men of the No. 2 (Scottish) Company of the Volunteers, positioned in the peninsula between Chai Wan and the Sheko Road, were ordered up to Tai Tam Gap after the fall of Sai Wan, but the eastern part of the Island was given up, as related below, before they saw further action.

The West Brigade commander, on news of the landings, ordered the Winnipeg Grenadiers up to Mount Butler, Jardine's Look-out, and the road junction by the filter beds just below and to the north of Wong Nei Chong Gap, to reinforce the No. 3 (Eurasian) Company of the Volunteers. This company, which had its headquarters on the slopes of Jardine's Look-out, manned pill-boxes on the slopes of that hill and on Sir Cecil's Ride and were spread out from the gap below Mount Butler in the east to the Wong Nei Chong Gap road in the west. These 250 men, Volunteers, and later, the Canadians, were soon in the thick of the fighting as the Japanese made their way up the hills towards the strategic Wong Nei Chong Gap, about three battalions strong, one advancing along the Ride, one going over the hill and one advancing south of the hill by Stanley Gap. The Volunteers held three pill-boxes covering the Ride until overwhelmed, the survivors retiring to other positions or escaping down the Happy Valley to the Middlesex Company on Leighton Hill. Two pill-boxes on the slopes of Jardine's Look-out held out all day on the 19th with superb heroism, until offered surrender terms by the Japanese at dusk. The company commander, Major Evan Stewart, held out in his company headquarters without food until 22 December when they had to surrender. A few stragglers reached Stanley but the company suffered 80 per cent casualties before being over-run, and it virtually ceased to exist as a formation after paying thus heavily for its heroic stand.

Great efforts were obviously being made to defend the Wong Nei Chong Gap which was a crucial strategic point from which roads radiated to every part of the Island. Here too, the Island was narrowest along a north-south line through the Gap and enemy control of this would threaten to cut the British defence in two. West Brigade's headquarters was established there. General Maltby was naturally anxious to hold the Gap and arranged for additional forces to be at Brigadier Lawson's disposal. He sent a force of 150 Royal Army Service Corps men to hold Bennet's Hill and then to go on to brigade headquarters. The naval commodore released a naval party of some 200 men, mainly from the beached destroyer *Thracian*, to take over the defences in the Little Hong Kong area, so as to relieve a company of the Grenadiers which had been ordered up for service at the Gap. R.A.F. personnel were also made available for ground defence, serving with the navy at Aberdeen. A Punjabi company was ordered to the Mound, and important foothill below and to the north of Jardine's Look-out, to link up the Grenadiers at the Gap with the Rajputs and Middlesex positions in the Tai Hang and Leighton Hill area.

By daylight on the 19th, only some ten hours after landing, the Japanese held the high ground from Mount Parker to Jardine's Look-out, and were joining their forces for an all-out attack on Wong Nei Chong Gap while the British held a line roughly from Tai Tam Gap along the southern slopes of the central ridge running the length of the Island, to Wong Nei Chong Gap, and then north to the Mound, Tai Hang and

Causeway Bay. In the course of a single night, the Japanese had secured an effective grip on the eastern half of the Island.

Early on 19 December Wong Nei Chong Gap came under severe enemy pressure, as was to be expected, and General Maltby ordered up more reserve troops to defend it. 'A' Company of the Royal Scots was sent up by road, and despite very heavy fire across the narrow valley from the direction of Sir Cecil's Ride, they eventually fought their way to within a short distance of their objective with severe casualties and the loss of all their officers, and a few even managed the desperate feat of reaching Brigade headquarters. Then a naval party from Aberdeen was ordered up to the Gap by road, but was ambushed and the few survivors managed to reach the shelter of a house, 'Postbridge', south of the Gap. The result was that when the West Brigade headquarters were attacked in force, the necessary reinforcements were not there, and Brigadier Lawson reported to General Maltby at 10 a.m. that he was surrounded and being fired on at point-blank range. He was killed, 'going outside to shoot it out', bringing lasting honour to himself and to Canadian arms. His own staff and the brigade artillery commander and his staff, together with some men of the Royal Scots who had earlier fought their way through to him, all shared his fate. Some 3.7-inch howitzers unfortunately fell into Japanese hands with stocks of ammunition, and were subsequently used against the defenders.

News of this reverse did not reach the General for some time because the Brigade Communications Centre was in enemy hands, and for twenty-four critical hours, West Brigade was without a commander, until Col. H. B. Rose, Commandant of the Hong Kong Volunteer Defence Corps, was appointed to the command on the morning of 20 December and Lt.-Col. E. J. R. Mitchell, a Volunteer himself, assumed command of the H.K.V.D.C.

On the afternoon of the 19th, the General ordered a co-ordinated counter-attack against the Japanese, north and south of the Gap. Two Punjabi companies were ordered to advance from Leighton Hill to Tai Hang Village where some Rajputs were still holding out, the Royal Scots and Winnipeg Grenadiers were to advance across the Gap eastwards in a line running from Sir Cecil's Ride to Middle Spur. Full artillery support was promised. The Punjabis reached Tai Hang Village and were then driven back with numerous casualties. The Royal Scots and the Grenadiers advanced on the northern and southern sides of Mount Nicholson until they were halted by intense fire from the Wong Nei Chong police station which the Japanese had captured. Despite the determined way in which they pressed the attack, they were unable to reach the Gap itself, where No. 3 (Eurasian) Machine-gun Company of the Volunteers was still holding out. The Field Company Engineers of the H.K.V.D.C. had been converted to infantry and attached to the Royal Scots, and took part with them in the attack on the Gap on the afternoon of the 19th.

In the east, Brigadier Wallis decided to give up Tai Tam Gap and withdraw to the Stanley Village and Stone Hill area, to regroup and prepare for a strong counter-attack on the Japanese on the morning of the 20th. He no longer had the Rajputs, the remains of which were at Tai Hang under the control of West Brigade, and was left with two companies of Middlesex, the Royal Rifles of Canada which had suffered some casualties, two companies of Volunteers and supporting artillery and other ancillary units. General Maltby, with surer judgement, had wanted him to retire towards Wong Nei Chong Gap so that the two brigades should remain in contact and act in concert, but he did not insist. It proved to be a great error, for East Brigade was eventually cut off and left to fight an independent isolated campaign, and the Japanese were allowed to deal with the defence piecemeal. Brigadier Wallis, despite the lessons in speed and aggressiveness given him by the Japanese in the mainland fighting, appeared to be confident that the coast road from Stanley to Aberdeen would remain available to him. Unfortunately, in falling back on Stanley, an important howitzer battery was lost because the order to withdraw was misinterpreted by an Indian officer, who had assumed command after his British commanding officer had been killed, as an order to destroy the guns. There were a number of similar instances where the loss of an Urdu-speaking British officer threw communication with his Indian Unit out of gear and the same difficulty arose in less degree over some of the French-speaking Canadians serving in the Royal Rifles. The whole of the Cape D'Aguilar peninsula had to be given up. Fortunately, the withdrawal of East Brigade was allowed to proceed without any strong enemy interference. Instead, units of the Japanese 229th Regiment moved west, along the south side of the central ridge, and, during the night of the 19th/20th, occupied Gauge Basin, Stanley Gap, Violet Hill, and Middle Spur overlooking Repulse Bay Hotel, and even reached Shouson Hill. The hotel, where some 150 civilians, chiefly women and children, had taken refuge, now came under an epic three-day siege.

Meanwhile the Navy made a bold attempt with the few ships available to stop the flow of supplies across the harbour. On the morning of the 19th the Commodore sent the motor-torpedo-boat flotilla in pairs into the harbour to make high-speed attacks on the Japanese supply craft. The first pair made a successful run, but the second two were heavily attacked and one was lost; the attack was then called off, though not before one boat made a dramatic solo attempt and was sunk.

Thus ended a disastrous day for the defence. The Japanese were firmly established on the Island on a line running from Repulse Bay, to Wong Nei Chong Gap, and then north to Tai Hang Village and North Point. The defenders could not be concentrated in sufficient strength or with sufficient co-ordination to make a decisive impact and the tragedy was that the heroic resistance of small bodies of men stubbornly holding isolated pockets could not be turned to better account. But Japanese pressure allowed no breathing space for re-grouping, which was desperately needed because the troops became separated by the fighting and unable to regain their own units and formations tended to become mixed. Heavy casualties also made some re-grouping necessary. The events of the 19th were decisive and thereafter the defenders were fighting a losing battle.

Despite having gained so much ground, the Japanese later admitted that the opposition had been stronger than they had anticipated, with the result that they were forced to spend the 20th consolidating their positions, bringing in fresh reserves, using mules and forced coolie labour to carry up guns, ammunition and stores. They were therefore content to hold on to their captured positions.

East Brigade's attack, planned for the 20th, on which so

much depended if the Japanese were to be driven from the strategic high ground, petered out. Brigadier Wallis sent a company of the Royal Rifles and two platoons of the Scottish Company of the H.K.V.D.C. to the Repulse Bay Hotel which had been under siege since 9.30 that morning. They cleared the road and the garage opposite the hotel and were then ordered to advance to Wong Nei Chong Gap by way of Middle Spur and the catchment channel to units holding out on the Ridge on the west side of Violet Hill, but in the absence of sufficient supporting artillery, they made little headway up the steep slopes above the hotel, to which they had to retire. 'Postbridge', near the Gap and defended by the naval party and the H.K.S.R.A., was now abandoned. Brigadier Wallis withdrew to the Stanley Mound area which was being threatened by an enemy force, and decided to resume his attack next day, using the more difficult route along Gauge Basin and Stanley Gap. Maltby was naturally worried by the Japanese thrust to Repulse Bay and ordered the hotel to be held at all costs.

On the western sector, General Maltby tried to free the Japanese grip on Shouson Hill and Repulse Bay by sending the Punjabis to advance from Aberdeen to clear the road. They made no headway and later Col. Kidd, the Punjabis' Commander, went to the area and took control; with a combined force of Punjabis and naval men, he attacked Shouson Hill, where he lost his life leading his men up the west slope of the Hill, and his force lost heavily. Two houses at the top of Shouson Hill, occupied by some R.A.S.C. and naval men, held out and indeed were still unconquered when the general surrender came five days later. A mixed force of Punjabis, Grenadiers and naval personnel occupied Little Hong Kong and the R.A.O.C. depot there, ensuring access to supplies of stores and ammunition. They were supported by the gunboat *Cicala* which gave covering fire from the Bay; she soon came under air attack and for a long time seemed to possess a charmed life, before she was ultimately holed and sank in the Lamma Channel.

At Wong Nei Chong Gap, West Brigade was ordered to secure the Gap and advance to the east beyond it. Sappers of the Fortress Royal Engineers were sent up to Wanchai Gap to take over defensive positions to free infantry for an all-out attack. Col. Rose used the day to reorganize his forces, planning to send in the Royal Scots and Winnipeg Grenadiers early on the 21st. Unfortunately, the top of Mount Nicholson was left unoccupied, the Royal Scots being to the north and the Grenadiers to the south. In the late afternoon, taking advantage of a thick mist, units of the 228th Regiment under Colonel Doi gained the summit without opposition, from which they were able to pour fire on the British troops moving forward to their positions ready for the dawn attack. This enterprising and aggressive move which appeared to be a snap decision in the field, comparable to the Colonel's earlier seizure of the Shing Mun Redoubt, proved a stumbling block to all attempts. by West Brigade to regain the Wong Nei Chong Gap. The Japanese also attacked the Mound, and a company of Royal Scots sent to assist the Punjabis there, suffered heavy casualties.

It was on this day, 20 December, that an announcement was made of the approach of 60,000 Chinese troops to relieve the Island; this was believed and helped sustain the morale of forces and citizens alike, but they were to be sadly disillusioned. The report was deliberately circulated by the British Military Headquarters, according to Capt. Freddie Guest, a staff officer serving there, as an antidote to the loss of the British battleships *Prince of Wales* and *Repulse*.

The winter solstice opened with high hopes for a concerted attack on the Japanese by East and West Brigades. Brigadier Wallis's planned advance on Wong Nei Chong Gap via Gauge Basin and Stanley Gap to co-ordinate with attacks by West Brigade was begun by the Royal Rifles supported by the No. 1 M.G. Company of the Volunteers. Some progress was made at Notting Hill, but the Japanese held the high ground at Bridge Hill and Red Hill from which they were able to bring such heavy mortar fire to bear that no headway could be made, and after suffering a number of casualties a general withdrawal was ordered to the Stanley area. While that attack was in progress, General Maltby called for a more direct attack by East Brigade forces on Wong Nei Chong Gap from the south, simultaneously with the attack on the Gap by West Brigade. A strong mixed force of Royal Rifles, some gunners and Volunteers assembled at the Repulse Bay Hotel and were sent up the road by lorry, supported by two remaining carriers of No. 1 Company

H.K.V.D.C. The Volunteer contingent was left to protect the hotel while the others pushed on. The two carriers were knocked out, but the party got to within a short distance of the Gap; unfortunately their Bren guns, which had just come out of store, failed to work properly, and as there was no sign of advance by the forces of West Brigade the troops retired to Repulse Bay again, and the hotel again came under close attack.

West Brigade's attack on the Gap also fizzled out. After a night of heavy rain, a company of the Grenadiers advanced along Black's Link, but since the Japanese held the high ground east and west of the Gap, it suffered heavily, losing all its officers and half its numbers, and withdrew to Middle Gap and then to Wanchai Gap. The Royal Scots Company on the northern side of Mount Nicholson, moved towards the Mound on the right of the Punjabis but they met very strong opposition and were forced back to the filter beds after bitter fighting. The Middlesex and Rajputs firmly held a line from Leighton Hill to the shore, the Rajput's Colonel having been transferred from Stanley to the northern sector by M.T.B. Some gunners from No. 6 Company (Portuguese) of the Volunteer Defence Corps were captured in the Causeway Bay area; they were then disarmed, but curiously allowed to return to the British lines to fight again.

Meanwhile, Japanese troops were moving from Shouson Hill to Brick Hill where they overran a H.K.S.R.A. Battery, and jeopardized road communication along the south of the Island. To meet this threat the General withdrew the Middlesex from their pill-boxes between South Bay and Aberdeen, where they were ineffective, and put them on a mobile basis, and the Punjabis manning pill-boxes on the northern shore were also now withdrawn into battalion reserve to meet the threat of a Japanese descent on the town from Mount Cameron. Substantially the defence had been cut in two and the chances of a successful resistance seriously reduced.

III

THE FALL OF HONG KONG

'Every man who could bear arms including some from the Royal Navy and Royal Air Force, took part in a desperate resistance. Their tenacity was matched by the fortitude of the British civilian population. On Christmas Day the limit of endurance was reached and capitulation became inevitable. Under their resolute Governor, Sir Mark Young, the Colony had fought a good fight, They had won indeed the "lasting honour" which is their due.'

Winston Churchill, *The Second World War*, Vol. III, p. 563

ON 22 December Brigadier Wallis was given full command of East Brigade in view of its isolated position at Stanley and the difficulty of controlling it from battle headquarters. This day saw the Brigade – now so sadly reduced in numbers as to make that term quite inappropriate – forced back on Stanley where conditions were becoming difficult because the water supply was cut, and supplies of food and ammunition had to be sent in by sea. Three lines of defence were hastily prepared with the grim determination to make a prolonged stand after the forward troops on Stanley Mound and Stone Hill had come under heavy mortar fire then infantry attack, forcing them to give ground and abandon the two hills. Early on the 22nd the Ridge, the R.A.O.C. headquarters just below Violet Hill and which was still stubbornly holding out, was attacked, and as food and ammunition were running short the men there were told to surrender or withdraw. Surrender proved impossible as the officers bearing the white flag were fired on and the men split into parties for the withdrawal to Repulse Bay. Some were captured and some reached 'Eucliff', the impressive stone mansion overlooking the Bay, and attempted to escape by sea but were detected by the Japanese and shot. The wounded at the Ridge had to be left behind and all were done to death by the invaders.

Repulse Bay Hotel was now closely besieged with the Japanese virtually at the doors and it was decided that the best chance of survival for the civilians caught there by the battle all around them was to evacuate its 'garrison' to allow the hotel guests to surrender to the Japanese. The guests suffered the ordeal of battle for some three days. They were shepherded each day into a drainage tunnel leading down to the sea, emerging only after darkness fell. It was intended that the troops garrisoning the hotel should use this same tunnel to make their escape; but after starting off, the noise of their equipment bumping against the sides threatened discovery of this escape route. The escape plan was changed and the troops were ordered to make their own way back to Stanley through enemy-held country. They marched off in stockinged feet and split into small groups, and all arrived at Stanley safely. The civilians left behind were unharmed except the No. 1 Boy who was bayoneted, and some wounded soldiers were saved only by the courageous protection of a British nursing sister. Early on the morning of Christmas Eve the guests were lined up and given five minutes to be ready to march to internment at North Point; and so a pathetic procession of men, women and children, with as much as they could carry, set off on foot for the long trek to North Point. It was a harrowing and gruesome experience because of the number of bodies of British and Canadian soldiers left lying unburied in witness to the severe fighting. Mercifully, the women, children, and elderly were taken on by lorry after reaching Wong Nei Chong Gap.

In the western part of the Island, the Japanese held Brick Hill and Shouson Hill and the defenders held the Little Hong Kong ordnance depot and some machine-gun posts barring the way to Aberdeen. The Winnipeg Grenadiers held Mount Cameron. On the northern side of the Island, the Royal Scots held a line from Wanchai Gap to the filter beds; and the Punjabis, Middlesex and Rajputs held a line from the filter beds to the shore at the west end of Causeway Bay; Colonel 'Monkey' Stewart of the Middlesex had up to this time maintained his battalion headquarters at Leighton Hill, virtually in the front line, and refused to withdraw until directly ordered to do so, when he set up new headquarters in a less exposed area in Wanchai. With the Middlesex on Leighton Hill were seven survivors of No. 3 (Eurasian) Company of the Volunteers.

During the day, the Punjabis were heavily shelled and forced to withdraw to the racecourse, and the Rajputs had to re-adjust their part of the line accordingly. On the high ground, early on the 22nd, a small party of the Grenadiers which had been holding out near the Wong Nei Chong Gap since the 19th, surrendered through exhaustion of food and ammunition. The Japanese later paid tribute to the heroism of the Canadians, who, half-trained as they were, seriously impeded the Japanese advance and upset their time-table. During the night of the 22nd/23rd, the Japanese attacked and overran Mount Cameron after an intense bombardment and the Grenadiers were forced to retreat to Wanchai Gap and then to Magazine Gap in some disorder. Nos. 4 and 7 Companies of the H.K.V.D.C. were brought forward to man the line there.

Brigadier Wallis began the next day, 23 December, by sending the Royal Rifles forward to attempt to regain Stone Hill and Stanley Mound, but under intense shelling, they had to be withdrawn to Stanley Peninsula; at the same time the Scottish Volunteers were brought back from the ridge running towards Chung Hom Kok.

In the west, the Royal Scots, reinforced by some Royal Marines from the Dockyard, beat off an attack on Wanchai Gap and even secured a lodgement on Mount Cameron. They maintained their part of the line to the racecourse, where the Rajputs under heavy pressure were forced to give some ground. Companies of the Middlesex still doggedly held on to Leighton Hill, under almost continuous attack. But this day was occupied by the Japanese mainly in regrouping their forces, bringing up guns and ammunition using horses, mules and impressed coolies, along a well-organized supply route, for an all-out attack the next day.

Christmas Eve came with the defenders everywhere in an unenviable position. In the Stanley sector, the Royal Rifles which had borne the brunt of the attacks in the east for five days and needed rest, were withdrawn into Stanley Fort, and replaced by men of various units grouped into improvised formations mainly under Middlesex and Volunteer Officers.

The Japanese brought up more troops with the obvious

intention of crushing the resistance at Stanley and made one strong attack on the road in from Tai Tam Bay in which they suffered heavily and were to learn that the assault on this last refuge of East Brigade was to cost them dear in casualties. Brigadier Wallis prepared for a determined stand on his three lines of defence. The first was forward of Stanley Village and was manned by the No. 2 (Scottish) Company who tried to hold a line to Chung Hom Kok, the Stanley Platoon of the Volunteers east of the Village, and some Middlesex and Royal Rifles between the Stanley Platoon and Tai Tam Bay. The second line ran across the peninsula close to St. Stephen's College and was manned by men of the 1st Battery of the H.K.V.D.C. with No. 1 Company of the Volunteers and a platoon of Middlesex. The third line straddled the narrowest part of the isthmus from St. Stephen's Preparatory School, to the Prison, and was manned by some gunners and the Middlesex troops.

Very strong attacks, supported by tanks, were mounted in the evening of the 24th and forced the Scottish Volunteers back to Stanley Village. The defenders were forced to retire to the second line but not until the Scottish platoons lost nearly all their men wounded or killed and the Stanley platoon lost some 50 per cent. Soon after midnight, the Japanese broke through on the east side towards the prison where the Volunteer gunners and the Middlesex inflicted heavy casualties and suffered severely themselves. By dawn, the Japanese were in Tweed Bay and the Preparatory School. Isolated units of the defence made their way back and withdrew into Stanley Fort. Preparations for a final stand were made at the approaches to the Fort.

In the west, the all-out Japanese attack planned for this day, and aimed at bringing about the fall of Victoria, was postponed for twenty-four hours to allow concentrated dive-bombing, shelling and mortar fire to have their softening-up effect. The Middlesex, attacked from three sides, were at last forced off Leighton Hill after a prolonged and resolute stand, and joined the Rajputs in a line from Mount Parrish to the north-west corner of the racecourse, and thence to the sea. The racecourse was virtually abandoned, but some Middlesex men held on to the top of Morrison Hill and remained in possession there until the end of the fighting.

The troops, volunteers and regulars, defending the gaps on the high ground were subjected to ceaseless bombardment and after five days of continuous fighting were becoming incapable of further effort, whereas the Japanese were able to bring in reserves to maintain the momentum of the assault. During the night of the 24th/25th the Japanese still allowed the defence no respite. Moreover, the naval dockyard, military headquarters and all military targets were heavily shelled.

Christmas morning dawned with the defence in a parlous state. Yet there was no hint of surrender. The Governor's Christmas message was a call to continue the struggle against the invader. It read: 'In pride and admiration I send my greeting this Christmas Day to all who are fighting and all who are working so nobly and so well to sustain Hong Kong against the assaults of the enemy. Fight on. Hold fast for King and Empire. God bless you all in this your finest hour.' The General sent greetings to all members of his forces adding '. . . Let this day be historical in the grand annals of our Empire. The Order of the Day is to hold fast.'[1]

However, the end was not far off, despite these brave words. In Stanley there was heavy fighting as the Japanese closed in from the high ground beyond Stanley Village, near St. Stephen's College. The Royal Rifles made a final assault on the Japanese positions in the afternoon and were virtually wiped out as the Japanese pressed their attacks regardless of casualties.

In the west, the Middlesex and Rajputs held the line from Mount Parrish to the shore in Wanchai a little to the west of the racecourse, which they defended tenaciously until the afternoon when Mount Parrish fell and opened the way to Central District along Kennedy Road. The Royal Scots, Grenadiers, and Volunteers, held out stubbornly at the gaps on the high ground but were showing the strain of days of continuous fighting.

On Christmas morning an informal truce was observed so that the defenders might consider the question of surrender. Among the civilians who were marched out of the Repulse Bay

[1]J. Luff, *The Hidden Years* (Hong Kong, 1967), p. 146.

Hotel on the previous morning were the Hon. A. H. L. Shields, an unofficial member of the Executive Council, and Major C.M. Manners, manager of the Kowloon Wharf & Godown Company. What they had been able to observe of the numbers of Japanese troops available, and the massive build up of artillery, mortars, ammunition, and supplies, convinced them of the futility of further opposition. Acting entirely on their own responsibility and in no way representing the Japanese, they secured permission to pass through the Japanese lines to the British Military Headquarters to urge a cessation of the fighting, reporting that in the face of all that they had seen further resistance appeared hopeless. But they returned to captivity without breaking the resolve of the Governor and Defence Committee to fight it out to the last. The Japanese did not observe the truce strictly, and indeed there had been no agreement between the two sides to establish a truce, and some bombing and shelling continued on a limited basis.

By the afternoon of Christmas Day, however, it was becoming obvious that further sacrifice of life would serve no useful purpose. In agreement with the Commodore, General Maltby advised the Governor that continued effective military resistance was not possible and the Governor, with the agreement of the Defence Committee, accepted the inevitable and all units were ordered to lay down their arms and surrender to the nearest Japanese forces. Brigadier Wallis, still confident that he could hold Stanley Peninsula, refused to believe the news and sent a staff officer to secure confirmation of the surrender order in writing. The result was that severe fighting continued at Stanley until the evening of Christmas Day in which Japanese casualties were heavy, in fact, the troops remained in battle positions until the following morning. The Governor's decision to surrender was taken at 3.15 p.m. on Christmas Day and a message was sent to Japanese Military Headquarters in the Peninsula Hotel, Kowloon. The Governor, his Aide-de-Camp, General Maltby and six staff officers went to Queen's Pier where Lieut-General Sakai and six Japanese Staff Officers landed from a launch, some British women being again brought over as hostages. The Governor was taken to Kowloon forthwith without being allowed an opportunity to collect a few personal requisites. He was confined to one room at the Peninsula Hotel without books, newspapers, or radio, allowed no exercise and permitted no visitors except some senior Japanese Officers who came to interview him in the first few days. A suitcase with clothes, toilet requisites, and books, was eventually sent in to him.

General Maltby in his Despatch put the British casualties at 2,113 killed and missing and 2,300 wounded giving a total of 4,413 for the army; the high proportion of killed and missing was almost certainly due to the inability to bring in wounded during and at the end of hostilities. Officer casualties were just under 40 per cent. The Royal Navy had 119 killed or missing out of a total of 148 casualties.[2]

Japanese losses were announced by the Japanese as 2,754 of whom 675 were killed. General Maltby estimated them in round figures at 3,000 killed and 9,000 wounded, based on the demand they made for hospital accommodation for 9,000 wounded. The Japanese English-language newspaper in Hong Kong, the *Hong Kong News*, in its issue of 29 December 1941, put the number at 1,996 killed and 6,000 wounded, and a Tokyo broadcast a few days later, gave the figures as 7,000 killed and 20,000 wounded. There appears to be no accepted figure. The Japanese troops taking part in the battle numbered about 13,000 men, and so some of the figures quoted can be immediately ruled out. Maltby's figures would have meant decimation of the Japanese 38th Division, an extremely unlikely happening as the 228th Regiment was sent to Davao in the Philippines on 18 January 1942 to join the assault force which sailed nine days later to attack Amboina. The 229th and one battalion of the 230th sailed for Camranh Bay on 20 January 1942 and left there on 9 February to take part in the campaigns in Sumatra and Java. These movements do not suggest decimation and though the units concerned doubtless had to be reinforced this was obviously not needed on such a scale as to cause much delay.

In the course of the fighting atrocities were committed by the

[2] Maltby, op. cit. Appendix. B, pp. 724–5. The detailed tables account for 1,332 wounded only, but those casualties were those treated in the British Military Hospitals. The approximate total of 2,300 included wounded in the hands of the Japanese.

Japanese for which there is overwhelming evidence, though the surprising fact is that survivors of the battle interviewed in 1968 and 1969 were almost uniformly loath to condemn the Japanese on this matter. After the fighting was over, British officers were surprised when senior Japanese officers were at pains to point out that they had fought the war in a civilized manner. Excesses are probably inseparable from war, for example prisoners of war are an encumbrance and have to be guarded. Where speed and unrelenting pressure are tactically vital to success, combatants are killed even if they have surrendered.

The 230th Regiment, soon after landing, occupied the Salesian Mission at Shaukeiwan, used as an advanced dressing station, and bayoneted the wounded; some prisoners were lined up by the edge of a nullah and met a similar fate. The women staff were unharmed; the two doctors and a medical orderly were marched across the hills and survived, though one of them, a Canadian doctor, Capt. S. M. Banfill, has related that they were from time to time lined up to be shot. Some twenty Volunteer prisoners, taken on Sai Wan Hill on the same night, were bayoneted.

On the morning of 20 December a number of British and Canadian prisoners were found roped together and shot at 'Eucliff', the large castle-like mansion near Repulse Bay Hotel; one of them, a R.A.S.C. Company sergeant-major, was luckily shot through the mouth and providentially escaped with his life. These men had been taken in fighting south of Wong Nei Chong Gap and on 'The Ridge', a spur on the west side of Violet Hill which the defence made strenuous efforts to hold. After the fall of Repulse Bay Hotel, the civilians were marched across the road to 'Eucliff' where they saw bodies of British prisoners tied together and shot, and they were forced to witness more shooting of captured men.

When the racecourse was abandoned on 24 December the Jockey Club premises, used as an emergency hospital, were occupied by Japanese; the Chinese nurses were locked in one room and four taken out and raped, but the medical officer managed to save the wounded. When the news of the outrage reached Military Headquarters, protests were made to the Japanese who allowed a British truck to pass through their lines to rescue the victims.[3]

Further up the hill, at St. Albert's Convent, used as an auxiliary hospital, nurses and staff were tied up and were on the point of being machine-gunned when the Japanese discovered one of their own wounded officers being treated and well cared for, and the staff were liberated.

The worst incident was at St. Stephen's College at Stanley, also being used as an emergency hospital. It was captured early on Christmas morning, and some fifty-six British and Canadian wounded were bayoneted in their beds and two doctors were shot trying to protect them. Four Chinese and three British nurses were raped and murdered, and next day the survivors were made to burn the bodies and blood-soaked mattresses. The Maryknoll Fathers and some wounded who had taken refuge in their Mission were also brutally treated. These incidents were probably caused by a breakdown in unit discipline. But even worse atrocities were reserved for the local population who were used for bayonet or shooting practice, or for jujitsu practice, being thrown heavily a number of times, and bayoneted when unable to move.

The fall of Hong Kong unpleasantly surprised the War Cabinet in England where a more prolonged stand had been expected. On 21 December 1941 Churchill had sent an encouraging message to the Governor asking that 'the enemy should be compelled to expend the utmost life and equipment', and urging all to win lasting honour by a prolonged resistance.

Why was the British resistance so short-lived? Britain was alone and struggling, and the dispatch of two battleships, *Prince of Wales* and *Repulse*, to Singapore without waiting until a more balanced naval force could be made available and assembled there, was an accepted risk designed to bluff Japan into more moderate courses. After their loss on 8 December Hong Kong's chances of early relief disappeared.

The garrison numbered 541 officers and 10,778 other ranks including 94 officers and 1,665 other ranks of the Hong Kong Volunteer Defence Corps; the Royal Navy and Hong Kong

[3] Freddie Guest, *Escape from the Bloodied Sun* (London, 1956), p. 41. This incident is not confirmed in Maltby's Despatch. Evidence given before the War Crimes trials at Tokyo by a Canadian chaplain and others confirmed accounts of these atrocities.

Naval Defence Force and R.A.F. numbered about 1,000 men so altogether there were a little over 12,000 men. On the Japanese side there were nine battalions of infantry, as against the equivalent of eight on the British side, comprising the 38th Division with all supporting arms with some additional artillery units from the 23rd Army[4] giving a total of about 13,000 men. They had overwhelming superiority in the air, at sea and in artillery, and their morale was boosted by the knowledge that three other divisions were available in south China if needed, sufficient to isolate the Colony from Chinese help.

There were specific weaknesses about the British defence, some of which have already been mentioned. There was a clear deficiency in the artillery. Many of the guns were sited to repel an invasion by sea and were useless for tactical infantry support. The general reorganization of the British artillery units consequent upon moving the mobile batteries to the mainland, was a long and complicated process and was incomplete when the fighting started, and so the artillery could not be deployed to the maximum advantage. Guns on Stonecutters Island were sited in such a way as to have few mainland targets, and the Royal Scots and Punjabis did not have on the mainland the artillery support they expected. The Hong Kong and Singapore Royal Artillery were much below strength and a number of local personnel had to be recruited, some of whom proved to be unreliable under the severe pressure they had to meet.

Next there was insufficient ammunition, and some of it was of 1918 manufacture and unreliable. Worse still was the lack of 2-inch and 3-inch mortar ammunition. Some supplies arrived in the Colony so late that ammunition did not reach the units until after the retreat from the mainland. Some infantry had little training in the newest mortars as very few practice rounds were allowed. This shortage of equipment was of course understandable after Dunkirk.

Military transport, which had never been adequate, generally broke down. Under the pooling system, there was sufficient only to move one company at a time, and when three battalions had to be moved, there was a breakdown. The mules had to be

[4] S.W. Kirby, *The War against Japan*, Vol. 1, Appendix 6.

left on the mainland and during the fighting on the Island, guns and ammunition had to be dragged by the gunners. Many locally-recruited drivers deserted and men fully trained for other tasks had to be pressed in as drivers.

The defence plans were changed late in 1941, and time ran out before some of the units could be adequately trained in new roles. Exceptions were the Middlesex who were well-trained and well-equipped for their role in manning the pill-boxes, and the Punjabis who were intended from the start to serve on the mainland. The two Canadian regiments were fairly raw, listed in Canada as 'not recommended for operational consideration', and were without their transport, rifles, mortars and machine-guns; but they learnt the hard way and earned the respect of the Japanese. The Volunteers emerged from the ordeal with honour and were justly praised by General Maltby for their steadiness in face of the enemy.

British intelligence proved to be consistently ill-informed and was a most important factor in the defeat. The British Embassy in Japan advised that a Japanese attack on Britain and the United States was improbable, or, if the Japanese did attack this was unlikely to be before the early summer of 1942, by which time the outcome of Hitler's attack on Russia would be clearer. There was no sense of urgency in December 1941; the Canadians were thought to have time enough to train, and indeed their arrival induced a dangerous wave of optimism. Worse still, as already stated, British intelligence rated the Japanese as poor-quality soldiers from whom there was little to fear. They were supposedly supported by a badly-equipped air arm served by second-rate pilots. This 'intelligence' proved wide of the mark; the failure was quite unpardonable and contributed to the catastrophe.

The British commanders were mostly new men; the General was a recent arrival and the two brigadiers were of course very new to their jobs, having been appointed only some three weeks before the fighting, and they had hardly time to get to know their staff officers, let alone the tactical problems facing them.

Whether General Maltby could have made more effective use of his forces is a matter for the military experts. He cannot be held responsible for the belief that war was not expected;

he claimed in his Despatch that there was no proof that war was imminent, and he did not blame the civil authorities for not implementing many of the precautionary measures called for by the Civil Defence Plan. There was some excuse for believing that the Japanese were bluffing and would continue to bluff, for the Japanese did not make up their own minds to attack South-East Asia until July 1941. The General did however receive sufficient warning to allow him to have all his forces in their battle stations before the attack came.

The General referred in his Despatch to those points in which the British generally, and by implication he himself, were misled, points which have already been mentioned. He seriously underestimated the strength of the Japanese landings and counter-attacks were not mounted in sufficient strength.

General Maltby felt that he had to deploy his forces to be ready to repel a landing from any quarter, and this necessitated a spreading of his forces which made it difficult to concentrate sufficient strength at any threatened point. It meant dispersal of food and supplies and placed a great strain on transport and communications, and in the event, in trying to prepare for all contingencies, he was ready to meet none. The result was that the British advantage of defence on difficult terrain was neutralized by the fact that the initiative rested with the Japanese, who were able to select their objectives and concentrate overwhelming force against each one.

As to the belief that the Japanese were wooden and stereotyped in their methods, the boot was on the other foot. The Japanese advanced across country, suitably clad, shod and equipped. The British tended to be road-bound; for example, East Brigade retired to Stanley by road, attacked Bridge Hill by road, and Wong Nei Chong Gap by the Repulse Bay road, and the Royal Scots were sent to the Gap by lorry. The Japanese on the other hand made for the high ground straight across country, often closing in silently on their objectives by night, whereas British troop movements were all too frequently made obvious and invited counter measures.

The withdrawal of East's brigade headquarters to Stanley against the General's better judgement was, in the words of Major-General S. W. Kirby, the official historian of the Pacific

War, 'a major tactical error', with the disastrous result of allowing the defence to be cut in two.

When Brigadier Lawson was killed, there was a breakdown in communication as the news did not reach the Battle Headquarters for twenty-four hours. Again, the chain of command did not appear to work smoothly; on a number of occasions, the General appears to have organized and ordered attacks independently of the brigade commanders, as for example, the sending of the Punjabis to Shouson Hill and of the Naval party to the Gap. The chain of command became more blurred, and according to the official British history of the campaign there was a sad 'lack of co-ordination which probably affected the whole course of the operation'. During the whole seven days' fighting on the Island, no successful counter-attack was made. Acts of gallantry by individual men or small units remained uncoordinated and unavailing. It is, of course, easy to be wise after the event, and it may well be that any attempt to collect men in strength would have invited dive-bombing and shelling. The impression left is that on the British side the battle lacked that close direction and planning necessary to hold the Japanese for any length of time. But it has to be admitted that they were fighting a battle that could not be won, and many must have felt this.

The Japanese, on the other hand, were well-trained seasoned fighters with some years' experience of campaigning in South China. They had control of the air, command of the sea and overwhelming artillery superiority. The men were supremely fit, able to negotiate the steep uneven hill paths by night as well as by day, being well-trained in night operations. They were imbued with the cause of Japan's great destiny and regarded death for the Emperor as the highest honour. The attack was well-planned and well-executed. They seized the initiative and, because they kept up incessant pressure showing the highest discipline and driving their men to the limit of endurance, they never lost it. They advanced on their objectives, often at night, sensibly equipped, avoiding roads, carrying such weapons as were necessary for the immediate objectives, operating for days on concentrated foods. Their seizure of the Shing Mun Redoubt in the Gindrinkers Line and of Mount Nicholson was typical of their aggressive spirit, daring and willingness to use unorthodox methods, backed by accurate intelligence.

Their success was also partly due to the building in Japan of a formidable fighting machine based on dehumanizing the soldier in the interest of ruthless fighting efficiency. One observer who had spent most of his life in Japan wrote:

> Trained in the grim philosophy of death, compelled to sell his life against impossible odds, condemned to blow himself to pieces with his last grenade retained for the purpose . . . rather than submit to capture, the Japanese soldier was brutalized from the day he entered the service . . . . For all the shame which the Japanese nation was to endure for its treatment of others, yet no greater condemnation could be made than of the manner in which it allowed a system to develop which condemned its own sons to live and die in a mockery of human dignity.[5]

[5] Louis Bush, *Land of the Dragonfly* (London, 1959), p. 196.

IV

HONG KONG TWILIGHT

'There was never for a moment any weakness on the part of the people, and all did their part to the fullest extent – but there was no enthusiasm.'

Fr. T. Ryan, *Jesuits under Fire in the Siege of Hong Kong* (London, 1944)

It is now time to go back and see how the civilian people fared during the battle.

Immediately on the outbreak of war against Japan on 8 December 'The Emergency Powers Order in Council, 1939' was applied to the Colony, authorizing the Governor to make regulations to secure public order and public safety, maintain supplies and services essential to the life of the community, to detain persons, take possession of any property or undertaking or acquire property except land, and to suspend or modify any ordinance. The most urgent problem was feeding. People had been officially advised to lay in a store of food, but with the coming of war there was no chance of further stocking-up. All food supplies were now placed under strict government control, and institutions with resident inmates, such as hospitals, children's homes and boarding schools, were supplied direct from Government depots, and a specified quantity was allocated to each person sufficient for three days. This meant going to the Food Office, filling in forms, being interviewed and calculating the amount to be claimed. Members of the auxiliary defence services were able to obtain meals provided by the Government at certain restaurants, on signing the necessary docket and producing identity cards showing the Service to which they belonged.

The very poor, chiefly coolies paid by the day, whose employment now disappeared, were fed from public food kitchens. It had been intended to arrange for the supply of hot cheap meals on a large scale, free of charge, but the coming of war had caught the Government unprepared and the plans had not been fully completed. A few kitchens were ready, including that in the basement of the Wanchai Market which had been operated by the Equitable Rice Sales Fund Committee; the largest were in the Central Market, where long queues formed and several thousands per hour were served throughout the day, each person being given one bowl of rice and some soya beans, without charge. Even so, Fr. Ryan noted that there was some starvation for a few days until an adequate number of kitchens could be improvised. In another section of the market, people were given cheap uncooked rice. Kitchen staff had to be recruited on a voluntary basis at first, and University professors, lecturers and students of both Hong Kong and Lingnam Universities as well as some clergymen, including the Jesuit Fathers, gave their services. The Chinese did not relish soya beans, despite the many attempts by Dr. Selwyn-Clarke to convince them of their high food value.

The rest of the civilian population had to buy their rice in the shops at government-controlled prices. The authorities had intended a full rationing scheme, but during the seventeen days' fighting there was no time to work out the details, let alone organize its administration and so improvisation was necessarily the order of the day. Food supplies were rigidly controlled, as Fr. Ryan reported, but that control was exercised mainly through price, the calculation apparently being that people would not buy in the black market at soaring prices if they could get the rice they needed more cheaply from the authorized distributors in the controlled shops. Rice shops closed on the outbreak of war because shopkeepers anticipated higher prices, and the Government had to compel owners to keep them open; in addition, the official rice depots offered supplies and were soon besieged by masses of people. Most Europeans were engaged on war service, either in the armed forces or in one of the defence services and were fed from official sources; the few left drew supplies from the main European stores.

The movement of vessels in the harbour was strictly regulated, banking hours were restricted to two hours from 10 a.m. to 12 noon, and power was taken to issue Bank of China $5 national currency notes over-printed 'Hong Kong Government $1' if and when necessary. All Civil Defence Corps were called out, a permanent black-out at night was imposed and, on the 9th, food shops were ordered to remain open from 8.0 a.m. to sunset. By an order issued on the 12th, unattended road vehicles had to be immobilized and four days later private motorists had to obtain official permission to keep their cars on the road. Those not permitted were requisitioned for official use. A curfew was imposed from 7.30 p.m. to 6.30 a.m. on the 15th.

The war came too suddenly for the Government's emergency defence plans for the civil population to be completed, and some administrative chaos was inescapable. Fr. Ryan observed that buildings which had been closed, now opened, disclosing newly-created Government departments already functioning in them.

The Government had drawn up an elaborate scheme of dispersal of the civilian population into so-called safe areas and large rice kitchens were built there, for example, one was in Hatton Road above the Western District and another was in Wong Chuk Hang near Aberdeen; again the Jesuit Fathers were asked to help, since they were neutral and exempt from compulsory service and so formed a valuable source of reserve manpower. However, the dispersal scheme was dropped when the war started. There were serious billeting problems because the Government had undertaken to rehouse the families of those in the various defence services in safer areas, and particularly it had an obligation to look after dependants living in Kowloon before the planned evacuation of the mainland. There was on paper an elaborate billeting scheme with cards, reception centres, time-tables, billeting officers, billeting transport officers and movement officers, but this was scrapped because there was no time for it even to be put up for approval, and makeshift arrangements once more had to be made. Again the Irish Jesuit Fathers and students in their Seminary were called in to help. The work was arduous and dangerous and was continually interrupted by air-raid warnings which sounded at frequent intervals throughout the day. Transport became almost impossible as drivers deserted and difficulties arose over repairs and fuel, but eventually, despite the cessation of the ferries, Kowloon dependants were brought over in police launches and billeted in commandeered empty houses, many of them in May Road. Some went into the Italian Convent and St. Paul's Convent. It was calculated that 20,000 people were affected by the billeting scheme, but not all chose to move.

The coming of war brought business to a standstill and forced many last-minute recruits into one of the defence or essential services; arm-bands proliferated.[1]

The Chinese emerged from their seventeen days' ordeal of fire with no little credit and all eye-witness accounts pay tribute to their discipline and good-humour in the face of danger. 'There was no panic at any time, the proverbial patience of the Chinese was fully demonstrated, and their unruffled calm in moments of danger and alarm won the unstinted praise of those not ordinarily given to praise,' wrote Fr. Ryan. 'The Chinese were orderly, there was no panic,' wrote another observer, and another commented on the orderly processions into the air-raid shelters, saying, 'The public shelters were filled to an unbelievable extent with Chinese who remained good-humoured and placid.' Many occupied the pavements in the Central District protected by blast-proof walls built between the archways of the street verandahs and many sought shelter in the corridors of the Gloucester Hotel.

The reaction of the local Chinese community to the British defeat was one of numbed surprise and sullen acquiescence in the new conditions, accompanied by a grim determination to survive; and of course, to the very poor, immersed in the problem of getting two meals a day and a bed-space, it mattered little who won. The mass of the Chinese had tried to continue their normal jobs, leaving the fighting to those whose business it was. With the Japanese victory their attitude showed little change, save for a hatred of the victors because of the suffering and chaos the Japanese had brought to China, rather than to themselves in Hong Kong.

The cessation of hostilities found the civilian population living under appalling conditions of overcrowding, failure of

[1] As Endacott suggests, the emergency schemes, which looked reasonable on paper, disintegrated under the stress of battle. One French observer, an administrator, who arrived in Hong Kong only on 2 December, was blistering in his condemnation of the emergency services. Only three (the Ambulance, Rescue and Demolition, and Fire Services) were efficient, the rest (A.R.P., Food Control, and Police) were inefficient beyond description. (F.O. 371/31671.)

public services, looting and general breakdown of law and order. The bombing and shelling had inevitably caused extensive damage to property, though Japanese gunners and airmen had appeared to concentrate on military targets and Government property. The homeless had to crowd in where they could. The supply of water had been cut off on 20 December when the Japanese controlled the main reservoirs, and supplies had to be drawn from wells or streams and boiled before use; toilets could not be flushed and all contemporary accounts refer to the repulsive stench which pervaded all buildings until water was restored in the Central District on 29 December. Electricity and gas had been cut off since 21 December, lifts failed, refrigerated food went bad until electricity was restored in the Central District on 3 January, and candles were in urgent demand.

Sporadic looting had occurred during the battle and had ultimately to be checked by shooting, but with the cessation of the fighting it appeared on a greatly extended scale, because neither British nor Japanese were in actual control. The homes of those absent on service with the forces or defence services were stripped and the contents brought down the hillsides to deck the hawkers' stalls and thus provide them with working capital to begin a business; afterwards the hawkers dealt in any commodity that they could buy. The fuel problem became acute, for rice must be cooked, and wooden furniture became more marketable as fuel than serving its original purpose. Looting British homes had some virtue in the conquerors' eyes of course, until the Japanese wanted billets themselves; they adopted arbitrary and equivocal methods to check this pillaging but made no attempt definitely to stop the abuse by putting a guard on residential areas. Looters were liable to be summarily shot on the roads, and it is surprising that they still continued to take the risk. John Stericker in his *Tear for the Dragon* has described conditions at the lower Peak Tram Station where the Japanese tied Chinese looters to a tree by their necks and hands, in groups, and left them to strangle, while others were strung up and hanged from lamp-posts. He also tells of looters having their hands pierced by bayonets and being thrown into the sea with their hands threaded together. Other observers have also left accounts of Chinese looters being tied up and tortured. Some Chinese attempting to glean a little spilled rice were thrown into the harbour and shot, yet a Chinese who was caught stealing quantities of telephone wire was subjected to the procedures of justice before he too was sentenced to death. It was all very arbitrary, perhaps necessarily so, until the new Japanese administrative machinery could get into its stride.

There was more looting, on an unsystematic individual enterprise basis, by the Japanese soldiers who tried to get whatever pickings there were after the Chinese had already been on the scene. They also operated on the streets and showed a particularly keen interest in watches; they would innocently ask the time from a passer-by and the victim, glancing at his watch to oblige, was forthwith relieved of it, and report had it that an ambition to have the whole of the arm straddled with watches was not uncommon among the Japanese soldiery. They also took jewellery and Professor Gawan Sewell wrote that his wife was forced to hand over her wedding ring to a Japanese soldier.

The Chinese devoted their energies to keeping alive, and their prime concern was food. Many shops closed because of insecurity, and uncertainty over the currency, and many owners preferred to join the rows of hawkers' stalls which soon lined the principal streets of Central especially Queen's Road, Stanley Street, and Wellington Street. Prices rose steeply as price control collapsed; the shopper might haggle but had to buy to eat, and bully beef rose to $3 a 12 oz tin and butter $12 a lb. compared with 1939 prices of about 33 cents and $1.30 respectively. Long queues hopefully waited outside the rice-shops.

One observer noted that numbers of bars opened in the Central District with Filipino bands and Chinese, Russian, and Eurasian prostitutes; they had a short life and were moved into specially allocated areas after the Japanese assumed full control.

The evidence shows beyond doubt that the Chinese were treated badly in many instances, and quite at variance with Japanese propaganda which stressed the theme of 'Asia for the Asians'. Propagandist leaflets were much sought after by the Chinese population, but report had it that the leaflets were put to an entirely different purpose from that intended. Phyllis Harrop reported that on 23 December she returned to her flat in Happy Valley to find her amah had been raped by soldiers, that fourteen persons had been bayoneted in a neighbouring flat, and altogether forty had been killed in the block of flats where she had lived.

On the other hand there were many recorded acts of kindness, particularly where people accepted Japanese ideas of courtesy such as bowing. Professor Sewell said he felt bowing was 'a natural courtesy and not a sign of humiliation as it seemed to Hong Kong dwellers'. He gave the Japanese visitors tea, and they in return showed all their traditional oriental politeness, and a Japanese major used to visit the family once or twice a week and bring sweets for the children. The Japanese were unpredictable, but accounts of this period all refer to their love of children and their kindness towards domestic animals.

After the surrender, the Japanese troops were given three days' leave and Wanchai district was more or less turned over to them. One American press reporter has stated that respectable families were not interfered with, that respectable women were not molested and that so-called rape cases were by consent, but he admitted that there may have been exceptions.

The Japanese had proved their preparedness in the field, but did not appear to have any prepared plan to meet the new situation created by victory. They had a small number of civil affairs officers in uniform to assist in the administration of the Colony but there seemed to be no blue-print of the sort of government they envisaged. No doubt the interests of the civilian population had to take second place to the more pressing needs of the war which was rapidly spreading to the whole of South-East Asia. In any case the military intended to retain full control though some delay was probably necessary while directives were sought from Tokyo. The result was a curious hiatus of eleven days in which the civilians were left very much to themselves.

The Japanese flag was hoisted in the Central District on 27 December and, as if at a signal, buildings were soon gay with flags, indicating that the Japanese had some sympathizers.

On the same day, the military descended on the Central District to take a count of Europeans, but this seemed to have been extremely haphazardly organized and was soon given up.[2]

On the following day came the grand Victory Parade. Over 2,000 men representing the various formations which had taken part in the fighting marched through the streets from Happy Valley to the western district in an impressive display of military might headed by their divisional commander, Lt.-General Sano, riding a white horse, wearing a long sword and accompanied by a strong bodyguard. The Chinese were encouraged to line the route and cheer and were supplied with small flags but they watched without any enthusiasm. Accounts vary, but all agree that a brilliant display of aerobatics by the Japanese Imperial Air Force added a thrill to the proceedings. The Europeans were kept indoors and forbidden to look down at the parade on pain of being shot, though some contrived to catch a glimpse.

One task which Japanese piety demanded be immediately done was the cremation of their dead in large funeral pyres. This was ceremonially performed in a long crematorium and the ashes were taken out with long steel chopsticks and placed in small white caskets, each bearing a man's name. Some of these were borne through the streets in a place of honour in the victory parade, and all were sent back to Japan. Memorial services were also held on the cricket field and on the battlefields. With inhuman and callous disregard of the feelings of their former foes, the British were not allowed to bring in their dead and wounded until the Japanese funeral rites had been completed; how many wounded men might otherwise have been saved is, of course, purely conjectural. It was impossible to compile lists of casualties for some time, and Mr. F. C. Gimson, who headed the British administration when the Governor was kept a prisoner, and who set up his office in Prince's Building, received no reply from the Japanese to his repeated requests for the names of prisoners of war in Kowloon.

[2] Recently the Hong Kong Government archivist, Mr. I. A. Diamond, has turned up, in official files, the list of 'European' civilians drawn up by the imprisoned Colonial Secretary, Mr. F. C. Gimson, and his helpers. P.R.O. Hong Kong, *H.K.R.S.*, 112.

Japanese booty was enormous. According to their English-language newspaper of 8 January 1942 they claimed to have captured 5 aircraft, 998 rifles, 1,200 machine-guns, 122 guns, 19 anti-aircraft guns, 'a large quantity' of heavy artillery, 18,300 rounds of ammunition, 10 armoured cars, 1,470 motor-cars and large quantities of fuel and supplies, as well as 11,241 prisoners of war. The Japanese collected the motor-cars on the cricket ground, the racecourse and at the Colonial Secretariat, and most were shipped back to Japan with other captured material. For days, ships sailed out of harbour with full cargoes; Gwen Dew, an American women journalist, crossing the harbour in late January, counted twenty-six Japanese fully loaded ships with deck-cargoes of motor-cars. Jan Marsman, an experienced businessman from the Philippines, who built the Hong Kong air raid tunnel shelters and was caught here by the war, estimated from what he saw and heard that some 2,500,000 tons of freight worth US$250 million were taken from the godowns and shipped to Japan at the rate of 300,000 to 350,000 tons a month.

The European civilians, many of them wives trying to find the whereabouts of their husbands, soon began to venture on to the streets, which they found littered with debris and broken glass, while steel helmets, arm bands and gas masks were scattered in profusion, having been jettisoned by Chinese members of the civil defence services who, after capitulation, sensibly got rid of their uniforms or arm-bands and merged into the community. The foreigners seemed to have been able to walk about quite freely. The main hazard was passing a Japanese sentry or check-point, and they were very soon taught that a bow was necessary, each bow being invariably acknowledged with a smart salute in return. Some went to visit wounded friends in the British Military Hospital, and some ventured back to their homes on the Peak or mid-levels to retrieve what remained of their possessions. In her book, *Twilight in Hong Kong*, Ellen Field describes how she went to a Japanese information office in the Hong Kong Bank on the 27th and secured a permit to return to her home in Kowloon, and the same afternoon she and a group of women walked to North Point in a vain attempt to see their prisoner husbands. She crossed by ferry to Kowloon the next day to find that her home had been stripped of everything except two trunks which were taken care of by a neighbour.

This freedom could not of course last indefinitely and on 4 January 1942 all British, American, and Dutch residents were ordered to assemble on the following day at the Murray Parade Ground and bring overnight bags. They were given too little time to prepare, many never received the mimeographed notice, or saw the announcement in the Press; some in the know brought blankets and all that they could carry, but few suspected that this was to be the start of a three years and eight months' internment. It was drizzling, and chaos resulted from Japanese attempts to line people up according to size but they were eventually marched off in indiscriminate batches of about a hundred to water-front hotels which catered normally for a less-demanding clientele accustomed to renting the rooms by the hour. One American journalist, George E. Baxter, has given a vivid picture of his experiences. There were 142 internees in his batch and they were marched to a boarding house in the Western District, a narrow four-storey building with windows at the two ends; the middle of the house was gloomily dark. Each floor had a corridor, with cubicles 6 feet by 9 feet leading off. These were formed by wooden partitions that did not reach the ground or the ceiling. There were two 'squat' toilets for 142 persons. They were given no food the first day and ate only what they had happened to have brought, but they were allowed out in the evening to what he called 'a dirty restaurant' under an Indian guard. They were charged 50 cents a day for food, and the hotel charged 50 cents a week for service. They were allowed exercise on one half of the roof, 40 paces by 8 paces, the other half overlooking the harbour being barred, presumably for security reasons. Chinese friends brought food, and a former Japanese Consul-General brought bread and milk to the children; another example of the acts of kindness done by some of the Japanese. They were also able to buy food and drinks from Chinese vendors on the roof of the adjoining house. But the black market tended to be unreliable and good money might be paid for an apparently sound tin of peaches only to find later that the contents were spinach. The Japanese did not supply rice for forty-eight hours.

The groups moved off on 20 and 21 January by sea to Stanley Peninsula. They assembled at a pier in the Western District and were to be searched, but instead the order went out that all who had radio sets, fire-arms or maps were to fall out. None did. The boats were dangerously overcrowded but arrived at Stanley without mishap.

A number of people remained out for a little while longer. The University community which had been running an auxiliary hospital in Eliot Hall remained in the campus, and residents on the Peak were allowed to stay out because the Japanese accepted the Chief Justice's offer of his personal guarantee on their behalf. There were also the bankers, restricted to certain lodging houses, and in addition some isolated families such as the Sewells who had secured exemption through the friendly offices of a senior Japanese officer whom they knew or accidentally met. Then there were the Medical and Health Department officials under Dr. Selwyn-Clarke who received permission to remain out to assist in health work. Most of these people came into Stanley a few weeks later in early February, except the bankers and Health Department officials who remained out until 1943. There were also a number of friendly aliens who were not interned in Stanley but who found living at large in Hong Kong offered a very illusory freedom.

The civilian refugees from the Repulse Bay Hotel were the first to experience the rigours of internment by the Japanese and to have a foretaste of Stanley Camp. As already related, they had set off on the morning of 24 December in a procession that was soon strung out over half a mile, and in the evening reached a paint factory at North Point, in which they were temporarily housed. They were given water and sugar, the only food they had that day. Next day, Christmas Day, after a breakfast of Japanese vegetable stew and some tea, they were taken across to the small Kowloon Hotel, at the rear of the Peninsula Hotel. No preparations had been made to receive them and they were haphazardly distributed from four to ten in a room without regard to sex or age. For weeks they had only rice and water with raw cabbage as an occasional extra. They were not allowed to look down on the Japanese, whose military headquarters were on the opposite side of the road in the Peninsula Hotel, and they were forced, not always successfully, to cover their windows. They were taught to bow Japanese style and failure resulted in having the face slapped. The Chinese room-boys were willing to sell food, but notes of large denominations, which most people had because they made it convenient to hold larger amounts of cash, were unpopular with sellers of goods, because of the difficulty of giving change, and a $100 note fetched only $60 in value. Many others were later billetted in the same hotel, which became grossly overcrowded.

On 24 January the party moved off to Stanley Internment Camp, except four press reporters who were kept out with the hope of inducing them to work for the Japanese. A Japanese press man, Ogura, was already known to one of the persons in the hotel, Gwen Dew, and he used to bring her fruit, another of the many instances of kindness shown to the prisoners and internees.

Gwen Dew was for a short time allowed to move about freely until her refusal to work as a journalist for the Japanese resulted in her being abruptly ordered into Stanley, and she was thus able to record some impressions of the early stages of the Japanese take-over. The fall of Singapore in February 1942 was celebrated by a general holiday with lion dances and lantern processions, and the Chinese were given extra rice. British signs and names were already being taken down and British offices, public and commercial, were being occupied by the Japanese. Chinese and Indian police were operating, the former carried long staves and the latter wore large badges. Villagers brought in supplies of vegetables early in the morning, stores were beginning to re-open, and every street was lined with stalls, though money was chaotic, with prices in dollars at a nominal exchange rate of two dollars to one Japanese yen. British bankers were pressed into service to assist the Japanese in handing over the banks, and processions of bankers being marched to and from their quarters were observed by this same reporter. Silk Street still had plenty of silks and sea-food stalls were common with supplies plentiful. Fuel was obviously chopped-up furniture. The Hong Kong Hotel housed Japanese officers; the Gloucester Hotel, already renamed the *Matsubara*, was select and expensive, with Japanese food. The Japanese had already declared their intention of reducing the Chinese population by a million, and she noted that prices for assistance in getting out of Hong Kong were quoted from $200 to $2,000. Members of the Medical and Health Department who had been allowed to remain at their posts to help prevent epidemics told her that some 200 bodies were picked up from the streets every day as a result of starvation, disease and in some cases, bullet wounds. She also noted that numbers of prostitutes aged between 14 and 20 were appearing on the streets with their amahs.

V

JAPANESE ADMINISTRATION IN HONG KONG

'There is no question that Hong Kong belongs to Japan, but consideration will be given to Chinese and other Third Nationals living here in the way of administration, which will be based on the new order of Greater East Asia. . . .'

General Rensuke Isogai on assuming the Governorship of Hong Kong, 20 February 1942

HONG KONG's status remained unchanged except that the Japanese replaced the British in control. Whatever may have been the hopes of the puppet Wang Ching-wei in Nanking, there was no hint of its retrocession to China similar to that of the British Concession at Shameen in Canton, which was handed over to the Chinese in March 1942. The former British Colony came under direct Japanese military rule under the designation 'The Captured Territory of Hong Kong'.

Reporting on the appointment of Lt.-General Rensuke Isogai as Governor, the Japanese-owned *Hong Kong News* commented that Hong Kong would not be governed 'in the same category' as Korea or Formosa, but would be run as a fortress. 'The first use of Hong Kong is as a centre for supplies for the troops. But under the rule of the new Governor it is hoped that Hong Kong will rapidly take its place as the heart of South China.' Hong Kong's eventual role in the Greater East Asia Co-prosperity Sphere therefore remained obscure, and probably no decision could have been expected at a time of total war. Japanese policy and administration, in Hong Kong as elsewhere, were subordinated to the urgent and immediate task of winning the war, and must be examined and judged in that context. This was especially important in regard to Hong Kong which, with its naval base, ample barrack accommodation, ordnance depots, artillery sites, fortifications and airfield, possessed substantial military value. So the garrison was maintained at some 25,000 in addition to naval forces. Notices of artillery exercises, frequently with a warning of live ammunition, appeared almost weekly in the Press during the whole occupation period, additional fortifications and defence works were constructed and more intensive air-raid precautions built up. Military requirements demanded a drastic reduction in a population heavily swollen by refugees from across the border; these immigrants had shown their lack of the co-operative spirit by fleeing from the Japanese armies to the hoped-for security of the British flag, and so could expect little sympathy from Japanese authorities in Hong Kong. Clearly, under these various circumstances the normal modes of civil administration could not apply in Hong Kong, and control firmly rested with the military backed by martial law.

The Japanese seemed in no hurry to re-establish law and order which broke down after the British defeat, partly because they were chiefly concerned with the security and welfare of their own troops, but possibly to encourage the Chinese to be co-operative, since the disorder harmed the Chinese civilians more than the Japanese military. On 1 January 1942 the Japanese set up a 'Civil Department of the Japanese Army', generally called the Civil Administration Department, under Major-General Yazaki which assumed responsibility for protecting the lives and property of the Chinese and non-enemy aliens.[1]

Their first step to obtain public support was to hold prominent members of the Chinese community incommunicado in their homes or in hotels and subject them to great pressure voluntarily to co-operate. There was no ill-treatment but the veiled threat of continued detention virtually ruled out a refusal. Among them were Dr. W. W. Yen and Eugene Chen, formerly Foreign Minister of China, who were detained in the Hong Kong Hotel. Then on 10 January 1942 Lt.-General Sakai invited 133 leading Chinese, referred to as 'former Chinese Justices of the Peace and other distinguished leaders representing all sections of Chinese Society' to a lunch at the Peninsula Hotel, attended by many senior Japanese officers. The General emphasized that Japan had made war in Hong Kong not against

[1] See J. Lethbridge's article, 'Hong Kong under the Japanese Occupation' in Agassi, J., and Jarvie, I.C. (eds.), *Hong Kong, A Society in Transition* (London, 1969).

the Chinese, but against the British, with the object of securing the prosperity of the races of Greater East Asia. He urged that the Chinese and Japanese, being of the same race, should collaborate and asked them to form a committee to assist in this. He suggested recruiting Chinese police to help the military to maintain order and called for Chinese co-operation in dealing with rice and fuel supply problems. He asked all to return to their jobs so as to get business going again. Hopes were expressed that the currency problem would shortly be resolved. Sir Robert Kotewall, the senior member of the old Executive Council, and now always referred to as Lo Kuk-wo since the Japanese frowned on British titles, replied promising Chinese help in restoring trade and employment, and he was supported by Sir Shouson Chow, now called Chow Shou-son.

On 12 January 1942 the Chinese Chamber of Commerce, which had on 31 December petitioned the Japanese military drawing attention to various difficulties such as the disruption of supplies and public utility services, the currency problem and the evils of prostitution, formed a committee of nine (increased to twelve on 5 February) called the Rehabilitation Committee (later the Rehabilitation Advisory Committee) to put forward their views. Its chairman was Sir Robert, with Sir Shouson as vice-chairman, and its membership comprised the principal leaders of the Chinese community, including all the Chinese unofficial members of the old Legislative Council. They held two prolonged meetings and discussed their proposals with the Japanese military administration on 14 January.

On 21 January the Japanese set up new government agencies called District Bureaux or Offices; there were twelve for Hong Kong Island, and some days later, six for Kowloon. Each was under a Chinese and was made responsible for public health, business, repatriation and welfare of the residents of the district and generally represented their needs and wishes to the Japanese authorities. A District Affairs Bureau was set up in the Civil Administration Department to act as the link between it and the district bureaux. A prominent Chinese lawyer, Sin Ping-hsi, was appointed head of the Central District Bureau and also became Director of the District Affairs Bureau, and was popularly referred to as 'The Mayor of Hong Kong'.[2] The other eleven Island district heads were named on 27 January and the six for Kowloon a week later. Early in February a scheme for dividing each district into wards was announced, on a basis of thirty families for each ward. The Central District Bureau went ahead immediately and named 131 Chinese ward leaders.

This district administrative machinery using local Chinese officials enabled the occupation authorities to have close contacts with every part of the conquered territory, and had the merit of reaching down to the people. It was therefore able to counter-balance the influence of the Rehabilitation Advisory Committee which represented the more substantial element in the community. The district bureau organization was new in Hong Kong and proved to be an extremely effective part of the occupation administrative machinery.

On 20 February 1942 Lt.-General Rensuke Isogai assumed office as Governor of Hong Kong, a post he retained until recalled to Japan at the end of 1944. He was a well-known student of South China, with strong political leanings. The occasion was marked by an 'Order of the Day' which called Britain the public enemy of mankind, whose loss of Hong Kong was a matter for rejoicing. It called on Hong Kong people to help achieve victory in the Greater East Asia War, to eschew 'easy practices' and to elevate the life of the place to Japanese levels in the light of 'the Kingly Way', as set out in the Confucian classical writings.

At an inauguration ceremony in the King's Theatre where he was welcomed on behalf of the community by Sir Robert Kotewall and others, the Governor referred to Hong Kong as having been long 'an important base for furthering the decadent materialistic civilizations based on selfish individualism' and he threatened to 'eradicate' all who wanted to remain slaves of the British.

The arrival of the new Governor was the signal for important administrative changes. The Japanese consulate was closed since Hong Kong was now Japanese territory, and at a

[2] See 'HongKong Administration', Office of Strategic Services, U.S. Department of State, Office of Intelligence Research, dated 12 January 1945, reproduced in Appendix 8.

farewell party the Japanese military paid warm tributes to the Japanese consul-general, Mr. Seiki Yano, whose detailed knowledge of Hong Kong greatly contributed to the preparation of the assault plans.

At the centre, the Civil Administration Department disappeared and was replaced by the 'Governor's Office', or Secretariat, responsible to the Governor and headed by a high-ranking Japanese military officer, Major-General Ichiki, assisted by a Japanese civilian, and Major-General Yazaki was recalled to Japan. It was organized into departments or bureaux. There was a Civil Affairs Bureau which seems to have been a policy-framing body, exercising control and supervision. Other sections or bureaux dealt with foreign affairs, education and culture, economic affairs, finance, land and houses. Three bureaux, namely those of Communications, Information and Repatriation, came more directly under the Chief of the Governor's Office since these were important matters affecting Japanese security, propaganda and relations with the Chinese. Finally there were some functional departments dealing with public works, water, medical and health services and electricity, the last dealing with telephones besides its more obvious duties.

Japanese experts and administrators were employed in the Governor's Office and its various bureaux, and one observer estimated that they numbered 800 at least, a figure that seems too high in view of Japan's expanding administrative commitments elsewhere, and particularly when compared to the 900 experts employed in Japanese-occupied Burma. But there is no doubt that considerable numbers were brought in as experts in administration, banking, education, law, land and housing, medical and dental services and economics, and these naturally occupied all key positions, carrying out a policy to accord with Japanese war needs. But the number of Chinese associated with the administration was also large, comprising the middle and lower ranks of the Government service and the officials in the eighteen district bureaux and wards. These were all drawn into the Japanese orbit ever more firmly as they became personally interested in making a success of their job as a matter of 'face'.

In relations with the Chinese the Governor replaced the

Rehabilitation Advisory Committee by two councils, the Chinese Representative Council and the Chinese Co-operative Council, both occupying an important place in the machinery for securing Chinese co-operation. The former comprised three Chinese; Sir Robert Kotewall was chairman, and Lau Tit-shing, who had been educated in Japan and was strongly pro-Japanese, and Li Tze Fong, a banker, were the other two members, all appointed by the Japanese. It met every day and was the main advisory body on relations with the Chinese community from the members of which petitions were invited. It selected the twenty-two members of the Chinese Co-operative Council which consisted, as Sir Robert Kotewall explained, 'of the leaders of the various organizations to secure the opinions of all sections of the community working under the leadership of the Chinese Representative Council'. The regulations for the Co-operative Council dated 28 March 1942 also provided for appointed members, named by the Governor to represent the people as a whole. This distinction between elected and appointed members was never again mentioned, either in the Japanese-controlled press or in official pronouncements, and seems to have been dropped. The Chinese Co-operative Council worked under the direction of the Chinese Representative Council, the members of which attended its meetings and put up questions for it to discuss; then in the light of the discussion, the Chinese Representative Council had to put forward its own considered recommendations to the appropriate departments of the Governor's Office. The Co-operative Council met on 2 April 1942, and usually sat twice a week; it elected Sir Shouson Chow as its chairman and Li Koon-chun as vice-chairman. These two councils enabled the Japanese to work through a small influential group of Chinese representing the main interests of the Chinese community.

The district offices were retained under their Chinese leaders, but a system of three area bureaux was superimposed on them on 16 April 1942, linking them with the Civil Affairs Bureau at the Secretariat. They included one for Hong Kong Island and neighbouring islands as far as Cheung Chau, a second for Kowloon and Tsuen Wan, and the third for the rest of the New Territories.

These area bureaux were important in the administrative

system and detailed regulations set out their duties and personnel. Each had three sub-offices: a General Office for general business, finance, education and culture, an Economic Office for the economy, communications, transport and the development of raw materials, and thirdly, a Health Office for public health and medical services. The staff comprised a chief, a deputy chief and three assistant chiefs who were all Japanese; the remainder of the total of forty-two personnel were Chinese. The three area bureaux were made responsible to the Chief of the Governor's Office for the execution of the decisions of the occupying Power, and as such formed an essential part of the machinery by which the Japanese governed the Colony. Chinese opinion on matters of general policy was available through the two councils, which had advisory powers only, and the district bureaux kept the Japanese informed regarding the impact of the administration on the life of the people. The district bureaux were expected to work through the area bureaux, where the authority really rested, but their Chinese heads enjoyed the right of independent approach to the Governor's Office, and therefore never became just cyphers.

The administrative machine as re-designed by Governor Isogai, no doubt under instructions from Tokyo, continued without substantial change for the rest of the occupation period. When a new Governor, Lt.-General Tanaka, took over in February 1945 the critical war situation absorbed all available attention and ruled out further constitutional experiment. Again probably on orders from Tokyo, General Tanaka streamlined the Governor's Office, which was divided into only two departments instead of the former three, namely Commerce and Industry, subdivided into three sections dealing with Civil Affairs and Education, Manufacture, and Finance; and secondly, Transportation, also with three sections dealing respectively with Trade and Sea Communications, Shipbuilding and Posts and Telegraph. The change clearly reflected the pressing war needs. The functional departments, mentioned above, continued as before.

There were naturally some developments in the machinery regarding co-operation with the Chinese community as set up by General Isogai in February 1942. The two Chinese

C. OCCUPATION

1 The statue of Queen Victoria being pulled down. (*Hong Kong News*)

2 The local population reading Japanese proclamations. (*Imperial War Museum, London*)

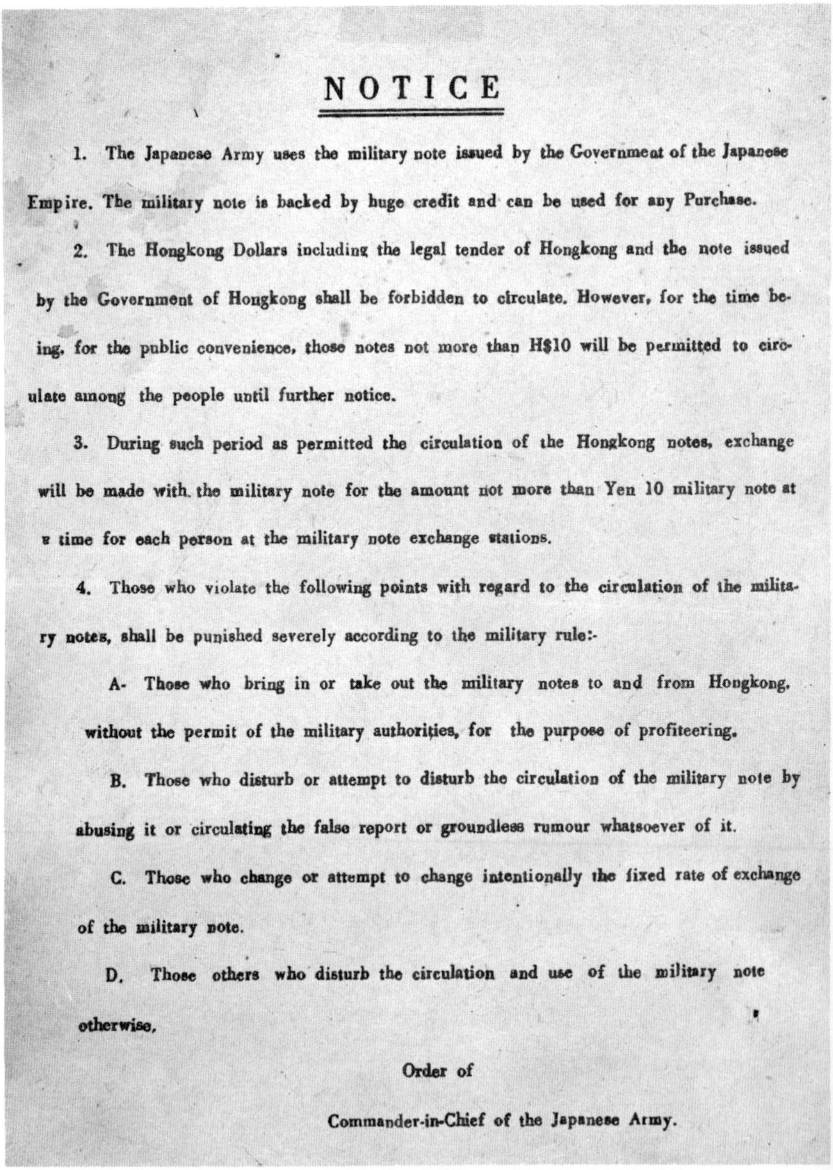

NOTICE

1. The Japanese Army uses the military note issued by the Government of the Japanese Empire. The military note is backed by huge credit and can be used for any Purchase.

2. The Hongkong Dollars including the legal tender of Hongkong and the note issued by the Government of Hongkong shall be forbidden to circulate. However, for the time being, for the public convenience, those notes not more than H$10 will be permitted to circulate among the people until further notice.

3. During such period as permitted the circulation of the Hongkong notes, exchange will be made with the military note for the amount not more than Yen 10 military note at a time for each person at the military note exchange stations.

4. Those who violate the following points with regard to the circulation of the military notes, shall be punished severely according to the military rule:-

A- Those who bring in or take out the military notes to and from Hongkong, without the permit of the military authorities, for the purpose of profiteering.

B. Those who disturb or attempt to disturb the circulation of the military note by abusing it or circulating the false report or groundless rumour whatsoever of it.

C. Those who change or attempt to change intentionally the fixed rate of exchange of the military note.

D. Those others who disturb the circulation and use of the military note otherwise.

Order of

Commander-in-Chief of the Japanese Army.

3 Notice issued by the Japanese authorities. (*in possession of the author*)

4 A photograph of internees at Stanley, taken in 1945. (*Imperial War Museum*)

5 Stanley Grams—an example of internment camp humour. (*By courtesy of Dr. W.J. Wylie*)

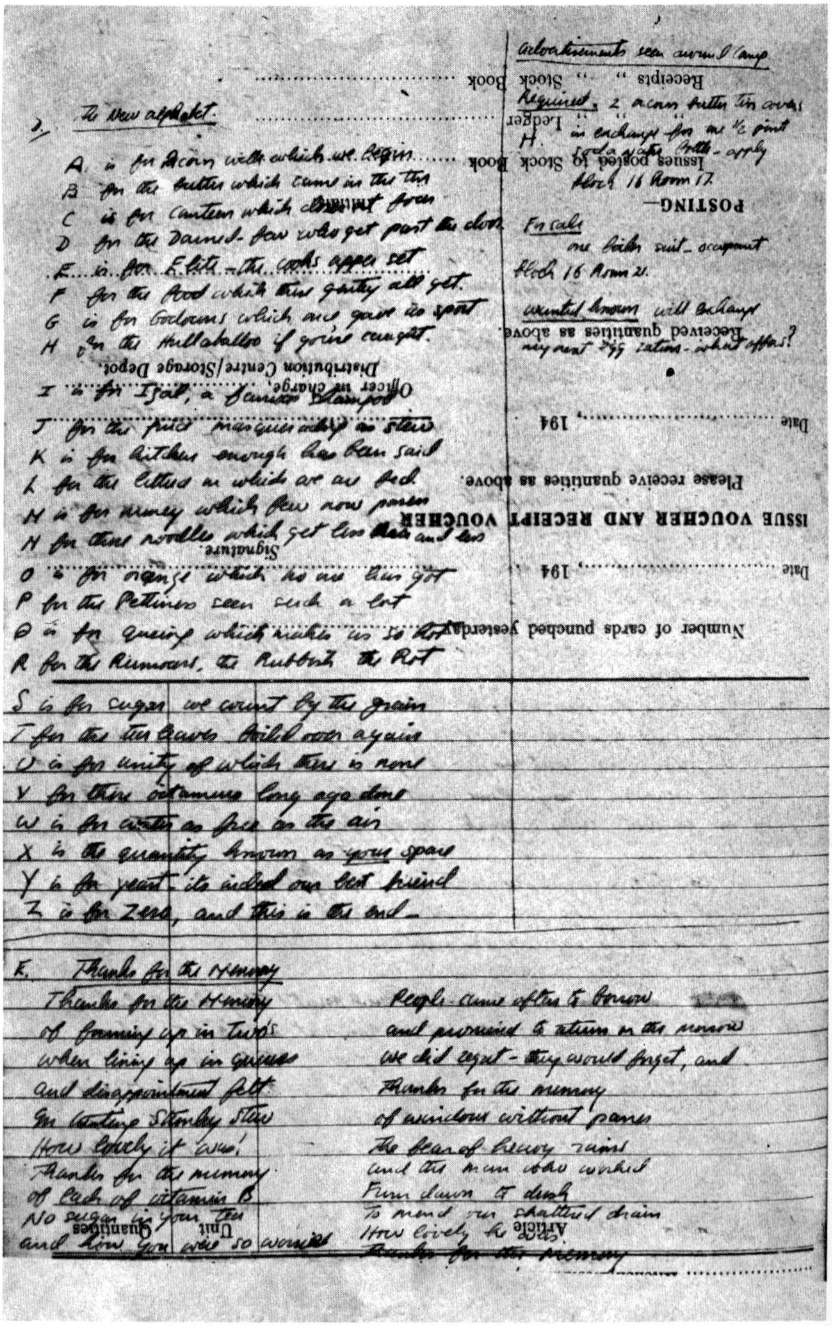

J. The New alphabet.

A is for Acorn with which we begin
B for the butter which came in the tin
C is for Canteen which [illegible] from
D for the Darned-few who get past the door
E is for Elite – the cooks upper set
F for the food which they gaily all get.
G is for Godowns which are good to sport
H for the Hullaballoo if you're caught.
I is for Isolation, a [illegible]
J for the [illegible] as stew
K is for kitchens enough has been said
L for the Lilies on which we are fed
M is for money which few now possess
N for those noodles which get less and less
O is for orange which no one has got
P for the Pettiness seen such a lot
Q is for queuing which makes us so hot
R for the Rumours, the Rubbish, the Rot
S is for sugar we count by the grain
T for the tea leaves boiled over again
U is for unity of which there is none
V for those vitamins long ago done
W is for water as free as the air
X is the quantity known as your share
Y is for yeast – its indeed our best friend
Z is for Zero, and this is the end –

Allotments seen around Camp

Required: 2 acorn butter tin covers in exchange for one ½ pint soda water bottle – apply Block 16 Room 17.

For sale one boiler suit – [illegible] Block 16 Room 21.

Wanted known will exchange my next [illegible] rations – what offers?

E. Thanks for the Memory

Thanks for the Memory
of forming up in twos
when lining up in queues
and disappointment felt
for [illegible] Stanley Stew
How lovely it was!
Thanks for the memory
of lack of vitamin B
No sugar in your tea
and how you were so worried

People came often to borrow
and promised to return on the morrow
we did regret – they would forget, and
Thanks for the memory
of windows without panes
the fear of heavy rains
and the men who worked
from dawn to dusk
To mend our shattered drains
How lovely it was.
Thanks for the memory

6 The Stanley Camp alphabet. (*Searle MSS. Bodleian Library, Oxford University*)

7 Japanese War Memorial—a victory shrine which was to have been erected in Hong Kong. (*Public Works Department, Hong Kong Government*)

8 Staff of the Economic Affairs Administration of the Japanese Military Occupation Forces. (*by courtesy of Mr. R. Ribeiro*)

9 A Japanese 100-yen note issued during the occupation. (*in possession of the author*)

10 The Japanese presence—Decorated Trams in Central. (*Hong Kong News*)

councils were increased in membership but otherwise continued with little change. The strongly pro-Japanese Chan Lim Pak, a former chairman of the Chinese Chamber of Commerce, joined the Representative Council on 17 April 1942, increasing its number to four, and remained a member until he was killed in an air raid in December 1944. In February 1945 General Tanaka increased the membership to five, and after the death of Lau Tit-shing in April 1945, the council was increased in number to six. Sir Robert Kotewall remained its chairman, and while in that position was forced to support the Japanese line, though his public utterances became increasingly devoted to purely Chinese community interests, and in 1945 he absented himself for some time on grounds of ill-health.[3] The Chinese Co-operative Council continued to work under the direction of the Representative Council. In February 1945 its number was increased to twenty-four and changes in membership inevitably occurred, though Chow Shou-son remained as chairman.

The district bureaux developed strongly. As early as 1 March 1942 they were made responsible for rice rationing and their control of the census, on which the rationing was based, followed automatically. From 15 April 1942 they gave free service and advice in completing the very numerous forms by which the Japanese sought to control every side of Hong Kong life, a service which had to be prolonged beyond the two months originally suggested.

On 20 July 1942 appeared new regulations for the district bureaux by which the chief and the vice-chief were appointed by the Governor, and the remaining staff by the chief. District councils of from five to ten members selected by each district chief from among the residents to approve his decisions, were also provided for. These unpaid councillors were to serve for two years and could resign only by permission of the Governor. The regulations also arranged for the residents to contribute to the expenses of their district bureau, the amount and method of collection being subject to the Governor's approval. At the

[3] His broadcast in December 1943 on the occasion of the second anniversary of the Japanese conquest is an interesting example of formally toeing the line, but surely its lack of enthusiasm must have disappointed its Japanese sponsors. (CO129/591/54112).

same time the two Chinese councils were empowered to advise the district bureau and help them keep in touch with the Secretariat, so that Chinese habits and customs could be given more consideration. The names of the district chiefs and vice-chiefs were announced on 23 July 1942. The regulations also set out more explicitly what ought to be the functions of the district bureaux. They were 'first-line administrative bodies carrying out decisions of the Government at a level of direct contact with the people; secondly they were autonomous bodies with power to raise funds locally and vote them for local purposes; thirdly they should assist and supplement the work of the two Chinese Advisory Councils'. In fact, the district bureaux never became fully autonomous, for the Governor's Office continued for some time to pay all their expenses and naturally retained control, and it was not until June 1943 that the Secretary-General announced at a press conference that the district bureaux were to be self-supporting and invited suggestions as to how the funds were to be raised. In November the issue was still undecided, and the bureaux were described as a trial step, which, if successful, would be handed over to district control. In December 1943 all the district bureaux chiefs met to discuss plans for compulsory education, and in June 1944 they had to register all births and deaths. The first real pressure to allow the bureaux to raise their own funds came from the bureaux themselves and then not until October 1944, when the rise in living costs brought demands for increased salaries, but the Japanese administration refused to treat the officials of the district bureaux differently from Government employees generally.

After the new Governor, Lt.-General Tanaka, had taken office, it was finally agreed in March 1945 that each District should collect funds for its own expenses, and that roughly each family should contribute Y30 per month. The collection was begun, but poverty soon imposed obvious difficulties and the amounts collected varied from Y30 to Y5 according to the circumstances of the family, while business firms had to pay anything up to Y300 a month. This was how the position rested, until the defeat of Japan a few months later brought the bureaux to an end.

The district bureaux were important elements in the

Japanese administration of Hong Kong. Although, just before their defeat, the Japanese discussed giving more self-government to Hong Kong, and earmarked the district bureaux as the organs through which the wishes of the people could be effectively ascertained, they were a most effective way of establishing collective local responsibility for individual behaviour and obedience to the Japanese regulations. As such they were hated by the local inhabitants.[4]

The Japanese at first placed Hong Kong under martial law since that was clearly required by the military situation, and it was not until General Isogai became Governor that attention was given to introducing a system of law and organizing law courts on a civil basis.

A Court of Justice, with civil jurisdiction only, was set up on 10 March 1942 in the old Supreme Court Building, and a Civil Law Office came into being soon after, which dealt with all litigants. English practices such as trial by jury and presentation of cases by barristers were of course brushed aside. Instead, an officer of the court enquired into the case, questioned both parties and judgement was pronounced. The Japanese appeared to wish to respect the laws and customs of the Chinese, but the way in which this was to be done was never properly worked out. Costs were fixed at 5 per cent of the amount or value of the property involved. Early in 1943 the rule against the employment of lawyers was rescinded, and Japanese, Chinese and neutral attorneys were allowed to act for clients and practice in the Court. The latter dealt mainly with conveyancing, company law, administration of estates of deceased persons, and property disputes, and administered English law in these matters, being advised by the Hong Kong lawyers. The Chinese lawyers formed their own association in April 1943.

Criminal law remained firmly under military administration and criminal offences were tried in military courts, or, in the case of military prisoners, by courts martial. The criminal law was concerned mainly with safeguarding the Japanese military personnel and war effort generally, and with breaches of local

[4] In the New Territories, in the Saikung area, the name (and possibly the notion) of a self-governing committee given to it by the Japanese was retained after the war, until it was suppressed by the British administration.

military regulations. Decisions of the civil and military courts were enforced by the *Kempeitai* (Military Police). In October 1943 the jurisdiction of the civil courts was expanded to include criminal cases, leaving martial law still in force for all cases involving military security and members of the armed services, and regulations governing the courts martial were issued.

Control over the movements and economic activities of the local people was further detailed in a notice promulgated on 28 March 1942 and headed 'Laws for the Rule of the Captured Territory of Hong Kong'. All persons entering, leaving, residing in, carrying on business or establishing a business in Hong Kong, had to obtain permission of the Governor of the Captured Territory of Hong Kong. Certain categories of persons such as enemy nationals or those with enemy leanings or unreliable towards the military or public safety, were to be refused permission; in fact, power was given to exclude anyone whom the Japanese thought undesirable. Those already in business had to apply to be allowed to continue. The last day for registration was 30 June, but the demands were largely ignored by the Chinese, and less exacting ones and a more simplified procedure had to be substituted and an extension of dates made, despite appeals by the two Councils and others to co-operate.

The maintenance of public order under martial law was automatically assumed by the Japanese Army immediately on the surrender. But in fact for some days public order broke down while the army was given licence to celebrate its victory. The result was every man for himself. Gangs seized the opportunities for extortion, demanding protection money, levying a toll on looters, charging fees at the wells after the failure of the public water supply, selling water from public fountains and often extorting money by wearing Japanese arm-bands. The Chinese with typical realism paid one gang to secure protection against other predators and organized street guards.

Early in January former members of the Hong Kong police, Indians and Chinese, were recruited into a re-formed police with new uniforms. Under General Isogai's reorganization of February 1942 the Japanese gendarmerie, which up to then had dealt with military security and political suspects, assumed direct responsibility for the police, water police, and fire services. They took over all police stations and organized the police in five divisions, East Hong Kong, West Hong Kong, Kowloon, New Territories, and Water Police, with their headquarters in the former Supreme Court Building. The civil police now had the backing of an organization which inspired terror in the hearts of the civil community because of its reputation for ruthlessness. The *Kempeitai*, according to evidence given in a War Crimes trial in May 1946, numbered 150 officers and non-commissioned officers and 200 auxiliaries, besides some 1,500 to 3,000 Chinese and Indians assigned in small groups to each warrant officer or N.C.O. to secure information. Crimes such as robbery, burglary and murder were regarded as not being so serious as the more political offences such as working against Japanese, impeding the Japanese war effort, espionage, communication with the enemy, and refusal to adopt the new 'Kingly Way'. On 29 April 1942 the street guards and private protection guards were disbanded by order, on the ground that the police were now able to take over the protection of the community.

The preliminary orders issued on 10 March 1942 directed the gendarmerie to deal with offences such as sedition or any action directed against the Japanese army, espionage, or conduct endangering the army or affecting its military operations. On 31 May 1942 the Government issued 'Regulations for Police Punishments' applicable to all persons living in Hong Kong, including Japanese, if 'there is no other Nipponese law to be applied'. It listed seventy-four offences punishable with a fine not exceeding 500 yen, or not more than three months' imprisonment. These included such offences as making a false statement to officials, giving false information, lying down or getting drunk in the road-way, dancing, singing or making other noise at night, failing to chain up a fierce dog, spitting in a public place, making water in any open place and burying the dead without permission.

The Japanese recruited and trained successive batches of Chinese at a training school at the old police headquarters in Boundary Street, Kowloon, and experimented with women police, but police organization proved to be unsatisfactory because of the amount of crime, and later, the severe air raids. Lt.-General Tanaka took control of the police out of the hands of the gendarmerie, and set up a police bureau in the Governor's Office, and thereafter the police operated independently. New residence certificates were demanded in an effort to combat crime, and a police committee with Chow Shou-son as chairman was set up to ensure Chinese co-operation. Then in April 1945 special protective guards were recruited, given some police training, and in May an Emergency Police Corps was formed. In July the police force and the protective guards were merged, and these were the men encountered by the British Military Administration in the following September. They were scathingly described by the local population as a lot of brothel-keepers and their runners.

The Chinese sullenly accepted the Japanese domination. The feeling was one of dazed surprise at the British débâcle and a sad disillusionment with the British. Huge numbers had flooded into Hong Kong to escape the Japanese, and now found themselves worse off. As an editorial in the *Hong Kong News* put it, '. . . the vaunted supermen of the white race have melted like butter. In eighteen days of conflict it was all over, a horrible muddle of inefficiency and helplessness which has bequeathed a miserable aftermath.' But disillusionment with the British did not mean acceptance of the Japanese, despite the propaganda of Asia for the Asians. Outwardly, Japanese rule was accepted and by some with warmth, but the ruthlessness with which the Japanese conducted operations against China, the rape of Nanking, and, in Hong Kong, the arbitrary shooting or bayoneting of Chinese offenders, left a legacy of hatred for the Japanese. So they were faced with every form of subtle obstruction and forced continually to modify and simplify their administrative requirements.

There is no reason to believe that these administrative requirements did not adequately serve Japanese objectives. Control rested firmly in their own hands as was necessary in time of war. At the same time, the Chinese could nominally put forward their views. War pressures permitted the military administration in Hong Kong little discretion in carrying out policies decided in Tokyo, and it is safe to assume that the Japanese ability to implement Chinese wishes was strictly limited. The use of the district bureaux as their main local government agents showed clearly that the Japanese had no intention of riding roughshod over the Chinese community. This is also demonstrated by the intense pains taken to publicize and explain their policies. The regular series of press conferences given by the Governor, the head of the Administration, the heads of the various central government offices, the head of the gendarmerie, and by members of the two Chinese councils is quite impressive.

The Japanese administration was intensely bureaucratic, and every activity was regulated and supervised, although this did not always make for efficiency and consistency of action. Everybody had to have a pass to move around. Laws issued on 28 March 1942 for the control of Hong Kong affairs strictly controlled people entering, leaving or residing, also the importing or exporting of goods and the setting up or conducting of any business; people had to make a full report of themselves, or if there were any change, to apply to the Gendarmerie Headquarters in quadruplicate. The local population had to register their requirements for water, gas, electricity and telephones. All house-owners had to register their property, and get permission to undertake repairs. Doctors, lawyers, herbalists, hawkers and market stall-holders had to supply particulars and register. All religious bodies and schools had to supply information and register. All house property had to be re-registered for tax purposes. Changes of address and the possession of radios had to be registered with the gendarmerie for security reasons, and registration was of course essential for rice rationing. The tally of registrations could be greatly expanded, and it created massive requirements for queueing for forms, permits and licences and filling them in. Moreover, as noted, regulations and orders were amended from time to time making for wearisome repetition. The Japanese patiently explained the orders and their need, and induced the district bureaux and Chinese councils to urge Chinese to co-operate, but no wonder that there was little enthusiasm and orders had to be amended and simplified, and periods for registration extended. The *Hong Kong News* regularly complained about the apathy of the Chinese in complying with these demands.

This weight of bureaucratic interference in daily life naturally created bribery and malpractice among the officials, and the Chinese citizen eventually could not get very far without it, however much the senior Japanese officials might inveigh against it.

Finally, as part of the Japanese apparatus of government, all Western influences and evidence of former British rule were obliterated. British street and district names and all street signs were replaced by Japanese; even the race horses at Happy Valley were not immune from this renaming process. Japanese had to be taught in the schools, the Japanese calendar used, Japanese history and institutions studied, Japanese national festival days observed. This was not done to make everyone Japanese; the policy was to allow Asians to use their own language and encourage the general use of Japanese as the lingua franca of communication throughout East Asia. The policy in Hong Kong was to propagate Japanese influence as much as possible.

In conclusion, the Japanese administration in Hong Kong was, from the Japanese point of view, painstakingly devised for the purposes for which it was designed, bearing in mind Hong Kong's role as an important strategic base and the demands of all-out war.

VI

LIFE IN HONG KONG UNDER THE JAPANESE

'The previous condition of Hong Kong must be swept clean before it can take its position in the East. The present strength and culture of the place must be elevated to the same spiritual stream in order to attain the Kingly Way which will shine upon the eternal basic prosperity of East Asia.'

Lt.-General Rensuke Isogai in
the 'Order of the Day', 20 February 1942

As this was a traumatic experience for Hong Kong and potentially of lasting consequence, it is important to examine further how the Japanese administration affected the life of the community. One drastic change was the very severe cut in its numbers. The huge refugee immigration, originating in the China incident from 1937 onwards, had impeded the British defence, undermined military security, created a colossal food problem and hindered attempts to enlist the Chinese in the war effort because so few regarded themselves as belonging to Hong Kong. The Japanese saw that effective defence demanded a drastic reduction in population, and measures to repatriate the Chinese were introduced immediately and continued throughout the occupation.

A Repatriation Bureau was set up as part of the Civil Administration Department and was advised and assisted by a Chinese Repatriation Committee composed of representatives of clan and district associations who were expected to help shoulder the costs. In the first week of January 1942 the Japanese gave notice that all who had no residence or employment would have to leave, after having first obtained a repatriation permit from the district bureau, a ruling which threatened most people with an uncertain future because of the economic stagnation brought about by the war. In addition, applicants for a permit came under the scrutiny of the gendarmerie, which most were anxious to avoid, with the result that many preferred to leave secretly via the underground, provided they could pay the required protection money to the guerrillas. Others, especially property owners who could not abandon their houses, managed to preserve an anonymous existence in Hong Kong, fatalistically accepting the risk that the alternative to compliance might be starvation.

The story of repatriation is long and complicated, since the regulations frequently changed and scarcity of transport caused delays. Generally, the Japanese encouraged repatriation on a voluntary basis after shipping became available in the middle of January, when they were able to advertise sailings at prescribed fares to Canton and the Delta ports, to Macao, and along the coast to Swatow and beyond; applications were invited and passengers selected from the lists of applicants.

Bureaucratic controls made the process of leaving a protracted one, involving long queues for the necessary exit permits, for the required vaccination and inoculation certificates, and for certificates of health from the Anti-epidemic Bureau, all of which had to be produced before the passage tickets could be bought. As tickets were available only one day before sailing, their purchase normally entailed queueing for about forty-eight hours and since the number sold bore little relation to the available accommodation, passengers usually had to go to the wharf the previous night to ensure getting on board. They were searched on the quay and their luggage examined, an arbitrary process of emptying everything on the ground leaving them to retrieve their possessions as best they could. It all required monumental patience and persistence.

At Canton, passengers were kept on board for twenty-four hours for an additional medical check, during which time they had to provide their own food. From Macao boats were available to French Kwongchouwan where the Japanese, who were in effective control, turned a blind eye to those crossing into Free China. The ships left packed, but could not cope with demand, and so large numbers had to go overland, on foot and by river. After due advertisement, batches for the overland route were made up and departure dates publicized, the chief destinations being Swatow, the Chiu Chow area, Amoy, Shanghai, and Chekiang and Kiangsi Provinces. They took the train to Taipo or Shum Chun and then went by foot to the East River trusting a river vessel or barge might be available. Food carried was limited to five catties of rice, but free rice was distributed at Taipo or Shum Chun, and provincial authorities along the route were asked to provide transport for the old and sick and give general assistance to the others. All repatriates leaving by train had to use Yaumati Station, and in June 1942 a special daily repatriation train was put on, again starting at Yaumati, where the usual formalities regarding health and exit permits and searching of baggage were insisted upon. Many walked all the way to the East River and eye-witness accounts refer to the long processions plodding up the Taipo road. At first repatriates were allowed to take no more than they could carry, but this rule was later relaxed and they were given help in selling personal and household effects, and allowed to take out jewellery to meet expenses.

In July 1942 free repatriation was offered to destitutes wishing to return to China, and free food and accommodation were provided in three North Point restaurants which by 1 August had 3,000 inmates awaiting passages. Those who could afford it had to continue to make their own arrangements, but it was noted that some claiming to be destitute had so much luggage that doubts arose about their indigence.

In the following March, the Japanese stepped up repatriation in a determined effort to reduce the number of mouths to feed by a thousand a day, and amended the limited free repatriation scheme in favour of an assisted scheme applicable to all. The Tai Ping Theatre at Sai Ying Pun was made into a temporary shelter for repatriates awaiting a passage, who were given MY4 as expenses. Those without ration cards or who were evading Japanese residence regulations were given until 30 April to take advantage of the new scheme, but the date was extended a number of times. Those found after 30 September 1943 without a residence permit or ration card were to be handed over to the gendarmerie for forcible repatriation, but this date too was extended a number of times. After repeated warnings, destitutes, unemployed and beggars were rounded up, taken aboard junks and put ashore on uninhabited islands south of Hong Kong and left to shift for themselves; those who survived told a grim tale of their harrowing experiences. In the autumn of 1944 free repatriation for destitutes was still being offered, and in May 1945 cheaper fares were offered on small ships and the exit procedure simplified. In July 1945 the North Point Camp was opened for vagrants and others being compulsorily repatriated.

The reduction of the population was a Japanese war measure; how well it succeeded the figures eloquently reveal. In December 1941 the population was estimated at 1½ millions, some 200,000 less than what it had been six months earlier. A quarter of a million were said to have left in the first month, that is by February 1942, and a census in February 1943 gave a figure of 968,524. By August 1945 the population was estimated at between 500,000 and 600,000, indicating a reduction of some 23,000 per month throughout the whole occupation, or rather under the target of one thousand a day which the Japanese had set.

The Japanese set out systematically to destroy all trace of former British control, and the Hong Kong Government records were not sacrosanct unless they served a clearly useful purpose. About 80 per cent of the registers of births and deaths covering the years 1871 when registration first began, to 1941 were saved by loyal Chinese officials. The rest did not survive. The Japanese refused to continue the British registration system for some months, and the 1942 vital statistics are necessarily incomplete. The figures given by Dr. Selwyn-Clarke in his *Report on Medical and Health Conditions under the Japanese Occupation* are: for 1942, 10,343 births and 82,435 deaths; 1943, 20,732 births, 40,117 deaths; 1944, 13,687 births, 24,936 deaths; and 1945, (eight months only) 3,712 births and 23,098 deaths.

Hong Kong people were mainly concerned with sheer survival and for most this meant rice. The British administration's monopoly stocks were seized, but the sales depots were not opened until ten days after the surrender and were immediately besieged by enormous queues, for example, at the Central Market the queue stretched three abreast to the Queen's Theatre, each person being allowed to buy 40 cents' worth. In early February a hundred more rice shops opened and each person could buy two catties at 60 cents a catty, but there was no individual check and dishonesty on the part of the buyers plus squeeze by the traders made rationing essential. A Chinese lawyer, Mr. P. H. Sin, was put in charge and suggested a scheme which came into effect on 15 March 1942 by which, until a full census could be taken, the number of persons living in each flat or house was noted, and each family received a ration card from its district bureau allowing 4 catties daily per person at 40 cents a catty and one member of the family was permitted to collect three days' rations for the family at a time. The ration was stated to be the same as that in Japan. There were 57 rice depots in Hong Kong and 41 in Kowloon, each catering for about 11,000 persons living in specified streets and houses, but much queueing was required to get the card, to pay for the rice and to take delivery on presenting the receipt. There were difficulties, and a new census was taken to circumvent false declarations, and scales were placed in all rice depots to stop short weight; permits were even required for the supply of coffins in order to check on the dead and prevent relatives claiming for them. Restaurants were supplied with rice direct at first, but this was later cancelled because they charged excessive prices for meals. Indians were rationed through the Indian Independence League, the Portuguese through the Club Lusitano, and in June 1942 Eurasians were supplied through the Eurasian Mutual Aid Society.

The system was amended to ease the queueing, but scarcity drove up the price of rice to 75 cents a catty in August 1943, and 75 sen or $3 in January 1944.[1] The rice ration scheme was cancelled as from 15 April 1944 because of the war shortages, and only those directly concerned in the war effort continued to receive a ration; in the following November even their families were excluded from the ration, which now applied only to essential workers themselves. The price rose to MY8.80 a catty in August, by the end of the year it was MY18 a catty, and by July 1945 reached MY90 a catty and it is small wonder that Government servants and eventually teachers and journalists had to be paid in rice. The rice occasioned much complaint because it was glutinous and often broken. The poor were helped with limited supplies of cheap rice by the H.K. Peoples' Food Co-operative Association and Chinese philanthropists

[1] 100 sen equal one yen. See pp. 149–50 for the conversion of H.K. dollars to military yen.

distributed rice at cost to orphanages and other charitable bodies.

Sugar was rationed in June 1942 through designated shops using the rice ration card, and each person received one-third of a catty per month at 55 sen a catty. Peanut oil for cooking was also rationed at three-fifths of a catty per person per month at $3.20. Flour was rationed for those not receiving rice, and salt had to be rationed in June 1944 because of the long queues. Steeply rising prices, the interruption of supplies, and lack of stocks, caused the rations to be suspended or decreased from time to time and there was much adulteration, so that by 1945 all rationing was virtually at an end.

An attempt was made to control fuel, a commodity just as essential as rice. In January 1942 dealers in fuel had to register and supply fuel at 40 catties for MY1; this was virtually disregarded, and one resident described fuel regulation as a racket. A Fuel Syndicate was set up in March 1943, and in August 10 catties of fuel were allowed to each rice-card holder. Prices rose to MY60 a picul by September 1944, and people relied on the black market or on cutting trees in the hills or looting houses for wood. War shortages obviously made rationing difficult and price control was ineffective, forcing many to rely entirely on the black market and to regard rationing as a bad joke. In fact, survival became impossible without resort to the black market.

Food remained dear and scarce. Meat which came largely from Kwongchouwan and the Canton Delta was allowed to find its own price level. For a time there was one source of local supply, unfit race ponies were slaughtered for food advertised at MY2.70 a catty. Cats were extremely valuable and had to be carefully guarded against theft for the pot. One Jesuit Father described his meals as rice gruel for breakfast, some rice and a little corned beef for supper, one tin of the latter having to last four men for a week, and pine needles were placed in the tea to add some vitamin. Philanthropists like Aw Boon Aw supplied rice to the needy below cost, and the Ruttonjees gave rice from time to time.

Under these conditions people's health inevitably declined and symptoms of malnutrition appeared. There were damaged drains and derelict houses, and garbage heaps piled up in

Kennedy Town, Queen's College and the Southern Recreation Ground as well as some back streets, breeding flies and cockroaches. Rats foraged among this garbage for food. From 10 December 1941, night-soil had to be dumped in the harbour since lighters could not leave port during the fighting, and the Japanese continued this practice though they also had built the maturing tanks at Castle Peak and Tsun Wan, a scheme which the British had talked about for years. Yet, despite all this, the Japanese can claim credit that no serious epidemic occurred in Hong Kong except cholera in 1942 and 1943.[2] An Anti-epidemic Bureau was set up in February 1942 and a vigorous campaign was launched with free inoculation and vaccination using University medical undergraduates. Further campaigns were conducted in January 1943, May and August 1944, and June 1945, accompanied by propaganda talks, touring vans and posters educating the public on health measures. A fly week was held from 14 to 20 February 1942, during which the offer of one catty of rice for two taels of flies was made to the public. This brought in a total of 306.8 taels of flies. The Japanese also enforced house cleansing campaigns each year. All persons leaving the territory were checked for disease, and inoculation and vaccination certificates had to be shown before receiving a rice ration card, as well as when travelling to and from Kowloon by ferry. Inoculations were unpopular among the Chinese and a lucrative trade in the clandestine sale of certificates grew up, in which a number of unfortunates succumbed to an excessive number of injections as a result of a too thriving business in this respect. Barbers were inspected, there were anti-spitting campaigns, and a rat week was held in April 1945. The spread of malaria was perhaps the most serious failing on the part of the Japanese in the field of public health; the authorities were quite unwilling to examine broken water-pipes in damaged buildings and to locate and treat stagnant pools, until they were themselves threatened. Their neglect ruined years of valuable anti-malarial work.

The Director of Medical Services, Dr. Selwyn-Clarke, with

[2] *Hong Kong News*, 18 November 1943, Article 'Prevention of Epidemic in Hong Kong'. Cholera: Showa 15 (1941) affected cases, 945; fatal cases 626. Showa 18 (1943) 211 and 105 respectively.

the support of the Japanese senior medical officer, Col. Eguchi, induced the Japanese military to exempt him and his staff from internment in Stanley to deal with casualties and community health, but he was allowed to retain only two health officers, one medical officer, six sanitary inspectors and an accountant. Despite Japanese obstruction, he sent medicines into the various camps, looked after the dependants of the Volunteers and families of other emergency services. He worked through an Informal Welfare Committee which, after much persuasion, the Japanese allowed him to establish, to do in part some of the work normally done by the International Red Cross which was denied permission to operate in Hong Kong until early 1943. Its funds came mainly from prominent local Chinese and local Indians such as the Ruttonjees and the Ebrahims also subscribed generously. Many local people owed their survival to Dr. Selwyn-Clarke's unsparing efforts. It is highly probable he had supplies of drugs from China, via the underground, because relief of all kinds would not have been available locally on the scale he wanted. The result was that on 3 May 1943 Dr. Selwyn-Clarke was arrested for communicating with the British outside, tortured and sentenced to death. This was commuted to imprisonment for life and he was sent to Stanley Prison; later, in 1945, he was transferred to Ma Tau Chung Camp and was joined by his family. His European staff were interned in Stanley Camp.

There were few hospitals available to the civilian population. The Japanese army took over Kowloon Hospital and the temporary hospital in the Central British School, and the British wounded were moved to St. Theresa's Hospital until 1943 when this was taken for Japanese sick. Queen Mary Hospital was used as a Japanese military hospital and then as a military barracks and was left at the end of the occupation in a lamentable condition. The Japanese navy used the Tung Wah Eastern Hospital. Dr. Selwyn-Clarke induced the Japanese to re-open the Sai Ying Poon and Tsan Yuk Hospitals but they were closed again in 1944, and the Kwong Wah and some small private hospitals, like the Precious Blood Hospital, were the only ones open to the Chinese community during the whole period. The old public clinics and dispensaries were closed, but eventually the Japanese began a scheme of free medicine for the poor and one hundred free beds were made available at the Kwong Wah Hospital, and by May 1945 there were thirty-eight free treatment dispensaries. Work at the new Wu Hop Sek cemetery in the New Territories was stopped, but the Japanese allowed burials at Aberdeen, Pokfulam, Applichau, Stanley, and other public cemeteries. There was much trouble because of shallow burials and also much grave robbing in search of gold ornaments and teeth fillings.

Public utility services were restored with speedy efficiency. Water reached all districts by 20 January 1942 when meters had to be registered, and charges were fixed at 15 sen per 100 gallons, later reduced to 45 sen per 1,000 gallons, plus a deposit of MY25 for family residences and up to MY100 for factories. The collection of water-rates began in March. For the poor there were 120 street fountains giving a free supply.

Street lighting came back on 11 January, and electricity charges for private users were fixed at 26 sen per unit plus a deposit varying in amount according to the number of bulbs used; gas supplies began on 23 January at MY6.6 per 100 cubic feet. By the middle of February, the telephone system was back to 90 per cent of its former capacity and regulations of 28 April prescribed charges consisting of a deposit of MY50, an installation charge of MY25, and an annual fee of from MY120 to 250 according to the distance from Central. Registration was slow, and by November only about ten thousand phones were in use compared to 170,000 pre-war. All these public utility charges were prohibitively high, and the Chinese Rehabilitation Advisory Committee was able to secure some reduction in early February the following year.

Trams were restored on 27 January 1942 between Causeway Bay and Western Market and by 18 March all routes were in use with thirty-eight cars running, employing women as conductors, at fares of fifteen and ten sen. On 25 January four bus routes with sixteen buses were in service, the minimum fare being five sen, and Kowloon services soon followed. The buses were invariably overcrowded, long queues formed at the terminals, and in April the Kowloon Motor Bus Company sought an order prohibiting people from boarding the bus by climbing through the windows, and spikes were suggested for sides of the trams to prevent people travelling by clinging to the outside.

The ferry service to Kowloon was resumed on 10 January, that to Cheung Chau in May and three large vehicular ferries were salvaged and put into service with fares about double those of pre-war. The badly-damaged Peak Tram was in operation by 5 June at fares ten times as high as formerly. Private cars, which had all been commandeered by the Hong Kong Government, were collected and shipped to Japan, but a few were run by Japanese officials and officers and by such essential users as doctors, who had to take a Japanese driving test which included a written examination. The British section of the Kowloon-Canton railway had been made largely unusable by the retreating British in the war, but within a week of the surrender repairs were begun, the Kowloon tunnel patched up temporarily, and the whole line was ready with six trains a day on 24 March 1942 when the Governor made a ceremonial journey to the border.

Kai Tak airport was repaired almost immediately and plans for a much overdue extension of the airfield were put in hand. The co-operation of the 20,000 Chinese living there was enlisted by means of 'an association for the assistance of the authorities in the enlargement of Kai Tak airport', through whom full information about occupants of land was collected and alternative plots allocated; the farmers were promised compensation with farm land in model villages at Sheung Shui and Kowloon Tong, and each family given MY200 as compensation. Those living on the north-west of the field had to move by 10 August 1942 and the rest by 31 December 1942 and on 10 September 1943 the enlargement was officially inaugurated. The Sung Wong Toi, commemorating the refuge of the last Sung Emperors, was removed at a ceremony attended by Buddhist priests and a promise given that it would be re-erected elsewhere. Wireless communication was re-established for the public on 1 February for Japan and Canton, and later Rangoon, at rates which penalized the English language in favour of Japanese.

The public utility services gradually deteriorated because of lack of fuel and replacements due to the war scarcities, and charges rose steeply. By the end, the railway service was down to one precarious daily train each way; electricity distribution was suspended a number of times in 1944 and 1945, and the hours of supply were progressively shortened and quotas imposed until a supply of wood as fuel allowed a still limited but more regular supply from July 1945. Electricity shortages naturally affected other services such as the trams, the Peak Tram and the water-pumps. In July 1943 the bus services had to be curtailed and some routes suspended to save fuel, and soon after, in September 1943, bicycles fitted to carry pillion passengers appeared. In Kowloon horse-drawn carriages had already begun to ply in December 1942, but this service terminated a year later because of financial loss. In fact, transport became almost impossible and those taking food parcels to prisoners in Shamshuipo found it simpler to walk. These public services were run by the Japanese, using the former company organization, and personnel were subject to strict control.

The Post Office re-opened on 22 January 1942 with Japanese postal experts in charge. Mail was accepted only for Japan, Formosa, Macao, China, Manchukuo, Indo-China and Thailand as well as for local delivery, using Japanese stamps of 2-, 3-, 4-, 10- and 30-sen denominations. There was no registered mail or parcel service. Deliveries, at first restricted to the Central District, were gradually extended as men were taken on or retrained, and a promise was made to deliver all mail accumulated during the hostilities and the occupation. On 1 April all postage rates were increased in line with similar increases in Japan. Mail had to bear the sender's name and address and stamps had to be affixed in the top left-hand corner of the envelope, but that for foreign countries had to be handed in unstamped and postage paid at the counter. Street collection-boxes were increased in number and stamps made available at each.

The Japanese issued currency notes in military yen, printed on one side only, unnumbered and valid in Hong Kong alone. The exchange rate was arbitrarily fixed on 5 January 1942 at two dollars to one military yen, and the two currencies circulated side by side for some time though, as the result of a rumour apparently spread by the Japanese during the fighting that they would not recognize dollar notes above $10 in value, notes of higher denominations were at a substantial discount. In July 1942 the yen was revalued at four dollars to the yen thus automatically doubling dollar prices and the yen was made sole tender for official purposes. Prices of articles for sale had to be marked or stated in yen. Still, there remained considerable faith in the Hong Kong dollar because it was believed to be fully backed in London.

The three note-issuing British banks were ordered to increase their note issues by releasing reserve stocks of notes without any additional backing. In fact, heavy withdrawals during the emergency had threatened serious depletion of note stocks, so much that the Hong Kong Government prepared to issue five-dollar Chinese National currency notes, over-printed for use in Hong Kong to ease the situation.

Japanese banking experts were sent to liquidate enemy banks, whose staffs were conscripted to assist this operation. Incidentally, they were able to keep secret records which greatly eased the re-establishment in 1945. Some sixty British, American and Dutch bankers, ten with families, were billeted in a small hotel near the Macao Ferry Wharf under similar conditions to the other internees, except that they had more space, better food, and were kept there some eighteen months until May 1943. They were given rations of rice, peanut oil and brown sugar and allowed a weekly medical visit by a British doctor, and later allowed passes into the town and even into the countryside at week-ends. They were marched to and from the banks in Central under military guard in the morning and afternoon of every working day. The Americans were soon repatriated and the Belgians released as neutrals.

Some bankers were suspected of being in communication with the enemy via the underground and one, C. F. Hyde, was amongst those executed in October 1943. Sir Vandeleur Grayburn, head of The Hongkong and Shanghai Banking Corporation, and his assistant, D. C. Edmonston, were imprisoned in Stanley Prison where both died from the ill-treatment they received.[3] Money had been smuggled out of the

[3] See below p. 211. M. Collis, *Wayfoong, The H.K. & Shanghai Banking Corporation* (London, 1965) pp. 224–9. 'Considerable sums of money were raised from our Chinese friends . . . somewhere in the region of HK dollars two million in all. This money was used by Dr. Selwyn-Clarke and others to buy supplies of food, drugs, bedding, clothing, cooking utensils for the internment camps and hospitals.'

bank in breach of Japanese regulations but the penalty suffered by these men was outrageously excessive. The liquidation of the sixteen enemy banks appeared to have been completed by 31 December 1942 when all further payments from them ceased, but the bankers were not interned in Stanley until June 1943, being given the extra six months of comparative freedom through the influence of the staffs of the Japanese banks who knew many of them personally. They received a pleasant surprise in Stanley Camp on Christmas Day 1943 in the form of parcels from their Japanese colleagues. It was later found their banks had been debited with large sums for these presents.

In January 1942 two Japanese banks, the Yokohama Specie Bank and the Bank of Taiwan, re-opened after being closed on 8 December 1941 and by early February twenty-two Chinese banks were open. In January, Chinese, Indians, and neutrals were allowed to draw $50 from their accounts with enemy banks, and in May, up to $500. In July 1942 a dividend of 20 per cent was paid to all non-enemy depositors by the enemy banks under liquidation after any overdrafts had been liquidated. Many Chinese enterprisingly used yen realized on the sale of goods at inflated prices to repay the old dollar debts, for the new exchange rates meant a substantial devaluation of the dollar in terms of military yen.

In February the Chinese banks were allowed to pay out up to $300 to their non-enemy depositors, only newly-opened accounts being free from restriction on withdrawals. Access to safe-deposit boxes was given at various announced times but gold, silver and enemy currencies were retained by the Japanese with a promise of the payment of their value in military yen. A Chinese Bankers' Association under Lau Tit-shing as chairman was formed and worked closely with the Japanese; money-changers continued in business and a Gold and Silver Exchange opened on 20 February, on a cash basis. Remittances to families in China up to a maximum of MY100 monthly were permitted but only through Japanese banks.

The Chinese were anxious from the start to get trade going again to re-establish Hong Kong as an entrepôt and the Chinese Chamber of Commerce put up a number of proposals to the economic section of the Civil Administration Department, but the dislocation of markets, the uncertainty regarding the currency, the lack of shipping and the Japanese war-time controls all created big problems.

On 29 March 1942 under the 'Laws for Rule of the Captured Territory of Hong Kong', already mentioned above, the Governor's Order No. 9 set out in detail the controls considered necessary over 'all persons entering and leaving, residing in, transporting goods in and out of, and establishing businesses or carrying on businesses with commercial activities in the areas ruled by the Governor of the Captured Territory of Hong Kong'. In every case, permission had to be obtained, meticulously detailed information supplied together with a plan of the premises, or a detailed statement of personal information, all of which had to be reported to the head of the gendarmerie. Permission had to be obtained to employ any manager or take a partner. This was interpreted and probably intended to be interpreted as an invitation to take Japanese business partners. In fact, the difficulty of form-filling, of vouching for all statements made, and securing permits, drove many to abandon their enterprises and flee to China. All British and Allied firms were taken over, including the Hong Kong Brewery, though its Indian owners continued to reside in Hong Kong.

Some Japanese, holding official positions, gained control of some businesses, for example a gendarmerie official ran the Nan Yang Tobacco Company, and some Japanese re-started the British-American Tobacco Company. In May 1942 Japanese firms were encouraged to start up; also Chinese firms, provided they handled essential products such as food or textiles. By June nineteen Chinese insurance companies were operating. A Hong Kong Trade Syndicate consisting of Japanese firms was set up in October 1942 to control all overseas trade, except that with the ports of Kwangtung Province, and Amoy, Macao and Kwongchouwan, all of which were free ports. In September 1942 Hong Kong and Canton merchants made a commercial agreement listing goods to be exchanged and this was renewed at three-monthly intervals.

In January 1943 the Green Island Cement Company was re-started, mainly to supply cement for the local fortifications and so save Japanese shipping space. The Hong Kong Trade

Syndicate was replaced in September 1944 by a Hong Kong Trade Association called the Hong Kong *Koeki Kosha*, under a Japanese chairman, to import food and exercise general trade control. In 1945, as the end drew near and difficulties mounted, a number of joint Sino-Japanese trading syndicates were formed to assist the war effort and deal with essential commodities, but war scarcities and the large amount of 'squeeze' required by Japanese officials made any real revival of Hong Kong's trade impossible. Ultimately, except for farmers and hawkers, all residents were forced to work for Japanese public or private bodies or to starve, unless they were fortunate enough to have a sufficient supply of gold ornaments.

The Japanese looked to the New Territories' elders to maintain order there and they set up district bureaux in the important centres, meeting administrative costs by a levy on agricultural produce collected at barriers on the road to town. Generally, they recognized Chinese law and custom and seem to have treated the villagers justly if strictly. The New Territories were vital in the declared policy of making Hong Kong self-supporting; nevertheless, the Japanese imposed no production targets, preferring to improve farming in the New Territories as part of a development policy. In November 1943 an Agricultural Training Institute opened at Fanling with an entry of thirty-four students though only twenty-one enrolled on the opening day. In March 1943 a Hong Kong Fertilizer Syndicate was formed and the Taipo experimental farm established under the Taiwan Engineering Company, which also prepared large irrigation schemes and distributed first-grade vegetable seeds and, in March 1944, an improved rice strain. Fish ponds for good supply were promoted, and roads such as that to Saikung were started; later to be completed by the British.

The Japanese took over the race track at Fanling and the air-strip at Kam Tin for their rice-growing experiments; but these were hindered by lack of water. They also discussed a scheme to reclaim Tolo harbour by a sea wall and use the bed for paddy, but the war pressures prevented any progress with it.

Despite these measures, the New Territories passed through lean times. There were restrictions on movement and visitors had to have a permit or an identity card, the export of rice was forbidden, lack of transport affected deliveries of vegetables which had to be done by hand-carts, and fishing was hazardous, and not surprisingly many young men drifted off to join the guerrillas as the only alternative to remaining at home semi-starved and in rags. The villagers, particularly the Hakkas, were subject to communist propaganda and a rift between the communist youth and the elders developed, especially when the latter promised to aid the Japanese in dealing with British agents, an undertaking they probably had no intention of honouring.

Some indication has already been given how the Japanese set out to destroy all trace of British influence and build up the Japanese language and culture, failure to conform being regarded as prima facie evidence of unwillingness to co-operate. The Japanese encouraged people to use their own dialect, with Japanese replacing English as the communication link, but for the time being English and Mandarin proved indispensable. English shop signs and advertisements were removed and on 20 April 1942 Japanese street names in Central replaced British, e.g., Queen's Road became Nakameiji-dori and Des Voeux Road, Katorido-dori. The Gloucester Hotel became the Matsubara, the Peninsula, the Toa, but the Hong Kong Hotel kept its name unchanged. The statues were removed from Statue Square to Japan for a metal drive, but were brought back after the occupation, little the worse for their trip.

The Japanese set out to humiliate the Americans and Europeans, particularly the British, who had the leading stake in China. Their propaganda pointed to the superiority of the Japanese way of life, of Japanese spiritual values and the evils of western materialism and exploitation of the Asians for their own profit, and declared the object of the war as the building of the Greater East Asia Co-prosperity Sphere to emancipate East Asia from Western control and to allow Asians to enjoy their own living space with higher living standards. The Japanese victories in war were adduced as proof of the superiority of the Japanese way of life, the 'Kingly Way' as set out in the Book of Rites. By way of contrast, a leader in the *Hong Kong News* of 5 June 1942 trenchantly attacked Britain's record as one of 'intrigue and plunder and of jobbery, robbery and snobbery'.

The Japanese naturally looked to education as a means of infusing Japanese influence and were anxious to re-open the schools, which were asked to register and supply particulars; but since they made the teaching of Japanese compulsory, the schools had to remain closed until enough teachers of the language were available. There was a rush to learn Japanese; the Military Administration ran courses, there were lessons over the radio, and numerous private classes, but it was not until May that sufficient teachers of Japanese were available and twelve schools opened. In early February 150 teachers were selected by written and oral examination, and given $20 and food, were enrolled in an officially sponsored two months' Teachers' Training Course comprising Japanese language, Japanese affairs, general knowledge and physical education; and further courses were held every three months until numbers began to dwindle. Many who successfully completed the first course were drafted into the general Government service and the rest went as intended into the schools. Students were also encouraged to study in Japanese schools and universities. A grant scheme for primary schools was introduced in December 1942, and in the following February the Chinese Representative Committee launched a scholarship scheme to benefit 400 pupils in selected schools, and this number was subsequently increased to 1,000. This was a significant social welfare project in Hong Kong for which the Japanese must take some credit. Rising living costs drove the schools to reduce staffs in order to pay the remaining teachers more money. This led to classes of up to sixty, and before the end of the war teachers had to be paid wholly or partly in rice to enable them to live.

There was much talk of re-opening the University; but nothing was done. However, an East Asia Academy giving special courses in Japanese language, history and culture by Japanese lecturers catering for teachers, government employees and students was set up on 1 April 1943 at St. Stephen's Girls' College, and gave some indication of what the remodelled University might have attempted. The University library was saved by the devotion of Chinese members of the staff, though the Japanese claimed that it had been protected by

Japanese guards. They decided to collect all the books from various sources and make one large library in all languages available to the public and it was opened in the Helena May Institute in December 1944, and a lending section was added in the following April.

The Japanese influence was also strengthened by the celebration of Japanese festivals, national occasions, victories and anniversaries. Mass processions, encouraged by the distribution of free rice, marked the fall of Singapore in February 1942, as well as a Japanese version of the harvest festival in October 1942, and the Yasukuni or Shrine Festival honouring the dead, in the same month. 25 December 1942 was celebrated as victory day and a shrine to honour the dead was set up on the cricket ground; there was also a Japanese Empire Day or National Foundation Day on 11 February 1943 centred around the worship of the Emperor Jimmu, the legendary founder of the Japanese state. The Emperor's birthday was celebrated on 29 April, and there were many other official holidays. Japanese flags had to be flown on each occasion and often the dimensions of the flags were laid down for the various types of premises. The press announced on 7 April 1943 that a 'Love the Horse Day' would be celebrated but there was no further reference to it.

The Hong Kong News, a pre-war Japanese-owned English newspaper, was revived on 1 January 1942. Its Japanese and Cantonese associates also appeared, and by the end of January ten local Chinese newspapers resumed under a press censorship, but by May these ten had been reduced by amalgamations to four. Radio sets were permitted and used for Japanese propaganda, but listening to Allied broadcasts was forbidden, and to enforce this, in November 1942, only long-wave reception was allowed and all sets had to be handed in at prescribed centres for free adjustment.

People were free to continue their religious practices and Sunday was declared a public holiday as from April 1942. Religious organizations had to register and seventy-one complied; pressure on the Christian sects to amalgamate followed and in February 1943 eighteen of the Protestant bodies did so. The Roman Catholic Church, predominantly Italian and Irish in its priesthood, was allowed to continue ministering to the remains of its flock but the Japanese forced the bishop to hand over the Cathedral bells for their metals drive. The British Anglican and Free Churches suffered. Services at the Anglican Cathedral of St. John continued for some months, and then the church ornaments and stained glass windows were removed, and in fact preserved, and the building converted into a social club. St. Andrew's Church was used as a rice distribution centre, then as a Chinese Anglican church and eventually became a Buddhist temple. Its communion plate had been preserved by being taken for use in Shamshuipo prisoner-of-war camp.

The Japanese built shrines to honour the war dead and one was erected in the Botanical Gardens as a centre for this worship, at which the Governor could be seen every morning engaged in his religious observances. On the first anniversary of the outbreak of the war, 8 December, the foundation stone of a monument to the Japanese war heroes was laid at a site on a spur of Mount Cameron, and one year later, a sacred sword was embedded in the base by Shinto priests dressed in white, at a ceremony attended by the Governor and leading Japanese and Chinese personalities. The monument, supported by twelve reinforced concrete legs, was designed to be 80 feet high with three Chinese characters meaning 'Heroic Memorial', each 15 feet high, engraved on its face. An adjoining indicator was to show the direction and distance of various eastern cities. The Japanese also proposed to erect a cenotaph to the Allied dead but this was not proceeded with. Appeals for subscriptions towards the Japanese monument's cost raised some MY750,000 mainly from Japanese firms and citizens and their Chinese staffs. Work on the monument lagged as the war went on, and despite Colonel Noma, head of the gendarmerie, setting an example of voluntary manual labour which was followed by many Japanese schoolchildren, at the end of the war it was still incomplete.

As well as the fund for the monument, there were other Japanese war funds inviting subscriptions, for example, that for the Japanese wounded and the Hong Kong Nipponese Soldiers' Welfare Fund; in June 1943 came the first gifts to the Japanese National Defence Fund and, in July 1943, a Japanese association began a drive for an aeroplane fund which raised over seven million military yen in its first two years; a War Weapons Fund was started in 1945. Prominent Chinese and Indians could hardly avoid making a donation but an examination of the lists of donors gives the impression that the chief donors were Japanese and their Chinese employees or associates, while the Chinese subscribed most heavily to the Chinese Relief Fund which was set up in April 1943 to assist the poor and the charitable institutions.

The Tung Wah, the chief Chinese charitable body, was badly hit and announced in January 1945 that it had to sell some of its property to continue to exist. There were flag days and public welfare lotteries for charitable purposes, and some philanthropic Chinese and charitable bodies distributed rice at cost price to the aged and sick, and in 1945 congee depots were set up to supply free cooked meals. The Japanese subscribed to Chinese relief funds too. When Governor Isogai took office in February 1942 he distributed 500 bags of rice to the needy. In September 1944 Yamaguchi gave MY100,000 to the Chinese Relief Fund, asking that half should be earmarked for education. On 20 February 1944, the second anniversary of the founding of the Governor's Office, one day's free rice was given to all the inhabitants. Governor Tanaka celebrated the third anniversary by donating one million yen to the Tung Wah. In fact considerable relief work was done under the Japanese.

Despite war conditions, amusements were there for those who could afford them. At first gambling houses and night-clubs were encouraged, but that phase soon passed, and two designated amusement areas, mainly bars and cafés, were marked out in Wanchai and Shamshuipo with segregation for Chinese and Japanese. From the prominent and repeated advertisements in the *Hong Kong News* for the treatment of venereal diseases, medical control of these areas appears to have been inadequate. Theatres opened for traditional Chinese opera. The cinemas, which had to adopt Japanese names, screened Japanese films only, chiefly war films including 'The Capture of Hong Kong', which appeared on the first anniversary of the attack; by June 1944 the shortage of electricity cut the screenings to once a night. A long drama on the rebirth of Hong Kong under the Japanese was printed by instalments in the newspapers, but it does not appear to have been produced on the stage. A curfew was imposed from 11.00 p.m. to 5.00 a.m. but, later, cuts in electricity and the black-out kept people off the streets at night in any case. In April 1942 mahjong was prohibited, except at home, and not even there after 11.30 p.m.; dancing was forbidden in July; fire-crackers were banned except for an occasional official display as a celebration; and all clubs' meetings were prohibited except funerals, sports fixtures, and associations devoted to charity, on the excuse that energies had to be concentrated on winning the war. Nevertheless, horse-racing was revived at Happy Valley on 25 April 1942 with cash sweep-stakes and the usual betting, and in December 1943 Japanese ponies were introduced.

The Japanese strongly supported the Indian Independence League as part of their pro-Asian propaganda exposing British rule in India as the enslavement of a nation. The League was founded in Japan and held the first Hong Kong meeting on 26 January 1942, when it was agreed to work for the freedom India and of Asia. The League's success was limited and only 400 joined out of some 3,000 Indians, despite a low entrance fee of $2. Regular meetings were held in a large cinema on each side of the harbour.

But Japanese regulations give little indication of the everyday life in Hong Kong during the occupation. Many people lived in shell-damaged houses with the minimum of furniture and equipment, making a daily trip to town to purchase food and necessities; most found rationing hopelessly wasteful of time and relied on the black market. They made for the hawkers' stalls in Central, mainly in Stanley Street and its neighbourhood, and spent much time in haggling over prices. If Japanese soldiers passed, the women discreetly took shelter in a shop. Neutrals received a subsistence allowance from their own or a friendly consul; others sold gold and silver ornaments, and as the price of these increased all the time, they were able to survive by selling a little at a time. Property owners had to establish their title and pay tax, but permission to repair war damage was restricted to the less seriously affected houses. Owners were entitled to charge rents, but if the house were in disrepair, or if the tenant were penniless, this was only a fictional right. The Chinese council discussed the problem repeatedly, but the Japanese steadily refused all their requests to enforce rent collection. Real estate changed hands fairly freely, the sales being carefully recorded by Japanese officials in a manner closely following British official usage.

Life was a hand-to-mouth existence. All water had to be boiled because there was no chlorination or filtering, permits were necessary to move around, but passing a Japanese military post was always an ordeal because of bowing and the possibility of suffering indignity according to the mood of the sentry. Women rarely went out alone, and never at night. The thoughts of those who had family or friends in the prisoner-of-war camps were dominated by 'parcel-day' which involved the search for food and its purchase, the long trek to the camp and the anxious moments when the parcel was being examined. One constant source of irritation was the *Kai Yin* siren, which the Japanese sounded whenever they were showing an important visitor around, at which all movement in the street had immediately to stop and pedestrians had to remain quite still until the all clear.

During the last months of the occupation life became desperate. The Japanese defeats made the yen quite valueless by July 1945, water and other services were cut off because of lack of fuel, and workers demanded to be paid in rice, because at MY240 a catty they could not buy it, and schools collected their fees in rice.

Many former government employees continued their normal duties under the Japanese. Former Chinese police were among those who served with the gendarmerie, after training at a Police Training School at Boundary Street in Kowloon; they were present at interrogations, but the questioning and tortures were done by Japanese. One Chinese man has described his life during these years. He joined Admiral Chan Chak's organization, getting $2 per day, and when the fighting was over he engaged in running a gambling-house for the short time allowed by the Japanese. He then used two ships he possessed to trade with his native Heung Sah, buying rice there, selling it to the Japanese at a quarter or fifth of what he paid, and recouping his losses by selling matches, oil and soap obtained from the Japanese to the rice farmers at a large profit. One manufacturer of metalware has related that he worked for the Japanese for eight months after which they closed his factory and bought the machinery.

One woman whose husband was a railway official in China, has related her hectic experiences in trying to cross the harbour to negotiate loans or shelter from friends. She had lost through looting all the valuables lodged in a Chinese bank. The threat of starvation drove all her family, comprising some two dozen persons, to make the trek to China with only $200 for the whole party; on the way, her son went back to Hong Kong to borrow more, but the money was stolen. They were ultimately rescued by the Tamshui magistrate who knew the family. In Hong Kong she used to go out dressed as a coolie to avoid being robbed and molested.

Friendly third nationals were given a stamped pass with a photo which had to be carried everywhere. The French community prudently declared itself 'Vichy' and so were classed as friendly aliens, though the majority are said to have been Gaullist, but third nationals generally were faced with problems of living as rigorous as those of the internees in Stanley.

Norwegians were 'friendly' enemies and had been allowed to remain out on condition they gave their parole not to escape. Two of them, a sea captain who had been caught in Hong Kong, and an employee of Thoresen & Co., did escape to Free China with the inevitable result that all Norwegians except for those over sixty or engaged in Christian missions were interned in Stanley in February 1943. The Norwegians received a monthly allowance from their consul who obtained it from the Swedish Legation in Tokyo. One woman married to a Norwegian has related that, while everything such as a fur stole, silk stockings or dresses had value, because trade was at a standstill, she had to rely mainly on selling gold, piece by piece, for example half a bangle, with which she immediately bought food. She was able to get messages into Stanley Camp via the underground, chiefly to find out what her husband needed, but such contacts were most dangerous and she was advised to drop them. She was threatened only once by a Japanese, an officer who kicked at the door which he saw her enter, but went away when the amah told him her mistress had a fever. The Japanese seemed to shun any form of illness.

She moved to St. Paul's Convent to avoid living alone and was given a cubicle there, but when St. Paul's Convent was hit in an air raid, she was glad to get a bed-space in the Club Lusitano, sharing a room with many others, as numbers of Hong Kong people had to do. She sent her daughter to Macao by junk, a journey which took three days.

Brooding over all the community was the sinister shadow of the gendarmerie. One young Eurasian woman, who helped Dr. Selwyn-Clarke with his work among families of prisoners of war and internees, was suspected of carrying messages from him to others who were subsequently implicated. She was arrested, beaten, tortured, and questioned at various times of the day and night but was eventually liberated. In the end she had to take a job with a Japanese firm supplying the Japanese navy; it was that or starvation.

Air raids added to the difficulty of life. Hong Kong was an important military centre which the Japanese showed every intention of defending, and intelligence supplied by the British Army Aid Group enabled the China-based United States 14th Air Force and, later, planes of the advancing American Pacific forces, to select their targets. The first raid was on the night of 24 October 1942 and the planes returned on the afternoon of the following day to drop incendiary bombs. This led to the imposition of black-out restrictions and the Governor announced that the injured would be given compensation. Ten months passed before the next air raid, when six planes came over on 28 July 1943 and ten appeared the following day, the Governor again promising compensation to the injured. Altogether there were nine raids in 1943. Thirteen planes came over on the morning of the 25 August, followed by another wave the next day, and another on 3 September; in each case the local press was silent on the matter of casualties. The black-out was strictly enforced and air-raid shelters constructed between the pillars supporting the verandahs in the main streets. There were further attacks on 3, 15 and 16 November, and on the afternoon of 3 December, when the Japanese press claimed that seven out of the 40 P.40s and 70 B.25s that came had been shot down.

There were nine air raids in 1944. The first was on 12 February, by twenty-seven planes of which four were claimed to have been shot down, and a wrecked P.40 was placed on display at a large Japanese store. Two further raids followed on 13 March and 18 April, and in the latter the crew of the one shot-down bomber was captured. In May there were attacks on convoys outside the harbour and in September compensation to the victims of a 'recent' raid was announced, but accounts of these raids appear to have been censored. Scores of fighters and bombers were reported over Hong Kong on 16 October; the target appeared to be the Kowloon dockyard but a school close by received a direct hit and there were heavy casualties among the children and other civilians. Further raids came on 20, 23 and 24 December, in the last of these a Soviet ship was sunk, as well as a Japanese passenger ship which suffered a heavy death roll.

In 1945 the Americans were able to step up the tempo with eleven air attacks. 'Many tens' of planes were reported in the press as coming over on the morning of 15 January, and again that night. A heavy raid by some 300 planes on 16 January, from 8.30 a.m. to dusk, caused casualties at Stanley Camp. The airfield was attacked on 17 January. Another severe raid occurred on 21 January, causing numerous casualties in Wanchai and bringing a race meeting to a halt. The Chinese Relief Fund voted $500,000 to help the victims for whom a memorial service was held at the former St. John's Cathedral, and injured Chinese dockyard workers were given MY30 to MY60 as compensation. The next raid was by two P.51 fighters on 15 March and fifty planes–P.51s, P.38s and B.24s–came over from noon to 3 p.m. on 2 April, followed by several waves which came over next day. On 4 April, about seventy planes bombed Wanchai and, aiming at the *Kempeitei* Headquarters in the French Mission building, they hit the French Mission Hospital instead, with heavy damage and numerous casualties; about 80 orphans from the French Convent were sent to Macao and 28 sisters and 122 orphans were cared for at the Canossa Institute. A severe raid occurred again the next day. The Japanese now had to organize First Aid and Rescue Squads and mobile assistance parties. On the 18 April a Yaumati Ferry was machine-gunned, causing one hundred casualties. The last air raid was by fifty-nine planes which dropped incendiaries on the Central district on 12 June, causing about one hundred casualties and making 2,000 homeless, who were looked after by Tung Wah. The harbour was now full of wrecks, and with the Americans in the Philippines and in Okinawa, Hong Kong was effectively neutralized.

Summing up, life under the Japanese was grim, and under conditions of all-out war perhaps little more could be expected. On the credit side it might be claimed that the Japanese carried out certain beneficial measures, for example, the health campaigns, the encouragement of medical and education facilities to the poor, and schemes to improve agriculture in the New Territories. They rebuilt Government House with its roof embellished in the Japanese style, and added a new tower. The building remains their most lasting and perhaps elegant memorial to their occupation of Hong Kong.[4]

[4] See Appendix 2 on the impact of the war, especially on the Chinese population. There can be little doubt that no one was sorry to see the Japanese liberators leave Hong Kong.

VII

PRISONERS OF WAR

'Shamshuipo was made up of two barrack blocks. In peacetime they had been Nanking Barracks and Hangkow Barracks . . . . To the men of the 1st Middlesex it was like coming home, for before the war they had occupied Nanking Barracks for three happy years.'

Tim Carew, *Hostages to Fortune*, p. 67

For the defeated British servicemen there could be no interval of freedom between defeat and incarceration. They were ordered to disarm and report to the nearest Japanese unit commander, after which it was a matter of following instructions. As in the case of the foreign civilian community the Japanese had no ready-made plans for prisoner-of-war camps, and the men were shuffled around until April 1942 when three camps were finally organized.

Following the surrender the prisoners were collected at various centres; the naval personnel were sent to the dockyard, whence some moved on to the Missions to Seamen building on the waterfront in Wanchai. One naval officer noted that thousands of troops were assembled along the harbour front, and he saw the survivors of two platoons of No. 2 Scottish Company of the Volunteers march in from Stanley with their hands tied behind their backs. The prisoners then boarded launches to the accompaniment of what some of them thought was musical honours provided by a Japanese military band which, in fact, was probably practising for the victory parade. They marched past the Peninsula Hotel in Kowloon, where a number of German officers, probably liberated internees complete with Nazi swastika arm-bands, were watching the procession. Then they trekked dejectedly along Nathan Road to Shamshuipo Barracks which was earmarked as a prisoner-of-war camp.

The Volunteers, except those from Stanley, were collected in the residential blocks of the military compound adjoining

Kennedy Road; next morning they were moved to the cricket-ground area, from which vantage point they had a good view of the preparations for the Japanese victory parade. They too were ordered across to Shamshuipo.

The British wounded had a hard time, because the Japanese understandably requisitioned hospital accommodation for their own casualities. Lt.-Commander Ralph Goodwin, R.N.Z.N.V.R., after being wounded, was moved from the Aberdeen Industrial School Auxiliary Hospital to Queen Mary Hospital and then to the University. After the surrender, the University buildings gradually ceased to be used as a hospital and Goodwin was transferred back to Queen Mary. He soon found himself in the Royal Naval Hospital on the Peak, but was shortly afterwards told to leave and was placed in St. Albert's Convent Hospital on Rosary Hill, from which he was finally ordered to North Point Camp where he arrived on 25 February.

The Japanese decided, either from policy or expediency, to put all the prisoners of war into one camp and so, by the evening of the 27 December, over 7,000 were crowded into the Shamshuipo Barracks where reception preparations were conspicuously lacking.

Life in Shamshuipo in these early days was grim. There was gross overcrowding. The camp had been shelled during the mainland fighting and, after the British withdrawal to the island, was looted so thoroughly that everything portable had disappeared. Doors, windows, furniture, metal pipes and electric fittings had gone, window frames had been prised from the walls and even the asbestos sheeting used for the ceilings had been taken, leaving most of the huts mere empty shells. There were no beds and men just lay on the concrete floors. The prisoners of war mostly brought their kit-bags with them, including blankets, but for any extras had to fend for themselves. There was some anxious bartering between the prisoners, for example some preferred to exchange their army boots for cigarettes and to go bare-foot.[1] One naval officer has recorded that he and his friends made a pact that they would share everything, yet one of his early experiences was

[1] James Bertram, *The Shadow of a War* (London, 1947), p. 146.

to lose all his washing from the line where it was hanging out to dry.

The General and the Commodore were present, and formal parades were held with the usual bugle calls, barrack square formality and a military band in attendance, to boost morale. Later, when the officers were transferred to another camp, to the great relief of the men this ceremonial was abandoned.

At first the Japanese camp régime was fairly liberal and the inmates were left largely to their own devices. Chinese vendors, many of them children, sold food freely through the wire and when, as happened on occasion, they took the money and ran off without handing over the goods, the Japanese tried to halt the offenders. After a number of escapes a much harsher régime was imposed.

The overcrowding was relieved on 24 January when some 2,000 men of East Brigade including a dozen or so survivors of a captured Dutch submarine were sent to North Point Camp at the Quarry Bay end of King's Road on the Island. Conditions there were appalling.[2] The camp had been originally constructed to house Chinese refugees in huts 120 feet by 18 feet with two tiers of bunks on each side. During the fighting the Japanese had stabled their pack mules there, and as the huts had not since been cleaned they were swarming with flies. Unburied corpses still lay outside the perimeter and a noxious stench enveloped the whole site. There was no cleaning equipment or materials, but the camp was somehow made habitable, and the men were packed in, two hundred to a hut, without furniture or furnishing. When dysentery struck, the victims were segregated and left to look after themselves. On 18 April 1942 the naval contingent was ordered to Shamshuipo, and they were soon followed by the Canadians and then by the Dutch.

Three prisoner-of-war camps were then organized, one at Shamshuipo for other ranks; one in Argyle Street, Kowloon, for officers; and the third at Ma Tau Chung for Indians. The Shamshuipo Barracks were spacious, with two large parade grounds and two broad avenues lined with trees and there was a block of flats called Jubilee Building on the water's edge,

[2] Conditions in the North Point Camp were the subject of investigation by the War Crimes Tribunal in Tokyo after the war.

which was used as sick quarters. Each naval and military unit was allocated to huts in proportion to its numbers and placed under one of its own officers who was responsible to the camp administration for discipline.

The food in Shamshuipo was appallingly bad,[3] consisting mainly of rice, 'rice bust' as it was called, that is, rice and the water it was boiled in, and the army cooks were scarcely at their best in cooking it to the proper consistency. There was some improvement following a number of deaths from dysentery or malnutrition, and some swamp cabbage or water chestnuts, normally used by the Chinese as pig feed, was supplied with very small portions of beef. Even then, later escapes from the camp were usually punished by cutting the extras and reducing the rice ration.

The result of this lack of proper food was eventually malnutrition and constant ill-health. Most men lost weight rapidly, 50 or 60 pounds being by no means unusual. Deficiency diseases soon appeared, including beriberi, and the men's bodies and limbs became seriously swollen making it difficult to sit or lie down. Pellagra, in which the skin reddened, dried, and cracked, and 'electric' feet, often called dry beriberi, which was a form of neuritis, in which the toes went numb followed by continuous shooting pains making it the most painful of all the malnutritional diseases, were other afflictions. Sufferers from these diseases could be seen painfully moving about during the night because sleep was impossible. There were cases of blindness, and dysentery was common. Severe outbreaks of diphtheria brought a very heavy death toll,[4] in the face of which the doctors were powerless because there were no medicines available. The Japanese simply allowed the epidemic to take its course and over a hundred men died before they brought in any anti-toxin.

[3] Food was the chief pre-occupation of everyone. Therefore it is not surprising that accounts such as those of Goodwin, Carew and others, record the uninspiring details of daily diet, e.g. the tasteless, non-nutritional lily-roots as a staple for empty groaning stomachs. See also sketches by Lt. A. V. Skvorzov, *Chinese Ink and Brush Sketches of P.O.W. Camp Life in Hong Kong*, 25 December 1941–30 August 1945.

[4] J. Luff, *The Hidden Years* (Hong Kong, 1967), p. 171. Citing a diary kept by Sgt. Millington, Luff writes that during the first year's captivity the total number of deaths was 352. In one month alone, October, there were fifty-five casualties due to disease and deficiencies.

The Japanese provided coffins for the dead, arranged a military funeral attended by a burial party at slow march, with buglers sounding the last post, and also sent flowers to grace the proceedings. To some, all this pomp seemed the extreme of cynicism as many deaths could have been averted with proper medical attention. This saddening sight was almost of daily occurrence. The Jubilee Building was converted into sick quarters and some iron cots were secured, making conditions there less primitive than those in the huts, but the British doctors and their staff worked in face of the greatest difficulties from an almost complete lack of equipment. The first six months were notoriously bad, but by the early autumn of 1942 some supplies of anti-toxin did reach the camp through the agency of Dr. Selwyn-Clarke, and the British Army Aid Group at Waichow was able to send in supplies of vital drugs which saved many lives. There was an inspection by a delegate of the International Red Cross, after which the inmates noted a considerable improvement and Red Cross parcels arrived. The first issue, made on 1 November 1942, included some foods obviously intended for Indians such as coarse atta flour for making chapatties, and ghee, or Indian butter, made from buffalo's milk.

Then, during the autumn and winter of 1942–3, three thousand men, mostly from the regular army and navy units, were drafted to Japan as prisoner-of-war labour. Just under two thousand were left in camp. These were three main groups, Canadians, Volunteers, and a group of rejects who for one reason or another escaped the drafts. There was more room for everybody, though the Japanese restricted the camp area by a new and stronger perimeter fence which was electrified and further secured by rolls of barbed wire along the top and bottom.

The Volunteers, whose young recruits were sent to Japan, now became the largest group in the camp and were able to exercise more influence in its internal running. Their regimental sergeant-major, a regular soldier who had been posted to the Volunteers just before the fighting and scarcely knew his men, insisted on smartness on parade, and though he was at first detested he later came to be appreciated as having helped many men to preserve their self-respect. The officers were all paid in yen at rates equivalent to their Japanese counterparts, and they contributed to the Camp Amenities Fund which was used to obtain food and useful camp accessories.

One source of improvement in the supply of food was the camp gardens which provided sweet potatoes and cabbages and made a welcome addition to camp rations. In fact, the second year in camp showed decided improvement, but afterwards, when the allied blockade became effective, conditions deteriorated all round for prisoners and the victors.

The Japanese allowed food parcels to be brought to the camp by relatives and friends living in Hong Kong, often at no little personal sacrifice to the donors. Saturday became the recognized day for parcels, which had to be laid on the ground between the hours of 11.00 a.m. and 1.00 p.m. in front of the camp guardhouse. They had to be opened for inspection. At first only food was permitted, but afterwards some clothing was allowed. It was forbidden to speak to the prisoners; and in any case the guard house was some distance from the wire and it was not always easy for the women to spot their menfolk.

In the first week of September 1942 the first batch of some 700 men from the camps sailed for Japan to work in factories and Japanese coal mines. On 27 September 1942 a second draft of 1,816 prisoners sailed on the *Lisbon Maru*, a Japanese ship of about 7,000 tons. The men were crammed into three holds, with the Royal Navy in the forward hold, the Royal Scots, the Middlesex, and other smaller units in the next hold, and the Royal Artillery in the after hold. They were under Lt.-Col. 'Monkey' Stewart, the commanding officer of the Middlesex Regiment. The Japanese Commandant of the Shamshuipo Camp, Lt. Hideo Wada, and a detail of twenty-five Japanese troops was responsible for guarding the party. There were also 778 Japanese troops on board. On the morning of 1 October the ship was torpedoed by an American submarine, U.S.S. *Grouper*, off the Chusan Islands at the mouth of the Yangtze, and sank about twenty-four hours later. Lt. Wada kept the prisoners battened down in the holds in foul air and without food or water because he feared that his men were quite incapable of guarding so many prisoners. Fortunately one of the officers forced an opening in the hatch cover and began to liberate the men and, equally fortunately, the ship rested partly on a sandbank and remained afloat long enough for the men to leave the holds. They were fired on from the bridge, and again as they were swimming or floating towards the land; some were picked up by Japanese and about 200 landed safely on the islands from which the Japanese collected them next day, with the exception of three who were hidden by the islanders and made good their escape to Chungking. Of 1,816 men, only 724 survived this catastrophe.[5]

The next draft, consisting of 1,000 men, left in January 1943 by a fast, new Japanese liner, and made the voyage in three days. A film was taken which showed the men on the gangway, each carrying a Red Cross parcel.[6] Other drafts followed, and the Japanese medical officer responsible for the health of the prisoners, Capt. Saito, 'examined' the men to ensure that every prisoner capable of work should be sent to Japan, but generally only young men under thirty were drafted.

The prisoners were also drafted on local working parties. There were always fatigue parties in camp, including ration parties which loaded 200 lb. sacks of rice onto a lorry and unloaded them in camp, others brought in loads of firewood. For this labour they were rewarded with extra rations. Working parties were popular because it meant leaving camp and seeing new sights and new faces.

The first job assigned to the working parties was to clear the demolition on the Taipo road.[7] But the main local project on which prisoners were employed was the Kai Tak airfield extensions which the British had discussed for some years, without anything being done until the Japanese decided to proceed with it. In the early summer of 1942 a large working force of up to a thousand men from Shamshuipo Camp was set to work. They marched the three miles, or were taken by lorry, and later went to and fro by sea in an overcrowded barge escorted by an armed Japanese patrol-boat. It made a

[5] G. C. Hamilton, *The Sinking of the 'Lisbon Maru'* (Hong Kong, 1966), p. 19. Hamilton himself was a survivor of this tragedy. Carew also gives an account based on survivors' accounts.

[6] Bertram, op.cit., p. 170.

[7] Bertram, op.cit., p. 160 complained that all he received for his extra work was a bowl of thin vegetable soup.

long tiring day, parading before dawn with an hour's passage each way and returning to camp generally after dark, but it meant a welcome release from camp, and above all the chance of seeing wives, relatives and friends.[8] This was, of course, a special 'treat' to the local volunteers with families in Hong Kong. The work lasted until the end of the year. The Japanese also used prisoner-of-war labour on their new sea-plane base at Aberdeen on the south side of the Island, where the men were employed moving 500-kilo bombs and drums of high-octane aviation spirit into store, or, when the allied bombing began, into shelters. This was heavy work; at first the bombs were handled with great circumspection, but familiarity bred contempt and these lethal objects were soon unceremoniously pushed about.

Camp life gradually became more organized around a number of varied activities, and while it continued mostly dull and drab yet there were lighter moments, and especially notable were those associated with the 'Shamshuipo Hippodrome'. The Japanese received a sum of $10,000, reported to have been sent by the Pope, and popularly known in the camp as the Pope's Fund, which was used to buy sports equipment and musical instruments. In this way the camp band, which was lost in the *Lisbon Maru*, was replaced at least in part, and led to a considerable cheering-up of camp life. Camp entertainment grew up spontaneously after a sing-song in the old N.A.A.F.I. building on the first Saturday night in camp, and the Saturday night concert became an institution, with turns coming from any one who volunteered. Performances were given in darkness until electric light came on some weeks later. The old camp concert-hall was eventually made available, the Japanese supplied a piano, and the 'Shamshuipo Hippodrome' came into full swing. A dance band was formed, also a camp orchestra under Captain (Dr.) S. M. Bard, consisting of three violins, one saxophone, one clarinet, two trumpets, one trombone, two guitars, drums and a piano, and the Royal Engineers manufactured a cello[9] from a 40-gallon oil

[8] Contact was also made with British Army Aid Group runners, notes being left in cabs of lorries. However, the Japanese discovered this leak and exacted heavy retribution against the organizers of this 'grape-vine'.

[9] *The Volunteer*, Spring 1962–63, vol. 29, p. 115, article on 'Entertainment à la Shamshuipo'.

drum. A signature tune composed in camp came into regular use. The Portuguese formed their own group and performed in national dress and then, in the New Year 1943, a Cossack Choir was assembled from the thirty Russian members of the H.K.V.D.C. After some time, the stage was enlarged, a cat-walk from the stage into the auditorium added, and scenery was obtained. Eventually some plays were put on with surprisingly elaborate costumes. The biggest hit was the Portuguese 'female' troupe for whom no great amount of dressing up was apparently needed, whose singing and dancing invariably brought the house down.

A few books were accumulated. The Camp Committee organized classes and lectures given by qualified men mainly from the University and the Education Department, the head of which served in the Volunteers as a member of the ranks.[10] There was a halt to these activities when a tunnelling party, bent on escape, was found to be using the class in Spanish as a cover. Meetings exceeding four persons were then forbidden except at church parades and concerts. Other prisoners played bridge, some formed small discussion groups, and one New Zealand pressman organized poetry writing and criticism sessions.

Argyle Street Camp, which in April 1942 became the temporary home of some 500 officer prisoners including the General and the Commodore, with a few batmen, was next door to the Kowloon Hospital. It had been built to house Chinese Nationalist troops who had sought refuge in the Colony from the Japanese and possessed the barest necessities. During the fighting the Japanese had used it as a prisoner-of-war camp, and at the surrender it contained about one thousand men, many of them wounded, who had slept on bare bed-boards raised on bricks. Food consisted of rice and vegetables, but the catering arrangements were haphazard and there would be food without fuel or vice-versa. A serious outbreak of dysentery had carried off some thirty men a day; further deaths were avoided only when the Japanese permitted the use of medicines from the hospital next door. When they were all removed to Shamshuipo in January 1942 the empty camp

[10] The Director of Education, Mr. C. G. Sollis, had been a lance-corporal in No. 1 Coy. H.K.V.D.C.

was systematically looted and stripped by the locals of everything movable.

No preparations were made to receive the officers when, in April 1942, they moved to the Argyle Street Camp. They too found it completely bare; there were no rice cookers and the first meal, inevitably of rice, had to be sent in. Gradually, by begging equipment from the Japanese, and pooling carefully-husbanded useful materials, the camp became less primitive. Conditions in Argyle Street were not greatly dissimilar from those in Shamshuipo. The officers refused to work, and were not forced to, but they agreed to tend a vegetable garden on the other side of the street adjoining Ma Tau Chung Camp, and later they kept poultry. They held classes; languages, which included Chinese, Mathematics, and Navigation, were the most popular subjects. All officers were asked if they would volunteer to go to Japan, but very few did, and among these was Lt.-Col. 'Monkey' Stewart, who preferred to be with his men.

Newspapers were smuggled in and translations were made by Capt. K. M. A. Barnett, H.K.V.D.C. These, with the news received by a secret radio, formed the basis of a daily news bulletin. They had the occasional Red Cross parcels, perhaps one parcel divided between four men. The full contents were never received as the Japanese took part of them. As in Shamshuipo, those with local families or friends received food parcels sent in under Japanese supervision and regulation. Rations came to include whale-meat, which was palatable once it was discovered how to cook it. There was little or no news of their families, even if the latter were at Stanley. Captives were allowed to write one letter a month from the end of 1942, but few of these reached their destination; as for incoming mail, three letters for the whole of the three years and eight months' imprisonment was a fair average. The Japanese had a passion for records and controls, and all letters outwards and inwards had to be translated and censored, and this proved virtually beyond the capacity of the staff available. In Argyle Street there were strict roll-call parades, partly because the numbers were smaller, and there were no escapes.

The men were usually fairly free of duties, and reading

and playing bridge were the commonest forms of relaxation. Magazines were produced; there was *Prisoners' Pie*, produced by a group of three journalists, which had articles of general interest as well as sketches; *View Point*, edited by a government officer which was slightly more technical; and *Within*, produced by an army major. *P.O.W. Art* published selected drawings and sketches. One officer wrote and produced a play.

In 1944, after successive drafts and liberations of Asians had reduced the ranks of the prisoners, the officers were moved from Argyle Street back to Shamshuipo and the Indian prisoners took over Argyle Street. The General and Commodore were removed from Argyle Street in August 1943 and taken via Japan and Korea to a camp near Mukden. After the surrender they were assisted by the Russians to make their way to Chungking.

The third camp was at Ma Tau Chung and became the home of the Indian prisoners. It was situated about 300 yards from the Argyle Street Camp on the opposite side of the street and set back some distance from it. About the last week in January 1942 the Indian regulars were taken there from Shamshuipo. The Indian members of the H.K.V.D.C. were taken first to Argyle Street Camp, where they found a motley crowd of prisoners, and then, after a day or two, they were taken on to Ma Tau Chung Camp where the Indian regiments were already quartered. Besides the Rajputs and Punjabis, there were Indians of the Mule Corps, the Royal Army Service Corps, the Hong Kong and Singapore Royal Artillery, the Indian Medical Corps, the Indian warders from Stanley Gaol who had been members of the Stanley Platoon of the H.K.V.D.C., and some Indian Police reservists.

There was gross overcrowding, about one hundred men to a hut, giving each man about two feet six inches of bare concrete to sleep on. Most men had carried their blankets and kit-bags with them, but even so their bedding was not warm enough for a Hong Kong winter. The food was not plentiful but was adequate, consisting of rice, vegetables and fish. Whale-meat was issued, but the Mule Corps men who drew and cooked the rations refused to touch this, suspecting some sinister design to get them to eat meat that was forbidden by caste rules. They generally got a ration of fish. The Indian officers drew their rations and cooked and messed separately. Those with local families or friends received parcels on a generous scale, two or three times a week, and though conversation with their families was forbidden, a kindly Japanese interpreter or guard occasionally turned a blind eye to these meetings. Red Cross supplies from India provided flour for chapatties, and ghee. So, on the whole, the Indian prisoners did not fare so badly. There was some beriberi and pellagra, caused mainly by switching to a rice diet to which most Indians were unaccustomed. They had more newspapers than their British counterparts, for example the *Nippon Times*. Since it was part of Japan's Grand Design for Asia to liberate India from the British imperial yoke the prisoners were frequently subjected to anti-British propaganda and pressure to collaborate with the Japanese. The Punjabis and H.K. and Singapore Royal Artillery were brought to Gun Club Hill Barracks for this purpose, but when all but a few refused to collaborate they were sent back to Ma Tau Chung and severely confined in three huts on bare subsistence rations. At the same time, that is about March or April, some Indian officers were taken to Shamshuipo police station and others to Stanley gaol, and again 'persuaded' to collaborate but with little result. All Indians were asked to sign a guarantee that they would not attempt to escape, similar to that signed by other prisoners of war, and also that they would collaborate even to the point of using arms. They all signed under duress, and were put on static armed guard duties at such places as Radio Hong Kong, Gun Club Hill Barracks, the Kowloon-Canton Railway, Kowloon Docks and some even went as far afield as Canton. For these duties they were paid a small sum. The men were treated as prisoners of war and were marched or taken to their guard duties or meetings under Japanese guard. Captain Ansari of the Rajputs, who came from a well-known Hyderabad family and held the King's Commission, refused to collaborate. The B.A.A.G. contacted him, and his escape could probably have been arranged, but he felt his duty lay in remaining with his men and he volunteered to go to Ma Tau Chung Camp to stiffen the resistance of the Rajputs to Japanese propaganda. His contempt for the Japanese led to his being arrested. He was tortured with revolting barbarity and ultimately beheaded at Big Wave Bay. His heroism was quite outstanding and gained for him the posthumous award of the George Cross.[11]

The Japanese encouraged the Indian Independence League, whose representatives visited the camp and also organized meetings at the King's Theatre on the Island and the Alhambra Theatre in Kowloon, which were well-attended mainly because they afforded a welcome, if temporary, freedom from camp. Indian sentries at Ma Tau Chung were sometimes seen in Indian National Army uniforms, but most wore their ordinary uniforms. The Japanese began to use Ma Tau Chung Camp as a Japanese troop transit camp, but no fraternization between Japanese and Indian troops was allowed.

In June 1944, when the officers were transferred from Argyle Street back to Shamshuipo, the Indians were switched over to Argyle Street. Later, many Indians from Malaya and Singapore were released and sent back to their homes in occupied areas; in addition, all local Hong Kong Indians who promised to work with the Japanese were sent home, so that by the time the war ended only three Indian prisoners, all of the H.K.V.D.C., remained in the Argyle Street Camp.

The camps at Argyle Street and Shamshuipo had some contacts with the outside world. Radio-receivers, though strictly forbidden, were assembled and news received from outside. In Shamshuipo, in the early days, a set was converted to battery operation because of the lack of electric power and the B.B.C. news was received, the moving spirit being Lt. H. C. Dixon, R.N.Z.N.V.R.[12] After moving to North Point he operated a small radio set brought in by the Canadians and hidden in a hole in the floor of one of the huts; in April the men moved back to Kowloon and the set was smuggled in with them.

In Argyle Street the Royal Corps of Signals attempted to create a set out of the most unlikely scraps; Lt. Dixon was brought in again, and after seven months of concentrated effort (with the encouragement of General Maltby and the Commodore) a set was once more in operation. In August 1943 the Japanese uncovered a network of communications between the camps and the British Army Aid Group (B.A.A.G.) working

[11] Ansari's head stone is to be found in Stanley Military Cemetery.
[12] Goodwin, *Hong Kong Escape*, pp. 26–7.

in South China and even, according to Goodwin, with Army H.Q. in New Delhi. This resulted in a thorough search of the camps and the seizure of radios in Shamshuipo. The Argyle Street radio was securely hidden in a tin container sunk in the ground below a flower plot outside one of the huts, and, when in use, under a tin of rice. It was accidentally discovered in September 1943, and those concerned, including Lt. Dixon, his senior officers, and Major Charles Boxer, Cdr. Craven, R.N., Lt.-Cdr. Young, R.N., were arrested and questioned with all the equipment used by *Kempeitai* to make people talk. They were confined under inhuman conditions in Yaumati and Shamshuipo police station cells, subjected to barbarous treatment, and at times deprived of the basic necessities. They were court martialled at the Supreme Court on 23 December 1943 and sentenced to fifteen years' imprisonment, subsequently reduced by the discretion of the Court to five.

The prisoners were sent to Stanley to serve their sentences, and were subjected to normal Japanese gaol discipline on very inadequate diet. Though suffering from malnutrition they had to sit cross-legged facing the wall of the cell for long periods, but were eventually allowed to join the prison working parties. Because of air raids and overcrowding, the European prisoners were taken to a Canton prison at the end of June 1945, from which they were freed in August 1945 on the Japanese surrender.[13]

It may be asked why men were willing to take risks merely to get news from outside. Only a few did so, of course, as in the nature of things radios had to be kept secret. It was a question of the importance of keeping up morale among men cut off from the world and the risks were accepted by brave souls who were convinced of the value of the service they were rendering to others, and who were encouraged by their superior officers who had to take responsibility; but there were many who felt that the risks of discovery outweighed the service rendered.

Contacts with the outside world were not confined to the radio. Even more hazardous were those established between

[13] Miss Constance B. Murray, who kept a diary in Stanley Internment Camp, noted for 22 August 1945, 'Heard Boxer in Canton in 3 years' solitary confinement, hair to heels and beard to knees'.

the Camps and the underground agents of the British Army Aid Group operating from Waichow. An account of the work of this Group together with an indication of its communications with the camps is given in a later chapter. Here, a brief summary must suffice and it is given mainly from the point of view of the effect of these contacts with the camps and on the individuals principally concerned.

First contacts were made at the site of the Kai Tak extensions between agents posing as Chinese coolies and the prisoner working-parties. These had to be carried on in the greatest secrecy because of the regularity with which informers tipped off the Japanese. The contacts were regularized and passed through Flt.-Sgt. R. J. Hardy, D.C.M., of the R.A.F., assisted by Corporal Bond of the H.K.V.D.C., to Capt. D. Ford of the Royal Scots[14] who assumed control in consultation with Flt.-Lt. H. S. Gray, R.A.F. as Hardy's commanding officer. In December 1942, when the working parties were withdrawn from Kai Tak, contacts ceased, but were resumed in January 1943 through a driver of one of the trucks bringing in the daily ration of rice and vegetables. Hardy continued as the chief go-between though the personnel of the ration parties changed. At the same time, in January 1943, the B.A.A.G. agents made contact with Argyle Street, again through a Chinese driver of a ration truck; Colonel L. A. Newnham took control and, after informing the General and the Commodore, assumed responsibility for the underground contacts at both camps because he felt that communications should be co-ordinated and decisions affecting all the prisoners should be taken at the highest level. The messages concerned war news, requests for news of conditions in the Hong Kong camps, appeals for medicine, and plans for escape. Progress was necessarily slow considering the three-way communication system and the long journey to Waichow. The contacts lasted barely six months, and in July 1943 the Japanese clamped down. On 1 July, Gray and Hardy and others were arrested, and on 10 July, Col. Newnham and Capt. Ford suffered the same fate. By this time well over seventy persons were in Stanley

[14] The 'Stickman' (the contact man) for these hazardous smuggling expeditions bringing in drugs and information from the B.A.A.G. is well-portrayed in Ford's novel *Season of Excape* (London, 1963).

Gaol as a result of their participation in this network. They included some civilians from Stanley Camp and others living in the town such as Dr. Selwyn-Clarke and two bankers.

For seven weeks they were kept in a separate prison block and were subjected to interrogation by the *Kempeitai*. This was carried out arbitrarily at any time of the day or night to the accompaniment of various forms of brutal torture to force them to speak. They were kept in solitary confinement, without change of clothing, on bare bed-boards without blankets, and with no break except when being taken for interrogation and torture. Under this pressure many broke down and the Japanese were able to get the information they wanted. The civilian prisoners were brought before a tribunal in Stanley Gaol and thirty-three were sentenced to death, the rest being given long prison sentences. The executions by beheading took place on Stanley Beach on 25 October 1943.

On 1 December the military prisoners were brought before a court at the Supreme Court Building and accused of espionage. The proceedings were extremely perfunctory; the charge was read to them in English after a long speech in Japanese by the prosecution and they were asked if they had anything to say. Newnham, Ford and Gray were sentenced to death and were shot on 19 December; Flt.-Sgt. Hardy and two others were sentenced to fifteen years, subsequently reduced to five. They were subjected to the usual Japanese prison routine, sitting cross-legged facing the wall for the day except during meals and washing out the cells, and were later joined by Boxer, Craven, Dixon, and Young who were sentenced shortly after, as already mentioned.

The prisoners of war generally were largely at the mercy of the Japanese camp officers and the camp guards; after the first weeks when the front-line troops were withdrawn, the latter were second-line troops, often Formosans, and were much disliked. The O.C. Prisoner-of-War Camps, Col. Tokunaga Toku, usually referred to as the 'Fat Pig', was unpredictable and ill-tempered, but it is doubtful if he was responsible for the harsh conditions, deaths, and executions in the camps. A Lt. Wada replaced the first camp commandant. At Shamshuipo he was described as being 'fair-minded and reasonable'; then he sailed on the *Lisbon Maru* in charge of the prisoners. One interpreter and a Canadian-born Japanese called Inouye Kanao, nicknamed 'Kamloops Kid' or 'Slap-Happy' was hated by the inmates whom he treated with obvious contempt.[15]

The Japanese interpreters were frequently moved around so that those bringing parcels could never be certain who would be on duty. There were cases of harshness but also many acts of kindness by the Japanese towards those less fortunate. One outstanding individual was a Japanese Lutheran Minister, the Rev. Kyoshi Watanabe, referred to as the 'small man of Nantaki' who did his utmost both to serve the Japanese cause to which he was loyal and, at the same time, to help the unfortunate by carrying messages and bringing medicines into camp at great personal risk. Another official was Lt. Takabayashi, who had been educated at Heidelberg and spoke excellent English, and who smuggled out jewellery from a prisoner to deliver to his daughter in town.[16] Such selfless actions were rare.

As related previously, the Governor, Sir Mark Young, and General Maltby, were ordered to go in person to the Japanese Military Headquarters in the Peninsula Hotel to confirm the surrender, under the threat that if they refused, the Japanese would continue with their planned attack. The Governor complied with the greatest reluctance, and they crossed over to the Japanese lines in the streets of Wanchai and were taken to the Peninsula Hotel in Kowloon, where they met General Sakai. General Maltby was allowed to return, but the Governor was kept incommunicado in one room in the hotel and his requests for information about casualties and even for additional clothes were all at first refused. On 17 February 1942 he was taken by air to Woosung, near Shanghai, though he was not told his destination until they were on their way to the camp after landing. Sanitary conditions there for the 1,500 inmates were bad. He and twelve other British personnel refused to sign a form promising among other things not to escape, for which he was given close confinement. He was kept there until

[15] At the War Crimes Trial after the Japanese surrender, he was to plead that he had renounced his Canadian citizenship. This was of no avail and he was sentenced to death on the charge of treason.

[16] Ellen Field, *Twilight in Hong Kong* (London, 1960), p. 81.

September of that year. Later, in Formosa, he did sign such a document.

While in the Peninsula Hotel he had written a despatch giving the story of the surrender and was able to carry it to Woosung, where it was committed to memory by a British naval attaché awaiting diplomatic exchange, who on reaching Capetown, South Africa, telegraphed it to London.[17] In February 1942 the Governor was moved to Kerenko Camp on the East Coast of Formosa where senior British officials from Singapore and Malaya, Sir Shenton Thomas, Sir Percy McElwaine, and Sir Harry Trusted, and also the Malaya Commander-in-Chief, Lt.-General Percival, and other senior officers were being held. Conditions there were disgraceful. They were badly under-fed, had to do forced labour and were frequently assaulted for some irregularity in saluting a sentry. Later, Governors, Generals, and men aged sixty or over, were allowed to herd goats instead of digging or other form of labour. Sir Mark was assaulted four times, and made written protest.

In September 1942 he was moved to a small camp at Tamzako where conditions were better, and in October 1944 all the senior officials and officers were sent to Moksak Camp, about twelve miles from Taipei. Here conditions were good, each having a small room, and forced labour ceased. The same month they were moved via Japan and Korea to Manchuria, and met General Maltby and the Naval Commodore, Captain Collinson, R.N., en route. But the sixteen senior prisoners were again segregated on 1 December 1944 and sent to Seian Camp, 200 miles north of Mukden. Conditions were again

[17] This was published in the *Hongkong Gazette* in a Special Supplement in 1948.

In 1944 the B.A.A.G. was in touch with the captured Governor. A communication made then (CO.129/591(54112)), confirms that Sir Mark Young wrote a two-page report on the Hong Kong campaign in March 1942 when he was in Woosung Camp, Shanghai but this was destroyed when he was recaptured (apparently after an unsuccessful escape attempt). The Ride report gives an important side-light on the surrender, viz. that the Governor was not in agreement with the G.O.C. about the time to do so. 'Sir Mark held out for twenty-four hours after General Maltby recommended the surrender but when on the 25th, they knew that the enemy proposed a big attack at 18.00 hrs. he knew there was nothing for it but to surrender.'

Sir Mark's anguish was acute. 'He felt very strongly that he was the first Colonial Governor to surrender his Command and he naturally was greatly exercised in his mind as to whether he had done the right thing.'

comfortable, with single rooms, but they were kept without news; they had little mail, letters were heavily censored and food cut down to starvation level from which they were only saved by Red Cross parcels. They learned of the end of the war from two American paratroopers, and with Russian help went to Mukden, then to Chungking and eventually to India via Kunming. The Governor summed up his impressions thus: '. . . I would say generally that the treatment which I experienced at the hands of the Japanese during my captivity was almost invariably inconsiderate, that it was frequently objectionable, and that it was on occasion positively barbarous.'[18]

[18] A private communication to the author.

VIII

ESCAPES

'Few greater adventures are open to mankind . . . and not to try to escape is like missing the chance of a lifetime.'

R.K.M. Simpson, 'These Defenceless Doors', p. 193

NOT all members of the garrison fell into the hands of the Japanese when the Colony surrendered on 25 December 1941. Two officers had earlier been sent out to China by plane to carry out general liaison and intelligence duties and report on conditions in the Colony. Captain H. G. Chauvin, a staff Intelligence Officer, left on the night of the 19 November 1941 and Col. H. Owen Hughes of the H.K.V.D.C. left for Chungking on 9 December by the last plane to leave Kai Tak before the Japanese occupied it, to act as liaison officer with the British Military Mission at Kukong, and to attempt to co-ordinate military action with the Chinese force of '220,000 troops of one sort and another' under the Command of General Yu Hon Mon to threaten the rear of the Japanese forces investing Hong Kong. Owen Hughes recalls, 'mine was a mission doomed to failure, because so far as I am aware, the Chinese never fought the Japanese anywhere'.[1]

One large mixed group, comprising Admiral Chan Chak and some of his staff, some British military and civil officers, the crews of the naval motor torpedo-boats and others, got away within a few hours of the capitulation in accordance with plans improvised as defeat loomed nearer. The Chinese Government had been given an undertaking that the Admiral would not be allowed to fall into the hands of the Japanese. So it was arranged that in case of emergency the motor torpedo-boats would be made available to evacuate him, his chief aide, Commander Henry Hsu, and his staff, and also Col. S. K. Yee. The Governor and General Maltby also chose certain officers to accompany the Admiral to give an authoritative account of

[1] Private communication to the author. However, it is certain that Colonel Hughes was referring to the events of that particular period.

the events in Hong Kong. They were Sq.-Ldr. Max Oxford, R.A.F., Mr. D. M. MacDougall, head of the Department of Information, Major Arthur Goring, an Indian Army Cavalry Officer, Supt. W. Robinson of the Indian Police and Capt. Peter MacMillan, R.A. At the last moment another army staff-officer, Capt. Freddie Guest of the Middlesex Regt., joined the party uninvited. He later explained[2] that a strong aversion to prisoner-of-war camps led him to try to escape, and he thought the sea offered the best chance. Three members of Force 'Z', F. W. Kendal, C. McEwen and M. Talan, were detailed to help to organize the getaway and be responsible for the safe delivery of the Admiral. The M.T.B.s. had to leave port on the afternoon of the 25th to avoid surrender, and when the Admiral and his party arrived at the Aberdeen Naval Base not one was in sight. They boarded a launch belonging to H.M.S. *Cornflower* and since the channel to the west was mined they had to leave Aberdeen by the eastern side of Applichau Island. The party was shot up by the Japanese from Brick Hill, and Admiral Chan Chak and others were wounded and one seaman killed. All dived into the water and swam ashore, except two who could not swim. Climbing over the island's sharp ridge they saw an M.T.B. in the cove below. Alas, it opened fire on the anxious party shouting to attract its attention and Guest had to swim to the boat to get aid. The five M.T.B.s, running the gauntlet of heavy fire from the defences, moved in from Stanley Peninsula and, after steaming for about two hours, reached Mirs Bay where there was the British island of Peng Chau half a mile distant from the mainland. Fortunately, the local headman had served in the Chinese navy under Admiral Chan; he was an independent guerrilla chief regarded by the Nationalists as a bandit, and the Admiral was able to enlist his aid in conducting them into Free China as far as Waichow by personally vouching for him with the Nationalists. The M.T.B.s were stripped and scuttled. The party was joined by the crew of a naval stores ship which had been en route to Hong Kong from Singapore when the attack began. This also had to be scuttled. The huge party of some seventy-five persons set off and in due course reached

[2] Capt. Freddie Guest, *Escape from the Bloodied Sun* (London, 1956).

Waiçhow without casualties, travelling by night and lying up by day to avoid the risk of being seen and reported. A guerrilla-controlled escape route had not yet been organized but Commander Henry Hsu had little difficulty in arranging day accommodation as the party passed through, showing thus early the goodwill of the villagers.

There were a number of escapes from Shamshuipo and North Point Camp, but none from Argyle Street or Ma Tau Chung. There were many problems to be faced in the attempt to escape, especially for non-locally-domiciled prisoners. They had to decide whether to go alone or team up with a party, whether to seek permission from their senior officers or make an independent bid. One extraordinary, and to some extent incredible, feature of the camps was the certainty with which news of planned escapes reached Japanese ears. The participants had to act in great secrecy it the Japanese were not to learn of their plans. For example, one British officer's preparations to escape were foiled by the Japanese being tipped off by a note from a fellow prisoner. The incident was related at the trial of Colonel Tokunaga in January 1947, the officer being identified as Lt. Hyland. There were also the problems of what to take, where to go and how to avoid the Japanese forces.

Among the first escapes from Shamshuipo[3] were those Portuguese, Asian and Eurasian members of the local volunteers who had families or friends in town, and who, once out of uniform, could disappear into the community with little trouble. Considerable research is necessary before a list of these can be compiled, but one H.K.V.D.C. Battery Commander kept a list of his men who escaped, and if his experience is assumed to be typical, then the number must have been considerable. These escapes all occurred early, for in August 1942 the

[3] Tim Carew, *Hostages to Fortune* (London, 1971) has recently given a characteristically vivid account of prisoners of war in Shamshuipo, of escapes and the *Lisbon Maru* atrocity.

Also J. A. Ford's novel *Season of Escape* (London, 1963), which is based upon the tragic experiences of his brother Major Ford, not only conveys the claustrophobic pressures of incarceration and the ebbing of morale through starvation and ill-treatment, he also tells in a realistic way the tenuous connexion with the B.A.A.G. outside the camp and the plan for a mass escape which was to result in Major Ford's execution by the Japanese.

Japanese liberated all local Chinese prisoners of war on condition they signed an undertaking not to endanger Japanese military security. This was part of their policy to treat Asians sympathetically for propaganda reasons.

Escapes from Shamshuipo became sufficiently numerous for some control to be necessary to prevent the situation from becoming chaotic. The senior British officers set up an Escape Committee under Col. L. A. Newnham as chairman, with representatives of other Services, but it was Newnham who really decided. Men wanting to escape were instructed to report to the commanding officers of their units who then, after discussion, put the case up to the Escape Committee and, if approved, the applicants would take their place in the queue to await their turn. The majority were local men with families or relatives in the Colony, or in China; they were told to try to get into Free China where they could be posted to other combatant units to continue the fight, but they were also told to look after their families as an immediate priority. Non-locally-domiciled men were instructed to make for Free China. Only one map of the New Territories, scale one in 20,000, existed in the whole of the camp and this was used to make tracings. The route recommended took them through the Hakka villages on the east side of the New Territories because the Hakka people were felt to be more sympathetic. The villages mainly used were those to the east of Saikung and Three Fathoms Cove. The villagers there, and indeed elsewhere, proved invariably helpful. The men were given a letter in Chinese, addressed to the elders of different villages, certifying that the bearer was a British serviceman, and promising a reward after the war for any help. All these promises were honoured in due course. They were also taught some phrases in the Hakka dialect to assist them find their way. Further assistance had to be given to the escapees by arranging for someone to answer for them at role call, to give them a chance to get away.

The Japanese replied by strengthening the camp fence by electrifying it, putting electric lights around and strengthening the guards. In May 1942 they also required from everyone a written undertaking not to attempt to escape, a demand that led to much searching of heart, for no such pledge could be given without flouting the duty of all captured members of the armed forces to attempt to escape. Prior to the special parade arranged for the signing, the men in Shamshuipo met and there was a general agreement that all should refuse to sign, though many argued that a signature given under duress was invalid in which case signing was of no consequence. The Japanese Prison Camps Commandant, Col. Tokunaga, in due course attended the parade and demanded a signature from everyone. When an artillery colonel refused to sign without General Maltby's consent, he was informed that the General and all the officers in Argyle Street had already signed under duress. A deputation of British officers from Shamshuipo was allowed to go to Argyle Street and obtained confirmation that this was in fact so. The result was that those in Shamshuipo signed likewise, except a small number of hardy spirits who tenaciously maintained a firm negative to all demands to sign. They were kept under armed guard and later taken out to Shamshuipo and other police stations to suffer such inducements to sign as the *Kempeitai* well knew how to apply.

Recent escapes had in fact brought such heavy reprisals that many doubted if escape was worthwhile in the general interest. Escape was followed for those left in camp by starvation diet, by keeping the men standing on parade for an excessively long period, even the sick were not excused nor were medical orderlies, so that deaths occurred in sick quarters for lack of attention. But in the main the Japanese applied great pressure on the escapee's friends, associates and hut-mates, who might be taken away and given the usual treatment to extract information. To save them the greatest secrecy was usually preserved. After October 1942 all escapes ceased, and in any case, the men were in no physical condition after months of utterly inadequate diet, to undertake the rigours of the trek to Free China. Lt.-Commander Goodwin's escape in July 1944 described in his book *Hong Kong Escape*[4] was quite exceptional.

In view of the harsh treatment meted out to those who remained, would-be escapers were faced with a special moral

[4] Ralph Goodwin, *Hong Kong Escape* (London, 1953, paperback, 1956).

problem. Was attempted escape justified when it was certain that retribution would fall on the whole camp in general and on their hut-mates and close friends in particular? The dilemma was a real one. Goodwin who successfully escaped from Shamshuipo after a relatively short incarceration there of a brief two months commented, 'The merits of attempting an escape were debated long and heatedly in the prison camps in Hong Kong. From the point of view of the escaper the problem was clear-cut and simple. Success meant freedom and a return to battle; failure meant torture and execution. For those left behind the problem was confused, unpredictable and therefore the more terrifying. Anything could happen, from a spate of tortures and executions of individuals, to a mass starvation of the whole camp.'

The problem was resolved only by men being physically incapable of making the necessary effort through lack of food. The young, those under thirty, were shipped to Japan to do forced labour, the rest eked out an existence in the camps. Besides, General Maltby ultimately reached the conclusion that escapes by individuals relying on their own efforts should be discouraged because the low standard of health made the attempt too hazardous and brought such severe deprivations for those remaining as to be fatal for many.

Plans for escape with outside assistance were never given up. General Maltby apparently came to the conclusion that the best chance lay in an attempted mass escape planned by the B.A.A.G. It was to break out all three camps simultaneously, using caches of arms, ammunition and food hidden in the hills and helped by diversionary guerrilla attacks. He calculated that about one-third might get through to freedom and renewed participation in the war, the remainder being either casualties or those left in camp as too weak to make the effort.[5] This mass break-out never materialized.

Some account will be given of individual escapes from Shamshuipo, but first it may be convenient to deal with those from North Point, from January to April 1942, whilst it was being used as a prisoner-of-war camp, mainly for naval and Canadian and Dutch personnel. This camp was situated at

[5] Ralph Goodwin, *Passport to Eternity* (London, 1956). Foreword by General Maltby, p. 6.

the eastern end of King's Road on the water's edge, which in fact made escape all the more tempting.

The first to escape from North Point were Lt. Ben Proulx, H.K.R.N.V.R., and two Dutch submarine officers captured when their submarine was stranded off the coast of Indo-China. Proulx discovered a sewer passing under the camp and the three used this effluvious means of escape, taking the risk, which proved justified, that there would be a small connecting storm-water drain to take them out on the slopes of Mount Butler. Hiding by day, they eventually got a boat across to the mainland, were concealed and fed by villagers, and conducted to Free China.[6]

On 26 January 1942 a second naval party, consisting of Lts. J. Douglas and J. W. Hurst, Lt. (E) G. Thompson, all R.N.R., and P.O. (Tel) Maxwell Holroyd, R.N., one night took a boat across the harbour to Kai Tak and made their way via Customs Pass to the Saikung peninsula, taking seven days to cover the ten-mile journey, travelling only by night. They were helped by villagers and conducted to Waichow by communist guerrillas of the East River Column.[7]

Among the first Europeans to get away from Shamshuipo, in January 1942, was a group of Hong Kong University men consisting of Lt.-Col. L. T. Ride of the H.K.V.D.C. Field Ambulance and Professor of Physiology, Lt. D. F. Davies H.K.R.N.V.R. and Lecturer in Physics, Lt. D. W. Morley, H.K.R.N.V.R., former lecturer in Engineering, and Pte. Francis Y. P. Lee (Lee Yan Piu), H.K.V.D.C., a clerk in the Physiology Department.[8] Francis Lee had local contacts through whom suits of clothes were brought into camp to aid the escape. The party was taken by sampan to the shore to the north of the camp whence they made their way to Tolo harbour via the Saikung area. They were hidden at great personal risk by two villagers from the villages of Sun Liu and Ngon Wor, and were eventually conducted to Waichow and Kukong where they were assisted by Mr. R. C. Lee, a Hong Kong businessman with influential Nationalist Govern-

[6] Benjamin A. Proulx, *Underground from Hong Kong* (New York, 1943).

[7] Ralph Goodwin, *Passport to Eternity*, p. 24.

[8] Brian Harrison (ed.), *The First 50 Years* (Hong Kong, 1961). Chapter by Sir Lindsay Ride, 'The Test of War', p. 75.

ment contracts. Francis Lee later joined the B.A.A.G. and returned to Hong Kong late in the same year, 1942, as an intelligence agent. He was captured and sentenced to death, but managed to escape a second time and continued to serve with the B.A.A.G., being promoted to the rank of captain.

Major Munro, R.A., F.O. Moore, R.A.F. and Capt. I. B. Trevor of the Railway Operating Detachment Cadre, H.K.V.D.C., arrived at Shamshuipo from North Point Camp on 23 January, and on 1 February got away from Shamshuipo by crawling along the breakwater, swimming to Lai Chi Kok and then making their way via the Shingmun River to Taipo. They were shielded and assisted by the Lin Ma Hang villagers on their way to Waichow where they were helped with funds by Mr. R. C. Lee. In the same month Lt. Fairclough, of the H.K.S.R.A., and Lts. Passmore and Wedderburn escape from Shamshuipo and again were helped by the Lin Ma Hang villagers.

A group of four Europeans, Capt. J. D. Clague, Lt. L. S. White, Lt. J. L. C. Pearce, all of the R.A., and Sgt. D. I. Bosanquet of an A.A. Unit of the H.K.V.D.C., escaped on 11 April 1942. Sgt. Bosanquet was moved from North Point to Shamshuipo on 23 January 1942 and set about organizing his escape immediately, intending to use the land exit, but was forced to look to the sea and link up with the others when the Japanese tightened the camp security system. The party discovered a man-hole giving access to a typhoon drain which ran under the camp for over fifty yards to the sea and after one or two false starts they got away by this tunnel and swam to some boat-building yards. Their objective was to make for the Kowloon hills and they had to spend a week hiding in the undergrowth on Lion Rock Hill. They were fed by two fishermen and sheltered in Chung Mei village on Tolo harbour, from where they boarded a junk which took them to Sha Yu Chung, a village on the north of Mirs Bay, from which they were conducted to Tamshui where they were handed over to one Yip Foo, described as 'a charming old rogue' who was later found to have left-wing connexions with Saikung in the New Territories. Eventually they were taken to Waichow and met up with other escapees at Kukong.

Capt. R. D. Scriven, of the Indian Army Medical Service,

Captain Hewitt and P/O Crossley, R.A.F., who was a New Zealander, escaped by sampan at four o'clock in the morning, and like so many others made their way to a Hakka village, Woon Yui, and were then taken by guides to Waichow. Two sappers, Ferguson and Howarth, who both gained the Military Medal, escaped in October 1942 after receiving shelter and attention to their badly-cut feet from the Siu Lik Yuen village, where they were given a note enabling them to contact the guerrillas for passage to Free China.

The New Territories villagers were promised rewards for helping British escapees. This promise was fulfilled when the British came back after the war and a committee with the District Officer of the New Territories as chairman collected the evidence and made recommendations which were accepted by the Supreme Allied Commander, South-East Asia Command. At a ceremony in Government House on 15 February 1947 money grants were made to the villages and certificates of merit to the individuals. One Chinese was rewarded for assisting S/Sgt. Sheridan, R.A.S.C., to escape to Kwongchouwan; no detail was given in the press account of the ceremony just mentioned, but presumably he went by boat or junk to Macao, possibly via Lantao, and got a ship from there.[9]

Four British servicemen were taken to safety from Kowloon by the B.A.A.G. underground. At the trial of an Indian collaborator in March 1947, another Indian described how he assisted a Lance-Corporal Cedric Salter, of the Royal Scots, to escape by putting him in contact with a B.A.A.G. agent. Salter had apparently remained outside, stoutly maintaining that he was a Swiss. Three others including Pte. J. White of the Royal Scots, who had been hidden in Kowloon by a friend, were similarly helped. Ellen Field has described how she was brought in to act as a foil in all four cases.[10] The agent and the escapee, the latter dressed in each case as a Chinese, went by bus late at night to the outskirts of Kowloon, and the agent, the same man on each occasion, then walked

[9] Cf. F.O. 371/31671/1. Report of escape by S/Sgt. Sheridan. He was employed by the Japanese as a baker and given a pass to go around Hong Kong. He says he asked for permission to go to Kwongchouwan, which was granted, and he left the Colony on 3 June 1942.

[10] Ellen Field, *Twilight in Hong Kong* (London, 1960).

along the road some distance before stepping off into the bush, discreetly followed at some distance by the escapee. It was after these escapes and an unsuccessful tunnelling attempt that in May the Japanese forced the inmates to sign an undertaking not to escape.[11]

The last of the escapes from Shamshuipo and perhaps one of the most spectacular, a feat of endurance, courage and great fortune, was that of Lt.-Cdr. Ralph Goodwin, R.N.Z.N.V.R. in July 1944. By then the camp had been surrounded by a strong fence, with four strands of electric wire, with coils of barbed wire at the base and at the top of the fence and more barbed wire on the outer side. A second electrified but less formidable fence was a short distance away from the first on the two landward sides of the camp. By wearing rubber-soled shoes and stepping on the insulators of the electrified wire fixed to the fence posts, he was able to climb over the fence and jump to the other side, and after negotiating the second fence which was only five feet high (as his vivid account of this desperate adventure reveals, this was only the beginning of an arduous exhausting escape), he made his way in pouring rain up Butterfly Valley and the Shingmun River to Shatin, then to Taipo and, by-passing Sha Tau Kok, to the northern shore of Mirs Bay. This stage of the escape took eleven days, at the end of which Goodwin was ill and exhausted. But again he was taken care of by villagers, the East River Striking Force, and the Kwangtung Peoples' Anti-Japanese Guerrilla Group, and his passage to Waichow was arranged by them.

Not all were lucky enough to succeed in their attempts to escape. Three British officers, one Indian officer and eleven other ranks were believed to have been shot for attempting to escape. Goodwin mentioned in his book that a party attempted to get away in October 1942, but were discovered and executed. Quite early on, four Canadians attempted to escape from North Point Camp, apparently before it was emptied of war prisoners in April 1942, but they were recaptured next day and later executed. This action was defended at the subsequent War Crimes trial of Col. Tokunaga on the ground that the men had signed an undertaking not to escape. The Colonel

[11] Luff, op. cit., pp. 193–4.

admitted in January 1947 that the four Canadians and also seven British prisoners of war had been reported shot while attempting to escape, though in fact they had been executed some days later. The seven British were sappers who were discovered in the act of tunnelling in September 1942. All were buried in the prisoner-of-war cemetery at Argyle Street, and a careful record of burials with the cause of death was kept by the Japanese which was later produced at the War Crimes trials.

Finally, mention must be made of a striking success by the B.A.A.G. whose agents, with help from the villagers of Lin Ma Hang, in March 1943 succeeded in liberating a large contingent of Indian troops to Free China.

A number of civilians managed to get away from Hong Kong during the occupation. Some escaped from Stanley Camp, and some evaded internment there and made their escape from town. Two parties escaped from Stanley on the same night, apparently unknown to each other, in March 1942. One party, including Police-Superintendent W. P. Thompson, Mrs. Gwen Priestwood, a lorry driver in the Defence Services, and others, made their way to Cape Collinson and were rowed across to the temple at Joss House Bay by six Shaukeiwan boatmen, whence they made their way to Saikung and by the usual route to Waichow. The second party consisting of F. W. Wright, Miss Elsie Fairfax-Cholmondeley, and three others, including an American seaman, O'Neill, escaped by sea and reached the village of Tong Fuk on Lantao Island where they buried their boat and hid for a time until a junk from Cheung Chau was organized to take them to Macao. They were led to Free China by the Macao underground. It was affirmed at a collaboration trial in November 1946 that the Hong Kong Government Defence Secretary, J. A. Fraser, organized one or perhaps both of the escape parties.

An American Missionary, Father Tooney, of the American Maryknoll Mission, who had refused repatriation in June 1942, escaped from Stanley in the following year because he found conditions there too bad. This was achieved through local contacts.

As in the case of the military, some civilian attempts were unsuccessful. Three policemen, a superintendent, a police cadet and a sergeant, and a member of the staff of the China Light and Power Company got away from Stanley Camp on 8 April 1942 but only enjoyed two days of freedom. They were discovered and confined for some time in the Happy Valley Gendarmerie, eventually sentenced, and kept in Stanley Gaol until 20 June 1944.

From the town there were a number of escapes. Professor Gordon King[12] with other members of the University, the buildings of which were used as an auxiliary hospital, had been allowed to remain out of Stanley to continue his medical duties. He already had experience of the Japanese in Chefoo in northern China, and decided to escape after some unpleasant incidents over the collecting of fuel at May Hall, where some five hundred people were being kept. Helped by Chinese friends and former students and shabbily dressed, he left on 10 February 1942, mingled with the crowd on the ferry and bus to Kowloon Tong, slipped past Kai Tak while the guard was being changed, picked up his guide at Customs Pass and with an escort of armed guerrillas reached Saikung and was lodged in a temple. There he met J. H. Marsman, and three others. Marsman, an American businessman from the Philippines, claimed to be a Filipino and so was allowed to live in town. His local business associates advanced him $25,000 and planned his escape by way of Customs Pass where he found coolies posted every 500 yards, leading him to the Saikung area where he met Professor Gordon King. They were kept five nights huddled in the bottom of a sampan before it was safe to cross Tolo harbour, and were then taken by guerrillas to Waichow. Mr. A. H. Bentley, a Government pharmacist, also one of the University group allowed to stay out, escaped on Chinese New Year's Day 1942, soon after Professor King, using the same contacts and the same route.

Four Chinese students attempted to leave May Hall at the University for Free China in 1943, but were discovered and accused of espionage. Three were executed and one died in prison.

[12] Professor Gordon King has recently given an account of this escape and of his subsequent work in China, assisting ex-Hong Kong students, in the Daphne Chun Memorial Lecture given in 1973. 'An Episode in the History of the University of Hong Kong', *Supplement to the Gazette*, Vol. XX, No. 6, 1 August 1973.

The bankers kept out to assist the Japanese in the financial take-over had been quartered in the Sun Wah Hotel, one of the less elegant hotels on the waterfront. Two of these, T. J. J. Fenwick, the Chief Accountant of the Hongkong and Shanghai Banking Corporation and a colleague, J. A. D. Morrison escaped in October 1942. The escape was engineered by the B.A.A.G. which was asked by the British Embassy in Chungking to get Sir Vandeleur Grayburn and his wife out of Hong Kong to attend to the bank's affairs in England. Sir Vandeleur had intended getting away to Singapore but had been caught by the suddenness of the Japanese attack. A plan of escape was prepared, but at the last moment Grayburn refused to go, and Fenwick and Morrison were assisted to get out instead. They followed a hawker at dusk out of the hotel, took a tram at the Supreme Court, made their way to North Point where a small sampan was ready and after a precarious trip were put ashore at Lyemun, where twenty armed guerrillas suddenly rose from the undergrowth and guided them to safety at Waichow where they arrived carrying their sole piece of luggage, a Hong Kong basket containing half a bottle of gin. They eventually made their way to Kweilin, India, and London.[13]

Many third nationals were able to leave without much difficulty unless they came under suspicion by the gendarmerie. Phyllis Harrop, who had worked for the Secretariat for Chinese Affairs and was able to claim German citizenship through a previous marriage, was able without much difficulty to take ship to Macao on 27 January 1942 from where she picked up Chinese contacts who helped her to get to Kwongchouwan, and so on to Chungking.[14] Ellen Field, who claimed to be Irish, got to Macao also by boat in 1944, and some of the Jesuit Fathers also went to Macao and thence to Kwongchouwan by sea.

A local resident, a newspaperman, A. C. Greaves, was reported in the *Hong Kong News* on 10 September 1945 as having escaped from Hong Kong, though no details were given. Like so many he took ship to Macao in 1942 and with the help of the British Consul there, went on to Kwongchouwan by

[13] M. Collis, *Wayfoong: A History of The Hongkong & Shanghai Bank* (London, 1964), pp. 228–9.

[14] P. Harrop, *Hong Kong Incident* (London, 1942).

ship and then reached Kweilin mainly by foot-slogging, where he joined the B.A.A.G., rising to the rank of Captain.

Chinese had no difficulty in getting out, because the Japanese encouraged them to leave; getting in again was the difficulty.[15] Even so, many Chinese preferred to slip away secretly rather than apply for an exit pass which meant enquiry by the gendarmes. Emily Hahn, an American who refused the offer of evacuation in June 1942 by claiming Chinese nationality, had little difficulty in remaining until she eventually accepted repatriation on 1 September 1944.[16]

Finally there must be recorded the case of three Scandinavians who were literally forced to escape, a rather amusing episode related in the newspapers of 4 June 1947. The three friendly neutrals decided to have a picnic in Customs Pass in the course of which they were surrounded by over-zealous guerrillas and conducted to Free China despite their protests and having made no preparations whatever. They were just forced to be free. Members of the B.A.A.G. who met them in Waichow in 1943 have vouched for the accuracy of this story.

[15] One Chinese lady has given an account of a dangerous and abortive mission to smuggle herself into Hong Kong in order to retrieve some valuable possessions. Liang Yen, *The House of the Golden Dragon* (London, 1961).

[16] E. Hahn, *China to Me* (Philadelphia, 1944).

IX

STANLEY CIVILIAN INTERNMENT CAMP[1]

'All are here from the first class passengers to the steerage: all are reduced to a certain equality.'

J.A. Stericker, 'Captive Colony' (unpublished MS.)

THE Japanese decided to concentrate local enemy civilians in an internment camp in the Stanley peninsula on the south side of the Island, using the prison officers' quarters and the St. Stephen's College buildings. A healthier site could not have been chosen. So, a cheerless fortnight spent by them in the squalid waterfront doss-houses was ended when about half of the internees moved out on 20 January 1942 and the remainder the following day. The site had been suggested by Dr. Selwyn-Clarke and accepted by the Japanese after consultation with Mr. F. C. Gimson.

Virtually nothing had been done to prepare the camp for the new arrivals. A small advance party had been able to achieve little except deal with corpses still unburied, though the fighting had been over for nearly a month. The reservation of accommodation proved futile as the number of internees greatly exceeded that anticipated, and it was thought friends would want to be together, with the result no detailed billeting scheme was ready. There were no cooking facilities, no furniture, little crockery or cutlery, toilet facilities were filthy, shamefully inadequate, and without water.

The accommodation consisted partly of the residential quarters of the European, Indian and Chinese prison officers, and the minor staff and their families. Other prison buildings such as the sanitorium, Tweed Bay Hospital, and the prison officers' canteen, and the neighbouring St. Stephen's College buildings and staff bungalows were also occupied.

[1] The most authoritative printed account is by J. Stericker, *A Tear for the Dragon* (London, 1958). Stericker was Secretary to F. C. Gimson, the 'official' spokesman of the internees. Stericker wrote a detailed history of the camp but this was not published. The manuscript is held in Hong Kong University library.

The Dutch and Americans soon settled in.[2] The former, numbering sixty, included a few Belgians and occupied a building adjoining the prison officers' canteen. The 291 Americans, including twelve children under three years, were put into a large block which formerly served as the European prison officers' bachelor quarters. The British, numbering 2,325 with ninety-one children under three, had the remainder, but had much greater difficulty fitting themselves in, and were milling around for some time. There were many more of them than expected, for it seemed that the Japanese intended the term 'British Nationals' to mean Europeans and were surprised at the number of Asians who claimed to be British. People tended to settle in where they could and left any adjustment arising, for instance, from obvious incompatibility, until later. This haphazard beginning tended to continue, based on an unwritten rule that everybody fended for himself or herself and no one asked or expected favours. On 30 January there were ninety-six new arrivals from St. Paul's College, and in the second week of February more crowded in. These were the residents from the Peak who had been allowed to stay out by friendly Japanese officers on the personal word of the Chief Justice, Sir Atholl MacGregor, and another group from the University who were now ordered into Stanley possibly as a reprisal for the escape of two of the number. In August 1942 nearly ninety nurses came in.

The result was ghastly congestion. For example, Professor Sewell's family of five, newly arrived from the Peak, was led to a room in a European prison officer's flat, to meet a chilling reception from its five existing occupants who made no move until directly ordered by the billeting officer to make room for five more. These ten persons, three men, four women, and three children, thrown together quite arbitrarily, lived and slept in this one room until the Americans were repatriated in July 1942, when the Sewell family was given a small room, 14 feet by 12 feet, to themselves. They considered themselves lucky. There were 501, nearly all men, in St. Stephen's College which normally housed 180 boys; they were comparatively well-off, with three to each cubicle 14 ft. by 10 ft. which was

[2] See Marian Dudley's typescript, 'Hong Kong Prison Camp', (1942).

equipped with cots. They also had some cutlery and crockery, whereas other internees had to make do with tin cans and tin lids as cups and plates. There were 780 internees packed into the Indian warders' quarters, with 82 sharing one toilet, and women could nowhere be given any privacy. The average space per person was 41 square feet, and as late as December 1942 there were still 700 without makeshift beds. The situation was eased by the repatriation of Shanghai residents to Shanghai in May, and of Americans in July 1942.

Sewage disposal was one immediate and pressing problem and was resolved by digging seven septic tanks, four of them outside the camp boundary. It was difficult to get men to volunteer for this essential work because, as Dr. N. C. MacLeod, the Deputy Director of Health Services, who acted as the Camp Health Officer, put it in his report on Stanley Camp, 'the typical Hong Kongite still regarded menial work as being the birthright of the Chinese'.[3] But as time went on volunteers came forward when work was seen to be necessary.

The average population over the whole three years and eight months was officially given as 2,500 plus 106 children under the age of 3. Older children seemed to have gone unrecorded because no special food or other arrangements were made for them, but they numbered altogether about 300. The British section included Chinese, Portuguese, Eurasians and people of various other origins, many being families of prisoners of war. The usual legal records of births and deaths were kept; the latter numbered 31 in 1942, 18 in 1943, 40 in 1944 and 32 up to 31 August 1945, a total of 152; while births numbered 22 in 1942, 10 in 1943, 13 in 1944, and 6 up to August 1945. The birth rate was low statistically, but as Dr. MacLeod's report wryly put it, 'by the nature of our circumstances it should have been lower'.

Camp life was a new way of life. Ill-clothed and hungry, people lived cheek by jowl, day and night, in grossly over-crowded conditions lacking the basic necessities of a civilized life. It is small wonder that many could not adapt themselves to this strange existence; quarrels, accusations, petty meannesses

[3] Dr. P. S. Selwyn-Clarke, *Report on Medical and Health Conditions in Hong Kong, 1st January–31st August, 1945* (London, H.M.S.O., 1946); Dr. MacLeod's report is to be found at Appendix III to this Report.

and suspicion were starkly manifested, and yet many showed patience, humanity, and helpfulness. One discerning and humane anglican priest has said

'. . . there were uglier aspects of internment than the heartaches, privations and near-tragedies. . . . There were cruelty, terror, things sordid and shameful, degradation and callousness. . . . There were broken bodies, broken lives, broken hearts and broken faiths. . . . Yet in spite of this there was manifested in the community, and I think made more available than in normal times, a quality of life which was nearer to eternal life.'[4]

As the years of internment went by and conditions became harsher, some remarked a growing moral deterioration that matched the physical, and many passed the point at which they could be strengthened by suffering and privation. As Professor Sewell, a Quaker, observed, 'It is impossible for any ordinary person to be moral under the desperate conditions of hopeless poverty.'[5]

The main pre-occupation was food. Daily food rations were fixed at: flour a quarter of a catty, sugar one-fiftieth of a catty and salt one-fiftieth of a catty per person, and coal one ton per hundred persons per month, and any extras had to be paid for, the committees being responsible for collecting the money. In the event, camp living conditions were quite different. The Japanese issued rations each day, and the internees did the rest. Kitchens had to be improvised out of nothing. At first, twelve were set up, each serving a block and dealing with the food as its inmates thought best, but later they were reduced to three to economize in fuel. In the early days the rations were sufficient to give each a bowl of rice, a spoonful of meat or fish, some vegetable and some bread for which the internees lined up twice a day, at 10 a.m. and 5 p.m., in queues which formed early in the chance that left-overs might yield a second helping for the lucky few who, having already consumed their first, were ready to line up a second time. Queueing for food and hot water might occupy anything up to five hours per day. Hunger gave rise to much petty dishonesty, and ration cards had to be issued and checked to prevent a person

[4] Revd. A. P. Rose in foreword to W. G. Sewell, *Strange Harmony* (London, 1946).
[5] Sewell, op. cit., p. 170.

from drawing more than one ration. During the last two years of the camp, conditions seriously deteriorated and the ration was reduced to rice and vegetables; meat and bread disappeared from the rations, and the inmates were faced with slow starvation.

The Japanese allowed individual gardens, but later required them to be put on a communal basis to supplement the official rations. The fuel ration expired and supplies were obtained during the last two years only by stripping the rooms of picture rails, floor boards and doors, and eventually, as a last resort, even heroically sacrificing the lavatory door.

The town water-supply was cut because shortage of fuel stopped the pumps from working. This added a new misery to existence. Water was cut back to a few hours a day and ultimately every fifth day, and as the hours of supply were often arbitrarily varied, washing and cleaning had to be done in good time to allow storing. After November 1944 the supply was cut off altogether and the camp had to rely on a local stream, helped by an official Japanese issue of two pints a day of boiled chlorinated water, though doubt was expressed whether this had in fact been properly treated.

The food was described in Dr. MacLeod's report as 'monotonous, unpalatable, unsuitable and scarce'. All rations were inspected by the Government Medical Department health staff, but since bad food was not replaced little could be done and risks had to be taken. Eating shellfish had to be stopped because of the fear of contamination, as town sewage was now being dumped in the harbour. Occasionally the rice contained godown sweepings, sand, stones, glass, cigarette ends, and cockroaches, but it was that or nothing. No special rations were supplied for infants, mothers, or the sick, until this was remedied by Dr. Selwyn-Clarke who sent in milk and special foods, but on a scale sufficient only to provide for children under five. A Camp Milk Board, under the chairmanship of the Deputy Director of Medical Services as the Camp Medical Officer, reported that they were never completely without some supply of milk.

The internees were saved from starvation by food from various outside sources. Friends sent parcels, as they did to the prisoner-of-war camps, leaving them open, at the Civil

Administration Office in the Hongkong and Shanghai Bank Building. A lucky few, but under 10 per cent of the total number living in Stanley, had weekly parcels from Chinese wives who were not interned, or from Chinese, Eurasian, or neutral European friends. Red Cross parcels from Britain in September 1942 noticeably improved the health of the camp, and according to one account the distribution amounted to two parcels each on that occasion. In 1944 a few bulk supplies of corned beef and dried milk and Red Cross parcels from Canada again saved the situation which was rapidly becoming desperate. Perhaps the greatest single benefactor to the camp was Dr. Selwyn-Clarke, who was allowed to visit the camp and always brought extra food. He organized in the town the Informal Welfare Committee which gave invaluable help to prisoners, internees and their families and was financed from sources in and outside the Colony. After Dr. Selwyn-Clarke was imprisoned in Stanley Prison in May 1943 his work was taken over by the International Red Cross.

Then there was the canteen at which could be bought extras such as sugar, chocolate, tinned meat, jam and beans. Long queues formed because late would-be purchasers were turned away if those who came earlier bought more than their share, until a system of numbered tabs ensured strict rotation. The canteen had been proposed and agreed to by the Japanese as early as 26 January, though many months passed before it materialized, but limited supplies of stock meant that its services were only spasmodic. People would start queueing at five in the morning until it opened at 1.30 p.m.; later, cards were issued for each building and one person could buy on behalf of four. Only one item from each food group could be bought, e.g. tinned beef or mutton, fruit salad or jam, coffee, tea, or chocolate, or, alternatively, soap or household utensils could be chosen. Prices were high, for example, half a pound of chocolate cost $8 and a pound of brown sugar $6. There was little small change, and a $100 bill was worth only $68 and a $50 bill only $27.

More important, in the last year when rations were at starvation level and the Japanese themselves were suffering because of the allied blockade, there was the illicit trade 'over the wire'.

This had gone on in some degree throughout the whole period of internment, often in the middle of the night to avoid detection. When money ran short, the guards accepted articles of value, particularly gold and jewellery which were in great demand, and they pocketed a handsome rake-off. Faces were slapped in the case of the more blatant offenders against camp regulations, but the Japanese camp administration made no serious attempt to halt the commerce altogether so the black market continued and kept many alive. During the last year of captivity the black market indeed burgeoned into big business by the use of cheques or I.O.U.s, payable after the war. Many internees had no money, and many others found their money and jewellery close to exhaustion by 1944. The simple process of writing a cheque or an I.O.U. produced ready cash and therefore food, if a middleman or agent could be found to accept it. The discount was naturally considerable because of the risk of the I.O.U.s not being honoured. A man's word had to be accepted and the terms varied according to his standing; members of large companies of international repute had 25 yen to the pound sterling, employees of big local firms 20 yen to the pound, professional men 15 yen to the pound, and so on down to doubtful risks who had to be satisfied with as little as 4 yen to the pound. Those still with valuables to sell could have a sterling cheque or the equivalent in food. Prices were outrageously high and £500 would buy about 25/6d worth of food at normal peace-time prices. People were driven by sheer desperation to pledge the future to ward off starvation. The middlemen, Chinese and Europeans, were of course essential to the proceedings which were euphemistically regarded as commercial transactions, and they cashed in handsomely. To regard people goaded by starvation as being free to make commercial bargains was of course plain hypocrisy, and to turn these exceptional circumstances to commercial advantage would seem to deny the morality basic to the decencies of community life. The justification, if there is one, lies in the fact that the I.O.U.s were generally honoured despite the fact that the Hong Kong Government after the war officially released all individuals concerned from the letter of their engagements. A few held out against the I.O.U. system on principle, and survived on the issued rations. It is estimated that about six million yen passed over the wire between October 1944 and March 1945.

The result of the bad feeding was malnutrition and its associated diseases. Beriberi and pellagra were kept down mainly because of medicines sent in by Dr. Selwyn-Clarke; home-made yeast was produced in an old ambulance van used as a laboratory and bran was purchased from the town. Cuts and scratches would not heal and remained septic; dried bones were used for calcium to treat rotting teeth, and the cutting of finger-nails and toe-nails was unnecessary, as they hardly grew. Vegetables were later boiled in seawater to overcome the shortage of salt. More frequently malnutrition resulted in inertia, giddiness, inability to concentrate, irritability, and obvious loss of weight, though this was perhaps not entirely disadvantageous in some cases.

The camp site was salubrious; but even so it is to the credit of some forty doctors, two dentists, six pharmacists and 100 trained nurses that no major epidemic occurred. Tuberculosis was serious owing to malnutrition, overcrowding and the absence of X-ray equipment in the leprosarium which was used as a T.B. hospital. There were three clinics in the three main residential areas, St. Stephen's College, the Indian quarters and European quarters, and also special clinics for nutrition, surgery, ear nose and throat and eyes, also dental clinics. Drugs and medical stores came from the hospitals, from Dr. Selwyn-Clarke, and from the Red Cross. The Japanese sent some medical supplies, but as Dr. Valentine, the Camp Medical Officer, caustically remarked, 'Perhaps the most valuable of their contributions was the supply of stationery . . .'! In fact, the Japanese, perhaps understandably, sent in supplies of whatever happened to be available, rather than what was needed. Dysentery was rife during the first year with 410 cases, after which there was little, and typhoid was rare because everybody had been inoculated. Malaria was more serious because the Japanese refused to allow anti-malarial work in the camp until nearly the end of 1942. Then parties were allowed outside the wire, but very irregularly, and none at all between February and July 1943, until the Japanese themselves suffered, when permission to work outside the camp was renewed. But malaria could not be eliminated, and there were 143 cases in 1942, 331 in 1943, 151 in 1944, and 57 up to August 1945.

Few of those who assembled on the Murray Parade Ground on 5 January 1942 guessed that they would not see their homes again for three years and eight months, and most were pitifully ill-supplied with clothes. The worst deficiency was shoes. Clogs or bits of board were worn with some attachment, however flimsy, over the bridge of the foot, while canvas shoes with toes protruding were common; soles were refitted with cardboard or any other materials that came to hand. Footwear remained the most serious problem, and by the last year many were reduced to walking bare-foot. The men wore shorts in summer, and Dr. MacLeod noted that, 'Some ladies wore little more than natural sun-tan.' The ladies showed remarkable ingenuity in producing embellishment out of the most unlikely materials, and relieving the drabness by some sort of design. The girls unravelled gunny sacks or canvas to get sewing thread, and cut up curtains to add to their wardrobes. Generally, since the same clothes often served by night as well as by day, neatness of dress was difficult to maintain.

For some time there was no soap or any cleaning materials, and only after much protest was a free issue of four ounces of soap a month made in the last year. Most men shaved, once the necessary art of sharpening a safety razor blade was mastered. The smoker for his requirements either expended valuable funds trading over the wire, or was forced to smoke pine-needles or sweet-potato leaves. Some just unblushingly went around picking up cigarette butts and acquired no little skill in rolling them in whatever paper they could come by. Beds were used as settees and a canvas bed repair shop soon became necessary; a shoe repair shop served those who could provide the materials, and there was a spectacle-frame repair shop and a soya bean milk factory producing about 50 pints a day. The Japanese supplied 400 *mintois* for the beds, but this was woefully inadequate.

There was no serious crime but much anti-social activity since, with a number of honourable exceptions, each person was out for himself. Petty larceny, prompted by need, was committed by people to whom it would have been inconceivable in normal times. Public order and the common interest required a camp controlling authority, and this was a matter on which the British internees were torn by dissension. The Hong Kong Government still regarded itself as responsible for good order and welfare of the British community and did not regard defeat and internment as abrogating either its right or its duty to govern, and considered disloyalty to it as amounting to disloyalty to the Crown. And, it must be conceded, government officials did excellent work; for example the medical and health officers undertook camp responsibilities as part of their official government duties, and vital statistics of camp births and deaths were kept as required by law as a matter of normal civil service routine.

On the other hand, the Colony's Government had made itself intensely disliked. There had been scandals over the Immigration and Air Raid Precautions Departments and an enquiry into corruption in Government generally had been started, while compulsory evacuation had created deep bitterness and charges of favouritism. Perhaps the most potent source of anti-government feeling was the humiliation of defeat. The Government was accused of inefficiency and of having called for futile sacrifices to carry on a struggle which it knew was doomed to failure from the start. Political dissension split the camp, and most inmates were adamant that Government officers should not be allowed to repeat in Stanley the fiasco they were accused of having perpetrated outside. Loyalty to the Crown was one thing but loyalty to a number of discredited officials quite another.

The camp had been going only three days when a Camp Temporary Committee was elected,[6] a tribute to the British instinct for law and order. The elections were a little haphazard but it was felt better to go ahead, rather than wait until satisfactory electoral arrangements could be worked out. Eight were elected and five more were elected in time for the second meeting next day, and there was only one Government officer among the thirteen. The committee appointed camp officials

[6] Editor's note: see my article, 'Confinement and Constitutional Conflict in Occupied Hong Kong 1941–5', *Hong Kong Law Journal*, Vol. 3, Pt. III (September 1973), pp. 293–318, reprinted as Appendix No. 5. This is based mainly on Sir Franklin Gimson's several own accounts and diary, covering part of the internment, now held in Rhodes House Library, Oxford.

and a number of Government officers also attended, until the committee numbered twenty-eight when it was eventually decided to restrict it to elected members only. Mr. F. C. Gimson, who was still in the town, attended personally or was represented by the Defence Secretary, J. A. Fraser. The committee voted its own demise on 18 February 1942 when new elections were held, resulting in eight members being elected to represent the various blocks or districts. A week later six additional members were elected to represent the camp as a whole, an experiment which was not repeated. The name British Communal Council was adopted. There was an executive committee and a number of other working committees, including co-opted members, which dealt with law, order, labour, the canteen, supplies, relief and welfare, billeting, medical sanitation and water, construction and maintenance, electric light and power, recreation, education and religion. The internees insisted on electing the chairman and vice-chairman which was done at a special camp election on 2 March 1942. The standing of the Colonial Secretary, who eventually came in to Stanley camp as an internee on 11 March, was safeguarded by his having the right to attend all meetings of the council and to represent the camp in negotiations with the Japanese as Camp Commandant. It was agreed that in internal matters the Executive Committee would work with the knowledge and consent of the Colonial Secretary and that in external matters the Colonial Secretary would work with the knowledge and consent of the executive committee.

The Colonial Secretary was not satisfied with this compromise and wanted to reserve what he claimed were the powers of the Crown. When the Americans left in July 1942 some re-shuffling of the accommodation occurred, and new elections were suggested. A petition from one district that a new council should be elected with the Colonial Secretary as *ex officio* chairman, which was supported by Gimson, caused acute dissension as many felt that the petition had been engineered and that discreditable methods were being used to oust the council and its elected chairman.

The new council, named the British Community Council, was elected on 15 August 1942 and was advisory to the Colonial

Secretary, who was now in effective control; the former committees generally continued, but under a camp officer appointed by him. The Japanese insisted on dealing solely with Gimson and refused to recognize any democratic British constitutional forms, but they forced him to drop the term Camp Commandant and call himself 'Representative of the Internees'. They refused to allow a British law court to sit in camp, and a Camp Disciplinary Committee dealt with the offences against camp administration, while a billeting Appeal Tribunal formed from a panel of well-known citizens dealt with accommodation grievances. The Japanese censored all committee minutes and camp notices, and to avoid this camp notices were often sent around by hand, giving decisions, explaining what was being done, and advising people on the regulations. The camp representatives were usually criticized for not doing enough, or not taking a strong enough line with the Japanese, and were often suspected of keeping ordinary internees in the dark about what was going on. The American section had an elected committee, but a tough 'boss' and his associates exercised power, and though his methods were seen to be discreditable, no one felt strong enough to interfere.

Because many internees had come into Stanley quite destitute, the British almost immediately set up an International Welfare Committee with two members from each national community, under the chairmanship of the Hong Kong Government European Lady Almoner. This first met on 4 February 1942. Its tasks were (a) to discover the specific needs of individual internees, (b) to distribute equitably articles received, (c) to distribute food on the basis of medical necessity alone and (d) to keep records of children and infants. In July 1942, after the Americans had gone, it was expanded by adding representatives of the four main blocks and the Colonial Secretary himself became chairman. The committee adopted a completely impartial stand, using need as the sole criterion. Dr. Selwyn-Clarke worked through the committee in sending money, food and clothing, and an advisory panel of doctors advised on medical needs. A small surcharge was made on each article sold in the canteen and the proceeds used to purchase extra food for distribution to the needy. There was also a Camp Relief Fund which helped internees in financial need. Just before the liberation the two committees amalgamated.

On 20 March 1942 five internees, including a police superintendent and Gwen Priestwood, a woman truck-driver of the Defence Services, escaped by night via Cape Collinson with the assistance of Chinese friends outside, and the same night, apparently by coincidence, another party, including Americans and Miss Elsie Fairfax-Cholmondeley,[7] who had been assisting with a left-wing Chinese journal advocating agrarian reform in China, escaped by boat to Macao. As a result, the camp area was restricted and wired in, an additional roll call imposed at 10 p.m., and all had to be in their rooms between 8.0 p.m. and 8.0 a.m., with lights out at 11.0 p.m. The inmates had up to this time enjoyed a surprising amount of freedom.

To round off the gloomy picture, the inmates had little or no personal or family news; wives at Stanley were kept in complete ignorance of their menfolk in the prisoner-of-war camps only a few miles away, a seemingly unnecessary piece of unfeeling inhumanity. The Japanese quite callously neglected to publish a complete list of the Stanley Camp internees and the first news relatives overseas had, in many cases, was that taken out by the Americans on repatriation in July 1942. In February 1942 they were allowed to send post cards to neutrals in the town, and on 10 April post cards could be sent to the prisoners of war, but since a strict censorship was imposed, it was weeks or months before they were dispatched. In May 1942 internees were allowed to send ten-word messages via Tokyo, but many of these never arrived, and in 1943 a monthly letter written in conventional phrases of twenty-five words could be sent. One internee had ten post cards during the whole period; he received his first letter from his wife after two years and three months, and had four overseas letters during the whole period of internment. Normal mail routes were disrupted, of course, but mail was held up largely because of the shortage of censors, nevertheless the inmates regarded this hold-up as deliberate. Another internee family had sixty-five letters while in camp, about half from England and America, and half local.

[7] Now Mrs. Epstein, who has remained in China.

Radio communication was forbidden, but, as in the case of the prisoner-of-war camps, dauntless men began to operate secret radio sets, braving the known risks, and spread news which helped to counter the feeling of isolation and despair. Two radios were quite secret and the inmates were kept in ignorance of them since the fewer who knew of these the better. John Stericker remarked, 'Most prison camps have their Judas who is willing to sell his soul. Ours was no exception.' In July 1943 the Japanese struck, as they did at Shamshuipo and Argyle Street, and some twelve inmates were arrested. At the same time, some British bankers living in town were accused of espionage, and put into Stanley Gaol with the other accused. On 19 October 1943 seven internees, including John Fraser, Defence Secretary, were sentenced to death, four others were sentenced to long terms of imprisonment. The death sentences were carried out on Stanley beach, visible from the camp, which was informed on 2 November. Altogether, thirty suffered the death penalty at that time. After that no one felt secure. The chairman of The Hongkong and Shanghai Banking Corporation, Sir Vandeleur Grayburn, was also accused of complicity in an espionage ring and sentenced to one hundred days' imprisonment, but he succumbed to ill-treatment and his body was handed over for burial. Edmonston, his deputy at the bank, also died in the same way in Stanley Gaol in August 1944. Dr. Selwyn-Clarke was imprisoned in Stanley Gaol, but was later released and joined his family in Ma Tau Chung Camp.

The camp cemetery occupied a casuarina-shaded plot which was an old military cemetery and adjoined St. Stephen's College grounds. Its oldest graves were those of British soldiers and their families, dating from the 1840s and the 1860s. For the new interments a single coffin with a false bottom had to serve for all occasions, for wood was impossible to get.

But camp life was not one of unrelieved gloom. Children were least affected in morale, and took the new conditions in their stride. They knew no other life and quickly acclimatized themselves to the limitations of camp existence, and temporarily carried some habits acquired there into freedom. 'They had to learn again the very art of using knives and forks,' wrote Gawan Sewell, adding delightfully. 'It was many months before Guy ceased to lick his plate and Joy refrained from peeping into dust-bins.' The children went hungry, but they became used to it and had a more communal life with their friends than would ordinarily have been the case. Birthday parties went on with tastefully produced invitations, and the fare was generally graced with some small carefully husbanded extra. Schools were soon organized with the voluntary assistance of the many teachers, and over fifty seniors met in St. Stephen's College Hall and over 100 juniors in the Prison Officers' Club Hall; at first scholars sat on the ground or on grass-filled sacks, but at the end of 1942 they used desks sent by the International Red Cross. The parents supported the education plans, but the camp community as a whole took little interest. One major difficulty was the shortage of writing materials, for paper was a distressingly scarce commodity; school reports, on the usual pattern, were given each term. Matriculation classes were held and two examinations taken, and freedom came just in time to forestall the third. The second class had many adults, including police officers.

Lectures and discussions were conducted by members of the university staff and others with professional qualifications.[8] Some subjects were cultural and some were aimed at a specific qualification, such as that of ship's officer. They attracted great interest, were well-attended, and created considerable discussion, but had to be suspended when a curfew was imposed, or allied air raids necessitated a black-out, or when the electric light failed altogether, at which times discussions were held in the dark. They were instrumental in maintaining and strengthening the group spirit, but the black-out generally was a great trial, particularly for those with sick children.

Then there was entertainment. It was said of Stanley, never was there a place with so little to do and so little time to do it. Internees had a limited access to the beach at Tweed Bay, which provided some of the finest sea-bathing in the Colony. During the first two years there were cricket, football, base-ball games, and health and beauty exercises, but during the last two years when food was deficient, these physical activities

[8] For example, see G. P. de Martin, *Told in the Dark* (S.C.M.P., 1946). This book, as the author says, reprints the talks given either in the flickering light of an inch of candle or, literally, in complete darkness.

had to be abandoned for lack of energy. The consumption of alcohol ceased abruptly on entering camp, apparently without serious adverse effects.

There were concerts and other diversions. One on 14 November 1942 was lavishly advertised in freehand coloured sketches as a 'Koncert', with 'Klean, Krazy, Kinloch's Kasino Kops' showing dancers being watched by an audience wearing the broad arrow clothing reminiscent of Dartmoor. Internees provided musical items, wrote and acted plays, performed ballet, sang, and danced. The Japanese censored all concerts and entertainments, for example in the masque of Pyramus and Thisbe they ruled out the hole in the wall through which the lovers whispered, as they thought the two fingers, representing the chink in the wall, stood for the 'V' for Victory sign. People tried to amuse themselves as in normal life until the last two years when survival took all the available energy, and the total black-out at night, in any case, made the normal evening concert difficult. Dancing was banned by the Japanese, as it was in town. Fortunately there was a good supply of books generally available and not a few, as Dr. MacLeod reported, 'in private and secret circulation'. Hardly to be classed as entertainment, a hunt had to be organized in May 1942 for a tiger which had escaped from a private menagerie. It was shot, and its hide was reported to have been sent to Emperor Hirohito as a present.

Church services were well attended. The different denominations, except the Roman Catholics and Christian Scientists, came together to form the United Churches. Holy Communion was taken in rotation, and celebrated according to the rites and customs of the celebrant's own church. This ecumenical arrangement was generally welcomed by the congregation and many wished it could have continued after the war. The first Easter was marked by a dawn service complete with choir, soloist, and instrumental accompaniment, after which most churches continued with their own denominational service.

The internees were at first regarded as enemy civilians taken into protective custody, and were held under military guard, mainly Indian and Chinese at first, and later, Formosans, under the over-all control of 'fat-pig' Colonel Tokunaga, the officer in charge of all prisoners' camps in Hong Kong. Stanley Camp was placed under a civilian administration and the first Camp Superintendent was one Yamashita, who had been a barber at the Hong Kong Hotel. Early in 1944 the Japanese discovered that the internees should have been considered prisoners of war according to an agreement with Britain, and the Japanese military assumed full control.

All inmates had to bow to the Japanese military and much slapping of faces proved necessary before this art could be correctly acquired. On meeting a Japanese soldier, all had to bow from the waist at an angle of at least 30 degrees and a man had to remove his cap and refrain from putting his hands in his pockets. Most important, no one was allowed to position himself that he could physically look down on the soldier, as this showed disrespect to the Emperor whose uniform he wore. The language barrier resulted in many internees being punished for misdeeds without knowing the precise nature of their offence. Most inmates hated bowing, and the old colonials had some difficulty in adapting themselves.

Repeated attempts to improve the conditions in camp, particularly the food, were unavailing; the Japanese received the representatives of the camp on numerous occasions, but with few results. A Swiss representative of the International Red Cross was appointed to Hong Kong and caused great offence when in March 1943 he reported to Geneva by telegram that the unfavourable reports regarding the health of the internees over the last nine months were unwarranted, and that deaths were due to diseases not necessarily connected with internment. He was told sharply that since January 1943 conditions had definitely deteriorated. There seemed to be little excuse for the bad food in the first years, particularly when godowns stored full of food were on the camp perimeter; but later, as the allied blockade became effective, all Hong Kong, including the Japanese, suffered shortages.

There were many acts of kindness. Many Indian guards, but not all, were friendly and helpful. Matsubara of the Matsubara Hotel, formerly the Gloucester, sent trunks of clothing and personal effects which had been left at the hotel, in time for Christmas 1942. The Revd. Watanabe, the Lutheran minister who did so much for the prisoners of war, also came to Stanley, not always in his role of interpreter, bringing news and such gifts as he could manage, as a matter of Christian charity.

The internees generally were buoyed up by an unshakeable faith in eventual allied victory; the only question was when, and unreasoning optimism led them to swallow the wildest rumours. The Japanese-sponsored English-language newspaper, the *Hong Kong News*, was supplied to the camp and at least they knew where the war fronts were. There was also the evidence of increasing American air raids. The first was in October 1942, the next in August 1943, and thereafter they became more frequent and total black-out was imposed as a security measure. On 16 January 1945 a severe three-hour raid over Stanley scored a direct hit on one of the College bungalows, killing fourteen persons and wounding four. It is a sad commentary on the state of the camp that by the time friends arrived on the scene, some looting had already occurred. The victims were buried next day in a communal grave. The bungalow was almost on the camp perimeter and near a machine-gun site, but in fact the camp had not been marked by white crosses as required by international convention. The Japanese made the inmates dig crosses in the ground on the next day and filled them with kaolin. Some of the camp officials were told to write a condemnation of the raid. At the risk of being accused of collaboration an account was handed over, but this was returned with a demand for a more strongly-worded censure; compliance with this criticism was encouraged by face-slapping.

Whatever the danger, the raids boosted morale; for clearly help could not be far away. On 10 August 1945 all the technicians and their families were suddenly and inexplicably removed to Ma Tau Chung Camp in Kowloon. On 15 August stores arrived for the canteen, the first delivery for months, and a free issue of cigarettes followed. Then everyone was astounded to receive a roll of toilet paper, a highly prized commodity in the camp, and dubbed 'victory rolls'. Next day the camp seethed with excitement. The atom-bomb attack and the entry of Russia into the war were known, and rumour declared that the fighting was over. The Japanese Camp officers remained silent but the *Hong Kong News* reported that an Imperial rescript ending the hostilities had been issued in Tokyo. Then Mr. Gimson asked for an interview with the Commandant and was officially informed that the Japanese had accepted the Allied terms. The internees were warned against making any demonstrations or attempting to leave, and advised to be patient; for, until the British relieving forces arrived, the Japanese were *de facto* in full military control. Extra rations were issued that evening, and a United Churches Service was held in thanksgiving. Two of the technicians added to the excitement by arriving at Stanley on a fire-engine, some officers from Shamshuipo arrived in a launch, neutrals and Chinese came out from town with gifts, and next day numbers of prisoners of war arrived for family reunions charged with all the pent-up emotion of over three and a half years' separation.

On 29 August British planes flew over the camp dropping parcels of food and medicine and warships appeared off the island, and on the 30th Rear-Admiral C. H. Harcourt entered the harbour in H.M.S. *Swiftsure* and landed at the naval dockyard. Next day, he and Mr. F. C. Gimson accompanied by a number of staff officers went to Stanley. To make a fitting ceremony commemorating the sad memories of the past and the joy of the present liberation a church service was held at which the Union Jack and the flags of every nationality represented in the camp were raised by a representative in a solemn and moving ceremony. Internment was finally at an end.

X

THE BRITISH ARMY AID GROUP

'A Colonel Ride was a prisoner of war in Hong Kong and managed to escape from camp and wanted to devote his time to assisting others and do the same. He organized a few people with this in mind and started it to work. For want of a better name, he called it the British Aid Group or the British Army Aid Group.'

Lt.-Col. Willis H. Bird to Major H. Stevens,
US Army, Chungking, 4 January 1945

ONE important by-product of the escapes from the prisoner-of-war camps was the British Army Aid Group, familiarly known as B.A.A.G., formed in March 1942 under the command of Lt.-Col. L. T. Ride of the H.K.V.D.C.[1] In relation to the whole Pacific War its role was a relatively minor one, and indeed the official British War History, *The War Against Japan*, passes it over in complete silence. But since it was recruited mainly from former Hong Kong residents who were deeply concerned with conditions in the Colony under the Japanese,

[1] In order to bring the story of the B.A.A.G. into a more accurate perspective in relation to the account of British intelligence activities in China and to incorporate new information from American sources as well as some suggestions from Sir Lindsay Ride, I have taken the liberty of substituting parts of my articles on this subject which first appeared in the *South China Morning Post*, 12 and 13 October 1973.

Recently, through the kindness of the Librarian of Oklahoma University I have come into possession of a lengthy, detailed, and substantially accurate account of the several British Intelligence Groups in China taken from the Patrick J. Hurley Collection. The report in question, drawn up by Lt.-Col. Jacques de Sibour of the O.S.S. S.U. Det. 202 China, is dated 5 January 1944. Three pages are devoted to the B.A.A.G. One of the most significant comments in the report, endorsed by Colonel Ride, reflects on the loyalty of the Hong Kong Chinese to the British cause. 'They . . . employ a great number of agents. These agents, for the most part, are formerly known by the British in the Hong Kong area. It can be assumed that the British must have a rather strong hold on many of these people for their wage is low, their treatment not particularly good and yet they seem to remain loyal.'

The counter-intelligence section was reported as having a very complete card-index of enemy agents, saboteurs, spies, etc., numbering well over 15,000 names.

its importance to any narrative of the war period in Hong Kong is clear and demands more than passing mention.

Hong Kong was lost, and soon afterwards all British-, French-, Dutch-, and American-controlled areas in East and South-East Asia were in Japanese hands. But the war was not yet over. It was some time before the Americans could build up their forces in the Pacific or the British could free men from the Western front for the inevitable Pacific campaign. In the meantime the Allies did what they could to strengthen China's resistance, support anti-Japanese underground movements, and gain intelligence regarding Japan's strategic plans and war supplies.

The history of these semi-secret war-time organizations operating in and out of China whose objectives, put more simply than they could be in practice, were to harass the enemy and assist his eventual defeat – in other words pursuing a military objective in the highly complex tangle of Chinese politics on the one hand, and the strategic requirements of the Indian Ocean chain of command on the other – is a subject which probably cannot be exhaustively treated in Hong Kong. It would be necessary to study the history of the operations of the war-time Ministry of Economic Warfare and of the British Special Operations Executive and of the U.S. O.S.S. organization.

Lt.-Col. Ride, in peacetime Professor of Physiology in the Medical Faculty of Hong Kong University, had commanded an ambulance unit during the brief campaign, but in company with other members of the gallant Volunteer Force he was made a prisoner of war in the Shamshuipo Camp. He has not publicly given an account of this escape; but other ex-POWs have told the now-amusing story of four POWs (one being Ride, the others staff members of the University) walking boldly out of the prison camp disguised as civilians. Apparently, outfits of clothing had been smuggled into the camp in the very early days of the Japanese camp administration.[2]

The gradual trickle of escapees from Hong Kong, whose flight from Hong Kong required determination, courage, and knowledge of the Kwangtung countryside and of its peoples,

[2] See Chapter V on 'Escapes'.

became a regular channel of escape for some of the students of Hong Kong University, as Professor Gordon King has recently described in his Daphne Chun Memorial lecture.

One of these was Rayson Huang, the present Vice-Chancellor of the University. At the home of the missionaries Dr. and Mrs. S. H. Moore in the Ho Sai Hospital, Kukong, the B.A.A.G. took shape. Ride went to Chungking and induced the British military authorities there to approve of his scheme for a group of these escapees to operate in a manner similar to Force 'Z'.[3] So the B.A.A.G. came into being some time early in 1942.

The B.A.A.G. was a unit of the Indian Army under Group E of the Headquarters Intelligence Branch, Delhi, and it did not therefore have a combat role. It comprised a uniformed staff of officers and other ranks, as well as civilians employed on a wide range of duties such as security officers, interpreters, clerks, orderlies, and specially-recruited agents for underground work in the field.

It took some time to find its feet, for the British army authorities in Chungking and Delhi had to be persuaded of its usefulness; its role had to be clearly defined and an establishment created adequate for the purpose.

Agreement with the Chinese military and civil authorities as to the scope and area of operations was of the utmost importance[4] because their political quarrel with the communists imposed a limit on what they could be expected to tolerate in the matter of allied forces operating independently in their territory.

Selection of personnel was not easy and anyone passing through from Hong Kong was regarded as a potential recruit; many escapees preferred to proceed on to India for combat

[3] There are, indeed, few indications in the Foreign Office files of the early moves to form the B.A.A.G.; as early as April 1942 the Military Attaché, Chungking, sent a brief report to London: 'We are negotiating with the Chinese for permission to establish a small military organisation in South China with the objective of carrying out work of M.I.9 as regards P.O.W.s in Hong Kong. *The present organisation under RIDE should form the nucleus and majority of extra personnel can be found locally* . . . (editor's italics).'

In February Colonel Ride had been ordered back to Kwangtung 'to facilitate the escape of P.O.W.s.' (F.O.371/31671).

[4] Sir Lindsay Ride has told me that he believed that the initial recognition of the B.A.A.G. by the Chungking authorities was because of the support of Madame Chiang for its humanitarian role in helping escapees and bringing drugs and medical aid to the war-stricken population of South Kwangtung.

service in more active operations, but not a few Chinese were glad to accept an offer of service with the Group because they had lost everything in Hong Kong.

It is difficult to give the precise numbers of those serving in the Group because they varied, there was considerable turnover and, of course, there was gradual expansion.

The maximum number of uniformed men at any one time was about 100 of whom some thirty were officers, but the total maximum strength including civilians exceeded 500. Its headquarters were at Kweilin, in Kwangsi Province, until the Japanese drove them out in 1944, when they moved to Kunming, and there were posts at Kukong, Ho Yuen, and an important one commanded by Capt. J. D. Clague at Waichow on the East River, the last being the most southerly and forward base with direct underground contacts with Hong Kong.

Another post was at Takhing on the West River, from which agents in Macao were contacted. Kweilin and Waichow were the two most important centres, one a headquarters and the other the main base from which operations in Hong Kong were conducted.

At Waichow there were some fifty to sixty personnel, mostly civilian Chinese, since the size of the uniformed military establishment could not be expanded until authorized from Delhi.

The B.A.A.G. was a mixed force comprising soldiers and civilians, Europeans and Asians, men and women, gathered from many walks of life. As the word 'Group' implies, it was an unconventional formation designed for specific tasks and operating under unusual conditions. As a unit of the Indian Army, its members were paid in rupees but received an allowance in Chinese yuan for living expenses.

The directive issued to the commander of the B.A.A.G. has not been published, but the Group's record is fairly indicative of its purpose. Broadly its role was to further in every way possible the military effort in South China. It assisted all allied personnel, whether in prisoner-of-war camps or not, to escape and to evade the Japanese while in transit to Free China. Escape and evasion sums up one important part of what it set out to do. Where escape could not be arranged, the aim was to provide medicines to help keep the captives alive, to supply news, and generally to bolster morale in the occupied Colony.

The B.A.A.G. was essentially an intelligence unit, so its second main objective was to gain information about Hong Kong and South China, and in fact it became the main source of military intelligence for that area.[5]

In this, it supplemented the work of other intelligence organizations working secretly in China such as Force 136, the British Military Liaison Office in Chungking, and the Ministry of Economic Warfare. This intelligence function was important in preparation for the long and costly campaign which was feared would be necessary before the Japanese accepted defeat.

Success depended upon ensuring contact between Hong Kong and its forward post at Waichow. This was no easy task. The two essential conditions were, first, strict neutrality in China's internal civil conflict; second, there had to be good relations with the guerrillas who controlled the routes to the Colony to permit contacts being made and maintained, confidence built up, services bargained for, and communications kept open.

The B.A.A.G. agents selected for underground work in Hong Kong had to be acceptable to each side in China's political struggle, for each suspected Chinese travellers of being agents of the other.

A promise was given that the B.A.A.G. would remain neutral regarding China's internal politics, and it was kept. It follows therefore that the B.A.A.G.'s relations with the guerrillas had to be very guarded.

[5] The U.S. intelligence reports referred to in the beginning of this chapter give the following fragmentary 'organization' chart of the B.A.A.G.:

Organization and Personnel:

BAAG is divided up into approximately eight sections:

'A' Section	Adjutant's Office	OC, N.K.
'B' Section	Budget Office	OC, Capt. Boyd
'E' Section	Escape	OC, Maj. Minshull-Ford, Capt. Morris Perrault
'H' Section	Translations	OC, Capt. Khan
'I' Section	Intelligence (Positive)	OC, Maj. Cowie
'M' Section	Medical	OC, Capt Lee
'S' Section	Counter-Intelligence	OC, Maj. Hall-Caine & Capt. Khan
'T' Section	Transportation	OC, Capt. Khan
'W' Section	? ? ? ? ?	OC, N.K.

Armed communist guerrilla bands were active in the New Territories as well as across the border, but the B.A.A.G. did not succumb to what must have been a strong temptation to supervise their training and use in the furtherance of Allied plans, as was done in Malaya to the later embarrassment of the British there.

To have kept communication with Hong Kong open during the remaining years of the war in face of the deep-seated suspicion and distrust of the Kuomintang civil and military authorities of any contact with the communist guerrillas, was indeed no mean achievement, attainable, perhaps, only by those who had lived among the Chinese, as was the case with many of the B.A.A.G.

While there were staff members of the B.A.A.G. engaged on sifting and collating reports for presentation to Delhi, on radio communications, interpreting and translating, interviewing refugees or escapees, much of the work had naturally to be done by agents working underground.

Their selection and training were entrusted to a young Hong Kong University graduate, Mr. Paul Tsui, who was interviewed by Col. Ride and by Mr. R. C. Lee and to whom he was able to give information about conditions in Hong Kong; he was recruited into the B.A.A.G. and posted to Waichow where he became chief Chinese aide to Capt. Clague. (The latter had made an independent escape from Shamshuipo, during which he contracted malaria. He apparently was approached by the British Military Attaché at Chungking to see if he would be willing to return to Waichow, and played an important part in the work of the B.A.A.G. there.)

The difficulties involved in recruiting agents were enormous. The man had to know Hong Kong well or they would be useless, they had to be acceptable to the guerrillas or they would never get through, and the work was exacting and dangerous, demanding a thorough training which could not be given in the time available nor with the expertise available.

Security was difficult to inculcate, yet it was essential to success. Many of these agents came forward as witnesses at the post-war collaboration and War Crimes trials, and these afford us a glimpse of the B.A.A.G. and its work. They were mostly people with considerable western associations such as teachers, clerks in government offices, or in offices of the big firms, or members of the police reserve.

There were women as well as men, some worked in groups, some alone. In the nature of things, the hazards were such that many paid the penalty of torture and death.

At one period at Waichow six teams of agents were successively sent out and only one individual survived. Many were never heard of again.

Much was gleaned from escaped prisoners and Chinese refugees from Hong Kong who were questioned by B.A.A.G. security officers.

Gradually the B.A.A.G. was able to build up a picture of conditions in Hong Kong, British casualty lists, conditions in the prisoner-of-war camps and at Stanley, the movement of shipping, the development of trade, the disposition of the Japanese garrison, the fortifications, air-raid damage, and general military intelligence. Copies of Hong Kong newspapers were smuggled out, and in fact the Japanese were hardly able to make any move without it becoming known. For example Lt.-Cdr. Ralph Goodwin, R.N.Z.N.V.R., who escaped in July 1944, was amused to read a Japanese version of his escape which had been smuggled out and reached him before he even arrived at Kukong.

The B.A.A.G. also disseminated information. The British Embassy's news bulletin was often delayed, and the B.A.A.G. posts gave out their own news-sheet distributed free to Chinese civil and military organizations and sent to Hong Kong; in addition Hong Kong Chinese, Japanese, and English newspapers were collected and made available to British intelligence.

The Group's agents came and went, though all declared that it was much easier to leave Hong Kong than to get back again.

The experience of one Hong Kong civilian, a lawyer, gives some indication of the work of the B.A.A.G. He began in Hong Kong during the occupation to pass information to British agents, but left for Macao in 1943 when the Japanese clamped down on espionage. He went by ship to Kwongchouwan, and joined the B.A.A.G. at Kweilin where he found some thirty-five uniformed officers and non-commissioned officers, some civilians, and a number of civilian agents coming and going.

He was employed as a civilian on security work, questioning Chinese arrivals, and because he knew the southern part of Kwangtung Province well he was able to detect any discrepancies in their replies.

Later he was commissioned as an officer and worked in the field with a radio transmitter, reporting back to Kweilin on Japanese troop movements and other military intelligence, working generally in the area Kunming, Kwongchouwan, Macao and Canton.

The B.A.A.G. devised plans to free the prisoners of war in Hong Kong. Its agents made contacts with the camps which have been described in Chapter VII, 'Prisoners of War'. The first contacts were made at the Kai Tak airfield extension works between agents working as Chinese labourers and Chinese-speaking members of the H.K.V.D.C.

The work of military intelligence was not left entirely to Chinese personnel and indeed, from time to time and in some areas, there were journeys and tasks which could only be undertaken by non-Chinese personnel because of the complex network of allegiances which characterized the various guerrilla formations.

One example was the inital extended reconnaissance of the New Territories, undertaken immediately after the setting up of the B.A.A.G. post in Waichow in the autumn of 1942.

This operation, led by Capt. D. R. Holmes, lasted for nearly two months and laid the foundation for the communications subsequently maintained throughout the war across the eastern New Territories; it carried out extensive photography from the Lion Rock against which later allied photographic reconnaissance from the air could be checked; and it established liaison with communist-affiliated para-military formations, which throughout hostilities was essential for any operations carried out in this area.

The B.A.A.G. also operated a line of communications between Macao and Kweilin via Takhing on the West River. The chief agent was a Chinese Macao businessman, who amongst his various activities ran a compradore's shop. He assisted many British nationals who had fled from Hong Kong and who had been able to take very little money with them by supplying food on credit, and his helpful attitude came to the notice of the consul to whom he appeared to have pro-British sympathies.

The consul asked him to assist by getting information about transport in the Chung Shan district with the aim of establishing a route to Free China and gaining contact with the B.A.A.G. He impressed Col. Ride who invited him to Kweilin in December 1942, where he arrived after an eighteen-day journey, five of which were spent in Japanese-occupied territory, and he was recruited into the B.A.A.G. as a civilian agent under the code name of 'Phoenix'.

In Macao his shop served as a cover which soon became a headquarters for the underground, and in February 1944 he was placed in charge of all B.A.A.G. work in Macao. His main tasks were to organize an escape route to assist allied personnel to reach Free China, to work with and report on the guerrillas, chiefly communist, and to gather as much intelligence as was possible in the relative freedom of Macao, on the Japanese war effort and conditions in Hong Kong and Macao.

He was successful in organizing a route to Free China, which despite much difficulty remained open for the rest of the war. Two U.S. airmen shot down in 1943 were smuggled out and three more in 1945. Escapees were limited to carrying with them a maximum of 20 lbs.

He had his own agents with each of the guerrilla groups, so the four hazardous days it took to reach Free China from Macao were always successfully negotiated and he claimed with no little pride that he did not lose a single agent or escapee to the Japanese.

He bought time on the Macao radio by which he sent coded messages to Kweilin and he operated a wireless transmitter on a junk which kept on the move to avoid detection; and, since the Japanese would not allow essential spare parts for transmitter sets to be sold in Macao, he was able, by flooding the basement of the Portuguese bank in which they were stored, to get his hands in the confusion on some spares and keep transmission going.

To lessen the risks of detection he saw as few people as possible, but was helped by two British Portuguese doctors.

He had to go to the B.A.A.G. headquarters annually to get instructions and discuss the operations but was never offered a commission, probably because living in Macao made it inappropriate.

The B.A.A.G. was able to contribute more directly to the war effort in other ways. About a thousand Chinese members of the H.K.V.D.C., the Royal Engineers, the Hongkong Chinese Regiment, and other army units, together with Chinese civilian employees of the Naval Dockyard, had made their way to Free China and were helped to find employment in British, United States and Chinese war organizations.

A volunteer unit of Chinese, Eurasians, and Portuguese, was formed from Hong Kong men, including some from the Hongkong Chinese Regiment, the H.K.V.D.C., and other units. It was trained, and eventually served with distinction in the Chindit operations in Burma. The Chinese Nationalist Army was also helped with demolition work, particularly during the Japanese advance on Kweilin.

Again, thousands of Hong Kong refugees fleeing from the Japanese in Hong Kong were helped financially and given medical care by the B.A.A.G. Later the British Embassy in Chungking assumed financial responsibility for this work through a Refugee Relief Department, and millions of dollars from the Red Cross, the Lord Mayor's Fund and Lady Cripps' Fund were channelled by the Embassy to the B.A.A.G. for such purposes as medical care, refugee camps, and soup kitchens.

The Chinese refugees fleeing towards Kunming after the fall of Kweilin in 1944 were similarly helped. When Kukong fell, Dr. S. H. Moore lost his hospital. He was recruited into the Indian Army Medical Service for work in Takhing to assist the Chinese and guerrillas with medical care and thus build up goodwill towards the British.

On the eve of the Japanese surrender the B.A.A.G. was poised to assist in the take-over. Col. Ride made an unsuccessful attempt to fly into Hong Kong in an American plane from Canton. A plane did land at Kai Tak with a B.A.A.G. officer a day or two after the news of the surrender, but since the Japanese were in full control, little could be done except to report.

Even before the surrender the British Government in London

had felt that British authority should be urgently restored in Hong Kong and that contact should be made with the senior Hong Kong Government official, the Colonial Secretary, who was a prisoner of the Japanese, to set up a provisional administration.

The B.A.A.G. had to be brought in as the only body with contacts in Hong Kong, and their chief agent in Macao was entrusted by the B.A.A.G. with the highly important official instructions to be transmitted to Mr. F. C. Gimson in Stanley Camp.

The agent had no credentials, but went to Hong Kong on a Japanese ship and delivered his message to Mr. Gimson on 23 August.

He meanwhile had left Stanley Camp and established himself in the town at the Missions Étrangères, adjoining the Colonial Secretariat. The message also instructed him to demand the release of all prisoners of war and internees, the protection of all British personnel, and the halting of all Japanese war activities.

As Col. Ride has written in *The University of Hong Kong, First Fifty Years, 1911–61*, 'The B.A.A.G. set up relief camps and food kitchens and organized famine relief for thousands, many of whom were refugees from Hong Kong. . . . Besides all this work amongst the Chinese in the unoccupied forward areas, medical supplies, urgently needed in Hong Kong, were sent by underground routes to the doctors who were still permitted by the Japanese to carry on their work among the Chinese of Hong Kong.'

Thus the B.A.A.G. played a truly decisive role in the survival of the war-ravaged occupied Colony and in its restitution as a British outpost of empire. The Commandant's farewell message to his men when the B.A.A.G. stood down on 31 December 1945 is a fitting tribute to its distinctive and many-sided role.

'You tended the Chinese wounded and sick; in famine you fed their helpless and starving; you came to know the full measure of their lavish hospitality and you learned to understand and appreciate their point of view. As a result of all this you built up a fellowship with Hong Kong's neighbour that will not be easily made to cease bearing fruit; therein lies the lasting value of your labours.'

XI

LIBERATION

'How much elated? The bewilderment of that tragic Christmas Day when our world came to an end, returns to us. Can this be it? Can this be deliverance? Ay, this is Peace – this is The Day in faith whereto throughout those interminable months we refused to die.'

South China Morning Post, 1 September 1945.
Editorial by the late Mr. Henry Ching

THE Japanese surrender came with dramatic suddenness, and yet in Hong Kong the reaction was not so much one of surprise as of numbed relief, people hardly daring to believe that deliverance had come. Optimism, fed on rumour and exaggerated by wishful thinking, had been so often belied that freedom seemed incredible. Hong Kong had never been completely cut off and news of the outside world filtered through via the B.A.A.G. underground network, through the radio, and also by way of Macao which maintained its freedom by favour of the Japanese. Besides, the Japanese English newspaper, *The Hong Kong News*, gave details of the fighting and though these told a tale of unbroken Japanese victories and crippling American losses, they did not disguise the fact that the fighting was coming closer and had reached the Philippines in late 1944. The increasing occurrence of air raids was an additional and obvious pointer to the fact that Hong Kong's turn could not be long delayed; it was also known that Russia had entered the war and that Hiroshima and Nagasaki had been devastated by a new and powerful type of bomb. By mid-August rumours that Japan had capitulated spread through Stanley Camp, and on 16 August men making the victory sign kept passing outside the windows of the room where the Camp Council were in session.

The Allies at the Cairo Conference in November 1943 had agreed to impose unconditional surrender, and when the Japanese attempted to negotiate terms, including the preservation of the Imperial system, the Allies at the Potsdam Conference of July 1945 adhered to their original demand, leaving the Japanese no choice but to accept or face the threat of destruction by atomic weapons. On 15 August 1945, on the personal intervention of the Emperor and with the object of preventing further bloodshed, the Japanese accepted unconditional surrender, much to the relief of the Allies who feared that they might suicidally continue the conflict to the last.

In Hong Kong the Imperial Rescript was read on 16 August by a Japanese officer outside the Hong Kong Hotel, first in Japanese and then in Chinese. Everyone present was subdued, the Japanese for obvious reasons, and the public from fear because they were still at the mercy of the Japanese and did not want their faces slapped, the mildest of the punishments they had come to expect.

In Stanley Camp the internees had no authentic news until F. C. Gimson, Colonial Secretary, asked for an interview with the Japanese Camp Commandant on 16 August at which he was told of the surrender. He at once approached them with the object of setting up a provisional Government under himself as the senior Hong Kong Government official present. This move had been long discussed by high-ranking Government officers and others in the camp, and various plans to re-establish British authority had been made to meet varying contingencies, in fact a message had got through to London via Macao asking that Hong Kong currency notes should be printed in readiness. The British Government were also preparing plans through a Planning Unit in London to set up a Military Administration in the Colony under a Military Civil Affairs Unit. The surrender came before its personnel could get to Hong Kong and in the meantime, to avoid any delay in restoring British authority, Mr. Gimson was instructed to set up and assumed control of an interim administration, provided he were liberated and the Japanese placed no obstacle in his way. This message was sent to Chungking on 11 August and then relayed to the British Army Aid Group. They passed it to their chief underground agent in Macao, who brought it to Hong Kong and delivered it personally to Mr. Gimson in Stanley on 23 August, though in fact he had no credentials to prove his identity or bona fides.[1] Mr. Gimson thereupon finally left Stanley Camp, taking with him key administrative personnel, some police officers, and also some former employees of the public utility companies who had the necessary expertise to try to ensure that the plant equipment and stock would be satisfactorily safeguarded, repairs begun, and possible sabotage averted. He established himself in the French Missions Étrangères building made available to him by the Japanese, whose main administrative offices were across the road in the Hong Kong Bank building, and with him were senior Government officials and all the European members of the Executive Council. The Japanese protested to Mr. Gimson on the ground that they remained responsible until the surrender had actually been made and it was of course true that their large armed garrison was in effective control until the British forces arrived. They also correctly argued that the surrender should be made to the Chinese, as Hong Kong lay in the Chinese theatre of war. Nevertheless they agreed to unofficial contacts between him and their own civil and military authorities, and in fact they behaved correctly and co-operatively during the interval before the British forces took over. Mr. Gimson accepted this arrangement as the only one possible, as he himself had no means of ensuring the maintenance of law and order. He was able to observe and report regarding conditions in the Colony, and also to get utility companies' employees at work preparing for the rehabilitation.

On 28 August Gimson broadcast over the old Z.B.W. radio station on the top of Gloucester Building. 'As the chief representative of the British Government now resident in Hong Kong, I have already established an office in the City of Victoria, with the concurrence of the Japanese, and have in preparation the essential steps towards resuming the British administration on the arrival – which I trust will not be much longer deferred – of the British Forces to take the surrender of the Colony.'

[1] This has been confirmed by the reminiscences of F.W. Shaftain, O.B.E., who, in an unpublished paper, 'An episode dealing with the re-occupation of Hong Kong' (R.H.K. Police records), refers to the arrival at the home of Lo Man Kam in Robinson Road of a Chinese aged about thirty, immaculately dressed in a white silk robe. He stated he was an agent of the British Government and had arrived in Hong Kong with vitally important verbal instructions to the Colonial Secretary (Mr. Gimson). He gave his name as Mr. Leung.

The glad news came to Shamshuipo Camp also on 16 August, and the senior British officer, Lt.-Colonel S. M. White, M.C., of the Royal Scots, raised the flag at a ceremonial parade of the whole camp. In view of the Japanese military presence and because there were no suitable accommodation or facilities for obtaining food in the town, the men were told to remain in camp until satisfactory arrangements for moving out could be made. The Stanley internees, except those required for immediate duty with the Gimson administration, were also told to remain where they were for the same reasons.

On 18 August people in the town saw with delighted surprise a large Union Jack unfurled on top of the Peak. Apparently this was the work of two Public Works Department officials interned in Argyle Street, A. F. May and J. C. Brown. They set out at midnight, rowed across the harbour in an old, leaky boat which was prevented from sinking only by ceaseless bailing, and managed to reach the Island. They climbed the Peak and unfurled the Union Jack at precisely 9 a.m., the previously appointed time. The Japanese were naturally annoyed and ordered the offending flag to be taken down. Some Indians appeared, having been organized as part of the escapade, and after some discussion, the flag was eventually lowered at about 1.30 p.m. The Japanese showed remarkable forbearance.

The International Red Cross organized transport to take relatives and friends to Stanley, and the prisoners of war from Shamshuipo were brought there by motor launches. Many happy reunions of families and friends followed. British planes appeared and gladdened the hearts of the Stanley internees by dropping supplies, and with extra rations from the Japanese the captives were able to wait in good heart for their final release.

The Admiralty detached units of the British Pacific fleet, under Rear-Admiral C. H. J. Harcourt, with orders to take the surrender of the Japanese at Hong Kong. This fleet was delayed in Subic Bay, the American base in the Philippines, while the Admiral's precise official position was debated, and he was not given definite orders until 30 August, by which date he was in the neighbourhood of Hong Kong. He had signalled the Japanese that he would send a plane to Kai Tak airport at a stated time and asked that Japanese representatives should meet it, to discuss the take-over arrangements and the entry of the fleet. The Japanese objected, but eventually they detailed an officer, and Gimson selected a member of his administration, and the two were flown back to Harcourt.

The British Naval Force was a powerful one, comprising the battleship *Anson*, two aircraft carriers, *Indomitable* and *Venerable*, cruisers including the *Swiftsure* and *Euryalus*, destroyers and submarines with the submarine depot-ship H.M.S. *Maidstone*. The Admiral made his entry at 11.0 a.m. on 30 August, with his flag transferred to H.M.S. *Swiftsure*. The triumphal fleet was preceded by minesweepers clearing a channel. It was felt that safeguards had to be taken against mines, mainly American, which had been dropped from the air to deny the use of the port to Japanese shipping, though they were designed to be inoperative after 1 July. All ships were at action stations. There was no opposition from Japanese guns, but three small motor torpedo-boats seen moving out from a nearby island were attacked and sunk because it was feared they might be on a suicidal strike mission. Naval parties landed and took over the Naval Dockyard. Machine-gun and small-arms fire were heard as isolated pockets of Japanese threatened to resist, but this was not serious. Some patriotic Japanese preferred what was to them a more honourable way out by *hara-kiri*, some were attacked in the streets and killed by vengeful crowds. Mr. Gimson came on board H.M.S. *Swiftsure*, and later in the day the Admiral and Acting Governor went out to Stanley, where national flags were raised and a thanksgiving service was held. Armed British naval parties were sent ashore to take over military and important civilian installations. When the Island had been taken over, Kowloon followed and the Japanese forces were interned, after which British control was gradually extended to the New Territories. There the take-over process was necessarily slow, and it was not until the third week in November that the last Japanese outposts were relieved.

The surrender ceremony was fixed for 12 September 1945, but had to be postponed when Generalissimo Chiang Kai-shek protested against the British intention to receive the surrender of the Japanese in Hong Kong, since Hong Kong lay within the

Chinese war zone. Eventually the surrender ceremony took place at Government House on Sunday, 16 September, at which this contentious issue was avoided by Admiral Harcourt receiving the surrender on behalf of both Britain and China.

To the naval men of the liberating force the Colony looked desolate and grim as if the atmosphere of defeat still prevailed; the harbour was full of wrecks and the hillsides were scarred by the gaunt roofless shells of what formerly had been European homes. Admirably as the Japanese behaved, they could not prevent the outbreak of extensive looting. One eye-witness recorded that gangs were looting the University buildings and that the neighbouring King's College sounded, as he passed, 'like a shipbreakers' yard'. British naval parties patrolled the streets, but the looters waited until they passed and continued as before. Nobody was firmly in the saddle at this juncture and the looters seized the opportunities wide open to them. But the looting was different from that of the earlier period of the British surrender; then, looting was for furniture and food, all of saleable value, now the looting was the work of people driven by hunger and despair to get fuel for cooking, and they ripped out floor-boards, stair-cases, window-frames, ceilings, and left the buildings an empty shell.

The Chinese welcomed the British as allies. British and Chinese flags appeared everywhere, and fire-crackers testified to the feeling of celebration. One officer visiting the New Territories reported, 'They stop as they see us, momentarily disbelieving; then rush forward with loud cries and great broad grins. If we have been doubtful about our welcome back, we are so no longer. The hand-shaking and dazed happiness is so completely natural and spontaneous that we are faintly surprised.' The feeling seemed to be that of pride in being one of the victorious allies. There was deep hostility to the Japanese who had obviously failed to win over the local Chinese to the pan-Asiatic ideal, as well as a strong pro-Chinese nationalist sentiment born from the long fight against Japan. There was no anti-British feeling.

The European prisoners of war and civilian internees, and indeed the neutrals who lived out, were all suffering from malnutrition and sadly in need of a period of recuperation. An American journalist who came into Hong Kong with the

Royal Navy said he could spot a Hong Kong war internee a block away by his gaunt legs and arms. The strain of those years had taken its toll, and the internees working to rehabilitate the Colony were described as 'not being capable of great mental effort, had no power of decision, short memories and made frequent minor mistakes in conversation'. The hospital ship *Oxfordshire* sailed for home with the more serious cases, and the *Empress of Australia* left on 17 September with about one thousand people. The rest went home as shipping became available and at public expense. Very few elected to remain in Hong Kong. All looked to the future with some misgiving, fearing that after the upheaval life for the European in Hong Kong would never be the same again. British colonial policy had already begun to take on a new look, aiming at greater self-government, and raising native peoples' living standards. This was referred to by Mr. Gimson in his farewell message to the Colony on 15 September, the day before he left for Britain, in which he spoke of British policy of fostering self-government institutions throughout the Empire. He added that there was great need for reform on the social side as well as on the political side. This note was taken up in the Press and there were demands for more urban and district councils, and for the Government to take over the public utility companies with compensation to the shareholders.

The Japanese were all ordered to leave the Island and they were interned in Whitfield Barracks, Kowloon, and in adjoining houses along Nathan Road. Several hundred Japanese women and children assembled at Queen's Pier, early on 1 September, with as many of their belongings as they could carry, reminiscent of their European counterparts three years and eight months earlier, except that they were spared the many indignities suffered on that occasion. The Island was to be cleared of Japanese servicemen by 4.0 p.m. On 2 September Admiral Harcourt agreed to allow the Japanese flag to continue to fly over Admiralty House until that time. A submarine officer from the depot-ship *Maidstone* decided otherwise, for he drove to there in a jeep with two armed ratings at 11.0 a.m. that morning and without a by-your-leave raised the naval white ensign and took away the Japanese flag, and probably got away with nothing more serious than a

EXTRA

FLEET ENTERING

The first communique from the Hongkong Government to the people of Hongkong since December 1941 was issued this morning at 11 o'clock as follows:

"Rear Admiral Harcourt is lying outside Hongkong with a very strong fleet. The Naval Dockyard is to be ready for his arrival by noon to-day.

"Admiral Harcourt will enter the harbour having transferred his flag to the cruiser Swiftsure which will be accompanied by destroyers and submarines.

"The capital ships will follow as soon as a passage has been swept.

"The fleet includes two air-craft carriers Indomitable of 23,000 tons, and the Venerable; the battleship Anson of 35,000 tons and carrying 10 14-inch guns, the Euryalus and the Swiftsure carrying 10 5.2-inch guns; the merchant ship Maidstone of 8,500 tons, the merchant cruiser Prince Rupert, Canadian registry, and the Hospital ship Oxfordshire.

"A considerable number of other ships will follow in a day or two.

"The formal surrender is likely to follow the proceedings at Tokyo."

(South China Morning Post and The Hongkong Telegraph)
AUGUST 30, 1945.

1 *South China Morning Post*, Extra, 30 August 1945. The smallest newspaper ever issued? (*in possession of the author*)

2 Hong Kong reoccupied. The arrival of the Japanese emissary on board H.M.S. *Swiftsure*, flagship of Admiral Harcourt, Commanding the British Fleet of Liberation, 30 August 1945. (*Imperial War Museum*)

3 Japanese troops leaving the barracks at Fanling, New Territories. (*Imperial War Museum*)

4 Surrender of Japanese troops at Picnic Bay. (*J.S.I.S. G.H.Q. Hong Kong*)

5 Some of the 6,000 Japanese troops entering into captivity at the time of the surrender. (*Imperial War Museum*)

6 A group of released internees from Stanley Camp. (*Imperial War Museum*)

7 The Japanese representative signing the instrument of surrender at Government House, September 1945. (*Imperial War Museum*)

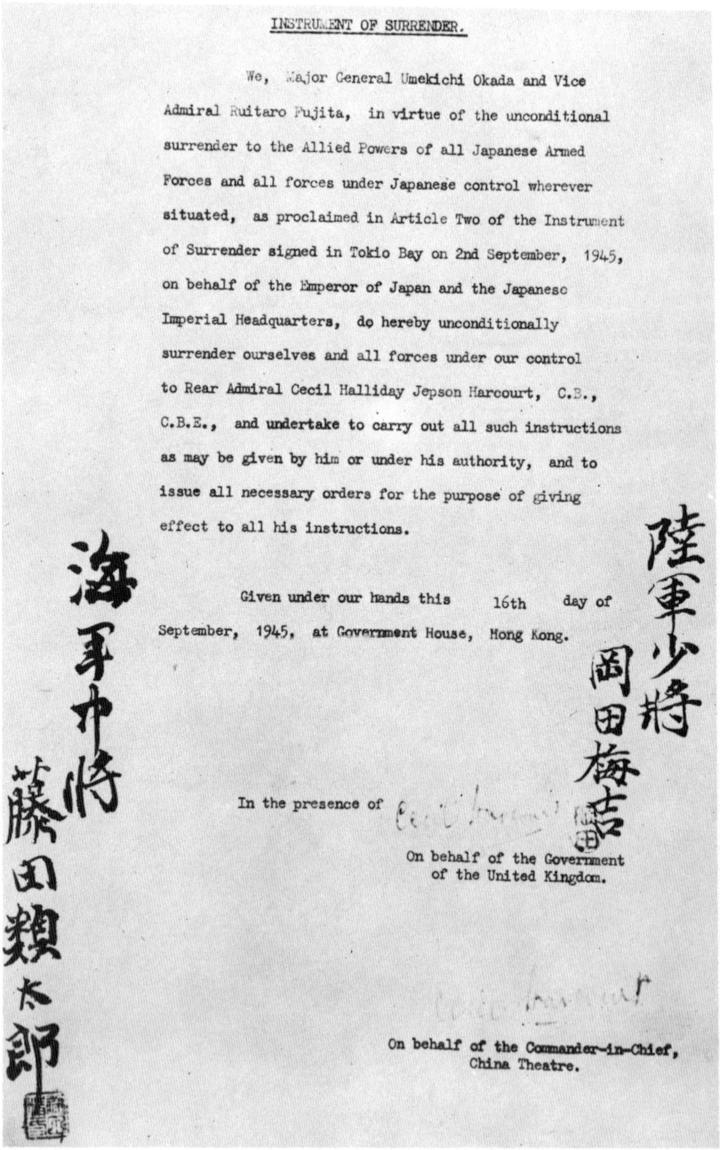

INSTRUMENT OF SURRENDER.

We, Major General Umekichi Okada and Vice Admiral Ruitaro Fujita, in virtue of the unconditional surrender to the Allied Powers of all Japanese Armed Forces and all forces under Japanese control wherever situated, as proclaimed in Article Two of the Instrument of Surrender signed in Tokio Bay on 2nd September, 1945, on behalf of the Emperor of Japan and the Japanese Imperial Headquarters, do hereby unconditionally surrender ourselves and all forces under our control to Rear Admiral Cecil Halliday Jepson Harcourt, C.B., C.B.E., and undertake to carry out all such instructions as may be given by him or under his authority, and to issue all necessary orders for the purpose of giving effect to all his instructions.

Given under our hands this 16th day of September, 1945, at Government House, Hong Kong.

海軍中将 藤田類太郎

陸軍少将 岡田梅吉

In the presence of

On behalf of the Government of the United Kingdom.

On behalf of the Commander-in-Chief, China Theatre.

8 The Instrument of Surrender. (*Imperial War Museum*)

9 The Victory Parade at the Cenotaph at Blake Pier, September 1945.
(*Imperial War Museum*)

10 The return of Sir Mark Young as Governor of Hong Kong, May 1946. (*Imperial War Museum*)

notification from the Admiralty of their Lordships' displeasure.

A curfew was imposed from 9 p.m. to 6 a.m. throughout the built-up area. A most welcome addition to the liberation forces was 3rd Commando Brigade (Royal Marines) which arrived from Singapore, and they played an invaluable role in maintaining law and order as it was found impossible to use Japanese recruited police because they were ill-trained and unreliable. University students were recruited as police, but they served more as interpreters and police liaison officers with the Chinese population, in which capacity they did excellently. Some Japanese were attacked when they rode on public trams, and there were clashes outside the dockyard, but generally the Japanese withdrawal from the Island was orderly. With the arrival of British troops, Kowloon and New Kowloon were taken over by 5 September. The strongly anti-Japanese guerrillas were still active in Cheung Chau, Tai O, and Silvermine Bay. They also created problems by returning to their villages bringing communist propaganda and generally disturbing the settled traditional village life and customs.

In one respect, the manner in which liberation had come was a matter of deep relief and thanksgiving, for Hong Kong was spared the military re-conquest which had been expected. The Allies feared that the Japanese would hold out to the last with that disciplined defiance and courage of which they had given such convincing proof. The people of occupied Hong Kong, as they watched military fortifications being prepared and A.R.P. tunnels extended, had every reason to fear the worst. Allied bombing had already caused heavy casualties and were a foretaste of the death and destruction that an attack on the Colony might have brought. From this, Hong Kong was mercifully spared.

XII

THE PROBLEM OF CONFLICTING LOYALTIES

'It is my opinion that in celebrating this second anniversary [of the occupation of Hong Kong by the Japanese Army] we should not simply eulogize the achievements of the Government: that is only a narrow view of the celebration. In short, as we have the privileges of residing in Hong Kong, we also have the duty of co-operating with the Government.'

Address of Chairman of the Chinese Representatives Council, 25 December 1942[1]

WITH the triumphant return of the British, the question of collaboration with the Japanese became a live and contentious issue in which accusations were freely bandied about. The Chief Civil Affairs Officer noted the disturbing currents of recrimination and denunciation giving rise to feelings of anger and distress in which 'loyalties were discounted and disloyalties excused on the shifting ground of expediency'. He found a world of what he termed 'grey men', with few outstanding renegades and equally few trustworthy leaders of the future, a world which he regarded as a legacy of oppression and repression and he explained 'for four years, the Colony has been turned in upon itself, and a kind of mental asphyxia has resulted'.

The word collaborator simply means one who works in conjunction with one or more other people but it has come to be used in a special sense, as in this chapter, meaning one who willingly assists the enemies of the State in active military operations, or helps to make more effective the policies of the enemy occupying power. The definition used by the Hong Kong Government in the objects and reasons for the Chinese

[1] C.O. 127/591/54112 Pt. I. *Kweilin Intelligence Summary No. 32.* This was regarded by the British Government as an apologia given by a leading citizen who had to walk the razor's edge between displeasing his present masters and betraying his fundamental loyalty to the Crown.

Collaborators (Surrender) Ordinance of 17 May 1946, by which Chinese collaborators taking refuge in the Colony were to be handed over to China in accordance with a United Nations decision, was one who had 'done any act or thing designed or calculated to benefit the enemy, or hostile or detrimental to, or designed or calculated to defeat, hinder or prejudice the cause of the United Nations or the prosecution of any war in which any of such nations were engaged'. Design and calculation are clearly the operative words here.

Collaboration with the enemy is an offence in English law which is fairly clear on this subject. The crime can be as serious as treason, historically a capital offence, which is defined as being 'adherent to the King's enemies in his realm, giving them aid and comfort in the realm or elsewhere', and can be committed (a) by any British subject in any part of the world, and also (b) by any alien if the latter voluntarily resides on British territory. Alternatively, the offence may be a breach of the defence regulations for which the maximum penalty was imprisonment for life and could be committed by anyone whatsoever and not restricted to the two categories of persons as in the case of treason. The Hong Kong Defence Regulations of 1940, based directly on the British Defence (General) Regulations of 1939, provided that 'If, with intent to assist the enemy, any person does any act which is likely to assist the enemy or to prejudice the public safety, the defence of this Colony, or any other part of His Majesty's dominions or the efficient prosecution of the war, then, without prejudice to the law relating to treason, he shall be guilty of an offence against this regulation and shall on conviction on indictment, be liable to imprisonment for life.' Briefly, the offence is doing any act with intent to assist the enemy.

Collaboration with the enemy was not a problem peculiar to Hong Kong or to the Second World War. All peoples in South-East Asia faced similar conditions and choices, as indeed the conquered have done in every age. Then, of course, there is always the question of conscience. Breach of the law is a clear and practical issue, but there have always been and probably always will be, people who are willing to break the law in pursuance of ideals to which they believe they owe a greater loyalty. There must have been many in Hong Kong genuinely attracted by the doctrine of Asia for the Asians, however much they might suspect that the Japanese were bent on substituting their own domination of Asia for that of the West. How many supported the Japanese cause is difficult to say. There was certainly no lack of volunteers for posts in their administration, including the police, but what evidence there is suggests that the vast majority of local people co-operated with the Japanese with reluctance and misgiving, and as a matter of physical survival.

Perhaps a distinction can usefully be made between collaboration during hostilities and that during the occupation. The offence remains legally the same, but in the former case the intent is obvious and the individual has made a deliberate choice. The enemy occupation posed different and difficult problems, because the Hong Kong Government could no longer give protection or enforce its laws[2] and the individual was left on his own and had to decide for himself what to do after weighing the possible consequences. Any course of action had necessarily to be a compromise.

The problem of collaboration was particularly acute in a colonial society where there was a racial cleavage between rulers and ruled. Collaboration in Hong Kong was quite different from that in a homogeneous community like France which, under Petain, was faced with the problem of collaboration with the Germans. Hong Kong was not one but a number of communities, each with its own loyalty, whose members were free to come and go and were held together only by economic self-interest. If the Chinese could secure the same economic opportunities under the Japanese that they enjoyed under the British there seems little reason why they should not accept the substitution of Japanese for British rule, since the purposes for which they resided in Hong Kong were equally served. Nobody was compelled to reside in the Colony except a few indigenous Chinese villagers. In such a society, collaboration could not be regarded as heinous as in a close-knit community like France. In any case, there were masses of newcomers fleeing from the Japanese who had had no time to develop any loyalty to Hong Kong, and the British made

[2] For a brief discussion of the legal issues and cases see the article, 'Confinement and Constitutional Conflict . . . '.

little attempt to enlist the loyalty of the Chinese until just before hostilities broke out, no doubt because of the high proportion of refugees among them. The Hong Kong Government was neither representative of, nor responsible to the people of Hong Kong, who did not look for political power as long as they could carry on their economic activities freely. This partly explains why no individual or group was prepared openly to confront the Japanese during the occupation as some French patriots did against the Germans. On the other hand, many men and women displayed loyalty to the British by flight to Free China and enlistment in the B.A.A.G. for dangerous underground work against the Japanese, in which a considerable number lost their lives.

One factor in the situation was that no one could be sure what the outcome of the war would be. The unbroken tale of Japan's successes and the range of her conquests could not fail to impress. The tide did not begin to turn until 1943. There must have been a gnawing doubt that the Japanese conquest of Hong Kong might prove to be permanent, in which case the prudent might well think it worthwhile to come to some terms with the occupying authorities. In this case, the search would be for the least harmful compromise until the situation became clearer, hoping that the future choice of action would not be jeopardized.

The essential element in criminal collaboration was the deliberate intention to assist the Japanese. In one sense, all obedience to Japanese regulations during the occupation was a form of collaboration, but the mitigating factor was the absence of intent. Often the individual had no choice, as for example when there was no option but to assist the Japanese or starve, since normal opportunities of employment were cut off. The mainland Chinese could and did return to their villages where, generally, the most they could expect was bare subsistence. Many, the Eurasians for example, had nowhere else to go; they might hold out until the supply of gold ornaments ran out and after that the alternative was service under the Japanese or starvation. Locally recruited Government officers were faced with this problem; they had been advised by the British to continue in their normal jobs to help the community and many did so, again mainly to earn a livelihood in the way they were accustomed. Many police, both Indian and Chinese, served under the Japanese and were undoubtedly assisting the enemy, but only a limited number did so with any enthusiasm. For most it was mainly a matter of the rice bowl. There could be no moral obliquity where a man acted under duress, whatever the law might say.

John Stericker, in his *Tear for the Dragon*, amusingly relates his forced collaboration with the Japanese when he was asked to write a piece on the air raid of 16 January 1945 in which fourteen inmates of Stanley Camp were killed. He at first refused, but was advised by Mr. F. C. Gimson, the British Camp Commandant, to comply; but to keep a copy of his contribution to the Japanese propaganda for future reference. 'In other words,' he wrote, 'if the Japanese did not shoot me now, my own side would after the war. My future appeared to be a trifle unsettled to say the least of it.' After some face-slapping he penned a compromise piece which the Japanese accepted. In fact he was acting under duress.

Some worked with the Japanese on matters which they considered did not conflict with their conscience. The bankers who marched to and fro under armed guard from their sordid quarters to their banks were presumably collaborators and could, and perhaps should, have refused to assist in the handing over of the banks, and gone into Stanley internment earlier than they did. But their remaining out enabled them to see that records were preserved and information about accounts and notes in circulation were up-to-date, and this materially assisted the British take-over in 1945. It was partly a case of 'duress banking' too, for the mortality later among the prominent bankers of the Colony pointed to what lay in store for them had they refused.

Again, there was the case of teaching the Japanese language in the schools. This was of course collaboration by assisting the Japanese design of imposing their own language and culture on the Greater East Asia Co-prosperity Sphere. Many religious neutrals who controlled schools conscientiously felt they could not object to teaching Japanese since it did not conflict with their main purpose, which was to educate Chinese youth in principles they believed to be right. They had taught English when the British were in control, and by the same token they could see little justification for refusing to teach Japanese under the new dispensation.

Dr. Selwyn-Clarke, the former Director of Medical Services, remained out of internment and co-operated with the Japanese. As a doctor he might have defended his duty to tend the sick to the utmost of his abilities in whatever circumstances. But his intention was not to assist the Japanese but to serve the community, the prisoners of war, and the internees. He argued that he could do more good to Hong Kong people by staying out, and that because the Government had assumed obligations to the families of the local volunteer forces and of the auxiliary and essential services, his first duty was to them. How well he performed his tasks, despite obstruction and humiliations and eventual imprisonment, has already been told.

Two professors of the University Medical Department were allowed to remain out because of medical commitments. One, Professor Gordon King, escaped in February 1942. The other, Professor R. C. Robertson, the Professor of Pathology, continued at the Bacteriological Institute under close Japanese supervision, doing laboratory work from which the occupation authorities benefited. This collaboration increasingly worried him, though unquestionably members of the community generally profited too; he became depressed and consulted a priest who reassured him of the value to the community of his work. Eventually on 4 August 1942 his body was found lying on the ground outside the Institute; he had apparently fallen from a verandah, and had apparently committed suicide. Such were the stresses to which sensitive minds were subjected during the occupation in trying to decide where their duty lay.

The main argument used to defend collaboration was that some collaboration was unavoidable in the interest of the people. A few rare Hong Kong Chinese citizens with a sense of social responsibility reluctantly thought that it was necessary to co-operate with the Japanese as the only way to serve their own community and so mitigate the severity and rigours of the occupation, and that somebody had to represent the interests of the people to make the views of the Chinese majority heard. A number of prominent people escaped this dilemma either on the eve of hostilities or, later in the occupation, by leaving Hong Kong. Those who apparently 'chose' to stay were in a very real sense making their loyalty to Hong Kong known, regardless of the unofficial requests by British officials to undertake this responsibility. Apparent collaboration in Hong Kong by such people was certainly fraught with more serious consequences than the inconspicuous deeds of comparatively unknown members of the public which often passed unnoticed. Members of the Executive or Legislative Councils could not escape the significance of their former official positions. In addition, the Japanese put great pressure on the influential members of the Chinese community to collaborate, particularly the unofficial members of the two councils and the leaders of commerce and industry. It has already been mentioned that they were rounded up at the beginning of the occupation,[3] confined in admittedly reasonably comfortable conditions, and then called to meet the Japanese authorities at a lunch, at which the Japanese appealed for collaboration on racial grounds. If the Chinese leaders refused to collaborate they inevitably laid themselves open to suspicion.

Sir Robert Kotewall acted as the chief spokesman for the Chinese under the Japanese occupation; he had been the senior local unofficial member of the Executive Council and it was clearly vitally important to the Japanese to secure his co-operation. Sir Shouson Chow, the first Chinese to be made a member of the Executive Council and another prominent local personality, also spoke for the Chinese, and it was of course equally important to the Japanese occupying authorities that he should do so. These two men were in a special category, not only because of their standing but also because they worked with the Japanese at the invitation and with the express approval of leading members of the Hong Kong Government. On 1 January 1942, R. A. C. North, Secretary for Chinese Affairs, J. A. Fraser, Defence Secretary, and C. G. Alabaster,

[3] F.O. 371/31671/1942. Telegram M.205 29 January 1942 from Military Attaché, Chungking. This reported that a Chinese puppet governor had been appointed. However, as well as local considerations, the Japanese had diplomatic motives in China for this treatment of prominent Chinese citizens. ' . . . About sixty prominent Chinese housed in Hong Kong Hotel in comfort, but subjected to political tutelage, with object of persuading them to join Nanking Government and influencing Chungking Government in favour of peace.'

Attorney-General, called on Sir Robert and Sir Shouson and requested them to act on behalf of the Chinese in Hong Kong where British officials were now powerless, and to promote friendly relations between Chinese and Japanese to the extent necessary to restore public order, protect life and property and preserve internal security.[4] Sir Robert and Sir Shouson therefore had reason to believe that the British had empowered them to co-operate with the Japanese to the extent necessary to enable them to do whatever was possible to assist the Chinese community.

How much they were in fact able to do for the Hong Kong community is difficult to say. They were treated in a cavalier manner, if not with disrespect, except in public where their 'face' was respected. The Rehabilitation Committee held fifty-nine meetings during its short life which ended on 30 March 1942, but it was not allowed to see Heads of Departments and could deal only with Japanese interpreters. Members were given orders for which they had to assume responsibility in public; they were ordered to make speeches and give radio talks and had to submit drafts for approval, and then had to endure seeing garbled versions in the press. When the British returned, Sir Robert resigned his membership of the Executive Council on the grounds that this was the honourable course to take. Sir Mark Young agreed, and wrote in warm terms commending him for his public services to Hong Kong.

Other prominent Chinese, including unofficial members of the Legislative Council and commercial leaders, found themselves forced into membership of the two councils but managed to keep in the background by toeing the line just sufficiently to allay suspicion. A few were undoubtedly whole-hearted collaborators. There was the Japanese-educated Lau Tit-shing, president of the Chinese-Japanese Returned-Students Association, and also chairman of the Japanese-sponsored Chinese

[4] See the account given after the war by Mr. R. A. C. North in *South China Morning Post*, 2 October 1945: He went to the China Building to see Kotewall and Chow 'and requested Sir Robert Kotewall and Sir Shouson Chow and their colleagues to take upon themselves what should have been my duty. These gentlemen in carrying out this task were abused and humiliated by the Japanese and were misrepresented and abused by some of their friends. I regret more than I can say that misunderstandings should have arisen over this matter and I sincerely hope that the true facts will now be realised.'

Bankers' Association. He was very pro-Japanese, as his speech of congratulation on the fall of Singapore reported in the *Hong Kong News* of 17 February 1942 clearly shows. There was also Chan Lim-pak, a prominent businessman, who later became a fourth member of the Chinese Representative Council and a well-known Japanese supporter who had been arrested by the British during the fighting on a charge of aiding the enemy. A larger number of Chinese collaborated with the Japanese in the districts where close contact with the people afforded greater opportunities of community service. Some no doubt acted from self-interest, others from a genuine belief in Japan's self-proclaimed mission of freeing Asia, but many more as a way to survive.

The British tended to take a broad and understanding view of collaboration with the Japanese, and in some cases it was condoned on grounds of political expediency. For example, the Burmese National Army had fought for the Japanese during the Burma Campaign, an active collaboration amounting to the clearest treason. Later the Burmese became less enthusiastic about the Japanese and deserted in order to fight once more on the British side. They were welcomed, regardless of the treason, mainly because the Burmese were fighting primarily for their own independence and it was felt politically undesirable to take punitive action.

The New Territories villages felt some effects of the collaboration controversies. Many of the younger men joined the communist guerrillas and had imbibed communist ideas, particularly in the Hakka districts in the Saikung area and also the area north of Tolo harbour. These returned after the end of the war and were proud of their record in resisting the Japanese and assisting the United Nations' war effort. They tended to be contemptuous of the old village elders who had remained behind, and whom they accused of collaboration.

Collaboration aroused deep and bitter feelings within the local community and resulted in a spate of accusations, mutual recrimination, and a strident demand for retribution against the guilty. The Military Administration set up a War Activities Committee to list suspected collaborators and enquire into their doings; it appealed to the public to come forward with information from which to build up evidence against them, and of course, in this connexion, the files of the B.A.A.G. and experiences of its underground agents were extremely important. By December 1945 over fifty suspected collaborators were being held in custody. There was considerable delay in bringing them to justice because of the shortage of police, the absence of witnesses, and a hesitation to bring these cases before the military courts under the Military Administration. The proceedings against the collaborators were quite different from the War Crimes trials of Japanese nationals, chiefly members of their armed services, which were taking place in Hong Kong at the same time before specially constituted Allied military tribunals. These were quite outside the control of the Hong Kong authorities, and dealt with crimes by Japanese against humanity and the accepted usages of war.

Collaborators, on the other hand, were charged on indictment with specific offences under English law such as treason or breach of the Defence Regulations, and it was considered preferable to bring them before the ordinary civil courts in due process of law, even if this meant waiting until normal civil government was restored. This arrangement also had the advantage of avoiding the awkward situation of some suspects being tried by the military courts under the Military Administration and others by the ordinary civil courts. However, when the restoration of civil government was postponed it became clear that further prolonged delay would be unfair to those in custody, and the collaboration trials opened on 17 February 1946 when six persons were accused of treason in public committal proceedings before a summary military court. According to newspaper reports, thirty-one persons appeared before the Military Courts up to 30 April 1946, when the Military Administration ended. One was sentenced to death and hanged in Stanley Gaol in the following July, after an appeal for clemency had been rejected. Another, a Eurasian, was acquitted but, immediately after the verdict, was banished for life, and the charges against two others appear to have been dropped, as their names do not appear in any subsequent newspaper reports of proceedings or in any official records. After the restoration of civil rule on 1 May 1946 a total of twenty-nine suspected collaborators, including one woman, appeared before the magistrates in committal proceedings. Of these twenty-nine, five were sentenced by the magistrate on a charge reduced from treason or breach of the Defence Regulations, and three were acquitted. The remaining twenty-one were committed for trial in the Supreme Court. During the period 1 May 1946 to May 1947 the Supreme Court Registers show that twenty-nine persons were tried in the Supreme Court for collaboration offences. This figure includes the twenty-one committed by the magistrates and presumably the remaining eight came up from the Summary Military Court. Included in the total was Inouye Kanao, the Japanese interpreter who was so much hated by the men in Shamshuipo. He had been tried for war crimes by the special Military War Crimes Court and condemned to death on 25 May 1946, but it was then decided that as a Canadian, he had been guilty of treason and would have to be re-tried on that count, and at the end of February 1947 he was committed for trial by the Supreme Court.[5] He claimed to be a Japanese citizen who owed no allegiance to the Crown, but was found guilty, sentenced to death on 23 April 1947, and was hanged in Stanley Gaol in the following August, after his appeal had been dismissed and leave to appeal to the Privy Council refused. One of the twenty-nine, a European who worked for the Japanese at the Dairy Farm during the occupation, was acquitted. The remaining twenty-eight were found guilty on one or more counts of their indictment and sentenced. They included six Indians, seven Europeans or Eurasians and fifteen Chinese.

In a number of cases heavy bail, up to $20,000, was allowed, as most of the accused had been in custody since September 1945. One Chinese jumped his bail while awaiting trial and apparently successfully evaded justice, since his name disappears from the records. The defence made in one case, that British sovereignty had ceased in Hong Kong during the occupation, was not accepted, and a plea of duress was rejected in another case because the accused's treatment of his victims showed a zeal quite incompatible with his defence. In November 1946, when a European stockbroker was found guilty, the jury added a rider to their verdict that it was inconsistent

[5] *Hong Kong Law Reports*, vol. XXX (1946–7), pp. 66–77.

with British justice that one collaborator should be punished when so many escaped unpunished. Indeed the trials attracted some criticism on the ground that relatively unknown collaborators were being charged, while more important figures, who were felt to be equally guilty, were allowed to go scot-free. In the previous March, instructions from London directed that future proceedings should be taken only against collaborators proved to have committed atrocities, a ruling that gave the collaboration trials even greater similarity to those conducted by the special War Crimes Military Courts.

Witnesses came forward with ghastly stories of tortures, particularly those inflicted by the *Kempeitai* to force confessions, brutal assaults, starvation diets, and confinement in filthy conditions, deprived of even the basic necessities of decent existence. One prominent Portuguese solicitor who had worked for the B.A.A.G., at a trial of a collaborator described how, on 21 June 1946, he had been confined for forty-seven days except when being interrogated. He had been beaten with bamboo whips, burnt with a hot poker, strung up for twenty-five minutes by his arms which were tied behind his back, and given the dreaded water torture.

As time went on the Court showed greater leniency, and in October 1946 directed that the sentence of three years' hard labour awarded in one case should commence as from the date of arrest of the accused in November 1945. The collaboration trials came to an end. The annual reports of the Judiciary show that no committal proceedings against collaborators were taken in the magistrates' courts during the year 1947–8, and the Supreme Court disposed of its last collaboration case in May 1947. Altogether, five accused received the death sentence, four from the Supreme Court and one from the Standing Military Court, and were hanged in Stanley Gaol after their appeals had been dismissed. The remainder, except one who was acquitted, received terms of imprisonment with hard labour as follows: two received fifteen years (one being reduced by the Appeal Court from a life sentence); two received ten to twelve years; seven, six to nine years; nine, two to four years; one, one year; one, six months; and two, including a woman, one day. Two distinctive features of the collaboration trials perhaps stand out. First, they occupied a relatively short period of time, a little over a year, from February 1946 to May 1947; and secondly, they affected relatively few persons, and a scrutiny of the newspaper reports yields only some thirty-six persons formally prosecuted in the courts. Proceedings against the remainder held in custody appear to have been dropped.

The two series of trials, for treason and breach of the Defence Regulations and for war crimes, occupied much official time and energy in the post-war reconstruction period. War Crimes trials took place before specially constituted military tribunals for which the British Government was responsible, and a press release in April 1948, by the Headquarters Land Forces in Hong Kong, gave a review of these trials.

Japanese prisoners of war who surrendered in Hong Kong in August 1945 were screened, and 239 were retained in custody in Stanley Gaol as suspected war criminals; fifty Japanese were brought from Formosa for suspected atrocities against prisoners of war there and ten were sent on request from Japan. Number 13 War Crimes Investigation Team, appointed by the British authorities, began operations in 1946, and a second team, Number 14, started work later in the same year to hasten the trials and avoid the prolonged detention of suspects awaiting trial. Photos of suspects were displayed and the public was asked to come forward to testify.

The first war crimes court sat on 27 March 1946, where fifteen Japanese were accused of atrocities at Lantau after a military post had been attacked by guerrillas at Silvermine Bay in 1945. The military courts were presided over by a Lt.-Colonel, usually of the Judge-Advocate-General's Department of the Indian Army, with two other officers of the rank of major and captain, also of the Indian Army, and two British officers were deputed respectively to be prosecuting and defence counsel. In the eighth trial in July 1946 a Japanese lawyer arrived to represent the accused, and at his first appearance as counsel received the court's congratulations. The trials were held in public, without a jury, and the charge was usually phrased as being concerned with specific acts 'in violation of the laws and usages of war', presumably referring to the Geneva Convention. The sentences had to be confirmed by the

Supreme Commander Allied Land Forces, South-East Asia, who occasionally, if rarely, refused confirmation.

Hong Kong was selected as the venue for the trial of Japanese accused of war crimes in Formosa, Hainan Island, in the old Treaty Ports, and on the high seas, and, accordingly, a second court began operating in September 1946.

Before these military tribunals was unfolded a shocking tale of torture, privation, denial of the ordinary decencies of life, and the imprisonment of 1,816 local residents of whom 181 had been executed, many arbitrarily. The trials lasted two years, the last judgement being delivered on 31 March 1948. During that period forty-eight cases involving 129 Japanese were heard, of which twenty-one were sentenced to death, twenty-eight received sentences of ten years' or more imprisonment, fifty-seven to periods under ten years, and fourteen were acquitted. The charges against the remainder were dropped. There were only two civilians, one of whom was Inouye who was handed over to the civil courts to be tried for treason, because as a Canadian he was subject to the Crown. Col. Tokunaga, commandant of all the Hong Kong camps and Capt. Saito, medical officer in charge, had their death sentences commuted to life and twenty years' imprisonment respectively. Among those executed were Colonel Noma, described by a Jesuit Father as ascetic, studious and gentlemanly-looking, but nevertheless the hated head of the gendarmerie, whose appearance so belied his occupation. Also his successor, Colonel Kanagawa, was executed. Lt.-General Ito, who commanded the Japanese 38th Division infantry, was sentenced to twelve years, and Major-General Tanaka, formerly colonel commanding the 229th Regiment, twenty years, but Major-General Shoji, formerly commanding the 230th Regiment in the attack on Hong Kong, was acquitted. Lt.-General Sakai was tried by the Chinese in Nanking and executed. Lt.-General Isogai, formerly Governor, was given a life sentence, also in Nanking.[6] The second Japanese Governor of Hong Kong, Lt.-General Tanaka, was executed in Canton in March 1947. The Captain of the *Lisbon Maru* was sentenced

[6] An effort has been made to trace the records of these trials held in China but it has not been possible to locate them.

to seven years. When the trials ended in March 1948 there were seventy-three still serving terms in Stanley Prison.

In conclusion it might be said: whether for reasons of expediency or through a humane appreciation of the dilemma of the Chinese in Hong Kong, the returning British authorities did not launch a policy of vengeance of recrimination. Some people might say that they were in no position to take that line. With the passing of the years into the new, more prosperous Hong Kong, the public memory of any shame or humiliation suffered at the hands of the Japanese has faded. Nevertheless, it has now been suggested that the subject itself is disturbing to the families of some of the principal protagonists of that time and therefore that the subject should not be ventilated at all. This is an unhealthy attitude. Indeed, it might be argued that the very fact of embarrassment today at the mention of the deeds of those, who it is clear had no choice but to do their duty, is itself an indication of the high sense of personal loyalty and honour felt by these families. The shame should be felt by those nameless opportunists who profiteered at the expense of their fellows during the war.

Finally, in Hong Kong, where the sense of public-spiritedness is a rare attribute, these examples of prominent men who put the responsibilities of their public office before their private, individual feelings and ends, need to be displayed to the community.

E. PERSONALITIES

1 Sir Mark Aitchison Young, G.C.M.G., Governor, Hong Kong, September 1941–May 1947. (*South China Morning Post*)

2 Major General C.M. Maltby, C.B., M.C., G.O.C., British Forces, Hong Kong, 1941. (*South China Morning Post*)

3 Admiral Sir Chan Chak, K.B.E., a special envoy of the Chinese authorities attached to the Allied forces to deal with pro-Japanese sympathizers during the hostilities. (*in possession of the author*)

4 Colonel L.T. Ride, C.B.E., Commandant, British Army Aid Group. (*courtesy of Lady Ride*)

5 F.C. Gimson, Colonial Secretary, 7 December 1941–6 September 1945. (*South China Morning Post*)

6 Lieut. General Rensuke Isogai, Japanese Governor of Hong Kong (1942-1944) during the Occupation. (*Hong Kong News*)

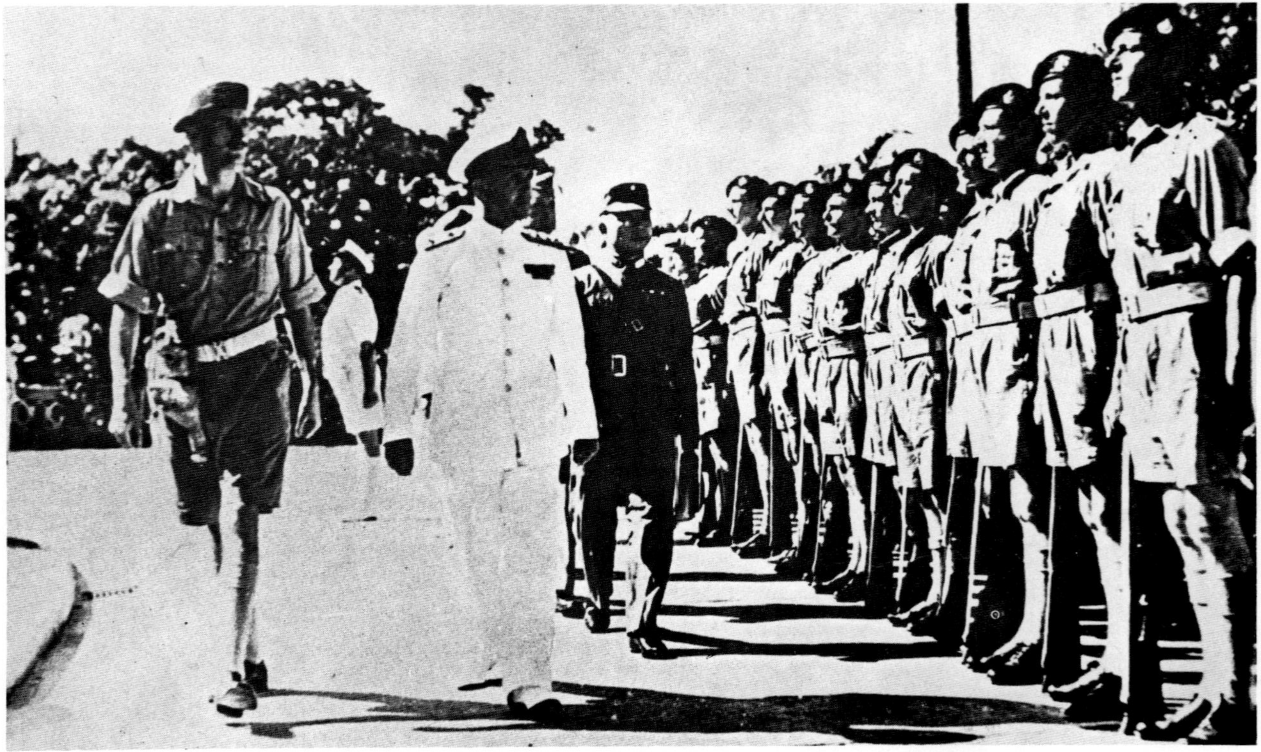

7 Rear Admiral Harcourt, C.B., C.B.E., Commander in Chief, British Military Administration, 1945-1946. (*South China Morning Post*)

PART THREE

POST-WAR

I

THE PLANNING UNIT IN LONDON

'Throughout the planning for the administration of the Far East colonial territories on their liberation, it was assumed that the war with Japan would not necessarily terminate with our return to those territories . . . . For this reason it was considered desirable that any statements of administrative policy should be formulated in that simple form which clearly would be most suitable for a Military Administration . . . . In the case of Hong Kong, there was the further complication that right up to the days immediately preceding the collapse of Japan, it was not known whether Hong Kong would be in a British Military Command or whether it might perhaps be an American or Chinese sphere.'

C.O. 129/54132/45. (Letter to Sir Mark Young from Downing Street, 13 April 1946.)

THE re-occupation of territory from which the enemy had been ejected by military operations posed the problem of how it was to be administered. In Burma there was also the problem of two administrations in the non-Japanese-occupied parts, one under the Governor of Burma and the other, where fighting was actually taking place, under the British Military Commander. Military rule was recognized to be unpopular with civilians, nevertheless it was decided that the administration of liberated areas must be assumed by the army, and in November 1942 the Allies decided to set up military administrations in all re-occupied territory. This was inevitable in war-operational areas, and equally necessary in rear areas which were being used as military bases because it was the only way to ensure that essential military considerations received priority when administrative decisions were being taken. It was arranged that the military commander in all areas should have a Chief Civil Affairs Officer who would be responsible to him for the administration of the civilians resident there. This officer and his staff were normally selected because of administrative experience, usually in the territory itself. Essentially, they were specialist administrative officials disguised as military officers, performing in military dress the same functions they would normally have done in peace time. The essential element was that the military commander had the authority to adopt and enforce such policies as the military situation might require.

There was much debate about whether the civil affairs officers should wear military uniform. It was argued that this was unnecessary as long as military needs were safeguarded. In operational areas these men had to be given military status in case of capture, and it was decided that they should be treated as members of military commander's staff like any other technical officer. Churchill was very much opposed to giving them any military rank, and wanted to safeguard the status of officers actually engaged in fighting. His powerful opposition temporarily held up the civil affairs planning arrangements, but it was finally ruled that all officers in the Civil Affairs Service should be commissioned and be subject to military discipline under the Commander of the appropriate Force, despite the fact that senior officers in this service would have to have high rank. Churchill fumed against 'hordes of sham Major-Generals', but the commissioning decision was upheld, subject to the concession that the commissions should take effect and uniforms be worn only when the officers actually proceeded to their duties in the field.

In any case the Colonial Office had to initiate plans for the Government of Hong Kong and other Far East British territories when they were liberated, and their plans had to fit in with those regarding civil affairs generally. In fact, in the summer of 1943, when the discussions about the administration of a liberated Hong Kong were set in train, a number of points about the Army Civil Affairs Units had still to be decided, but it was sensibly agreed that some donkey work was necessary by a planning unit before a civil affairs staff could operate.

In August 1943 it was proposed that a small planning staff should be assembled to plan for the Far Eastern colonies and protected territories, and that this staff should be commissioned and placed under a Civil Affairs (Military Planning) Unit of the War Office. The difficulty was that Hong Kong and the

Borneo territories were in the United States' strategic area, and the War Office was therefore reluctant to agree to anything which might suggest that it was assuming military responsibilities there. But whether the Commander of the Forces in the liberated colonies were American or not, it was still necessary that he should have a skilled staff to deal with civil affairs, and the Colonial Office proceeded accordingly.

The matter was then taken up with the Americans under the Allied Combined Civil Affairs Committee, and the Americans agreed that British civil affairs officers should undertake the administration of former British-controlled colonies and territories, under the local Allied Commander. But much discussion was required before the points at issue were determined. One difference of opinion between the British and Americans was over the implications of the method by which liberation was achieved.

The Combined Civil Affairs Committee in Washington had in the summer of 1943 issued a directive, or in United States' terminology a 'charter', laying down the general principles guiding the civil affairs units generally. Article VI of this charter stated that when an enemy-occupied territory of the United States, the United Kingdom, or one of the British Dominions, was to be recovered 'as the result of an operation, combined or otherwise', the directive to the Force Commander would include instructions regarding the policies to be adopted in the handling of civil affairs as formulated by the Government which exercised authority over the territory before it was occupied by the enemy. This seemed a clear enough safeguard for British control over her former territories. But in the autumn of 1944 the Americans put a construction on the words 'as the result of an operation' which caught the British by surprise. They took the view that if the territory concerned were liberated not 'as the result of an operation' but as the result of a general Japanese surrender without any military action being necessary, then no such directive regarding civil affairs would be given to the Force Commander. The British felt they had to accept this interpretation. It vitally affected Hong Kong because it meant that if Hong Kong were liberated through a military operation an American Force Commander would be there and that Americans would be responsible for civil affairs, including supplies and finance, though the officials administering civil affairs there might be British. If Hong Kong were regained as the result of a general surrender, then the Americans would not assume any over-all responsibility for administering Hong Kong. It was not in fact expected that Hong Kong would be liberated without an operation, and probably a costly struggle, but Britain had to be ready to take over full responsibility in case the surrender came without any direct military operation being necessary. The Hong Kong Planning Unit therefore assumed a new urgency.

Mr. N. L. Smith, who had just before the war retired from the Hong Kong Colonial Secretaryship, agreed to collect the Planning Unit staff and advise until a Chief Civil Affairs Officer was appointed. The Planning Unit was naturally to form the nucleus of the Civil Affairs staff who would administer Hong Kong. They would be commissioned when they were about to go out and work in the Colony.

For a long time the Planning Unit was small and nowhere near its intended strength. The problem was recruitment of men with suitable experience, as most Hong Kong Government officers were in prisoner-of-war or civilian internment camps. Some were available because they had escaped or happened to be out of the Colony when the blow fell, and some were taken out of retirement. Its directives came from the Colonial Office and its general policy was to take steps to set up an administration along pre-war lines.

The planners were confronted with a thankless and forbidding task. There were too many unknowns and yet they had to try to be ready to take over and provide a stable government.[1] They had to consider the possibility that those imprisoned in Hong Kong might not survive an outright allied assault, so they had to trace former government employees to see if they were available, and they had to take into account the purely material problems of rehabilitation, which might mean, if heavy fighting occurred, rebuilding virtually from scratch. Clearly they faced a difficult task in attempting to provide for all possible contingencies and to decide on priorities in recreating the essentials of a civilized community. There were

[1] But see Appendix 3, The liberation of Hong Kong.

important political decisions to be taken regarding the Chinese, such as restriction of immigration which had been imposed just before the war. Private enterprise, which formed the basis of the Colony's economic life, had to be rebuilt from scratch, and in fact businessmen were eventually sent out on twelve months' official salaries to get the Colony's commercial life restarted. Junior staffs such as clerks and mechanics were indented for, Hong Kong residents being preferred wherever possible. There was of course no active Hong Kong budget,[2] and the costs of the Planning Unit, including officers' salaries, were debited against the Hong Kong Government account in London until the Unit's personnel were seconded to the War Office in their military ranks, a fact which partly explains why the War Office delayed taking them over until the last moment. The Hongkong and Shanghai Banking Corporation, under the guidance of its acting Chief Manager, Arthur Morse, later Sir Arthur, played an active part by strongly supporting the Planning Unit financially by making available to it loans of up to £5 million without security or guarantee, mainly for heavy machinery and plant for the public utility companies and docks.

In September 1944, D. M. MacDougall, a senior Government officer whose escape from Hong Kong has already been mentioned, became Chief Civil Affairs Officer, in the prospective rank of Brigadier, with Mr. M. M. Thomson, a senior Cadet Officer, as his deputy in the rank of Colonel, and Mr. P. C. M. Sedgwick as his personal assistant. Others were T. J. J. Fenwick, in charge of Finance; J. Whyatt, Legal Affairs; Dr. J. P. Fehily, Health and Social Services; C. H. Sansom, Police and Fire Services; H. S. Rouse, Public Works; T. R. Rowell, Education, the last-named on a part-time basis.

It can be easily understood that they were not ready by V.J. Day, indeed, as one of the planners waggishly joked, they were rather praying that the war would not end just yet. After V.J. Day they were seconded to the War Office and put into uniform. Brigadier MacDougall, his deputy, and nine others were sent out at the earliest that transport permitted and arrived in Hong Kong on 7 September. Another eleven

[2] But accounts of disbursements to officials or pensions, etc., were kept in the Colonial Office during the war.

were sent out a little later, and the rest in batches, as transport became available. The sudden, and only partly expected, surrender of the Japanese had precipitated action and not only were the planners not ready, but the head of the Military Government itself had not yet been nominated.[3]

Still, the Planning Unit had done some valuable spade work and must take some measure of the credit for the rapid rehabilitation of the Colony.

Even if the planning had been complete that would not of itself have assured the restoration in Hong Kong of British rule. American opinion was strongly anti-colonial, a sentiment equally shared by President Roosevelt.[4] The President saw no place for Hong Kong as a British Colony in any permanent Far East Settlement and on a number of occasions he urged Great Britain to give it back to China as a gesture of goodwill, a point he particularly pressed at the Yalta Conference of February 1945. The Atlantic Charter of March 1943, urging the liberation of all peoples, was considered by Roosevelt to apply not only to victims of German and Japanese aggression, but also to colonial peoples, and he thought it inconsistent for the Allies to crusade for the freedom of peoples and at the same time leave the Colonial Powers in control of subject races.

There was also the American desire to build up China as a Great Power and assist her to take her full part in the war both operationally and in policy decisions. The United States and Britain had each made a treaty with the Nationalist Government of China on 11 January 1943. The British Treaty gave back to China the International Settlements at Shanghai and Amoy, and the British Concessions at Tientsin and Canton. Britain also gave up all extra-territorial rights including the special law courts in Shanghai and Amoy, and other special navigation rights such as those in China's coastal and inland waters. The Chinese regarded these privileges as the immoral gains wrested from her by the so-called 'unequal

[3] Formally this was the Commander-in-Chief, Admiral Harcourt.

[4] B. W. Tuchman, *Stillwell and the American Experience in China, 1911–45*, Macmillan (New York, 1971), p. 410. 'But let's raise the Chinese Flag there first, and then Chiang can next day make a grand gesture and make it a free port. That's the way to handle that.' (President Roosevelt, 1943). The views of Ambassador P. J. Hurley were perhaps an extreme example of this pro-Chinese attitude.

treaties' and their abrogation gave her special satisfaction.[5] Chiang Kai-shek, now that the war was over, also raised the question of the rendition of the New Territories which he regarded as coming within the 1943 Treaty, since they were leased territory and not definitively ceded as were Hong Kong Island and the tip of the Kowloon peninsula. Britain, however, regarded the New Territories as forming part of the Colony with which its administration was integrated, and claimed that in the exchange of Notes accompanying the Treaty she had made it clear that what she was relinquishing was 'all existing treaty rights relating to the system of Treaty Ports in China', a formula which did not embrace the New Territories.

Moreover there was the new spirit of national pride and claim to equal status demonstrated by the Kuomintang which vociferously demanded the retrocession of the Colony, and there was much talk among the Chinese in Hong Kong of its rendition to China.[6] British policy was to secure the restoration of Hong Kong's pre-war status and they therefore set in train a number of measures directed to this end.

Under these circumstances the Planning Unit and the proposed military administration of which it was the nucleus assumed an added urgency and importance in the take-over arrangements. Yet it took some time to get the decisions made, and Rear-Admiral C. H. J. Harcourt's entry was delayed for some time until his exact office and responsibilities were determined. In fact, as already mentioned, it was only on 30 August that his orders were signalled to him as he lay outside Hong Kong, designating him Commander-in-Chief, Hong Kong, and head of the Military Government under the direct orders of the British Chiefs of Staff.

Harcourt arrived on 30 August to find the Gimson administration already in being. This was retained as a temporary measure pending the arrival of the military administration staff, and its head was appointed Lieutenant-Governor, under Harcourt. Now that the war was over the question inevitably arose whether a military administration was still necessary or even appropriate; Mr. Gimson felt it was neither, and

[5] W. L. Tung, *China and the Foreign Powers . . .* (New York, 1970), p. 272.
[6] Sinimite, 'The Future of Hong Kong', *National Review*, vol. 128, no. 768, February 1947, pp. 148–56.

strongly urged the continuance of the civil administration established by himself by incorporating the proposed military civil affairs staff into it. The Admiral, in fact, on 1 September proclaimed a military administration under himself as he had been instructed and the British Government decided that this must continue as planned. No other course was possible since Mr. Gimson and his colleagues needed leave to recuperate from the ordeal of internment as soon as they could be relieved by the Civil Affairs staff. The advance guard, with Brigadier MacDougall himself, arrived on 7 September and began to set up their administration at once.

II

THE BRITISH MILITARY ADMINISTRATION

'. . . the real work of rehabilitation had of course to be, and was, done by the Chinese. We were able to give them freedom, food, law and order and a stable currency.'

Vice-Admiral Sir Cecil Harcourt, in a lecture to the Royal Central Asian Society, 13 November 1946

THE Military Administration was established in Hong Kong by a proclamation issued on 1 September 1945, over the name of Rear-Admiral C. H. J. Harcourt, and lasted for eight months until civil government was restored on 1 May 1946. Its personnel was largely made up of former Hong Kong Government officials, with others recruited from England or from the Armed Forces then serving in the Colony, supplemented by local professional and businessmen who helped out temporarily. It was a military administration mainly in name, in that the Commander-in-Chief assumed responsibility for the administration under the War Office and that normal constitutional machinery under the Hong Kong Letters Patent was in abeyance; in fact, since the principal administrative personnel had been recruited from former Government officers, pre-war civilian administrative patterns and normal colonial government procedures tended to be increasingly followed.

The take-over from the Japanese occupation authorities in Hong Kong proceeded more smoothly than in other British Far Eastern territories, the Japanese officials being co-operative in regard to handing over their departments, and the Japanese police and military maintained some degree of order. Mr. F. C. Gimson had been able too, during his interim administration as least, to do some spade-work in re-starting the main essential services of both Government and the public utility companies, and there was also less physical damage than had been feared.

The Military Administration faced great difficulties. Every side of Hong Kong life needed urgent rebuilding in order to re-create a healthy, growing community, a task complicated by a desperate shortage of skilled manpower and materials, and faced by an ever-present threat of failure through sheer lack of food. Liberation had been wonderful, but it did not solve the problem of feeding over half a million people.

The British Military Administration of Hong Kong was brought into being pending the restoration of civil government by Rear-Admiral Harcourt's Proclamation Number 1 of 1 September 1945, in virtue of which he assumed full legislative, executive, administrative and judicial powers over all persons and property throughout the Colony;[1] Japanese laws and regulations entirely ceased to have effect unless the Military Administration expressly thought it expedient for them to continue in force. The law, as it existed at the time immediately before the enemy occupation, was restored, subject to any proclamations which might be issued. All rights and property were to be respected, except that titles to property acquired under the Japanese were to be recognized only after investigation. The normal civil courts were suspended.

Mr. Gimson's temporary administration, however, was exercising the usual pre-war governmental powers derived from the current Letters Patent of 1917. To regularize his position, Proclamation Number 2 was issued on the same day, by which he was made Lieutenant-Governor, exercising the usual powers of the Governor, subject to any instructions from the Admiral.[2] The normal pre-war machinery of government, including the Executive and Legislative Councils and the Supreme Court and Magistrates Courts were thus theoretically revived, though in fact they never functioned, the sole purpose being to validate Gimson's actions, since he and his advisers had been meeting and taking decisions as members of the old Executive Council. These arrangements had been made purely on an *ad hoc* basis because, until the Chief Civil Affairs Officer and his staff arrived, the intended Military Administration could not in any case function, and of course Mr. Gimson and his team would shortly be leaving the Colony.

On 7 September the Chief Civil Affairs Officer, Brigadier

[1] *British Military Administration Proclamations, 1945–6.*

[2] This was shortly afterwards disallowed by the Colonial Office on the grounds that such office was incompatible with the existing command.

D. M. MacDougall, arrived with nine members of his staff and on 13 September the Military Administration was reconstituted by Proclamation No. 4 by which the Admiral delegated to him wide powers, subject to any directions from himself as Commander-in-Chief, including the exercise of the functions of the Executive and Legislative Councils and power to amend any existing ordinance or suspend its operation. He was authorized to make regulations on a number of specified subjects, for example he could prohibit or control the export of currency or securities, carrying on of any industry or manufacture, use or acquisition of all forms of transport, movment of persons in or out of the Colony, access to any area or premises, all publications, holding of meetings or demonstrations, any spectacle or entertainment, display of flags and symbols, use of roads and the harbour, and could call upon any person's services and fix the remuneration. He could institute a censorship, call for information, detain persons by written order if the preservation of public order required it, and could issue such an order against any person suspected of treason or any offence committed during the fighting or under the Japanese occupation, under the Defence Regulations of 1940.

By Proclamation No. 16 of 4 December 1945 there wa a further and embracing delegation of the Commander in-Chief's powers to the Chief Civil Affairs Officer, who was in turn empowered to delegate powers to any person he might think fit, and to authorize further delegation at his discretion. It was explained that this delegation of authority 'would assist the carrying into effect of His Britannic Majesty's Government to restore Civil Government at the earliest possible date. . . .'

The Home Government on 17 October 1945 amended its directive to the Head of the Military Administration to give the Chief Civil Affairs Officer wider responsibilities in rehabilitation. Under the original military directive his function was to administer the civil population, to avoid disease and unrest which might hamper military operations. Since military operations had ceased, he was now to be responsible to the Colonial Office in Whitehall for setting in hand the rehabilitation of the Colony. In fact, the new directive was largely a statement of long-term objectives, because shortages of men and supplies made it difficult to do more than the minimum originally aimed at.

Confronted with the forbidding task of setting up a government and restoring the life of the community virtually from scratch, the Chief Civil Affairs Officer was as short-staffed as he was over-worked. At the beginning of October 1945 seventy-nine names were officially listed as members of the Civil Affairs Administration staff. A number of appointments were announced, which for some reason were not included in the staff-list. Appointments continued to be made and the administration built up in numbers during the whole of the eight months, yet recruitment fell well behind that required, and Brigadier MacDougall reported on 15 November that he had only 18 per cent of the approved establishment. Some departments set up during the emergency, for example Censorship and Immigration, were wound up and the staff were freed for other duties; on the other hand, some departments not provided for in the plans for the Military Administration were nevertheless established.

This acute shortage of staff had one unexpected though significant result. The Military Administration was forced to rely much more on local Chinese and Portuguese personnel, who were now obliged to accept more responsibility than they had been allowed pre-war. Brigadier MacDougall paid tribute to the valuable assistance given by these Government officers, adding 'it can hardly be denied that they thereby established credentials which it would be difficult for any future Government to ignore'.

Immediate and formidable tasks were those to do with the repatriation and resettling of the prisoners of war and internees, the winding up of the affairs of the camps, and the demobilization of Hong Kong's own armed forces and auxiliary defence services. Most repatriates had to be sent home on recuperation leave. The most serious cases left by the hospital ship *Oxfordshire*, and by 17 September some 1,014 had been sent home by the *Empress of Australia* and a second hospital ship; by 6 October another six ships had taken 1,031 Europeans and fifty-three Indians, and in early December fourteen more ships took 386 Europeans and forty-seven Indians; another 126 were sent home by air; this left some 340, including dependants, remaining temporarily in Hong Kong to assist the administration or to deal with their own affairs. Of all those in the prisoner-of-war or internment camps only 120 elected to stay on in Hong Kong. Repatriation had been begun with commendable alacrity, before the Civil Affairs staff arrived, by an organization called 'Recovery of Allied Prisoners of War and Internees' (R.A.P.W.I.) which dispatched people off to Britain without much enquiry. Many claimed repatriation who were not entitled to it. It was one of the many tasks of the Military Administration to set up a Repatriation Office which scrutinized these claims more closely, keeping lists of those who had been given passages, and it also checked on those who had spent the war years in Macao, Shanghai, or Canton and who now appeared, wanting to be sent home at government expense.

A proclamation dealing with the demobilization of the Hong Kong Volunteer Defence Corps and Naval Defence Force was issued in October 1945, setting out the benefits to which a Volunteer was entitled on demobilization. This stipulated, amongst other things, passages only for those who were domiciled abroad. Those born in Hong Kong were to receive neither passages nor, as they reasonably claimed, cash in lieu. The Volunteers comprised various nationalities and as they had fought in the war with equal pay according to rank they now demanded equal treatment in demobilization. The position was made difficult by the fact that R.A.P.W.I. had allowed free passages to some Volunteers before the proclamation was promulgated; despite this, further claimants were dealt with strictly according to the proclamation. The cost of demobilizing Hong Kong's Volunteers was about $20 million.

The organization of law and order was of course a basic need. A number of gambling-house proprietors and their men had been given some police powers by the Japanese in return for their gambling licences; Gimson forbade gambling, but allowed these men to continue their police duties with pay to compensate for the loss of their gambling profits. This was quite unsatisfactory, and the Navy was ordered to take over police duties. On 11 September a Commando Brigade arrived and was immediately entrusted with arrangements for enforcing law and order, assisted by the existing naval parties under the general control of Col. C. H. Sansom, the Civil Affairs Officer in charge of Police and Fire Services. Only 98 police officers of the rank of Inspector and above out of a total of 321 were available, so that dependence on the military was inescapable. The local Chinese and Indian members of the Force gradually reported for duty as they drifted back to the Colony, or as they began to feel that service under the Japanese would not be held against them. They were generally found to be fit only for part-time duty and then only in company with one or more police officers. After some three months, more auxiliary police composed of Chinese students recruited by the Gimson régime were attracted into the Force by increased rates of pay. A Police Training School was opened to give refresher courses, but in practice it more closely resembled a convalescent home; police stations needed repair and there were no uniforms or equipment on hand. Fortunately there was no immediate widespread outbreak of crime. There were, of course, some criminal elements who took advantage of the absence of a trained police force to commit violent crimes and to stage holdups, especially in the New Territories, but the Chinese people generally proved themselves law-abiding.

The ordinary law courts were suspended and replaced by a Standing Military Court consisting of a President, Vice-President, and members appointed at his discretion by the Chief Civil Affairs Officer from among military officers and other legally qualified persons. The Court was organized in two divisions; as a General Military Court; and as Summary Military Courts, Class I and Class II, the number of such courts being decided by the Legal Adviser. The General Military Court, consisting of the President or Vice-President and two other members, heard the more serious cases of which there were 193 up to the end of March. Summary Military Courts of both classes consisted of one member of the Standing Military Court sitting alone, who was chosen from among those authorized by the Chief Civil Affairs Officer to hold a Summary Court. They were, in fact, mainly local barristers or solicitors. All military court proceedings had to be held in public unless the interests of justice or military security demanded otherwise. The penalties for Class I Summary Courts were limited to a maximum of five years' imprisonment and a fine of five thousand dollars, and those for Class II to one year or one thousand dollars' fine. The General Military Court's decisions were to be decided by a majority, except that in the case of the death penalty the majority had to include the presiding member. Counsel could appear on behalf of a defendant only if authorized by the Legal Adviser. The Courts dealt with criminal cases, as the civil side of the law was virtually in abeyance.

The currency question had to be decided immediately, to avoid chaos in the conduct of ordinary day-to-day affairs. It had been intended to refuse to recognize Japanese currency from the start, partly for reasons of prestige, and partly because the Japanese had flooded their occupied areas with military yen notes, far exceeding in value the amount normally circulating under British rule, and the yen had depreciated in value in anticipation of non-recognition. Still, it was impossible to abolish yen in Hong Kong unless there were sufficient Hong Kong dollars to replace the Japanese notes and, until new stocks of dollar notes arrived, there was no alternative but to allow the yen to continue to circulate temporarily.

Stocks of the notes of the three note-issuing banks, The Hongkong and Shanghai Banking Corporation, The Chartered Bank of India, Australia and China, and The Mercantile Bank of India, and of the dollar notes issued by the Hong Kong Government had been ordered and arrived on 11 September. In addition yen notes were over-printed locally but were never issued and held as an emergency reserve. Two days later, on 13 September, yen were withdrawn and ceased to be recognized as legal tender. The three banks had their note-issuing powers temporarily renewed and their notes became legal tender, except for a number of duress notes issued by the Japanese without proper backing;[3] some one-, five- and ten-dollar notes over-printed on Japanese and Chinese high denomination notes were also recognized, and there were also, of course, the Government-issued one-dollar notes. This drastic and sudden withdrawal of the yen depended for success upon sufficient dollar notes being pumped into circulation rapidly enough to prevent a breakdown. To ease the transition, on the same

[3] The banks, in fact, honoured their note-issuing liability, including the duress note issue.

day a general moratorium was declared on all debts previously incurred, except for sums under a hundred dollars, wages, salaries or fees for professional services, and Government debts. Financial institutions were closed temporarily and dealings in land forbidden. Hardship was undoubtedly caused by the sudden demise of the yen, but gradually the dollars circulated, though there were at first insufficient stocks to meet normal needs. The troops' pay helped, hoarded dollars circulated again, and some 40,000 labourers were employed on street-cleaning. The Government helped by giving its junior servants two weeks' pay in advance, by paying a dollar a day rehabilitation allowance to essential workers, by voting a sum of $150,000 for allowances to the destitute, and by making loans to fishermen to re-equip their vessels. The trouble was that general scarcities forced the price-level up to about ten times the pre-war normal.

To restore the Hong Kong economy, trade had to be revived, all else was merely a palliative, and the aim was to get trade flowing under Government auspices for six months and then to hand over to private enterprise. The Chinese merchant community in Hong Kong was impatient to restore private business, mainly because the Americans were willing to supply both goods and credit, and the Civil Affairs Administration acceded to their wishes. On 23 November 1945 private trading was resumed with a few exceptions and subject to licences being required for imports in order to safeguard foreign exchange, exports being free from control. Exchange transactions with sterling were allowed on 12 November and this freedom was extended to all foreign exchange on 4 December, subject to government exchange control. The first ocean-going private trading freighter did not arrive before mid-December, and trade had to be carried at first in junks and small ships. The revival of commerce was helped by the rendition of the Shanghai International Settlement to China which induced many firms to move to the Colony. Nevertheless, the remarkable resilience of the Colony in getting back to normal was due in no small part to the enterprise and resourcefulness of the Chinese.

The three British banks had been liquidated by the Japanese, all assets belonging to the Hong Kong Government and the

Bank of China seized, and the remaining assets of non-enemy ownership had been pooled and creditors paid in proportion to their claims. The Japanese compelled the three banks to issue their remaining stocks of bank-notes, without any further backing, to settle these claims, though there were not enough notes to meet them all. These 'duress notes' were the subject of a lengthy enquiry in which it was found that many of the notes had new dates and signatures forged on them. The Military Administration therefore decided to make a virtue of necessity and declared them legal tender on 2 April 1946.

The first industries restored by the Military Administration were those associated with absolute necessities such as food and those for which raw materials were available. A Fishery Co-operative Society was formed to control and centralize fish marketing and to offer better rewards to the fishermen. A Vegetable Growers' Co-operative Society did the same for the New Territories' farmer, and so the experiment of the Equitable Rice Sales Fund Committee, conducted before the war by some public-spirited churchmen and helped by Dr. Selwyn-Clarke, bore fruit in the post-war Hong Kong. The revival of industry was dependent on raw materials, and factories were helped by releasing to them such supplies as existed, with the result that some soap-making, flour and rice milling, boat-building, sail-making, tanning, and the production of matches and rubber shoes, all began in a limited way.

The food problem was pressing. Malnutrition affected about 80 per cent of the entire population, which had to rely on stores left by the Japanese, local produce, and food from Kwangtung, and the Chief Civil Affairs Officer admitted on 9 November 'from now on, unless supplies reach us, we lose ground'. People had little money to buy food until the economy revived. The administration was financially responsible for members of the Hong Kong Volunteer Defence Corps, with their families, until it was demobilized; in addition there were numbers of completely destitute persons, of whom about 25,000 had to be fed daily from the government rice kitchens free of charge. Numbers did not drop below 22,000 during the whole of the Military Administration. Food was supplied daily to all charitable institutions such as orphanages, which accounted for another 2,000 mouths to be fed, a further 3,000 were fed from depots under official supervision, where some received free meals, but others, who could afford it, received them on payment of a small charge.

Then destitutes had to be housed by the administration. This had been foreseen and planned for by the London Planning Unit which thought that about 100,000 Chinese destitutes would enter the Colony from China, and that a large number of permanent camps similar to those set up before the war would be needed; in the event, only about 10,000 Chinese destitutes were housed in camps and fed. Five centres for destitute non-Chinese were also operated with the help in money and personnel of the Council of British Societies for Relief Abroad. The British Red Cross opened a centre at Rosary Hill, and the Salvation Army, St. John Ambulance and the Government Relief Department helped with other centres. Bishop Hall established the Social Welfare Council, which voted $30,000 for the work and U.N.R.R.A. sponsored relief for about 2,300 persons in the Colony. Repatriates and prisoners of war from various parts of China passing through the Colony had to be cared for. In fact, the Military Administration was never relieved from relief work.

To add to the Administration's problem there was the influx of returning Chinese. By the end of 1945 the urban population was reckoned to have risen to about one million and Chinese were estimated to be returning at the rate of about 100,000 a month; the food supply naturally failed to keep pace with such growth, despite improved supply conditions and the restoration of private trade. At the same time a proposal to re-impose the immigration controls of 1941 was strongly opposed by the Chinese Government. Until the war, Chinese from Kwangtung and elsewhere enjoyed the right of free entry into Hong Kong. Finally, an understanding was reached with the Chinese Nationalists to allow free entry into the Colony in return for food being made available by the Chinese, a favourable bargain because in fact the Administration did not have an effective immigration organization to keep the Chinese out.

The Military Administration's food policy was strict control of stocks, stimulation of local produce, and equitable distribution based on controlled prices. Control of sugar, salt, peanut oil, and flour supplies, was little more than a gesture because shortages prevented its enforcement. Flour was borrowed from the three Services against expected shipments from Australia and a 'government' loaf of bread at 50 cents was baked and sold. Rice, as the vital food of most of the population, was subsidized and had to be rationed, being bought at 80 cents a catty and sold at 20 cents, at a cost to the Administration of some $150,000 a day. At first the ration was one catty daily, then eight-tenths of a catty per day and by mid-January 1946, the ration was further reduced to half that amount, but one-and-a-half catties of flour were added to the ration. In early March the Administration was forced by the large influx of immigrants to announce the issue of new ration cards restricted to bona fide residents of Hong Kong or to those engaged in essential work. A monthly ration of sugar was also organized.

Food and indeed all necessities were in desperately short supply. Pre-war supplies had been disrupted by the war, and shipping was still commandeered for the movement of troops and military stores. These shortages were widespread and not unexpected, and the War Office had arranged to distribute relief supplies temporarily to the liberated territories, Hong Kong having to indent for its share on the South-East Asia Command; but the cessation of hostilities had caught the War Office unprepared and 1 April 1946 had been the date set for supplies for Hong Kong.

To organize supplies in the immediate post-war Hong Kong became a massive exercise in improvisation, and the Military Administration had to fend for itself or go without. Officers were dispatched to neighbouring countries on buying missions; to the Canton Delta for the purchase of rice and vegetables virtually regardless of cost, to Borneo to buy wood for fuel, and to Shanghai and Indo-China to purchase coal. The attempts to purchase cotton from India and building materials from Australia met with little success. Two shipments, one of rice and one of coal, did arrive through the South-East Asia Military Command, but it was two months before any further supplies arrived from that source; a shipment of coal was also sent by the Occupying Authorities in Japan in return for sago. As time went on, and particularly in the New Year, the supply situation improved, but the Military Administration never felt secure and regarded itself as lucky to have more than ten days' reserve food in hand. In December and January one thousand tons of tinned meat and refrigerated meat arrived and helped to save the situation. It must be added that the three Services played an important part in food supply, for not only did all officers of the Administration draw army rations, since they were army personnel, but all Europeans in the Colony at first relied on the same source.

The housing situation was equally acute. The Services needed more accommodation on shore, and requisitioned hotels, schools and private houses, the furniture coming from stocks held by the Custodian of Enemy Property. Some 60 per cent of European housing was damaged and about 15 per cent in the Chinese areas; with no materials available for repairs, the Administration ordered all accommodation to be put to the maximum use, and hotel rooms were used as small dormitories. Rents rose steeply as the Chinese came crowding back and a Landlord and Tenants Proclamation No. 15 of 22 October 1945 became necessary. This froze rents at their 1941 level and provided for tribunals to decide claims to vary rents, to deal with evictions and to settle tenancy disputes. Up to the end of March 569 petitions were heard. The return of European women and children to the Colony was halted for six months, and European men were allowed in only if they were engaged on essential work.

Then there was the problem of health. The Japanese health measures had been limited by the demands of the war and in the case of malaria by a lack of concern. In any case their main interest in the population was to reduce it. The Report of the Chief Civil Affairs Officer refers to the Japanese neglect of health as the worst of his difficulties. Bad and inadequate food had led to malnutrition and lowered resistance to disease. The town was infested with rats. Tuberculosis was rampant, accounting for 40 per cent of all registered diseases. Little remedial work could be done without supplies and trained personnel, which did not arrive before February 1946; but the Armed Services helped to clean up the hospitals which had been stripped of all equipment and left filthy. By February 1946 there were 2,269 hospital beds available compared to

3,625 before the war, and the Military Administration assumed financial responsibility for the Nethersole and French Hospitals. Port Health machinery was working by this date and most of the Health Districts were again staffed and operating, but malaria was rife, due to neglect. Street cleaning had to be organized, garbage, which had not been disposed of because of lack of vehicles, removed from streets and back alleys, drains cleared, and sanitation arrangements improvised.

The Military Administration had to rebuild the school system. The grant-in-aid schools were in reasonable shape, particularly those run by neutral religious orders who had escaped internment; in October twelve of these re-opened with an enrolment of 6,000, and later in the month 52 private schools and 2 government schools restarted with another 12,000 pupils, but books and desks were hard to come by. Despite the fact that four large schools were still requisitioned by the Military, there were 274 schools open to 42,000 pupils by February 1946. It was estimated that about one-third of the children of school age were in school. Generally the single session system was adopted as an economy measure, whereby two primary schools occupied the same building for morning and afternoon sessions respectively.

The restoration of the public utility services, including those operated by Government, owed much to the steps taken by Gimson and his colleagues, and to many of the Utility Companies executives who delayed their departure to assist in restarting their services. The water supply system was in fairly good shape, except that the filter beds had been allowed to get filthy. Wood fuel was used to get the pumps working, supplies of water reached 25 million gallons a day by 15 November, at which date the collection of water rates was resumed. The Japanese had been reduced to running one train a day on the Hong Kong section of the Kowloon-Canton Railway. This meagre service was resumed on 6 September; a through service to Canton commenced on 14 November, the fare to Canton being $15.70 compared to one dollar pre-war.

Air services were restored at the enlarged Kai Tak airfield. It was considered to be still inadequate and the Air Officer Commanding was told to look for a new site for an airfield to serve both civil and military purposes, for which £150,000 was allocated from British Government funds. He chose the Ping Shang area in the New Territories where site formation began and a granite-quarry opened close by to give 600 tons of stone a day. However the proposed runway of 6,000 feet by 150 feet was well below the accepted international standard of 8,000 feet by 300 feet which was regarded in London as essential, and the work was therefore stopped in March 1946 and the project eventually abandoned. Kai Tak was then taken over for use primarily by Transport Command of the Royal Air Force, which controlled the airfield operationally until it was fully restored. Passengers were at first taken to the Peninsula Hotel for the customs examination. The China National Air Corporation was the first airline allowed to use Kai Tak and its first service touched down on 22 November.

Port facilities were poor. There were thirty wrecks in the harbour and one alongside at Holt's Wharf, while tugs and lighters were sunk at the piers and wharves. Only three of the Hong Kong and Kowloon Wharf Company's wharves were available, there were no usable cranes of any sort, and the godowns were full of confiscated Japanese stores. Not much could be done before the arrival of heavy equipment, but security patrols were organized, small wrecks raised, naval and civil anchorages marked out, buoys repaired, and harbour craft registered and handed over to commercial shipping lines and wharfage and harbour companies. The Ministry of War Transport office closed, and a Committee of Far East Shipping Agencies handled shipping on behalf of the Administration.

The public utility companies were all operating on a skeleton basis. It was intended that they should all be taken over temporarily and operated by the Administration. The two electricity companies agreed to operate under this arrangement for six months, receiving a rental and leaving the Administration to meet expenses and collect the revenue. The telephone, tramways, and gas companies were all put back on a commercial basis, but owed a great deal to the assistance given by the Armed Services' technicians. Taikoo Dock was repaired and began operating, and Holt's Wharf was put on a free commercial basis on 1 March. The Star Ferry had lost all its vessels, and the Hong Kong and Yaumati Ferry Company ran all the ferry services until 1 February, when the Star Ferry had repaired its piers and had raised sufficient of its sunken ferries to run a 15-minute service. Private motor-cars were all taken over for official use, and in any case there were no private supplies of petrol available until the first civilian cars arrived in February 1946. The R.A.F. was able to give the Administration 200 vehicles from its own large supply. Buses were few and far between, only six in Hong Kong and six in Kowloon; lorries had to be improvised with seats along each side; access was by means of steps at the rear, and they were used until 1947.

There was some trouble over labour and wages. With so much urgently needing to be done there was a labour shortage, and as wages had not kept pace with the soaring cost of living there was naturally much labour unrest. Wages were based on the 1941 rates plus a 1941 cost-of-living allowance, increased by a Rehabilitation Allowance of $1 a day based on the increase in prices between 1941 and 1945. Unfortunately, these arrangements resulted in the skilled worker being worse off than the unskilled, and further revision was necessary.

Whitehall during the war had initiated a new look at colonial problems. The policy was to raise living standards preparatory to self-government. Therefore the Administration paid special attention to labour conditions. A Labour Department was organized and a Permanent Labour Board was set up in November 1945, with a membership drawn from the Administration, the Services, and the large employers. It issued a schedule of hourly rates of pay for various grades of labour from skilled artisans to daily-paid coolies, increased the rehabilitation allowance from one dollar to $1.20 for coolies and $1.50 for skilled labour, and adopted a cost-of-living adjustment according to the price changes of ten articles of food and fuel instead of five as previously. Dissatisfaction continued and a number of strikes occurred which were settled without much difficulty, and compared to other British areas Hong Kong came off lightly. The lower-paid government servants were given a high cost-of-living allowance plus the rehabilitation allowance, as a temporary measure pending new salary scales which were not announced until prices looked like becoming more stable. In fact, the average price of the ten main items of food and fuel dropped by 1 December to roughly half, yet the cost of living was still nearly 500 per cent above the 1941 level.

The small amount of labour unrest was exploited by the Chinese Nationalists. American policy had been to boost China as one of the Great Powers, and this had intensified national pride and led the Chinese openly to discuss the retrocession of Hong Kong, a prospect which created an air of expectancy among a section of the community. The British Military Administration tried to establish good relations with China by lifting immigration controls and making further gestures of goodwill, including the handing over of twenty-seven Japanese ships and some Japanese stores well before the agreed time, but the Nationalists remained unpropitiated despite Admiral Harcourt's visits to Canton and Chungking. Numbers of delegations arrived from Canton, with the object of stimulating local Chinese patriotism, sometimes as many as fifteen at a time, all wanting accommodation and all claiming official status. Some doubtful cases were refused admission. At the request of the British Administration, the Kwangtung Government sent a senior Chinese government official, T. W. Kwok, from the Ministry of Foreign Affairs, to control the activities of all these unwanted and self-styled official visitors, and his office became a centre of powerful Nationalist propaganda. The communist press in Hong Kong at this time showed restraint and co-operation in contrast with the Chinese Nationalist press which magnified any incidents and exploited the difficulties.

In October the Chinese Government decided to send two armies to Manchuria after the Japanese had evacuated it and to prevent a communist take-over, and it was arranged that they were to go by American ships from Kowloon. The large numbers made this a prolonged operation, and throughout the period of the Military Administration there were Chinese military units permanently in the Colony and numbers of troops passing through, giving rise to the suspicion that passage to Manchuria to fight the communists may not have been their real object. For some time, Chinese Nationalists remained truculent and un-co-operative.

There were serious divisions in the community regarding collaboration with the Japanese, and Brigadier MacDougall reported 'bewildering cross-currents of recrimination and denunciation' as a result of the occupation. There was a great deal of correspondence in the press but little public spirit was revealed, the letters being mainly about personal claims and treatment; but one immediate unsavoury feature was the growth of an extortion racket which demanded money for not reporting incidents which might be alleged as collaboration, and the Hong Kong police had numerous enquiries to pursue and a special branch was set up for the purpose. Fortunately, the War Crimes trials and investigations were taken out of the Military Administration's control, but it still had to deal with some collaboration trials.

The cost of the Military Administration was heavy. Up to 28 February 1946 revenue was $27 million and expenditure $30 million, excluding the salaries of the Civil Affairs Officers which were paid by the War Office. Entertainment tax was collected from the beginning, but no other taxes were collected until 29 October, when the collection of rates on property was resumed; duties on liquor and tobacco, and Post Office charges and stamp duties, were also imposed. The net cost to the British tax-payer of the Hong Kong Military Administration was £254,183, but if the cost of relief supplies is included nearly a million pounds must be added to this figure. In addition, the cost of the administration borne by the War Office was £295,000.

On the whole the Military Administration had much achievement to its credit, though the Chief Civil Affairs Officer, with becoming modesty, reported that much was due to Chinese enterprise and resilience. The Administration was fortunate in its head, Rear-Admiral Harcourt, who showed tact, common sense, and balance in dealing with the Chinese staff as well as his own.[4]

The change-over to civilian government was fixed for 1 February 1946, but the Chief Civil Affairs Officer strongly urged postponement because adequate supplies had not yet arrived and the Administration was gravely deficient in staffing. The Colonial Office also pressed for a postponement, because it regarded the return of Sir Mark Young to take up

[4] Vice-Admiral Sir Cecil Harcourt, 'The Military Administration of Hong Kong', *Royal Central Asian Jnl.*, vol. 34 (1947), pp. 7–18.

his interrupted governorship as essential for prestige reasons, and it was necessary that his period of leave should be sufficiently long to ensure his return to health. Admiral Harcourt suggested that the hand-over should be on 1 April 1946, but continued Chinese troop movements in Kowloon and the need to observe due legal and constitutional forms in effecting the hand-over led to a further postponement to 1 May 1946. On that date, Sir Mark Young arrived and was sworn in as Civil Governor.

III

ADMINISTRATIVE RECONSTRUCTION

'Your return, Sir, we hope and believe, marks a new epoch in the history of the Colony. In a sense, it signifies the resumption of Civil Administration including the sittings of this Council interrupted in December 1941. But it means more than this. It marks a point in time at which . . . the Colony resolutely turns to post-war reconstruction and social betterment. It signifies the birth of a new Hong Kong.'

Sir Man Kam Lo in the Legislative Council,
16 May 1946

Sir Mark Young arrived by air on 30 April 1946 to resume his sadly interrupted governorship and was welcomed at Queen's Pier by the Navy, Army, and Air Force Chiefs; he then went to Government House where Admiral Harcourt's flag was lowered and that of the new Governor raised in a colourful ceremony, followed by an address of welcome by Sir Robert Ho Tung on behalf of the Chinese. The Chinese official party on that occasion included those prominent members of the Chinese community who had not accepted office or membership of any Chinese Council under the Japanese.

The Military Administration had achieved much, but much remained to be done. Transitional arrangements were urgently required to transfer power to the new civil government and there were thorny questions still remaining over from the war and the occupation. More exciting was what the Colonial Office in London referred to as the 'new angle of vision' expressed in the pledge given in July 1943 that Britain would guide colonial peoples along the road to self-government, and help to provide the necessary social and economic foundations for its fulfilment. Overshadowing everything were the pressing problems of re-creating the administrative machinery of civil government and formulating policies to guide the colossal task of rehabilitating every aspect of Hong Kong life.

The immediate need was to make constitutional provision for the continuance of such measures of the Military Administration as were obviously necessary, and for this purpose the Governor promptly convened a special meeting of the Legislative Council for the morning of 1 May to pass three ordinances through all their legislative stages. An Indemnity and Validating Ordinance confirmed legislative acts, court sentences, and administrative orders during the war period, prevented legal proceedings being taken against government officers in respect of acts done in good faith while performing their duty, and also validated contracts made with the British Military Administration. The Law Amendment (Transitional Provisions) Ordinance continued in force certain Proclamations, Notices, and appointments made or issued by the Military Administration, and discontinued others. The third ordinance, the Administration of Justice (Transitional Provisions) Ordinance, provided that all cases pending before the military courts were to be tried or continued in the restored civil courts. Briefly, the object of the three ordinances was to empower the Civil Government to continue in force as much or as little of the existing corpus of administrative and judicial arrangements as it judged necessary.

The most exciting but not the most pressing question was that relating to the Governor's announcement, made immediately on arrival, of the British Government's desire that consideration should be given to the best method by which the people of Hong Kong might be given a fuller and more responsible share in the management of their own affairs, 'the fullest account being taken of the views and wishes of the inhabitants'. Before the month was out the Government approached a number of representative bodies, and also invited individuals to express their views.

The response was not overwhelming, but the Governor did receive a number of replies to his invitation and in August 1946 he outlined his proposals which became known as the 'Young Plan'. He suggested a Municipal Council of forty-eight members, one third elected by Chinese voters, one third by non-Chinese voters and the remainder equally by Chinese and non-Chinese institutions, which was to take over certain limited functions in the urban area only, the New Territories being administered separately. He also proposed to reform the Legislative Council to include seven official and eight unofficial members with the Governor having both an *ex officio* vote and a casting vote, which would enable him to hold the balance between the official and unofficial sides. The new Municipal Council was to nominate two unofficial members, and other representative bodies four, leaving the two existing nominating bodies, namely the Unofficial Justices of the Peace and the Hong Kong General Chamber of Commerce, with one each as before. Again the comments of local bodies and individuals were asked for.

The Plan was well-received locally and in July 1947 a simultaneous announcement in London and Hong Kong indicated that it had been approved, except for some minor points. Sir Mark Young retired in May 1947, and it rested with the new Governor, Sir Alexander Grantham,[1] to work out the details, a process which occupied the next two years and eventually in June 1949 three Bills embodying the Plan appeared. Detailed examination of the Plan is unnecessary, because by this time conditions had changed radically. The Kuomintang regime was on the verge of collapse, and a flood of refugees from the mainland was transforming the character of the Hong Kong community so that even before these Bills appeared, the unofficial members of the Legislative Council voiced doubts and criticisms. On 22 June a motion was carried to delay the implementation of the Plan. Despite a petition from Chinese organizations for a more radical constitutional reform the Young Plan was abandoned and in October 1952 the Secretary of State for the Colonies announced in the Commons that the time was inopportune for constitutional changes of a major character. There the matter rested.

The plan of constitutional reform, though still-born, affected the resuscitation of the Executive and Legislative Councils and more particularly of the Urban Council, since definitive constitutional arrangements had to be postponed while reform was in the air. Provisional appointments to the Legislative Council, subject to the royal pleasure, were gazetted on 9 May and back-dated to 1 May. From the two 'electoral' bodies, the Hong Kong General Chamber of Commerce and the Unofficial

[1] See Sir Alexander Grantham, *Via Ports; from Hong Kong to Hong Kong* (Hong Kong, 1965).

Justices of the Peace, the former nominated its chairman on 29 April 1946, and the latter their member in the following October. At this date the Council comprised nine Officials and seven Unofficials. In 1951 the Council was increased to nine Officials and eight Unofficials, the local element being strengthened to include four Chinese and one Portuguese and by 1953 only two out of the eight unofficial members were Europeans. The appointments to the Council remained provisional until 1951 when they became annual and in 1953 a three-year term was adopted.

The Executive Council was revived on 7 May 1946 with seven official and four unofficial members compared to six and three respectively pre-war. The seventh Official was a former legal official who had retired in 1937 and had been brought back as Political Adviser, subsequently renamed Special Adviser, dealing with post-war constitutional and political problems. In November 1947 the Executive Council was reconstituted with six Officials and six Unofficials, the local element among the latter being strengthened to include three Chinese, and in 1948 a Portuguese was appointed leaving only two Unofficials of European origin.

The Urban Council was revived in May 1946 with five official and six unofficial members, the latter comprising three Chinese, one Indian and two British. In view of the proposals for reform, the usual election of two members was not resumed until May 1952 by which time it had become clear that reform would be delayed, and in October of that year, when the constitutional changes were indefinitely postponed, it was also announced that the number of elected members would be increased to four.

These Urban Council elections in the context of discussion of reform stimulated local interest and the formation of two political bodies, the Reform Club in 1949, and the Civic Association in 1955. So although the Young Plan came to nothing, local people were given more representation in Government Councils and more interest was generated in public affairs.

More important still was the new emphasis on local recruitment for the Civil Service, about which little had been done since this policy had been first advocated by the 1932

Retrenchment Commission. Under the Military Administration the local staff had more responsibility thrust upon them when the British went home to recuperate, and Admiral Harcourt pressed their claims to advancement, an action in line with British intentions expressed in a Colonial Policy statement in 1946, which urged the localization of colonial public services and the opening of all posts to suitably qualified local recruits. Answering criticisms made by Chinese unofficial members of the Legislative Council, Sir Mark Young in September 1946 had given an explicit undertaking in these words, 'The policy of Government is to ensure that every opportunity shall be given to locally recruited persons not only to enter but to rise in the service of the public up to the highest posts and to fulfil the highest responsibilities of which they are capable or can be assisted to become capable.' A number of posts in the Medical, Education, Police, Railway and Public Works Departments, which up to the war had been restricted to Europeans, were now thrown open to local people, a course strongly backed by the 1947 Salaries Commission which recommended that no expatriate should be appointed to any government post if a suitably qualified local candidate were available. Indicating the new policy, the first Chinese was appointed a cadet officer in October 1946, and in 1952 a locally recruited officer became head of the Medical and Health Department, the first such officer to rise to the position of departmental head.

A great deal needed to be done in reconstructing the administrative machine to serve post-war Hong Kong. The drastic rise in prices made pre-war salaries quite inadequate and from 1 May 1946 they were adjusted to give a 50 per cent increase for salaries up to £350 and thereafter diminished increases on a sliding scale to 10 per cent for those up to £1,500. The 1947 Salaries Commission broadly recommended a 200 per cent increase for the lowest grades, 30 per cent for salaries of $1,000 a month and 20 per cent on salaries of above $1,500 a month.

Some new departments were set up. A biologist from the University staff became Secretary for Development, a new department was created to develop the natural resources of the New Territories, and a Director of Air Services and

Airport Manager headed a new air communications department; other new departments were those of Supplies, Trade and Industry, Labour, which before had been part of the Secretariat of Chinese Affairs, Public Relations, and Custodian of Enemy Property. The old pre-war Botanical and Forestry Department was separated into a Gardens and a Forestry Department and two other departments, concerned with Agriculture and Fisheries respectively, came into being. Appointments had to be made as men became available, for example Father Ryan, S.J., became Agricultural Officer temporarily, and some local businessmen were pressed into service. Some war-emergency departments, those of Air Raid Precautions, Immigration, War Taxation and Censorship, were abolished, but some time was to elapse before the new post-war departments were organized on a permanent basis.

The finances of the Colony after 1 May 1946 could no longer depend on the War Office, and at the same time it was clear that, until trade revived, the expected revenue must be small and in any case difficult to assess. The balances in London in 1941 had not only disappeared but a large deficit had been incurred for war purposes. No wonder the Governor painted a sombre picture of the Colony's immediate financial prospects.

The Colony was faced with enormous and urgent rehabilitation expenditure, while rising prices and costs made for frightening increases in normal recurrent expenditure. The sensible course was adopted of meeting special capital expenditure for rehabilitation from loans, and ordinary expenditure from revenue, but even then the budget in July showed estimated revenue for the eleven months to April 1947 at $51,308,300, and expenditure at $160,751,665 subsequently increased to $167,854,576, leaving an estimated deficit of over $116½ million. The duties on imported tobacco and liquor, stamp duty, water charges and various official fees were all raised, and taxes on meals and intoxicants sold in hotels and restaurants and on sweepstakes were imposed. However, recovery proceeded much faster than anticipated and in the result revenue reached $82,141,556 with expenditure of $85,624,391 leaving a small deficit of just under $3½ million.[2]

[2] The original estimate included an item for $85.6 m. for rehabilitation expenditure. Some $30 m. of this was actually disbursed from a special loan. But the

The special war taxation of 1941 which the Government was naturally anxious to continue to meet the financial crisis, was not available because of a clause in the ordinance forbidding its collection subsequent to the year of assessment in which the European war of 1939 ended. A special taxation committee set up in September 1946 recommended taxes on earnings and profits similar to those of 1941, and these were incorporated in the 1947 budget. Briefly, income tax, to which there had been great opposition, was avoided by imposing four similar taxes on property, profits, interest, and salaries including annuities, that is, taxes were based on certain sources of income and not on total personal income. These four taxes were announced in March 1947. A Chinese newspaper published a premature report of the taxes and this sparked off a lively opposition, with protests of no taxation without representation. The Chinese community were bitterly opposed to the new taxes and petitioned the Governor three times, called on him at Government House, cabled the Colonial Secretary in London, and three unofficial members voted against the budget in an unavailing attempt to prevent this measure of direct taxation gaining a permanent place in the Colony's budget.

The estimates for 1947–8 showed revenue at $109,839,750, expenditure at $109,834,355 leaving a surplus of $5,395, but, in fact, actual revenue proved much more buoyant at $164,298,310 and expenditure came to $127,701,174 leaving a surplus of $36,597,136. The next year a budgeted surplus of well over a million dollars was realized as a handsome actual surplus of nearly $35 million.

The Government prudently delayed the floating of the Rehabilitation Loan until the price level became more stabilized and it could have a clearer idea of the amount of the special non-recurrent rehabilitation expenditure needed. The Hong Kong (Rehabilitation) Loan Ordinance of December 1947 gave authority to raise $150 million by 3½ per cent bearer bonds maturing 1973–8 and the first parcel of the $50 million loan was offered locally on 19 December. This was fully subscribed. A sinking fund was set up in July 1948. In fact

main reason for the cutting down of expenditure was the long delays and some lack of staff to implement post-war reconstruction plans.

this was the only section of the loan issued, and further expenditure on rehabilitation, earmarked to be set against subsequent issues of the loan, was met from buoyant revenues.

During the Japanese occupation and under the British Military Administration the Hong Kong Government liabilities had been shouldered by the British Government, and as was usual in such cases of colonial indebtedness the British Treasury consequently imposed a strict control over the Colony's finances through the Secretary of State for the Colonies. This caused some delays and detracted from the authority of the Legislative Council where the unofficial members questioned the authority under which emergency expenditure was incurred on behalf of the Colony. The sums involved were considerable, covering pay and allowances to Hong Kong Volunteers, maintenance and relief payments to families in Australia and Macao, repatriation passages for private individuals, *ex gratia* payments to civil defence workers, civil servants' salaries, and pensions to those who had retired. Some of this was contractual and so had to be met. It had been paid by the British Government simply because no Hong Kong Government was functioning. The total amount advanced by the British Government from January 1944 to March 1947 was £3,250,000. Some of this expenditure was debited to the Hong Kong Government account, and some was placed in a suspense account to await a decision on the respective liabilities of the two Governments. The unofficial members of the Legislative Council objected to Treasury control and also to war expenditure incurred by the British Government on behalf of the Colony as a unit of the British Empire, being debited to the Colony, since the latter had been overrun as a result of being involved in a British war. Therefore Sir Mark Young agreed, before he left, not to meet expenses which were currently under discussion between the two Governments out of the Colony's revenue without giving the Legislative Council opportunity to debate them. As a result of these representations and the desire to give each colony as much self-determination as possible, Treasury control from London was ended on 1 April 1948. The authority of the Secretary of State for the Colonies remained until October of that year, when he relaxed some of his powers of control in regard to supplementary estimates of small amounts and the writing off of claims, but his approval for the annual estimates, for supplementary capital expenditure of over one million dollars, or recurrent expenditure over $250,000, and decisions on important points of principle, as for example the salary structure, had still to be obtained. It was not until 1958 that the Colony was given virtually complete financial autonomy which was subject to consultation only.

The Government was faced with a great many decisions arising out of the war and its aftermath which the Military Administration had had no time to bring to a conclusion. For example, outstanding claims by some Volunteers and essential services workers were settled in June 1946 when all male civil defence workers who were interned received wages on an *ex gratia* basis for the duration of their internment, and those not interned received three months' salary if paid monthly, or forty-two days' wages if paid daily. In January 1947 another grievance was removed by the decision to pay family allowances to the families of prisoners of war who avoided internment and lived in the town during the occupation. *Ex gratia* pensions were granted to those who had to retire early because of impairment to health in the prisoner-of-war or internment camps, and additional *ex gratia* pensions were granted to those who suffered permanent injury to health under those conditions.

In March 1947 arrangements regarding demobilization pay and allowances to members of the Volunteer Defence Corps were finalized. The men were placed in one of four categories; firstly, those who returned home on 25 December 1941 received pay and allowances during the actual hostilities; secondly, those who were interned and escaped or were released, were considered demobilized ninety-eight days after their escape or release, and received pay and allowances accordingly; thirdly, those who went home, or escaped, or were released and who subsequently re-joined the Allied forces, were treated according to their war record; fourthly, those who were interned in the camps throughout the period, received full benefits in pay and allowances, plus forty-two days' leave, fifty days' demobilization leave, and overseas leave of one day for every month of service. In addition, ex-Volunteers whose studies at the University had been interrupted by the war received grants to continue their studies. In the previous November sums withheld from Volunteers' pay on account of allowances being paid to their wives in Macao were refunded.

Those suffering loss or damage during the hostilities in respect of ships, steamers, dredgers, cranes, and other harbour equipment, were asked to register their claims. Owners of motor-cars requisitioned by Government were refused compensation in October 1947 because their loss was considered a war risk, and the Government accepted liability only if it could be proved that requisitioning increased that risk. Claims for looted property removed from the Colony were also invited.

Then a difficult question came up relating to cheques and I.O.U.s signed in Stanley Camp for the purchase of food at exorbitant prices. Mr. F. C. Gimson had impounded these cheques on 1 September 1945 and, since so many of those who had signed these cheques were absent from Hong Kong, he had sent them to the Secretary of State in London. Questions were asked in the Commons. In August 1947 the Secretary of State decided against coercion and returned the cheques to the creditors, inviting them to consider whether the debts could not be equitably settled by smaller amounts than the face value, because of the completely artificial conditions in the camp. Creditors were invited to take the initiative and approach debtors to arrange an amicable settlement or, if the cheque had been banked, the bank was to approach the drawer, the basic appeal being to the individual's sense of fairness. If the two sides could not agree, they were recommended to seek the assistance of the Hong Kong Government, which set up an arbitration board of H. R. Cleland, H. R. Sturt, and the Revd. J. E. Sandbach. For the moment the debtors were protected by the general moratorium declared in September 1945, which remained in force until October 1948; in the event, many debtors simply honoured their debts on the ground that they very well knew what they were signing, some few refused, and some agreed to negotiations. There was also the question of the validity of divorce proceedings in Stanley Internment Camp. To remove any doubts, the judgement of a Stanley Court was regularized by ordinance in June 1947.

War cemeteries had to be laid out to replace the temporary

burial grounds in Argyle Street Camp and Stanley, and a roll of honour was compiled in July 1947. The military cemetery at Stanley was begun in April 1946 under the Military Administration, and a second cemetery at Mount Davis was suggested for graves from Argyle Street, China, and Formosa, but a site at Sai Wan was eventually preferred. Over 300 Canadian war dead were re-buried there on Dominion Day, 1 July 1947. The Canadians had suffered heavy casualties, losing 555 dead out of 2,000 men, of whom 127 died in Japanese prisoner-of-war camps, particularly in the camp at Niigata. About 70 per cent of the Canadian graves were transferred to Sai Wan.

In September 1946 a committee was set up to consider an appropriate war memorial. It recommended that it should take the form of a fund to help the dependants of those killed and the disabled; as a result a War Memorial Fund was established by ordinance, to which the Government gave dollar for dollar until 31 December 1947, at which date the total, including the Government subvention, stood at $3,733,840; the response was poor partly because those most interested were either repatriated or were struggling to re-establish themselves economically, but subscriptions continued to come in for some years, dwindling from $28,816 in 1948 to only $350 in 1961. The tall Japanese war-memorial monument on Mount Cameron was demolished on 26 February 1947. Its destruction gave unbounded pleasure to thousands of spectators on the streets.

The restoration of a sound economy was the most urgent task of Civil Government when it took up the burden on 1 May 1946. The War Office in London now ceased to be responsible for supplies but the abnormal situation continued in which the satisfaction of the community's needs through normal private commercial channels was not possible. To keep the community alive the Government had to continue to assume responsibilities for the supply and distribution of essential commodities for some time, despite private trading having been allowed in November 1945. There were serious shortages of essential goods, as well as a lack of shipping. International Government agencies apportioned commodities, such as rice, which were in short supply, on a government-to-government basis, and so the Hong Kong Government was drawn willy-nilly into playing an unaccustomed commercial role. The administrative machinery for this already existed in the form of the Department of Supplies, Trade and Industry inherited from the Military Administration.

There grew up therefore a complex administrative organization to purchase bulk supplies, control imports and exports, and distribute food and other essential commodities equitably and at prices ordinary people could pay, using methods as far as possible which did not prejudice the eventual resumption of normal commercial practices.[3] A wide variety of expedients of no little complexity had to be adopted and much had to be left to trial and error. The Department of Supplies, Trade and Industry formerly had had a transport section as well, but this had been hived off as a separate entity for a short time under the Military Administration. In April 1949 the Department ceased to exist under that name but continued its temporary supplies and control functions under the name of the Department of Supplies and Distribution, while its more permanent functions were taken over by an expanded Commerce and Industry Department, which twelve months earlier had taken over the work of the old Import and Export Department. On 1 September 1950 the Department of Supplies and Distribution was absorbed into the Commerce and Industry Department as its Supplies Division.

Supplies had been ordered by the War Department on an emergency relief basis virtually without regard to cost and they continued to arrive until well into 1947, but had to be paid for from Colony funds. Some of these goods proved unsuitable for permanent rehabilitation and had to be disposed of, because it was impossible to gauge Hong Kong's needs before the re-occupation. A section of the Planning Unit had remained in London to place orders for civilian needs. Rice, flour, sugar, and dairy products, still had to be imported from the Supply Departments in London under inter-allied rationing arrangements; for example, the sub-committee of the International Emergency Food Council in Singapore allocated rice supplies to the governments of the region.

[3] See Kenrick, op. cit., and Birch, 'The Control of Prices and Commodities in Hong Kong', *H.K.L.J.*, vol. 4, no. 2, 1974, pp. 133–50.

Because supplies were inadequate, bulk purchases by the Government had to be supplemented by requisitioning such local stocks as existed, and by purchasing supplies in the near-by areas. A Custodian of Enemy Property was appointed to take over unclaimed and enemy goods in godowns; motor vehicles, food, raw materials such as cotton yarn, paper, timber, textiles, machinery, furniture, soap, and candles, were the chief kinds of goods subject to requisition. In the case of flour, tinned milk, piece goods, and knitting wool, supplies imported privately were requisitioned when the shipment arrived, a form of requisition which was used mainly in 1946 to overcome the more desperate shortages and was less resorted to as time went on. Purchasing missions to neighbouring areas continued, and rice-importing firms were encouraged to purchase rice at virtually any price for sale to the Government at cost plus expenses.

The purchase and control of supplies involved storage and distribution. Some articles, such as firewood bought in bulk from Borneo, were stock-piled and distributed at $8 a picul whenever the shortage of commercial supplies drove the price above that figure, but the Government generally distributed its various supplies through wholesalers, who sold to retailers at controlled prices. The degree of control varied according to the importance of the commodity. The main difficulty was to see that supplies in bulk from the wholesaler did not get into the hands of hawkers and black market operators who would exploit any scarcity.

Rationing applied only to essential commodities and where supplies were inadequate, as in the case of rice, flour, peas, and peanut oil, and to a lesser degree, knitting wool, blankets, soap, firewood, sugar, and tinned milk. The last three items were distributed through Messrs. Butterfield and Swire, and the rest through a Chinese firm, Wing Wo Hing, each with its chain of retailers. Under the Military Administration new registrations were restricted in March 1946 to those who could prove seven years' residence before December 1941, but even so, at the return of Civil Government, there were 220,000 ration cards issued covering over a million persons.

In May 1946 there was a complete re-registration of persons for ration cards, but the same principle of one card per family was adhered to and each family had to draw its rations from a named store in its locality; the card being chopped as each ration was drawn. Non-rice-eating people, mainly Europeans, who had been fed on army rations under the Military Administration, were given a different ration card for flour, sugar, tinned milk, and butter, not excluding rice, and drew their supplies from the two principal European retail food shops. There were also special supplies to certain groups such as dockyard employees, police, and hotels. Bulk purchase by the Hong Kong Government and rationing continued until 1955, the return to normal trading practice being delayed by the victory of the communists in China in 1949, then the United States stock-piling and the outbreak of the Korean war.

Rice rationing continued until 31 July 1954, and Government purchases of rice ceased on 31 December of that year. In May 1946 the rice ration had to be reduced from 6.4 taels daily to 5.6 taels, and flour from 3.2 to 1.6 taels, but a ration of 1.6 taels of peas was added as compensation. The rice allocation was again reduced to 4 taels on 23 May, but flour increased to 3.2 taels. Deliveries of rice from Thailand proved insufficient to maintain the rice ration even at that low level and in July and September there were periods when the ration could not be honoured. However, the distribution of Red Cross parcels helped to overcome the shortages, and in the second break in ration distribution in September rice was issued for half the ration period and army biscuits for the other. Rice was also supplied to fishing families, hospitals, charitable organizations, and crews of ships. Rice was sold at 20 cents a catty,[4] increasing to 25 cents in July, to 30 cents in January 1947, and to 44 cents in March. The price of flour rose from 30 cents to 35 cents a catty in August 1946, to 40 cents later that month, and to 44 cents in January 1947. The rice ration was increased to 4.8 taels and then 5.8 taels in August 1947, but there were bonus issues from time to time as supplies increased. The price was reduced to 40 cents a catty in May 1947 and raised to 48 cents in November, and again to 54 cents in March 1948. The flour ration was reduced as the rice ration was increased to maintain a total ration of

[4] Sixteen taels equal 1 catty.

7.2 taels of cereals, and the flour price was raised to 56 cents a catty. In September 1948 flour was de-rationed, but Government continued to buy in bulk. The rice ration was increased to 7.2 taels a day, but prices varied from 45 to 60 cents according to quality, as free rice was reaching the market more plentifully. There were also special bonuses amounting to 19 catties in the year 1948–9. As from 31 March 1950 the rice ration was applied to all who had been in the Colony one year or more, and stood at 8.8 taels daily.

In 1952–3 the daily ration was 7.2 taels per person, collected every ten days. From February 1953 it ceased to be obligatory to take up the whole ration and people were free to buy on the open market more of the quality they preferred. During 1953 new ration cards were issued, and by 31 March 1953, reached a total of 351,830 cards covering 1,618,999 persons; by 31 March 1954, 483,523 cards were issued covering 1,419,099 persons, the ration remaining at 7.2 taels per person per day, and the price ranging from 51 cents to 80 cents. On 31 December 1954 the trade was partly returned to private hands and approved importers.

The sugar ration was increased in June 1946 to 4 lbs. per month per person from 1¼ lbs., but in July it was 3 lbs. and in August 2 lbs. at 40 cents per lb. in each case. In December 1947 it was not possible to issue the ration through lack of supplies, but the ration was resumed next month with an extra pound for that month. In 1948 brown sugar was issued for seven months at 35 cents a lb. and white sugar on five occasions at 45 cents a lb. Sugar was de-rationed on 1 April 1949, but bulk supply through the British Ministry of Food on Government account continued. In October 1950 sugar rationing had to be re-introduced because of shortages due to the Korean War, at 1 lb. white and 1½ lb. brown. In September 1950 the Taikoo Sugar Refinery came into production and supplied refined sugar locally. In January 1953 rationing at controlled prices ceased, but wholesalers were subject to control through purchases of Government supplies.

Butter was issued to non-rice ration card holders in 1946 at 1 lb. per month per person, but in January 1948 tinned butter was de-rationed, and in 1949–50 arrangements were made to distribute fresh butter bought through the Ministry of Food, and the two European stores guaranteed each person 1 lb. per month. Thereafter butter did not figure in the rationing scheme. The rationing of peas was a temporary measure which ended in August 1946.

Meat was imported on Government account through the Ministry of Food and sold at lower prices than those prevailing locally at the time. Canned meat, large stocks of which were taken over from the Military Administration, was also marketed in such a way as to keep meat supplies flowing evenly and no rationing was necessary. The shortage of refrigerated cargo space demanded the continued import of bulk supplies, and Government continued to import and distribute through selected wholesalers. It was not until July 1957 that the meat trade could be finally handed over to private commercial firms.

Other goods were rationed for short periods, such as knitting wool at 1 lb. per ration card, and cotton blankets and quilts were issued to ration card holders with five or more in the family in 1946, but this rationing was not repeated. In November 1947 there was talk in the newspapers of the Government sponsoring a European-type suit at $160, similar to the British scheme of utility clothing during the war, but no further reference was made to it. Coal was bought in bulk by Government, but was at first delivered to the electricity companies and factories and remained unrationed, as did liquid fuel.

Rationing in fact was applied to comparatively few essential commodities, mainly food. Government had other means of securing equitable distribution, one of which was control of the trade, and though this posed peculiar problems because of Hong Kong's entrepôt business, control was necessary to prevent scarce commodities being exported to get higher prices. The policy adopted by Government was to give the maximum freedom consistent with its international obligations and the welfare of the Hong Kong people. Import control was liberally administered. An attempt was made in 1946 to revive the entrepôt trade in flour and sugar, but the international allocation authorities ruled that no extra supplies could be given on this account, though this prohibition was later relaxed on the understanding that such exports were reported to them. All imports had to be licensed, partly to economize in hard currency, but import licences were issued freely for many classes of goods. In June 1947 the system was formalized by the issue of a general licence usable by all traders for all countries except for certain named categories of goods, and goods from certain named countries. The Korean War forced the Government to issue Essential Supplies Certificates to allow industry to import essential materials and equipment, and this system lasted until 1955. But some control remained, particularly over important strategic materials, the licences being more freely granted until they were absorbed in the wider quota controls of the 1960s.

Export control was taken over from the Military Administration but was revised on 1 October 1946, so that export licences were required only for specifically named articles, chiefly goods in short supply, such as food, piece-goods, bottles, fruit, glass, timber, and motor and printing accessories. Export control was administered flexibly. If the supply position permitted, certain percentages of stocks were allowed to be exported, but commodities under international allocation, such as rice, were exported only exceptionally. Again, for financial reasons, exports to certain areas were desirable to gain hard currency. Nevertheless, since there was a margin of some 25 per cent between the official and free market value of the American dollar, the export at open market rates of goods imported at official parities could not of course be permitted. Exports were further categorized as 'controlled' and 'restricted'. In 1950 the control of imports and exports passed to the Commerce and Industry Department. The Korean War complicated matters as the U.N. imposed restrictions on the export of strategic materials, but gradually licences were more freely issued, the main consideration being to preserve the sterling area reserves. Of course, controls had to be enforced when administratively imposed, and each year there were large numbers of prosecutions for unmanifested cargoes.

Price control was another alternative to rationing. The Military Administration had issued lists of controlled prices, but little enforcement was attempted because of shortage of supplies and staff. On 21 May 1946 there were maximum prices on thirty-one goods. By 31 March 1947 the list had swollen to 700 items giving precise descriptions of the goods, brand names for example, and specifying qualities. This was published in the *H.K. Government Gazette*. The policy was to fix prices high enough to induce co-operation by normal profit margins and low enough to protect the consumer. Retailers were asked to mark prices on the goods, a commercial practice at variance with the time-honoured haggling over prices characteristic of the East, and importers were persuaded by the Government into selling to reputable firms which had proved themselves co-operative and reliable.

Price control was enforced by inspectors who went around making checks, and numerous convictions were secured. But prices of goods not listed were also affected because all inward cargo manifests were inspected, and importers had to supply invoices for everything imported, whether price-controlled or not, and in the case of non-listed goods, maximum prices were suggested to the importer. Prices for fresh food, fish, and vegetables, were not listed, as supplies might have been withheld and because of seasonal variations, but a system of adding agreed percentages to the wholesale price of fresh fish and vegetables was evolved and prices published in the markets twice a day. In this price control policy, the Government was advised by a Price Control Advisory Board set up in October 1946, comprising the Director of the Department of Supplies, Trade and Industry, the Price Controller, the Deputy Price Controller, one Government representative, one each from the two Chambers of Commerce and four representatives of the general public appointed by the Governor.

Exchange control was an essential tool in the system of official controls of this period, and since it had existed in the pre-occupation period it was no novelty. The dollar was linked with sterling at a value of 1/3d and some twenty-three banks were authorized to deal in foreign exchange, subject to the Exchange Control Office which operated under powers given by the Defence (Finance) Regulations of 1940. Generally, British Government practice was followed except that the export of Hong Kong currency notes was not prohibited as they circulated also in South China. Hong Kong was expected to draw its supplies of foreign currency from, and pay its hard currency earnings into, the sterling area reserves the same as any other member of the sterling block. However, a free market in foreign exchange, particularly in American dollars, grew up for a number of reasons. Remittances in dollars by overseas Chinese to their families in China largely passed through Hong Kong, because Chinese emigrants came mainly from South China; then Hong Kong merchants often handled the sale of Chinese products, the proceeds of which were not subject to Hong Kong controls and could be retained; finally, there were considerable movements of capital into Hong Kong, seeking the security of the Colony from civil strife in China or from anti-colonial movements in South-East Asia despite strict controls against such transfers, and this money did not pass through the Hong Kong exchange control since it came in by clandestine channels. Thus a free market in various currencies flourished in Hong Kong at rates determined by supply and demand. The movement of gold was strictly controlled in Hong Kong but in response to strong Chinese demands a gold bullion market was legally operated. It is difficult to say what was the legal status of the free market in currencies; the Hong Kong Government did not interfere, and non-authorized banks dealt in currencies quite openly. The Exchange Control made exchange available to authorized banks for essential trading purposes, but exchange earnings deposited with the authorized banks under the exchange control permit had to be ploughed back into the sterling area, with the result that more trade passed through the open market where hard currency earnings could be retained. If a manufacturer bought his American cotton at the official parities under the Exchange Control, then he would generally be expected to sell through the Exchange Control too and dollars earned would go back to the sterling area. An industry obtaining foreign exchange at the official parity received in effect a subsidy, since the open market rate was at a premium of up to some 25 per cent, and the Government could therefore use exchange controls to encourage such industries as it judged were desirable.

IV

SOCIAL AND ECONOMIC RECONSTRUCTION

'Hong Kong has made greater progress towards economic recovery and in rehabilitation than any other city on the Chinese coast that suffered to anything like the same extent from Japanese occupation and wholesale looting. It has a stable currency, rigid price controls of all necessities and a police force which . . . still maintains reasonable law and order.'

Sinimite, 'The Future of Hong Kong',
National Review, February 1947

DESPITE all that the Military Administration had been able to achieve in its eight months of office, the tasks facing the Civil Government were so immediate and pressing that long-range plans for social and economic reconstruction had still temporarily to give way to the pressures of day-to-day decisions. Not least of the problems were those concerning food supply, food distribution, and general price control which have been dealt with in the last chapter, and which had to be solved before social and economic rehabilitation could make any headway.

One other matter which caused great concern was that of housing and particularly the repair of war-damaged buildings. Derelict houses were being occupied by squatters and were a hazard to health, while owners were looking to Government for financial assistance in making them habitable as part of the cost of the war. A Building Reconstruction Advisory Committee, appointed by the Military Administration, recommended in April 1946 that the Government should purchase and ration building materials, retain rent restrictions, refuse permission to women and children to return until they had accommodation, and set up a special department to deal with building reconstruction, the costs of which should be borne by the community; however, these recommendations were rejected. The damage had been great; of European houses, 1,808 had been destroyed and 400 damaged, and about 7,000 persons or 72 per cent of the foreign community were made homeless, and all had suffered badly from looting, while 569 Chinese houses of the better class had been destroyed and 162 damaged. The figures for other destroyed and damaged property were: tenement houses 8,079 and 8,217; offices 301 and 169; factories 274 and 141; and stores 155 and 361 respectively. It was reckoned that some 160,000 flat dwellers had been made homeless, mainly by allied air raids. These losses, aggravated by the numbers of people flocking back to the Colony, made serious overcrowding inevitable.

Much dissatisfaction developed because of Government's apparent unwillingness to help owners to rebuild their war-damaged properties. In reply to questions in the Legislative Council on 19 July 1946 the Government declared it was unable to accept responsibility for reconstructing damaged property, but would in specific cases rebuild for an owner and charge the cost to him, or lease and repair a damaged property if the owner was unable to meet the cost himself. It refused to advance funds for rebuilding, but agreed to approach the banks in suitable cases to grant a loan, though in fact up to 21 November 1946 only one loan was arranged through a bank.

The Government received only five applications in reply to a notice in the newspapers asking owners to notify the Director of Public Works of their plans and difficulties, and not a single landlord responded to the Government's offer made in the Legislative Council on 19 July to reconstruct properties on behalf of owners. On the other hand, owners were loath to build or repair on their own account because of high post-war prices, which they expected would fall as normal peace-time conditions were restored. The Government imported building materials but used them to repair its own staff quarters, of which 144 were ready by November 1946.

The Military Administration restricted rents on existing property to the level of those ruling in December 1941, except where varied by Tenancy Tribunals, but this was circumvented by the owners forcing tenants to pay clandestine 'tea' money or treating tenants as paying guests or even sub-letting at exorbitant rents. In April 1947 the Landlord and Tenant Ordinance allowed increases of rent up to 30 per cent of the standard rent as at 25 December 1941 for domestic premises and 45 per cent for business premises, new buildings and those which required very extensive renovations being exempt.

The rehabilitation of housing proceeded at snail's pace and the question was again raised in the Legislative Council on 3 July 1947 when Government was urged to treat the matter as urgent and to adopt a policy of rapid building for its own use, and encouragement of private building by removing all impediments to private enterprise. Trouble also arose over Crown leases when the Government announced in June 1946 that, in the absence of any provision for renewal of the existing 75-year Crown leases, the Crown would expect owners to surrender such existing leases as had fallen due and take out new 75-year leases on payment of the required premium. This ruling was regarded as harsh in the exceptional conditions of the aftermath of war and was strongly criticized. On 3 July 1947 the Government was severely taken to task over the lack of progress in solving the housing problem. A Legislative Council debate was marked by unusual outspokenness; and in the adjourned debate a week later the unofficial members unanimously voted against the Government, whose explanations were stigmatized as 'soothing syrup'.

In August 1947 a Government public announcement invited individuals to apply for permission to go ahead with housing schemes; twenty applications were made up to the end of March 1948, of which only nine complied with Government's conditions. Of eighty applications regarding individual housing sites nineteen were approved, and forty-eight were still being investigated. This delay was criticized in spite of the explanation of the Director of Public Works that it was due to the need for over-all planning of undeveloped areas as regards road drainage and public services, and to ensure that public amenities, for example access to shore areas, were preserved.

Gradually, building and repair work got under way as more building materials became obtainable, as Government made sites available, and more particularly when prices showed little tendency to fall and builders could see no advantage in further delay. During 1948, 3,041 plans were submitted for approval, involving 4,824 buildings, 513 of European type, 1,119 of Chinese type, 52 factories, 4 hotels, 5 theatres, 6 schools, 66 godowns, 45 site formations, and 2,909 rehabilitation and repair schemes.

The accommodation problem was made more acute by the number of Service personnel in Hong Kong. About 566 buildings belonging to the armed forces had been damaged or destroyed and the Military had had to requisition much civilian accommodation, thus adding to the pressure. The Government Quartering Authority was given power to requisition property, particularly empty houses, for public use. The four chief European hotels, which had been requisitioned to house government officers and returning European civilians, were de-requisitioned in June 1946 but continued to co-operate by using their accommodation to the utmost and three persons to a single room and seven to a double were not unusual. The Quartering Authority billeted returning Europeans, and austere overcrowded living conditions had to be accepted until new building eased the situation. In July 1947 a Town Planning Board was set up under the Director of Public Works in accordance with a 1939 Ordinance and Sir Patrick Abercrombie, the noted town-planner, visited Hong Kong to advise on general development. His report which appeared the following year in September 1948 made far-reaching recommendations regarding general planning, including the construction of a cross-harbour tunnel, re-siting the Kowloon-Canton Railway terminus away from Tsimshatsui, provision of open spaces, removal of military establishments from central areas in the Island and in Kowloon, and the creation of industrial and residential zones.

High prices and rents produced, as a natural corollary, labour unrest. Since wage levels lagged behind price levels, workers not unexpectedly demanded adjustments. The Military Administration had made some needful concessions but there was a reluctance to give all-round increases in wages because a fall in prices was confidently expected. The restoration of civil government was immediately followed by labour unrest and a wave of strikes as the cost of living reached its peak at that time.

The gas workers came out on strike on 10 May; a week later, the Hong Kong Electric Company's men went on strike demanding a 38 per cent increase over the 1946 wage scale which, with rent, household, and rehabilitation allowances, would mean a 100 per cent increase in earnings. This strike affected the trams and the big electric-power users. There followed a crop of similar demands on the part of ferry crews, cinema workers, and water-works employees, and soon after, 2,000 casual workers employed by a large godown company came out. The electricity workers' strike lasted fifteen days, and on 1 June the trams were running again.

The Kowloon Dock workers struck on 9 June, partly because of the introduction of piece-work for many workers instead of day work, and a week later one thousand of them were dismissed. The workers in the China Light and Power Company at Kowloon came out, but the strike did not last long because the new Labour Department's conciliation machinery allowed management, workers, and Departmental representatives to meet to work out acceptable compromises. The discussions led to the adoption of common standards in regard to working conditions and grading of workers by the two electric companies which was followed by other large firms.

The strike of the ferry crews in late July was more serious because the strike occurred while negotiations were being carried on. The Royal Navy was called in to keep the ferry service going, to prevent this major inconvenience to Hong Kong's citizens. After nearly a month, a Board of Arbitration, with a Supreme Court judge as chairman, was appointed and the service resumed. It recommended a slight increase in wages, a larger 'safe navigation' bonus, a seven-day working week of eight hours daily with two days a month leave, and a limited amount of sickness leave. Before the end of the year there were labour disputes affecting hospital workers, printers, and tailors. Wages were of course difficult to fix because of the uncertainty in the movement of prices; in May the price level increased to such an extent that the rehabilitation allowance was increased to 100 per cent above that originally fixed by the Military Administration.

Labour disputes continued throughout 1947 and affected skilled labour which had not benefited from the post-war pay allowances in the same proportion as the unskilled. In January the Peak Tram workers made demands and, refusing to back down after a five weeks' strike, were dismissed and new staff engaged. The Hong Kong Rope Works' men made similar demands, and after two months' strike and negotiation were replaced by other men, and in March 1947 the British Cigarette Co.'s employees demanded a 100 per cent wage increase but, after twenty-seven days on strike, decided to return on unchanged conditions. In the same month twenty-two labour unions unsuccessfully petitioned for a change in the method of calculation of the rehabilitation allowance in order to put this on a broader basis than 'food and fuel'.

Dissatisfaction over wages continued and a more general agitation for pay increases was organized by the Chinese Engineers' Institute which claimed to represent the skilled mechanics in the Government, the dockyards, and the utility companies, which demanded, in April 1947, a 150 per cent increase in basic wages for all skilled men. Other unions followed with demands for an increase in the rehabilitation allowance, and in fact there developed much inter-union rivalry which tended to confuse the situation. The negotiations dragged on until August, with the Labour Department trying to separate out the various negotiations and channel them to the several appropriate undertakings. On 16 August the Institute called a strike and was strongly supported with 11,000 of its skilled members coming out. A general strike seemed ominously near as skilled men from the railway, docks, cement works, Government services, wharf companies, and the Dairy Farm all came out; but the public utility companies were little affected. The strike lasted twenty-seven days and it ended with the skilled workers gaining a 50 per cent increase in basic wages, with adjustments in the wages of other workers to maintain wage differentials; but the variable rehabilitation allowance continued on the same basis as before.

This settlement naturally stimulated other workers to seek similar increases, and workers in all the utility companies, the two Electric Companies, the Gas, Tramways, Telephone, Bus, and Ferry Companies secured similar increases to those won by the members of the Engineers' Institute. In December 1947 the China Bus Company's men staged a twenty-eight day strike over conditions regarding the payment of an agreed retirement gratuity after ten years' service, but this was a dispute internal to the Company and without wider significance.

The labour unrest gradually subsided, partly because of the gains in wage rates, but partly because of the influx of immigrants from China flooding the labour market with industrious workers looking for work, many of whom were readily trainable to perform skilled work. The Government's policy was to build up a trade union movement on English lines to protect the workers' interests and it passed a Trade Unions and Trade Disputes Ordinance in 1948 which gave legal recognition to labour unions and employers' associations through registration, and it appointed an experienced trade unionist from Britain to advise trade unions on their organization and functions. But the old ideas died hard, and trade unions tended to continue to attract only a small minority of workers and to have strong political affiliations, either Nationalist or communist.

The post-war reconstruction was hampered by epidemics due to malnutrition, the uncontrolled refugee influx from China, the shortage of skilled medical staff and the neglect of health measures under the Japanese. In the summer of 1946 cholera became serious, so that in June servicemen had to be barred from Wanchai where 109 cases out of a total of 156 appeared in fourteen days, and during the year there were 514 cases of which 239 were fatal. Later in the year, smallpox appeared; in November alone there were 819 cases with 530 deaths, and over the whole year there were 1,998 cases with 1,305 or 65 per cent deaths, and an additional 1,032 were picked up dead in the streets, while a house-to-house search of affected areas revealed 315 hidden cases. Malaria claimed victims throughout the year with 2,422 cases of which 720 were fatal, and tuberculosis was also serious due to malnutrition and gross overcrowding, with 2,801 cases of which 1,752 were fatal.

As the Medical and Health Services were built up, so the incidence of these diseases declined; for example, in 1947 there was no cholera and no new cases of smallpox. Malarial areas remained for many years but vigorous anti-malarial measures reduced this threat; watercress cultivation was temporarily forbidden in an effort to stamp it out, and crops grown in defiance of the ban had to be destroyed. Tuberculosis remained the most serious disease because overcrowding prevented isolation and the Government set up an anti-tuberculosis clinic and an Anti-Tuberculosis Society secured the old Naval Hospital at Queen's Road East as a treatment centre.

Another pressing need was the continued rehabilitation of Government services, public utilities and communications, and here it was a matter mainly of continuing what the Military Administration had begun. The return of the European staffs, the training of new men, and availability of supplies combined to speed up rehabilitation. Water charges were increased in October 1946, and in May 1947 the Tai Lam Chung Reservoir scheme, first mooted eleven years earlier, was at last put in hand. Bicycles fitted to carry pillion passengers were banned in August 1946. This led to a series of protests by the riders who, after the third protest meeting in Statue Square, were allowed to continue until the end of September. The Government's intention was also to replace rickshaws by pedi-cabs or motorized rickshaws but these changes were never made because man-drawn rickshaws became a tourist attraction. Other decisions on road transport were taken. The change to right-hand drive for cars was discussed and rejected, as was the suggestion that the trams should be replaced by electric trolleys. In April 1947 a system of one-way streets was introduced in Central District, showing how rapidly traffic was reviving.

A decision had to be taken about the new airfield when the Ping Shan runway scheme was dropped. A mission from the British Ministry of Civil Aviation, believing that the Kai Tak site was incapable of further development on the necessary scale recommended, in March 1947, that Stonecutters Island should be levelled to form a new airfield. In November 1947 the Home Government announced that it was unable to make any financial provision for a new Hong Kong airfield and the Hong Kong Government then decided to retain Kai Tak though it was realized to be unsuitable for the needs of future aircraft already being envisaged. In 1948 new buildings for air traffic control, ancillary offices, hangars and workshops were erected, and the number of passengers, in and out, exceeded a quarter of a million.

The port presented a serious task in reconstruction.[1] Eleven

[1] See T.N. Chiu, *The Port of Hong Kong* (Hong Kong, 1973).

major wrecks remained in the harbour, which had to be cleared before normal facilities could be restored. A salvage adviser, a floating crane, and salvage vessels were procured from Britain and by the end of 1946 three wrecks were raised; it was estimated that the clearance work would take two years and cost a million dollars less the value of salvaged material. Of 48 commercial moorings only two survived, the rest being lost or removed to Japan, and by the end of 1946, 33 had been restored. All harbour navigation lights had been destroyed but all except two were functioning again by the end of 1946, and Waglan Lighthouse which had been bombed by the Allies was temporarily placed in working order pending the arrival of new equipment. By the end of 1947 only two major wrecks remained, all docking and repair facilities were back to normal, and during the year 1946–7, 46,547 ships of just over 13.8 million tons entered and cleared the harbour compared with 74,617 of nearly 30.9 million tons in 1939.[2]

The Port Trust, advocated in Sir David Owen's Report of 1940 on the future control and development of the harbour, was not proceeded with after a local enquiry had advised against it. Instead, a Port Committee comprising British and Chinese shipping and commercial interests as well as representatives of the Harbour, Public Works and Railway Departments, was placed in control. In many other respects the Owen Report's recommendations were adopted.

Trade began to revive strongly despite Government controls. In 1946, and excluding Government-sponsored cargoes, it was about 50 per cent of the pre-war volume, but in dollars it was more than double, with China remaining as the best customer in both imports and exports. In 1947 the Colony's exports were $1,200 million and imports over $1,500 million, and trade with Japan began to develop. In 1948 total trade was valued at $3,659 million and in 1949 at $5,068 million or a 38 per cent rise. Thereafter, Hong Kong trade recovered strongly except for the period of the Korean War when the embargo on trade with China, Hong Kong's best trading partner, caused a slump. As industry developed in the 1950s, the Colony came to rely more on domestic exports and less on the entrepôt trade and

[2] Ibid., p. 81. These figures include the coastal junk trade.

trade with China, as a percentage of the total, declined proportionately.

The banks, particularly The Hongkong and Shanghai Banking Corporation, recovered from severe war losses in personnel and premises to play a notable part in the post-war reconstruction. In order to prevent its assets being frezen in the United States following the Japanese occupation of Hong Kong, The Hongkong and Shanghai Banking Corporation's head office was transferred to London by an Order in Council of 13 January 1943 retrospectively to 16 December 1941, and Mr. Arthur Morse assumed control as from this latter date, acting under a letter of authority from the Colonial Office until the Order in Council regularized his position. An Order in Council of 15 May 1946 moved the bank's head office back to Hong Kong, and a local Hong Kong Ordinance of 20 June 1946, passed through all stages in a single session, allowed an Annual General Meeting to be called, there being constitutionally no directors to call one, and permitted the General Manager to be a director of the bank, a provision which resulted in Morse becoming Chairman. At the same time the fiduciary issue was increased from $30 to $40 million. The bank's 'duress notes' issued by the Japanese without backing had been made legal tender by the Military Administration in April 1946 and, it must be added, with the full support of the bank itself which felt that for the sake of its own good name it should honour all its own notes. These notes were now made the subject of a Bank Notes and Certificates of Indebtedness Ordinance in August 1946, which provided that the loss incurred in honouring the bank's 'duress notes' should be shared in part by the Government; the bank paid £1 million into the Hong Kong Exchange Fund, and the Hong Kong Government issued certificates of indebtedness to the amount of $103,800,000, with additional payments by the bank under a complicated compromise formula. The note-issuing banks had their note-issuing powers temporarily restored, and in July 1947 these were extended for one year and then confirmed.

Most merchants had lost all their stocks, and had to start business again from scratch. Many former directors of firms had no standing because there had been no annual general meetings of companies for four years. Morse was a man of great foresight and saw that orders for reconstruction materials could not wait until the companies could appoint directors and supply collateral security, and he had no hesitation in committing the bank to advances for plant and materials by opening confirmed credits guaranteeing payment to shippers without waiting for the companies to regularize themselves. Acting on the principle that what was good for Hong Kong was good for the bank he went ahead with faith, even without being absolutely certain that Hong Kong would remain British. As the Governor, Sir Alexander Grantham, said of him on his retirement in 1953 '. . . he did things which from the purely banking point of view could hardly be justified, but which certainly could from the point of the Colony as a whole'. Undoubtedly under Sir Arthur Morse's leadership the bank's part in the revival of business in the post-war Hong Kong was quite outstanding.

The moratorium on all debts incurred before the issue of the proclamation on 13 September 1945 proved unpopular, and in July and August 1946 there were a number of unavailing attempts in and out of the Legislative Council to induce Government to lift it, and there was some easing of the position in December 1946 when Government assumed power to exempt from the moratorium certain classes of debts. The moratorium was not entirely lifted until November 1948. A Debtor and Creditor (Occupation Period) Ordinance of June 1948 set out certain principles to be applied in dealing with problems arising out of the settlement of debts in yen, including those collected by Japanese liquidators of the banks. A debt settled during the occupation in Hong Kong currency was regarded as properly discharged, even if the creditor did not receive the money. A debt incurred before or during the occupation and settled with the creditor, was regarded as properly discharged unless it were settled in Japanese occupation currency or accepted under duress. If a debt were paid to the liquidators during the occupation in occupation currency, the debt was regarded as partially discharged; the amount paid in yen was converted to dollars according to a scale laid down in the Ordinance and the debtor remained liable for the difference between the value of the debt and the amount shown on the scale. The Ordinance, which also settled problems such as contractual obligations and bank accounts in military yen, was passed in June but could not of course operate until the moratorium was lifted, and various negotiations delayed this until November 1948.

One pressing task was to develop primary production in the New Territories. On 15 September 1946 there was introduced, as a temporary measure until the farmers could organize their own co-operatives, a Government-controlled vegetable marketing scheme for Kowloon to give the growers and consumers a fairer price. The scheme applied only to Kowloon, leaving the farmers free to sell on the Island in the traditional manner, and though the marketing scheme proved unpopular among the New Territories farmers, the preparation of a co-operative marketing scheme went ahead despite this opposition. A scheme of producing rice and fish on the same plot by raising the level of water by six inches did not get very far because of heavy flooding in 1947. Some progress was made in developing improved pig-breeding, and more vegetable growing. The ban on watercress because of malaria must have been soon reversed, as the report for 1950–1 of the Agriculture and Fisheries Department gave a figure of just under 1,148 tons of watercress locally produced in the year 1947–8.

After the occupation the urgent needs were fertilizer and replenishment of livestock. Maturing tanks built by the Japanese were operated to give twenty tons a day and rice-growers also received rations of peanut cake for manure, new vegetable seeds and insecticides were sent from Britain and Australia, and new strains of rice were introduced. The Japanese heavy-yielding Taiwan rice proved a failure because the thick stem sheltered a parasite from which the existing strains had hitherto been free. Progress with the planning of farming and fishermen's co-operatives proved eventually to be one of the most fruitful pieces of economic post-war reconstruction.

The main feature of post-war Hong Kong was undoubtedly the extremely rapid growth of the population. The Chinese flocked back to the Colony in large numbers and the British defeat was forgotten in the rush to reach the Mecca of hoped-for economic betterment. There are no precise population figures, but the official estimate at the end of 1946, based on the figures for rice and other rations issued and the amount of water consumed, as well as registrations of births and deaths, was 1,600,000, or roughly a million more in the sixteen months since the British returned. In December 1947 it was estimated at 1,800,000, and twelve months later the estimate was still at that figure, showing that the influx rate had steeply declined. In November 1946 it was estimated there were 20,000 street sleepers and there was talk among the Chinese of repatriating them. It says much for the wish to establish good relations with China that the frontier remained open until 1950, when the flood of immigrants threatened chaos.

The problems of housing, food, and restoration of public services have been described and it now remains to deal with some of the social problems of post-war reconstruction. One unfortunate result of the new influx was the steady rise in serious crime. Robbery with violence became common. A running gun-battle between police and armed thieves occurred in Central in early June 1946, and a police inspector was killed while investigating a flat robbery, railway trains were held up by armed men and passengers robbed, and in January 1947 a senior British Government officer was killed on the train when he bravely offered resistance. There were occasional bomb outrages, and bandits robbed people in a large department store in May 1946, travellers in the New Territories were held up at gunpoint and hikers robbed, two being killed in February 1947.

The rebuilding of the education system continued. By the end of the Japanese occupation only a few thousand children were in the schools, many buildings had been destroyed, school furniture had been taken for fuel, and textbooks, where they existed at all, were exorbitantly priced. The schools of neutral Christian Missionary bodies had been allowed to operate during the war and so were able to preserve their facilities and resume teaching early, but they were inadequate to meet the great demand for education which traditionally was the main Chinese avenue to advancement. By the end of 1946 there were 52,000 children in primary schools and 1,205 in secondary schools in the urban area, compared to 78,151 and

14,109 respectively in 1939. In 1947 Government expenditure on education rose from $6 million to $9 million, nearly half devoted to subsidies, but even so an estimated 60,000 children were thought to be without any education. A school meals service came into being, the old Trade School was re-opened and re-named the Technical College, and in 1948 the Central British School, hitherto reserved for European children, was re-named King George V School and opened to any child with the requisite knowledge of English. Primary education made a good recovery, but secondary education lagged behind with only 20,802 pupils compared to 37,355 before the war due to the failure of the private secondary schools to revive and the shortage of premises. Expenditure on education increased in 1948 to over $13 million and it was then estimated that of 225,000 children between the ages of five and twelve only 120,000 were in school. The system of making one building serve two primary schools continued as a regular practice. Private school fees were so high as to prevent expansion, but free evening classes and the Government regulations governing the fees of aided schools helped to counteract this.

The University suffered heavily as a result of the war.[3] There had been battle and internment casualties among the staff, the loss of equipment, and looting of buildings; all these losses presented a forbidding problem of rehabilitation. The library survived with a small depletion of its books, and some buildings used by the Japanese survived. The University Senate had continued to meet in Stanley Camp on an emergency basis and students moved into Free China to continue their studies under members of the University staff in Chinese Universities, including Lingnan University at Canton which had once been sheltered in the University of Hong Kong. In 1946 the Hong Kong Government voted $20,000 towards the rehabilitation of Lingnan in gratitude for the assistance given to Hong Kong University students during the war.

The coming of peace did not necessarily mean the restoration of the University. The Home Government set up a temporary controlling body, the University Provisional Powers Committee, to deal with immediate problems such as staff salaries, but in

[3] See B. Harrison, *The First Fifty Years* (Hong Kong, 1961).

fact shortly before this, in December 1945, it had set up a Committee to determine whether the University should re-open at all and if so what should be its objectives and underlying policies. The Committee, which made its report in July 1946, recommended re-opening; but no decision was taken until March 1948, when the Secretary of State accepted the need for a University in Hong Kong. Financial provision was left mainly to local sources, in contrast to the generosity bestowed at the time on other colonial universities. The University was thus again condemned to that indigence which had dogged its fortunes since its commencement in 1912.

In fact, the University anticipated preparations to open up in anticipation of the Home Government's eventual agreement. A matriculation examination was held in the summer of 1946 and classes started on 23 October 1946, with 109 first-year students, of whom 31 were women, in four faculties, arts, science, medicine and engineering, under the control of a University Interim Committee and a Board of Studies. It was an act of faith, fortunately justified in the event. The residential halls were rehabilitated and Sir Robert Ho Tung donated a million dollars to erect a women's hall of residence. The Government created a capital fund of $4 million and increased the annual grant to $1,500,000.

The Churches had to repair and re-equip their buildings. The Governor attended a service in the Anglican Cathedral on the first Sunday in May 1946, and was presented with a bible to commemorate his last previous attendance when he read the lesson on that ill-fated Christmas Day in 1941. The Union Church met in the old Volunteer Headquarters, as its building had been destroyed, but the Kowloon Union Church was able to re-open in October 1947.

Public statues were restored, except that of Governor Kennedy which used to be in the Botanical Gardens. The erection of a statue of King George VI, ordered before the war, was delayed until Sir Patrick Abercrombie had presented his town-planning report, and in the event it was never mounted. The remaining portion of the old City Hall site was sold to the Bank of China in April 1947 and a new City Hall was promised, though considerable pressure had later to be brought to induce the Government to fulfil its undertaking. The Sino-

British Club was founded in July 1946, largely by the members of the British forces, and took the lead in sponsoring cultural activities until its various branches formed independent bodies.

One interesting experiment of a temporary kind was the setting up of a Peoples' Canteen in a hut on a plot adjoining the Supreme Court where office workers could obtain a cheap midday meal. This followed the pattern of the public messes set up by the Military Administration in the Hong Kong Hotel for European meals and in the Kam Loong restaurant for Chinese. The canteen did not last long and the hut was used for Government offices and other public purposes.

Perhaps more significant was the legislation abolishing the last vestiges of residential racial segregation. The Peak District Reservation Ordinance of 1904, restricting residence on the Peak to Europeans, had been amended to allow residence to the Chinese under prescribed conditions and was finally removed from the statute book in July 1946; similarly the Cheung Chau Reservation Ordinance of 1919 restricting residence on the southern part of the island without permission was also abolished. In fact, there was little racial segregation in Hong Kong and little anti-Chinese prejudice, possibly because so few of the old colonials returned and so many new Europeans came to take their places. Racial prejudices and usages tended to be broken, for example buses were used equally by Chinese and foreigners, to the surprise of visitors from some other colonies.

Relations with China were chequered. There had been much talk among the Chinese of getting back Hong Kong, as had been advocated by the Americans and as a corollary of the 1943 treaty with China, renouncing extra-territorial rights and concessions. Anti-colonial feeling was in the air and British eagerness to shed colonial responsibilities encouraged Chinese aspirations. Despite the Nationalist agitation in Hong Kong centring around T. W. Kwok's office which campaigned to get the Colony back, relations between Hong Kong and China continued on a friendly basis; General Chang Fa-kwei, now the personal representative in Canton of the Generalissimo, made a friendly visit to Hong Kong in August 1946, and in April 1947 the Governor, Sir Mark Young, paid an official visit to Canton where he presented General Chang Fa-kwei with the

C.B.E. for services to the British during the war and particularly for the help given to the B.A.A.G. during the forced evacuation of Kweilin. The next Governor, Sir Alexander Grantham, also visited Canton twice in 1947, in August and November. General Chang Fa-kwei again visited the Colony in September 1947, and Dr. T. V. Soong, Governor of Kwangtung Province, paid a three-day official visit in November. The British authorities in London and Hong Kong were ready to assist China in her post-war problems. A financial agreement was made at the end of 1947 and was followed by a Customs Agreement in January 1948, by which China was assisted in regard to currency control and smuggling, and in a most significant concession the Chinese Maritime Customs were given facilities to operate collecting stations in the Colony; an Ordinance of October 1948 gave effect to the agreement, the delay being due to the demarcation of areas where Chinese patrol vessels were to operate. Hong Kong also assisted China in regard to the gold yuan currency introduced in 1948. In this same year representatives of the two Governments met at Shataukok and arranged to replace the old boundary stones marking the boundary along the middle of the main street. These had been removed by the Japanese.

Unfortunately a number of incidents created ill-feeling among the Cantonese, always susceptible to the treatment of Chinese in Hong Kong. A Chinese peanut hawker was killed by a policeman, who was charged with manslaughter but acquitted, and both on the news of the death and of the subsequent acquittal there were organized boycotts of Hong Kong goods in Canton. One notable source of trouble was Kowloon City. In the lease of the New Territories, Chinese magistrates were allowed to continue to function in Kowloon City, subject to a clause which empowered the British to take over control of the City if the defence of the harbour required it. This clause was invoked six months later, and by an Order in Council in Whitehall Kowloon City had been taken over.[4] This unilateral proceeding was never accepted by the Chinese, who continued to claim jurisdiction over Kowloon City, and Canton people were particularly sensitive on this point. During

[4] See the article by P. Wesley-Smith, 'The Walled City of Kowloon', *H.K..J.L*, vol. 3, no. 1 (1973), pp. 67–96.

the Japanese occupation the walls of the City disappeared and squatters took up residence. When the latter were ordered to leave, under a Government plan to convert the old walled city into a public park, T. W. Kwok issued a statement early in December 1947 that China had never waived her right to the City, and they refused to move, necessitating an eviction order being secured from the courts. Kwok went to Nanking and returned with instructions to seek an amicable solution, but when the evictions began soon after the New Year in 1948, the Nanking Government protested. Two men were arrested for resisting the police and at the trial the defending counsel's plea that the Hong Kong Government had no authority in Kowloon City was rejected by the Court. Demonstrations in Canton and Shanghai followed and the British Consulate in Shameen was damaged. The British policy was to soft-pedal the Kowloon City issue in the interest of good neighbourly relations, so the plan to convert the old city into an open space was forgotten and it has continued with its maze of narrow alleys to be a squalid survival of China in Hong Kong.

V

THE SUMMING-UP

THE sweeping Japanese victory, whatever excuses for it there may have been, inevitably struck a blow at British prestige and badly shook that confidence in the security offered by the British flag which both British and Chinese had taken for granted. So, as the prisoners of war and 'Stanley-ites' sailed home on their repatriation ships, mingled with the bliss of freedom there was an instinctive foreboding that Hong Kong would never be the same again. However, few had any clear idea of what the changes might be.

Uppermost in the minds of many was the futility of the war. The British lost about 1,860 officers and men killed and missing, as well as civilians, in the defence of the Colony, and the question was naturally asked if anything had been gained by their sacrifice. The British Government knew that the Colony could not be relieved and must sooner or later fall to the enemy; on the other hand, if one excludes the Chinese who mostly stood aloof from the conflict, opinion in Hong Kong tended to the belief that the Colony could and would defend itself, with a sporting chance of holding out until relieved by the Fleet from Singapore or, more problematically, by Chinese forces from across the border. The Governor called for all-out defence, having really no choice, because this was the decision of the War Cabinet in London, and he himself set an example of courage in visiting the forward areas during the fighting. The armed and auxiliary defence services undoubtedly responded nobly. The decision was probably justified because the over-all Allied interest demanded that the Colony be defended, despite the inevitable outcome, since allied morale partly rested on the implicit confidence that men in one theatre of war, whether at Dunkirk or Malaya, or later in North Africa and Normandy, should meet the enemy with equal resolution. Hong Kong was the first British bastion to fall to the Japanese, and though it must have boosted the latter's self-confidence and induced a corresponding depression in the

War Office in London, yet it has to be admitted that the battle for Hong Kong had no significant effect whatever on the outcome of the war. The Hong Kong battle had therefore the character of Greek tragedy in which men's steadfastness in the path of duty and refusal to betray their trust led inevitably to the predestined end, exacting its toll of human life and suffering.

The loss of British prestige could not of itself create a new Hong Kong. The factors behind this must be sought elsewhere. The first question which naturally arises is whether the Japanese contributed anything significant during their occupation of three years and eight months. For the most part Japanese influence in the creation and character of post-war Hong Kong seems to have been virtually nil; none of the Japanese administrative institutions survived; they left behind no new theories of government, and their practical reforms in social welfare, education, and health did not survive the British take-over. The reasons are fairly clear. Japanese hostilities against China over a period of eight years, together with the record of excesses committed in the fighting, left a legacy of Chinese hatred of the Japanese and all they stood for. Secondly, in Hong Kong the population was reduced to 600,000 at most, possibly less, and so relatively few had the opportunity of imbibing Japanese ideas over any length of time, and they were swamped by the huge post-war Chinese immigration. Finally, the Japanese ability to govern constructively was never tested in Hong Kong, owing to the demands of the war.

One significant factor was the outlook of the Chinese who flocked back to the Colony in their hundreds of thousands to take up residence in the traditional way and for traditional reasons, namely economic self-betterment with a view to retirement to the family village in China. They occupied themselves with the import-export business of the entrepôt trade, with small-scale light industry such as the manufacture of torches, sand-shoes, rope-making and ship-repairing, with clerical and manual employment, and with retail business. But this time they brought back a more truculent nationalism and if they showed little anti-British feeling it was because they displayed a more pro-Chinese sentiment, as in the strident Nationalist propaganda centred around the Nationalist envoy.

The significant feature of a new Hong Kong was the strengthening of the traditional attitude of the Chinese of looking upon themselves as Chinese, moreover there was little evidence of any desire on their part to build a separate independent Hong Kong community as an amalgam of East and West. The new Hong Kong was dominated in numbers by Chinese who intended to remain Chinese, and only a relatively small number of Eurasians, Portuguese, Indians, local Chinese, and foreign families of long standing, felt themselves to belong to Hong Kong.

The most formative influence in shaping the post-war Hong Kong was the 'new angle of vision' adopted by the Colonial Office in Whitehall, the main features of which, the granting of self-government, development of local resources, and raising of colonial living standards, have already been mentioned. This was no new revolutionary British colonial policy; for example, Lord Lugard, then Sir Frederick, had established the University of Hong Kong as a necessary step in preparing the Colony for eventual self-government, just as he later advocated preparing the Nigerians for the same end. Radical opinion in Britain during the inter-war years, shared by Dr. Selwyn-Clarke and his wife, took the same line that the interests and aspirations of colonial peoples should be advanced and that Britain should step down when they were ready to take over.

The war brought the issue to a head. The British people were called upon to shoulder enormous sacrifices which the colonies were expected in part to share, and their loyalty to Britain in the hour of need made a great impact on British opinion. In giving the necessary war-time guidance to the colonies on the control of currency and trade, restriction of imports, and economy in consumer goods, British authorities were brought up sharply against the poverty among native colonial peoples whose standard of living was so low that talk of sacrifices by them to meet the demands of war was hollow. Therefore, in calling on colonial peoples to play their part in the war, British policy held out to them the goal of greater self-determination and rising living standards. So it came as no surprise that Sir Mark Young's first statement after landing on 1 May 1946 contained a promise to Hong Kong people to give them a more responsible share in their own affairs, soon to be followed by a promise of greater local recruitment for the Government service. Some care for the people's living standards was also shown, for example by the new Labour and Social Welfare Offices, co-operative marketing schemes, and the attempts to create a trade union movement.

But Hong Kong fitted only with difficulty into this 'new angle of vision'. Hong Kong was not a community in the ordinary sense, but an agglomeration of individuals seeking their own economic salvation as they had always done, and asking only to be left alone. Again, there were few local resources to develop, and Hong Kong lived by commercial expertise which could not be democratized or reorganized in the interest of the community as a whole except by some form of nationalization, which was anathema to a commercial free-enterprise society. The war-time controls imposed by the Government had little permanent impact and were continued only so long as necessary until the traditional *laissez-faire* resumed full sway. Some direct taxation in the form of a salaries tax and taxes on property and business profits was re-imposed in 1947 and met with prolonged Chinese protests. Some liberal-minded observers urged the Government, in letters to the press, to use the opportunity of the post-war rehabilitation to place the public utilities under some form of Government ownership and control, but the *laissez-faire* climate, favoured by both Chinese and foreign businessmen, was too strong and the opportunity was lost. It was significant that the Chinese Nationalist propaganda was not allowed to interfere with business.

Perhaps one key factor in the evolution of the new Hong Kong was the greater economic opportunities open to local people. Political uncertainty and British impoverishment through the sacrifices of the war discouraged the inflow of British capital into the Colony and the Chinese increasingly expanded small family businesses, often generating their own capital for expansion out of frugally hoarded profits. Increasing numbers of Chinese entered the professions, such as law, medicine, and accountancy, partly because the Government had opened professional posts to them. Chinese self-respect was enhanced by their success in competing with Europeans in the professional examinations and in gaining high academic qualifications in overseas universities, achievements which made it impossible to deny them a correspondingly enhanced status in the Colony. At the same time the Hong Kong foreign community underwent great change. War casualties, deaths in imprisonment, and early retirement caused by privations, meant that a great number of Europeans never returned to the Colony and the old colonial element was considerably diluted by newcomers from Britain who brought a more liberal attitude to non-white peoples. The customary loud shouts of 'Boy!', by clients in bars and clubs, gradually ceased. The war spelled the end of what may loosely be termed the 'colonial' era. It had lasted almost exactly a hundred years, during which period the administrative control had been firmly in the hands of the Colonial Office in London, exercised through a local civil service recruited, except for clerical and minor grades, exclusively from those claiming pure European descent and directed broadly to the maintenance of British imperial and commercial interests. Local Asian peoples were protected against the grosser forms of exploitation under a white minority in that all were equal under the law, and particularly after 1865 when the Governor was forbidden by his instructions to agree, without the sanction of the Colonial Office, to any ordinance whereby persons of African or Asian birth might be subjected to any disabilities or restrictions to which persons of European birth or descent are not also subjected. But the unspoken assumption was that Asians, and in particular the Chinese, were not forced to come to Hong Kong, and if they did so that was their own affair and they must accept conditions as they found them. There was virtually complete freedom of economic opportunity regardless of race, and many local people prospered under the British flag; nevertheless, important businesses, banking, insurance, and the professions, were mainly in European hands.

The war inevitably temporarily undermined Britain's economic strength and impaired her influence in the world while Asians developed greater national self-consciousness which led them to challenge colonial regimes in Asia, particularly when Britain began actively to divest herself of imperial responsibilities. Hong Kong naturally felt the impact of these new influences. The local people secured greater influence in the counsel of the Government, through greater representation on the Executive and Legislative Councils, and through localization of the Government service. At the same time they began to hold the dominant stake in industry, commerce, real estate, and the professions.

All these factors making for change worked fairly slowly in producing the conditions from which the new Hong Kong gradually and perhaps unostentatiously emerged. These changes came more into the open when the communists came into power in China in 1949, and hundreds of thousands of refugees crowded into the Colony and forced the closure of the frontier. This allowed a Hong Kong community to develop its roots, and this circumstance has gradually forced the Government into a policy of extending its fields of action, in the interest of providing for the people the basic essentials of a reasonably civilized life. The war and its aftermath were perhaps the seminal influences in the orderly evolution of this preponderating local influence in the daily life of the Colony, in which the interests of the community as a whole, and not of one influential minority, had to prevail.

The post-war Hong Kong stood out conspicuously, together with the very much less important Macao, as the last remaining embodiment of those unequal treaties imposed by the West on China during the period of her political weakness, and has been eyed jealously by Chinese Nationalists and communists, but there has been no threat of the use of military force to disturb the status quo, and Hong Kong's existence as a separate entity has not been openly challenged. The threat has rather been that of a take-over by a subversive leftist element from within.

Hong Kong has therefore theoretically remained a Crown Colony in which sovereignty rests with the British Parliament, but in practice it has become autonomous financially and administratively, with Britain retaining control only of its foreign relations, leaving the Colony free to organize its own economic and social life and develop social and state services to an extent consistent with the satisfactory continuance of those economic pursuits which were the only reason for its existence. In the post-war period Hong Kong has triumphantly demonstrated the success of this rationale.

APPENDIXES

1. PRELUDE TO WAR

A recent study of British policy in China during the time of the Sino-Japanese war has concluded that Hong Kong and Britain's other Chinese interests there became an anomaly. Ironically enough, this contention is deduced in part from the reliance of Britain upon Singapore as the main line of defence. Nevertheless, there can be no argument with the other conclusion that Shanghai, Tientsin and Hong Kong 'became simply hostages to an Asia which was beginning to claim its own'.[1]

Yet, though understandably in the context of a discussion of world-wide British foreign policy during World War II by Sir Llewellyn Woodward, Hong Kong does not figure prominently – Hong Kong's importance and threat to the Japanese was primarily as the channel for imported war supplies for Chiang Kai-shek's armies – the 'special undeclared war' exerted new pressures on the British presence in the Crown Colony. A deterministic view of events from 1937 would conclude that the chain of incidents threatening Hong Kong was but a prelude to the final onslaught of 8 December 1941. However, since the situation was not as simple as a ready acceptance of Clifford's thesis might suggest, it is worthwhile to examine the nature of the impact of Japan upon Hong Kong during those four-and-a-half years.

In 1927, China had published the 'Tanaka Memorial' in which Japan was supposed to have openly declared its mission in Asia. Although scholars have thought this document to be spurious,[2] in Hong Kong some people believed throughout the 1930s right up to the invasion, that it gave an accurate representation of Japanese intentions. The idea of the southern advance, in fact, seems to have its origins in the early 1930s with the programme of Ishihara who wrote, in 1933, that in order to establish an East Asia League,

[1] N. R. Clifford, *Retreat from China: British Policy in the Far East* (London, 1967), p. 159. See also Bradford A. Lee, *Britain and the Sino-Japanese War 1937–1939* (Stanford, California 1973). Lee, however, cites Lord Cadogan's opinion that Hong Kong was important beyond its immediate context. 'Any abandonment of Hong Kong would have the most far-reaching effects not only on our position in the Far East but throughout the world.' (Lee, op. cit., p. 100, fn.)

[2] The Memorial itself is confined to plans for the Japanese colonization of Manchuria. However, in the 'High Lights of the Memorial' (supplied by '*The China Critic*') other points were put forward:

the Japanese army and navy should co-operate in attacking the Philippines, Hong Kong, Guam and Singapore.[3] As Iriye, the Japanese commentator on these war documents, says, however, this plan was more hypothetical than real.

By the Washington Conference agreements of 1922 Britain had engaged not to strengthen the fortifications of Hong Kong. This agreement, as Barbara Tuchman argues, was to have important consequences for the fate of Hong Kong.[4] But in any case Hong Kong was considered to be strategically of little consequence.[5] In fact, in the 1930s, British Cabinet and Foreign Office papers reveal that the role of Hong Kong as a military bastion was considered and that Chiang Kai-shek made offers to assist in its defence against the Japanese as early as 1936 and again in 1939. Neither offer was taken up. In April 1938 the Committee of Imperial Defence decided that the counter-bombardment defences of Hong Kong were to be reduced by half. This was in tune with the expectation that any Japanese threat would be by sea and that Singapore, the new naval base, would be the headquarters for British forces in the event of an emergency in the Far East. The Chiefs of Staff, in 1936, in fact, reviewed the position of Hong Kong and concluded,

---

(1) For settling difficulties in Eastern Asia, Japan must adopt a policy of 'Blood and Iron'.

(2) 'In order to conquer the world, Japan must conquer Europe and Asia, in order to conquer Europe and Asia, Japan must [*sic*] conquer China . . . . Japan expects to fulfil the above programme in ten years.'

(3) . . . .

(4) 'Japan believes wars in the near future with U.S.A. and with Russia are inevitable . . . .'

[3] A more incredible link with the actual dénouement is suggested by D. Bergamini in *Japan's Imperial Conspiracy* (New York, 1971), pp. 317, 854–7, where he suggests that the Crown Prince made an intelligence mission out of his visit to Hong Kong in 1921. But see also A. Iriye, 'Japan's Foreign Policies between World Wars – Source and Interpretations', *Journal of Asian Studies*, vol. XXVI (1967), pp. 677–82. In this context he refers in particular to vol. VIII of *Gendaishi Shiryō, Nit-Chū Sensō*, 'The Sino-Japanese War'.

[4] Barbara Tuchman, *Stillwell and the American Experience in China 1911–45* (New York, 1971), p. 85.

[5] S. Roskill, *Naval Policy between the Wars*, vol. I (1919–1929) (London, 1968), pp. 278–9, cites the remarkable report by Admiral Jellicoe, after a visit to the Far East in 1919. Here he pointed to the ultimate aim of Japan to invade Australia, involving the seizure of bases in the East Indies, and the attack on British bases, notably Hong Kong and Singapore. Roskill comments, 'His appreciation of Japanese strategic intentions was very precisely fulfilled in 1941–2.' C. Thorne, *The Limits of Foreign Policy* (London, 1972), p. 241, cites the opinions of the Navy's Director of Planning that Hong Kong was denuded of five out of the six battalions needed for defence (plus five squadrons of aircraft). None were available. The guns, mines and anti-submarine defences of the island were non-existent or quite inadequate.

first, that no matter how long the garrison of four battalions held out, the port would be effectively neutralized by Japanese aerial attacks from Formosa, and second, that Hong Kong, although important, was not a vital outpost. Nevertheless, some attempt was to be made to defend it as long as possible in order to give the Fleet sufficient time to reinforce the Singapore naval base.[6] In 1938, with the ever-nearer threat of the Japanese army in Canton, there was, as we shall see, some modification of these views. The outbreak of the European war, as Hong Kong's military commanders came to recognize, meant that the problem of Hong Kong's defence became an embarrassment which the Chiefs of Staff, preoccupied with threats of an impending German invasion of Britain, wished to ignore. There would be no reinforcements for the Colony.[7] However, in 1940, with the appointment of a Commander-in-Chief Far East, an optimistic view of the defence capabilities of Hong Kong was put forward.[8] A case was argued for reinforcements of two more battalions to enable Hong Kong to withstand a siege

[6] W. R. Louis, *British Strategy in the Far East* (London, 1971), p. 212, writes that submarines were to be given the job of defending Hong Kong for the requisite forty-eight days necessary to this operation. There were moments of anxiety and concern for Hong Kong in London during this period. Lee again quotes Lord Cadogan urging the Chiefs of Staff in December 1937 to consider what could be done in the event of a Japanese strike to the south. The strategists admitted Hong Kong's vulnerability, concluded that with Japan's shortages of money and materials and her international weakness ' . . . it seems scarcely conceivable to us that she [Japan] will deliberately do anything at Hong Kong which is bound to involve her in war with the British Empire'. Lee, op. cit., p. 100, quoting from CAB 53/35.

[7] 'A Presentation on the Fall of Hong Kong' (Commander of British Force Army Headquarters, October 1964). S. W. Kirby, *The War against Japan* (H.M.S.O., London, 1951), p. 56, quoting W. S. Churchill, *The Second World War*, vol. III, p. 157.

'If Japan goes to war with us, there is not the slightest chance of holding Hong Kong or relieving it. Instead of increasing the garrison it ought to be reduced to a symbolical scale . . . . Japan will think long before declaring war on the British Empire and whether there are two or six battalions at Hong Kong will make no difference to her choice.' People in Hong Kong gained some inkling of this assessment and there were murmurings among the British business community that it should be declared an open city. However, in order not to discourage Chiang Kai-shek, the authorities ruled this out of court. In October 1937, according to Lee, the Air Ministry had warned that 'the problem of the effective defence of Hong Kong against the maximum scale of air-attack which Japan could bring to bear against the fortress and base is virtually insoluble' (pp. 86–7).

[8] G. Long, *Australia in the War of 1937–45, Series I*, Army: vol. IV, L. Wigmore, *The Japanese Thrust* (Canberra, 1959), p. 58, points out that Brooke-Popham advised the War Cabinet that 'although the defences of the mainland part of Hong Kong might be overcome shortly after war began, the island could defend itself for at least four months'.

until relief was available. But the view was still taken in London that such measures would be 'frittering away our resources on an untenable position'. Nevertheless, General Grasett, having handed over to General Maltby as C.O.C. Hong Kong, did finally manage to secure approval for the dispatch of the two Canadian battalions, which were to arrive in the East as sacrificial victims to the idea that this might deter the Japanese from attacking the colony. In effect, Hong Kong was given the job, as Churchill put it, of exacting a heavy toll from the enemy. 'The enemy should be compelled to expend the utmost life and equipment.' It was, in all the circumstances, a desperate task without hope of the victory for which armies fight.

The threat, the dangers and the untenability of the British position had then long been recognized. The question arises, therefore, might things have gone differently? It may be that Japan might have agreed to respect British possessions in China if Britain had been more ready to meet Japanese demands. The large question of the origins of the Pacific War is, of course, relevant to this issue. In the ample discussion of both the Japanese and Allied foreign policies in which scholars have engaged and, with the mounting flood of source material, the simple interpretation of Japanese aggression, inspired and driven by the military clique, has been rendered less clear-cut. This is not the place to survey these alternative interpretations which now range from blaming a Roosevelt-Cordell Hull conspiracy[9] to the legitimist justifications of Japanese nationalism put forward by the American scholar, James Crowley.[10] What is clear, with regard to the marginal issue of Hong Kong, is that Britain, through her military and naval weaknesses on the one hand and her unwillingness to let down China on the other, was in a dilemma from which there was no easy escape.[11] As we shall see, the Japanese repeated the pattern of provocation and unofficial harassing of Hong Kong shipping and British aircraft, and of violating the border, which had brought it some success in China.

[9] A. Kubek, *How the Far East was lost: American Policy and the creation of communist China, 1941–1949* (Chicago, 1963). In this seemingly far-fetched interpretation the author's anti-communism leads him to suggest there was another nigger in the woodpile – Harry Dexter White. Thus the United States was the dupe of the Russian international communist conspiracy to fight Japan.

[10] J. B. Crowley, *Japan's Quest for Autonomy: National Security and Foreign Policy, 1930–1938* (Princeton, 1966).

[11] FO 371/20779, *Cabinet Committee on British Shipping in the Far East* (Secret). 'In maintaining British rights, especially in trade, in the present conflict in the Far East, it is clearly desirable to avoid as far as possible either causing offence to China or, or the other hand, unpleasant incidents with Japan. British trade and shipping would suffer in either eventuality.'

In the cases where these were not disclaimed as an excess of zeal by individual Japanese officers, the official justification was the necessity for Japanese forces to mount a blockade around Hong Kong to prevent war supplies being sent from the entrepôt to Chiang Kai-shek's forces.[12] The chapter of incidents on land in Southern Kwangtung – culminating in the capture of Canton in October 1938 – and the sinking and seizing of junks and customs vessels is given in the chronology attached to this introduction.[13] The aim, until 1941 when the Japanese judged that their preparations for the attack were ready,[14] was to tighten the economic noose around Hong Kong. One cannot think that British protests or diplomatic rejoinders impressed Japanese officials unduly. Well might Halifax, the Foreign Secretary, instruct Craigie, British Ambassador in Tokyo, to inform the Japanese Government: 'As regards Hong Kong His Majesty's Government will take such measures as they deem necessary to prevent the infringement of its

[12] Lee, op. cit., pp. 90–1 mentions that following the *Panay* bombing, there was a move in Roosevelt's cabinet and from the Naval Chief of Operations, Admiral William Leaky, to set up a joint British-US naval patrol between the Aleutians and Hong Kong. The blockade, to be instituted after the next grave outrage by the Japanese, would be designed to keep raw materials from reaching the Japanese. The British response was that the blockade proposals were naive and downright bewildering.

[13] See pp. 341-3. FO 371/20980 (1937). Report of Commission on sinking of Chinese Fishing Junks by Japanese Naval Forces. Nine out of twelve junks were lost, 106 fishermen and their families dead. 'The junks were wantonly attacked 20 miles off the Chinese Coast by an armed ship of war', cf. the statement of the Japanese minister of Marine reported in *Japan Chronicle*, 4 October 1937, 'In such cases [alleging that the junks fired on the submarine], the Japanese side needs to take such steps as are necessary to subdue the attackers. If in these encounters Chinese junks suffer losses, they merely take the consequences of their own deeds.' (Some of the junks were 'armed' with ancient cannon.)

There were two cases of Chinese Maritime Customs' cutters being attacked by Japanese naval vessels. In one of these incidents the victim was forced to run aground at Castle Peak beach in Hong Kong waters; whereupon the Japanese sent a landing party ashore to tow off the stranded vessel. In a note of protest the British Government remonstrated, 'The Japanese Government will doubtless agree that the actions of the Japanese destroyer was in all respects wholly unjustified and illegal. The illegal nature of these violations of British sovereignty and jurisdiction is so clear that H.M.'s Government can only suppose that the local Japanese naval authorities are in ignorance of the correct course of conduct in such cases . . . .' (21 December 1937).

[14] J. Toland, *The Rising Sun: The Decline and Fall of the Japanese Empire 1936–45* (New York, 1970), p. 157. In 1940, Major Kumao Imoto was dispatched to investigate the feasibilities in South-East Asia. His itinerary included Hong Kong and Singapore. 'Upon his return he drafted invasion plans for both Hong Kong and Singapore.'

territory . . . by either party to the conflict',[15] but at that time the British preoccupation was to avoid anything which might provide Hitler and Mussolini with an excuse for extending their adventures in Europe or Africa. The history of the British economic role in supplying armaments and munitions along the Kowloon-Canton railway and up the Pearl River estuary is a phase of the pre-war period which deserves to be told in greater detail.[16] There is ample information on the shipments sent through the port, sufficient to justify Medlicott's estimate that 75 per cent of China's war materials came that way. At the same time the diplomatic records reveal that, despite Japanese demands and one agreed closure for three months in 1938, the flow continued. Japanese impatience was understandable. To reinforce any diplomatic bargaining in the years from 1937 Shum Chum was temporarily occupied by Japanese troops, and at other times Lowu and Shum Chum, near the border, were bombed. There was one report that Japanese troops pursuing 'pirates' had actually gone ashore near Shamshuipo to apprehend the fugitives. Thus, in addition to the several warnings of Japanese intentions passed on to the British Government by the United States consular officials in China and Japan,[17] there were these clear indications that the Japanese were prepared almost totally to

[15] E. L. Woodward and R. Butler (eds.), *Documents on British Foreign Policy, 1919–39*, 3rd Series, vol. VIII, Doc. 169, F 11075/10717/10 of 21 October 1938. The key to the British position was given shortly afterwards again by the Foreign Secretary, this time to Clark Kerr, Ambassador to China. '. . . So long as Japan remains neutral, even malevolently neutral, we shall do everything possible to prevent them siding actively with the enemy powers.' Quoted in W. N. Medlicott, *The Economic Blockade* (London, 1952), vol. I, p. 386.

[16] Lee, op. cit., p. 60, fn. 'It has been estimated that from July 1937 to November 1938 an average of 60,000 tons of munitions was shipped every month through Hong Kong to China.'

[17] For instance, see *Foreign Relations United States*, vol. IV, 1940, pp. 661–2.

The report of Consul-General Myers, in Canton to the Secretary of State U.S. Government gives details of the approach of the Japanese forces to Hong Kong. 'Five Japanese detachments landed at Poon early on June 22, and began the occupation of the border areas for the purpose of cutting the routes over which supplies from Hong Kong were reaching Chinese forces . . . . This movement seems to lend support to the growing belief that the Japanese intend sooner or later to occupy Hong Kong and French Indo-China.'

In the same month a report of the Japanese Director of Military Intelligence was passed on stating that Britain was impotent in the Far East. 'There is now nothing to stop Japan from seizing French Indo-China, the Netherlands Indies or Hong Kong or all of them.' This assessment, which was not taken seriously by the British, was expressed when a demand was made by the Japanese Government for the immediate closing of the Hong Kong frontier.

disregard British authority in and around the Colony.[18] Inevitably, these threats had their effect on the morale of the Colony. The writing was on the wall for Hong Kong; a decisive Japanese military move to take the Colony seemed inevitable. As Endacott indicates, there were some attempts made by the British authorities to increase the power of resistance of the defence, but the forces Britain was able to spare were quite inadequate to defend the Colony except perhaps if the Chinese could have mounted an immediate and massive counter-attack on the rear of the Japanese forces. Inevitably too, there was self-delusion on the part of those Hong Kong citizens, British and Chinese, who vainly believed that the worst would never happen. One wonders how many people took note of the *South China Morning Post*? 'That the Colony would be defended no one doubted, but at times it has seemed that its defence would be more heroic than protective.'[19] The not distant future was to bear out the accuracy of this prophecy.

[18] Anyone interested ironically in collecting ostrich-like opinions expressed by the Hong Kong spokesmen of the day could find choice examples in the press. After the Bias Bay landings in December 1937 'high military and naval officers' said, 'We are completely unable to confirm the report and *we are only mildly interested*.' In the same year Reuter reported, 'Hong Kong is destined to become a second Singapore as regards the impregnability of her defences'. (Report in the *North-China Herald*, 13 April 1937, 29 December 1937).

[19] *S.C.M.P.*, 16 November 1941. Col. Lindsay Ride in a 'Report on the conditions in Hong Kong subsequent to the surrender, and on the events which led up to my escape from the prisoner-of-war camp in Shamshuipo'. (FO 371/31671) was of the opinion that 'Outwardly Hong Kong fell on 25 December, because its garrison was outfought; actually it fell weeks, months before, psychologically defeated.'

2. *THE SOCIAL AND POLITICAL IMPACT OF THE WAR ON HONG KONG*

A great deal of research must be done into the social, economic, and political structure of Hong Kong in the pre-war period. But at least it is clear that the Colony, even if it was primarily a trading post, was not like the Shanghai of the old days, an international concession, a cosmopolitan city; yet paradoxically the permeation of government into the everyday lives of the inhabitants, residents, refugees, expatriates – was far less than at present. Even among the top echelons of society, among the taipans and the top officials, as Lethbridge suggests, there was little contact and even conflict.[1] Perhaps as Agnes Smedley, herself a temporary refugee from the mainland, said, echoing the Japanese attitude, socially Hong Kong was an effete outpost of Empire 'like a rotten fruit' ready to drop into the plunderer's hands.[2] It was a divided community, united only by the tangential interests of commerce. Indeed, a newcomer to the Colony, F. C. Gimson, the Colonial Secretary, with a long career in Ceylon behind him, was shocked at the lack of identification of the Europeans with the welfare of the place where they made their wealth. And what of the poor, who previously had shared this 'bird of passage'[3] mentality, but who now were trapped in an insecure permanence as Kwangtung became more and more a waste-land of destruction? It would seem, even without the added burden of penniless starving refugees, that Hong Kong was recognized as a place where 'more than half [of] the Chinese population of the Colony – that is over 400,000 people – exists in a state of semi-starvation'.[4] These were, as the *North-China Herald* correspondent wrote, 'The products of the social system of the colony, which does not provide wages on which the average Chinese family can subsist.' And, if this is thought to be a journalistic exaggeration, the facts of utter destitution were undeniable in the embarrassing shape of the many thousands of pavement-sleepers who, day and night, huddled on the only space to which they could lay claim.

This might seem to depict a scene ripe for the revolution of the have-nots: but, of course, this did not happen, chiefly because this condition of existence was a common fact of life on the mainland.

[1] H. J. Lethbridge, 'Hong Kong during Japanese Occupation: Changes in Social Structure' in J. Agassi and I. C. Jarvie, *Hong Kong, A Society in Transition*, pp. 77–81 (London, 1969).

[2] A. Smedley, *Battle Hymn of China* (London, 1944), p. 357.

[3] The phrase is Gimson's.

[4] *North China Herald*, 23 June 1937, p. 496.

But, one might ask, these sufferers would surely respond to the liberating ideals of the Pan-Asiatic brotherhood propagated by the Japanese in China? The balance of the evidence indicates that the Japanese did little to secure the voluntary co-operation of the local population, apart from a few Eurasians, and the Indians who were mainly members of the police force and therefore vitally necessary for the control of the territory.[5] The first aim of the occupation forces was to cow the residents into submission by brutality and terror. The overriding objective was to cut down to the minimum the needs of the local population which even at that time was not self-subsistent and very much dependent on imported food supplies. This was done by strict measures of administration and hygiene, e.g. no one was entitled to a ration card unless he was in employment, and by lax control of emigration regulations to the mainland. As many Chinese families as possible were encouraged to leave the Colony. As the Allied blockade became tighter these pressures became greater; to remain in Hong Kong became a luxury not easily bought by working to aid the Japanese war effort. As Tanaka, the second Japanese Governor of Hong Kong in 1944, promised his subjects: 'If rice is available, the people will have rice to eat. If there are only sweet potatoes, they will only eat sweet potatoes, and if there are only beans, they will eat beans.'[6] With little work to earn a living, with no ships calling at the port, with few or no public amenities such as electric power or public transport, with fuel or firewood almost unobtainable, and the people dying daily of starvation, the B.A.A.G. report was undoubtedly accurate in declaring, 'The occupying Japanese authorities have nothing to offer except vague promises of Utopia around the corner.' The promises were by now threadbare and barely credible.[7]

In view of this it is difficult to attach great significance to other reports, for example that even early in the war, on the celebration of the fall of Singapore, there was great jubilation in Hong Kong. Then there were processions of Chinese in the streets, but the participants (probably Chinese government employees who could not refuse to be present) had been given a cake each as a 'present'.[8] On the contrary, in the words of one report: ' . . . As if in full

[5] The study of Hong Kong's Indian population by K. N. Vaid, *The Overseas-Indian Community in Hong Kong* (H.K.U.P., 1972), says very little about this episode. As he shows, the Indian community has never been fully integrated into Hong Kong society.

[6] CO 129/591. Intelligence Report No. 68, 28.8.1944.

[7] FO 371/31671 (1942). Report by an Australian-Chinese lady (Mrs. Gwen Priestwood?).

[8] Ibid.

expression of their sentiments thousands of Chinese residents packed their scanty belongings and made for their homeland – Free China.'

In a later similar report the writer, Count R. de Sercey, a Frenchman from the Chinese Postal Service who left Hong Kong in April 1944, confirmed anti-Japanese feelings in even stronger terms. He thought the Hong Kong inhabitants had more confidence in the British than in the Chinese Government. They had great faith in 'a not distant allied victory'. (In this respect the practical Chinese were voting with their precious money, hoarding their Hong Kong dollars.) This neutral observer also pleaded extenuating circumstances for the prominent Chinese citizens forced to be members of the puppet Councils; it was the extreme necessity to keep their families from starving which bound them to their masters.[9] On the other hand, the Japanese administrators did meet resistance. There was the passive unwillingness of school teachers, for example, to provide propaganda material. Questionnaires issued to schools for pupils to fill in questions such as, 'What would you do if the British came back to Hong Kong?' were skilfully parried with answers, 'We would do what our parents told us to do.' Similarly opinion polls about 'the present war' produced results which can only have been disappointing to the framers of those questions.[10]

Resistance of a more active kind was represented both by the Chinese members of the B.A.A.G. and the guerrillas of the East River Company. Both of these aspects have been covered by Endacott, but an article written just after the war by an author, H. C. K. Woddis,[11] amplifies that account. This article appropriately enough begins with the burning question, 'On which side lie the sympathies of the people of Hong Kong?' This seemingly authoritative account of the exploits of the East River Column and the Hong Kong, Kowloon, and New Territories Independent Battalion – controlling the New Territories against 'bandits' and Japanese forces alike; in posting up proclamations at the entrance of the Central Market in Hong Kong; rescuing allied soldiers and airmen; in intelligence work – claims that these irregulars played a vital part in helping to defeat the occupying armies of Japan.[12]

[9] CO 129/591, Intelligence Report 1944. In that month the Japanese were unable to maintain the supply of rice rations, and the official distribution was abandoned.

[10] Father S. J. Ryan, 'Steering in troubled waters'. (unpublished MS.)

[11] H. C. K. Woddis, 'Hong Kong and the East River Company', *Eastern World*, vol. 3, no. 7, July 1941.

[12] Woddis also claims that these irregulars were the first allied troops to march into Kowloon after the defeat of Japan. The presence of an irregular force is confirmed by several Foreign Office papers. Indeed, as Chan has told the story,

The million or more Chinese who flocked back into the Colony after 1945 at the rate of 100,000 a month provide some evidence that Hong Kong under British rule did appear to have some merits. Realistically, of course, one should take into account that some of those returning to Hong Kong calculated that British administration offered greater security for their lives and property than China, still in tumult after the Japanese defeat.[13]

According to Lethbridge, despite defeat and the eradication of the Japanese occupation – taking down the Japanese street signs and the demolition of the Japanese war memorial – 'The Japanese succeeded in establishing the foundations of a New Order in Hong Kong'.[14] In other words, the occupation worked ultimately to the benefit of the leaders of the Chinese community. Through the British failure in the Far East, the Chinese were able to make the Government of Hong Kong their own government. How this came about is conveyed again in Lethbridge's words: 'The British mandarinate collapsed in 1941: it has never been replaced.' The 'Peak mentality' and colonial arrogance were put aside. As for the Chinese, 'The local population . . . seem to have acquired greater trust in the Administration. They were impressed by the speed with which the rehabilitation of the economy was achieved, by the establishment of law and order and of a milieu favourable to the acquisition of wealth. The Government honoured its pre-war debts and obligations and compensated its former employees. Its post-occupation record was admirable – it believed in business first.'[15]

This reading of the Colony's transformation at that time, of course, does depend very much on the interpretation that the present day Hong Kong is a Colony run for a small group of Chinese and European businessmen. To discuss the whole complex body of the Hong Kong Government policy and administration in the years after 1945, in order to test this premise, would take this discussion beyond its intended objectives. However, it is a truism of Hong Kong's development that as a Colony it is debarred from the evolution, hastened by the Pacific war elsewhere, to independent nationhood. Thus politically, whether there is greater welfare for the people than previously is in a sense irrelevant. However, even here, as Endacott has described in this book and in his *Government and the People*, the returning Governor of Hong Kong, Sir Mark Young, did attempt, though abortively, to introduce a more

the imminent liberation of Hong Kong by these 'Chinese forces' appeared as a threat to the British plans for the re-occupation of Hong Kong.

[13] This point was made by Li Shu Fan in 1944.

[14] Lethbridge, op. cit., p. 78.

[15] Ibid., p. 127.

advanced stage of municipal government to Hong Kong. Where the blame should lie for this failure is again not a question to be debated here: however, the intention to introduce reform was there. Indeed, my own subsequent research into the Colonial Office papers suggests, albeit sketchily, that immediately after the war the British Military Administration looked for candidates 'to dispute local leadership with the established order'. What was ultimately in view, whether a more representative system or something more limited, is not known. In the mind of MacDougall, at least, there was every intention to start anew, as the following quotation from his informal report shows: 'We have dusted out the marriage chamber, cleaned the windows, put in some (almost) fresh linen and turned back the covers. But there is no sign of the bride and the groom grows restive.'[16] As subsequent attempts to introduce reform into Hong Kong Government have shown, it is because of the special characteristics of the local population that the democratic development so earnestly espoused in other ex-colonies is difficult to encourage here.

[16] CO 129/591 54132/45. F. C. Gimson, the retiring Officer Administering the Government, in a broadcast on the eve of his departure from the Colony also expressed the need for reform: 'I look forward to an era of rapid progress in ameliorating the methods of public administration here in accordance with the settled policy of His Majesty's Government to foster the development of self-governing institutions throughout the Empire. There is great need in Hong Kong for reform on the social as well as the political side; and we are now presented with the opportunity of a clean sheet on which to sketch for early implementation schemes for educational, medical, housing and town-planning improvements. Not least should attention be paid to the problems connected with the promotion by legislation and otherwise of better conditions for the people of the labouring classes.' (Gimson MSS. Rhodes House Library, Oxford.)

3. THE LIBERATION OF HONG KONG

ENDACOTT in his Chapter I of Part III 'The Planning Unit in London' has given a broad account of some of the problems and the thinking which moulded the administrative arrangements for setting up a civil affairs unit for Hong Kong in preparation for the end of the Japanese occupation. He has also pointed to the major diplomatic threat in the form of Chinese expectations and American sentiment to the British resumption of the Colony. Elsewhere he has correctly emphasized the determination and role of the Colonial Secretary, F. C. Gimson, a captive in Stanley, in planning some essential preparations, such as the ordering of new paper money, and in setting up a provisional administration immediately after the Japanese surrender, but before the arrival of the British fleet under Admiral Harcourt on 30 August 1945. However, since then some of the official records of the Colonial and Foreign Offices have become available and therefore the account given in the book can be amplified.[1]

Whatever the state of disarray the Hong Kong Government and the British were in during the early months of defeat, in a supreme gesture of optimism the Colonial Secretary, as early as September 1942, had smuggled a message out of the internment camp to Shanghai to the Foreign Office asking not to be evacuated and to be allowed to form a nucleus of an administration as soon as the Japanese withdrew.[2]

This was also the time, as another chapter records, of the formation of the British Army Aid Group which established an exiguous channel of communication between China and Hong Kong.[3]

[1] In my article 'Confinement and Constitutional Conflict in War-time', *Hong Kong Law Journal*, September 1972, using F. C. Gimson's papers, now deposited in the Rhodes House Library, Oxford, I have examined the legal and political implications of Gimson's stand that Hong Kong remained British though temporarily occupied by the enemy. All this underlines the key importance of Gimson's actions, especially when, through difficulties of communication from London, via Chungking via B,A.A.G to Hong Kong, the Colonial Secretary had to take the decisive step on his own initiative. Also Dr. K.C. Chan of the History Department, Hong Kong University, in a survey of the diplomatic questions involved, has convincingly linked the burning question, whether Hong Kong should revert to China, with the debates in America and Britain which took place from 1942 onwards. In other words it would be a mistake to regard the years 1942–August 1945 as a hiatus in the discussion about the future of Hong Kong.

[2] FO 371/ F 6872 message dated 2 October 1942. It was then the request for $100 million of new currency was made.

[3] See in particular Professor Gordon King's Daphne Chan Memorial Lecture 'An Episode in the History of the University of Hong Kong', *Supplement to Hong*

This was primarily an intelligence unit but it strove to establish links with the British internees and prisoners of war in Hong Kong, sometimes in a way not altogether approved by the Foreign Office. For instance, the link with the bankers, notably Sir Vandeleur Grayburn and his deputies in the Hongkong and Shanghai Banking Corporation, is an important episode in the history of assistance to the inmates of Stanley – one which ended tragically with the deaths of Sir Vandeleur and Mr. Edmonston at the hands of the Japanese. A not very heavily disguised invitation to the inmates of Stanley from Col. Ride, of the B.A.A.G. to escape,

> This the 1st of exchange, 2nd & 3rd to follow pending on negotiability of market .... Am attempting to arrange monthly letter of credit for hotel guests .... How many guests would be interested in Liberty Bonds? They are for sale (Parkhurst rates apply) money promised by interested promoters ... L.T.R. 10.11.42.

was sent to Edmonston. But he, obsessed with personal arrangements to provide money for the internees, failed to pick up the hint. In fact, the Japanese seized suspected contacts and message carriers, and were able effectively to cut off this contact.

In 1943, when the American forces were planning to launch the major land offensive in the East – operation 'Buccaneer' – it appeared for a time that Hong Kong might be the target for an attempt by the allied forces to liberate the Colony and then relieve occupied China and South-East Asia; however, this scheme was shelved in favour of the 'Overlord' Normandy landings.[4] In the years 1944 and 1945 nevertheless, this possibility affected the thinking of the War Office planners about the role of the B.A.A.G. As time went on and the hold of the Japanese on the Colony grew more tenuous and especially when Chinese forces, both regular troops and guerrilla irregulars, looked like mounting a campaign against the occupying troops, it became more urgent for Britain to prepare for this contingency. Already, through intelligence reports coming in from Chungking and through interviews with influential Chinese escapees from Hong Kong, such as Dr. Li Shu Fan, it was clear that China expected the rendition of Hong Kong. Moreover, the fact that the major effort in liberation would be American exacerbated fears of American political intervention against colonialism in the East. The full examination of this issue cannot

---

Kong University Gazette, vol. XX, no. 6, dated 1 August 1973, and FO 371/31671, pp. 117–23, report of Gordon King dated 18.3.1942. There exist other reports by escapees to China in this file as well as various military and intelligence reports on conditions in Hong Kong sent on from the B.A.A.G. at Waichow.

[4] M. Howard, *Grand Strategy*, vol. IV (H.M.S.O., London, 1972), p. 447.

be carried out here, and Dr. Chan in her article[5] has surveyed the diplomatic exchanges resulting from this contingency. Col. Ride, commander of the B.A.A.G, was however more outspoken than these official exchanges. In April 1945, after receiving a proposal from London that British Civil Affairs officers should recruit pro-British Hong Kong Chinese in South Kwangtung to infiltrate into Hong Kong, he ruffled a few feathers in the Colonial and Foreign Offices with the following representation from which only a few salient extracts can be given.[6] In support of his firm conviction that the B.A.A.G, which, according to him, had been and should continue to be carefully non-political and confined to a rescue operation, he stated,

> In 1942 we were derisively known as the 'Run-Away-British'.... For the last three years we have repeatedly told the Chinese that we are in this with them to the end . . . if, when Hong Kong is retaken (by the Americans!) and handed back to the British on a platter, and the BAAG packs up and returns to Hong Kong, it will take British prestige a generation to live it down.

The most important role for the B.A.A.G. even after liberation, he argued, was to continue to promote Sino-British relations. The real and continuing danger to Hong Kong would be the underground activities of the communist guerrillas in Kwangtung. Therefore, 'The longer we keep our intimate contact on friendly terms with them [the KMT] in their own territory, the better we can serve Hong Kong'. This 'remarkable report' was not accepted. Ride was criticized for over-stating the case; nevertheless, partly through the rapid development of events, the infiltration plan was shelved. Yet this gave an even greater urgency to the need to get in touch with the Colonial Secretary in Hong Kong to instruct him to forestall any consequences of a military liberation of Hong Kong by re-forming the existing administration there.

The B.A.A.G, through its medium of its link man in Macao, was the means of conveying this instruction to F. C. Gimson, although Col. Ride had warned London that it could not guarantee safe delivery of the missive or its speedy dispatch. In fact, this message did not reach Stanley until 27 August. Meanwhile, in a significant gesture of patriotism, a group of internees left Shamshuipo Camp and succeeded in allaying the Japanese unwillingness to recognize the British as the rightful recipients of their surrender. For a few

[5] Chan (Lau) Kit-ching, 'The Hong Kong Question during the Pacific War (1941–5)', *Journal of Imperial and Commonwealth History*, vol. II, no. 1, October 1973, pp. 56–78.

[6] FO 371/46251, 'BAAG and the future of Hong Kong'.

hours on 18 August the Union Jack flew at a masthead on the Peak where it might be seen by virtually all the Colony's population. Later it had to be removed as a premature development. On the initiative of Dr. Selwyn-Clarke, who had left another internment camp, Ma Tau Chung, on the 18th, a meeting was arranged between the Colonial Secretary and the senior military officer, Col. White, at the offices of the International Red Cross in Hong Kong 'with the object of sending a wireless message to the Secretary of State for the Colonies in London, asking for information concerning the future status of Hong Kong'.[7] It seems, understandably, that there was a crossing of messages. Nevertheless, the directive to Gimson from London, dispatched on 17 August, instructed the Colonial Secretary to assume responsibility for an administration. This was to be done to certain guidelines:

a) Policy of HMG is to restore British sovereignty and administration immediately . . . .
b) It is open to you to assume administration of government under existing letter patent.
Your duties will be to work accordingly with full support of H.M. Government till such time as force commander . . . arrives with authority to establish military administration.[8]

Gimson's reply of 27 August informed the Secretary of State that he had already done this.

> I have taken up residence in Hong Kong in a building near the Hong Kong Bank provided for that purpose by the Japanese. With me are all European members of the Executive Council as well as other Senior Government officials. Japanese have agreed to facilitate unofficial liaison with their civil and military organizations, but maintain the attitude they remain responsible until surrender takes place.[9]

Even so, in practical terms of law and order and running the day-to-day administration of the Colony, Gimson's organization was practically helpless. Indeed, at that stage, with Chinese guerrillas in the New Territories and armed gangs operating in Kowloon, Gimson was justified in expressing his apprehensions that 'an attempt to set up formally a British civil administration before the arrival of our forces would be unwise'.[10] Yet Gimson took the oath of office as Officer Administering the Government in Stanley and,

[7] John Luff, *The Hidden Years* (S.C.M.P., Hong Kong, 1967), p. 226.
[8] Copy of message in possession of H.K. Government.
[9] Legally, of course, the Japanese were correct in this position because of the British surrender in 1941.
[10] Message F. C. Gimson (O.A.G.) to Secretary of State, 27 August 1945.

as we know, weathered the crisis until the arrival of the British forces.

Political sentiments may be the ultimate forces determining the framework of society; however, in conditions of acute economic hardship the question of where the next meal is to come from dominates all others. As MacDougall, Hong Kong's Chief Civil Affairs Officer in the new military administration, observed in an unusually frank and direct letter to a friend in the Colonial Office, 'When the fleet sailed in, tens of thousands of Chinese lined the waterfront. A man who was there told me they didn't remark whether the ships were British, American, Russian or Chinese: all they said was, "Now we will eat"'. MacDougall went on to admit the precariousness of the liberation expressed in these fundamental terms: 'By shifts and evasions we have carried on nine weeks to conceal the essential weakness of our position, which is that the larder is bare, that the godowns are empty, and that the liberators brought nothing that fills stomachs or furnishes houses.'[11]

Endacott relates the administrative measures taken to tackle this grave problem and reminds us that it was necessary to re-impose rice-rationing as late as 1955. D. M. Kenrick also, in his detailed study of price-control in post-war Hong Kong,[12] shows how the compromises between the encouragement of free enterprise and the enforced controls were administered. Nevertheless, as the political issue forcibly reminded the civil servants in Whitehall, Hong Kong was a Colony. Colonialism was discredited, not only in the minds of colonial subjects, but more important from the point of power, in the foreign policies of the United States, the chief liberator of the Japanese-enslaved peoples. To be fair to the British politicians they were aware of the implications of the war upon colonial policy as early as 1942. But principles are one thing, practical implementation is another. Researches in the Colonial Office records, in fact, reveal that although the speed of the process of liberation overtook the slow planning of the committees, there was time to issue to MacDougall a set of policy directives, sketchy indeed, but providing for a new beginning of colonial government in Hong Kong. This is, in many ways, a foundation document of the post-war Hong Kong.[13]

... Your objectives are the maintenance of law and order and the prevention of disease and unrest. This will involve among other things:

[11] CO 129/59 54144/43/3. The letter dated 7 November 1945 was marked personal and confidential.

[12] D. M. Kenrick, *Price Control in Hong Kong* (Hong Kong, 1954). See also any article in *H.K.L.J.* vol. 4, no. 2, 1974, pp. 133–50.

[13] CO 129/591 54144/22. Top Secret Telegram AMSSO to SACSEA (MacDougall) dated 31.8.1945.

i) The establishment of a police force . . .
ii) The establishment of military courts
iii) The control, so far as possible, of the influx of civilians by land and sea
iv) The establishment of relief camps and the provision of relief for distressed persons
v) The provision of medical treatment in these camps in hospitals or elsewhere
vi) The taking of adequate measures of public health and sanitation
vii) The restitution and maintenance of essential public services
viii) The control and distribution of supplies

* Paragraphs omitted refer to control of ex-enemy property, dealing with quislings and renegades, censorship, etc.

xii) The establishment of currency, banking and fiscal arrangements . . .
xiii) The control of prices and wages
xiv) The greatest possible use of local resources

Further, the Civil Affairs Officer was briefed:

In carrying out your duties you will bear in mind the long term objective of Colonial policy. This will involve

1) The reconstruction of the Colony's financial and fiscal structure
2) The re-organization of civil courts, police and prisons
3) The rehabilitation of commerce and industry, including agriculture and fisheries
4) The reconstruction and development of public and private utilities, and in particular of the post and air services
5) The re-organization of hospitals and the public health and sanitary organizations
6) The re-organization of the educational system of the Colony

* Paragraph 7 refers to other aspects of policy of H.M.G. for colonial administration and development.

8) Preparation for the transfer of the administration to a civil government.

The vital period of reconstruction, with its myriads of far-reaching problems is, of course, worthy of full-scale study in itself, and will doubtless be the subject of books by future historians. Most of these policy directives, of course, were designed to cover the immediate contingencies of restoring a working system for the economy and government. However, in this document and in a subsequent briefing to the Governor, who resumed the Civil Government in Hong Kong in 1946, it is possible to see the germs of the social welfare policy which was to be a major part of British colonial policy in the post-war years.

Programmes of departmental activities should form an integral part of a general plan for social welfare, based on the ascertained needs of the community and so constructed as to give proper weight to the requirements of both urban and rural areas.[14]

It is possible to see in these carefully chosen words the approval for the post-war administrative policies which are, even today, physically and socially transforming Hong Kong.

[14] CO 129 (1945–6), 54132/45.

4. *CHRONOLOGY OF EVENTS DURING SINO-JAPANESE WAR AFFECTING HONG KONG 1937–1941*

1937

7 July	Marco Polo Bridge incident. The period of the special undeclared war.
September	*Asama Maru* (Japanese wireless 'spy-ship') aground in Saiwan Bay.
5 "	Seizure of Chinese Maritime Customs' ships by Japanese in Hong Kong waters.
13 "	Bias Bay area bombarded by Japanese.
1 October	Pearl River blockaded by Chinese.
12 "	Junks destroyed around Hong Kong.
11 December	Chinese Maritime Customs' vessel *Cha Hsing* captured by Japanese in Hong Kong waters. British note of Protest to Japan.
13 "	Japanese landing at Blackhead Point, Kowloon.
15 "	Shum Chun bombed.
22 "	Reported landing of Japanese troops at Bias Bay, New Territories.

1938

February	Imperial Airways' plane fired on by Japanese near Hong Kong. Japanese bombing near Sino-Hong Kong border. Attacks on junks in Hong Kong waters.
21 May	Two new units of H.K. Volunteer Defence Corps formed.
September	Trial blackout in Hong Kong. British Army and Navy manœuvres.
October	Pearl River again closed by Chinese.
10 "	Colony receives news of Japanese landing in Bias Bay. Garrison alerted.
13 "	Kowloon-Canton road closed.
15 "	Chinese section of Kowloon-Canton Railway in Japanese hands.
19 "	Seizure of junks bringing livestock to Hong Kong.

21 October	Fall of Canton. Flood of refugees into Hong Kong.
27 "	Major Matsutani, representing Japanese Commander-in-Chief, makes calls on Governor and G.O.C. British troops. First formal contact between British and Japanese at Hong Kong since hostilities in South China. Gives reassurances about limited nature of Japanese moves.
17 November	Visit to Hong Kong of Japanese cruiser *Myoko*, flying the flag of Vice-Admiral Shiozawa, Commander 5th Cruiser Squadron, 'for an important exchange of views with Vice-Admiral Sir Percy Noble, Commander-in-Chief, China Section'.
26 "	Fall of Shum Chun.
December	Opening of new Burma Road to traffic.

1939

10 January	Japanese occupation of Hainan Island.
21 February	Lowu bombed. 12 killed, 18 injured. Japanese Government pays $20,000 compensation.
March	Anglo-Japanese agreement re shipping on Pearl River.
April	Japanese annexation of Spratly Islands.
3 June	S.S. *Ranpura* boarded and searched by Japanese.
21 "	Anti-Japanese strike by Hong Kong students.
July	Conscription of all male British subjects in H.K. up to 41 years of age.
August	Bombing of Shum Chun.
September	Easing of tension. Colony appeared no longer under shadow of Japanese invasion.
November	Forty-four Vickers tanks landed at Hong Kong.

1940

March	Air-raid wardens' recruiting campaign.
20 "	Legislative Council approves War Taxation Bill, including £100,000 gift to U.K. and $5 million expenditure on construction of warships to be presented to Britain.
April	New Defence Regulations.

May	The 'Hughesiliers' Unit (H.K.V.D.C.) formed.
25 June	Return of Japanese forces to H.K. border. 500 Japanese troops occupy Shum Chun. Demolition by British of Shum Chun River bridge. Japanese demand cessation of export of arms to China via Hong Kong.
July	Anglo-Japanese agreement. Burma Road to be closed for three months. Plan for evacuation of British women and children put into effect. General Norton, Acting-Governor of Hong Kong.
August	Arrest in Hong Kong of alleged Japanese spy, Yamaguchi.
September	Food price control.
November	Entry of refugees into Hong Kong restricted.

1941

June	Centenary celebrations. Appointment of Sir Mark Young as Governor (arrived September).
July	Japanese assets in Hong Kong frozen. Emergency Regulations applied to everyone.
14 November	Arrival of two Canadian battalions of troops.
8 December	8 a.m. Japanese attack on frontier and aerial attack on Kai Tak airport. Five (?) 'planes destroyed.
8/9 ”	Japanese attack launched across Tide Cove, New Territories.
9 ”	Fall of Shing Mun Redoubt.
11 ”	Withdrawal from Kowloon via Star Ferry. Japanese attack on Lamma Island.
12/13 ”	Evacuation of British and Commonwealth troops from mainland via Lyemun.
13 ”	Japanese ultimatum to Governor to surrender.
17 ”	Second Japanese ultimatum.
18 ”	Japanese assault on Hong Kong Island. Triple landings at North Point, Taikoo Dockyard and Lyemun.
19 ”	R.N.V.R. motor torpedo-boats in action in harbour.
25 ”	Truce and further Japanese parley. 3.15 p.m. Governor delivers message of surrender to Japanese H.Q. and enters into captivity.

5. *CONFINEMENT AND CONSTITUTIONAL CONFLICT IN OCCUPIED HONG KONG 1941–1945*

Alan Birch*

THE story – albeit heroic and abortive – of the resistance of the British, Canadian and Chinese forces to the onslaught of the Japanese thrust to the South has been told many times. So, too, many accounts have been given of the long, seemingly endless grind to exhaustion, both physical and mental, of the military and civilian prisoners of war who were imprisoned in the Shamshuipo, Argyle Street, and Stanley Camps. And whilst the reader can still be moved to shock at man's inhumanity to man or to pride at the heroic fortitude of the narrators in the face of these grim experiences, inevitably the passage of time appears to reduce these epics in significance. Now, thirty years or more afterwards, 1973 is apparently a world away from these barbarities.

Of lasting relevance, however, is the question of the political future of the Colony of Hong Kong. Is it to remain a lingering relic of British imperialism in the East? Does it hold the possibility of constitutional development towards self-determination as other British colonies have done or does the future lie not too distantly with China?

It is precisely in this area of constitutional development that there was an episode in this war of the Empires in the East which, though

* M.A., Ph.D. (Manc.); Reader in History, University of Hong Kong. Most of the research for this paper was undertaken when I was Senior Associate Member during Michaelmas Term 1972–3. I have to thank the Warden and Fellows of St. Antony's College, Oxford, for the stimulus and helpfulness of the College. I have also to thank the Superintendent and Librarians of the Rhodes House Library at Oxford for making material available to me, as I do Sir Franklin Gimson, K.C.M.G., who also very kindly answered several important questions arising from my researches. Dealing with a subject which was and perhaps still is controversial, where in the cleansing of the stables of war much essential evidence in written form was cast aside, I am very much aware of the dangers of reading too much into remarks made at the time. I hope that my subsequent comments on the duty of the historian trying to be objective about this situation do not appear to be over-sententious or too trite. In Hong Kong I have to thank Mr. Ian Diamond of the Public Records Office of Hong Kong for helpful advice; Mr. Malcolm Quinn of the University of Hong Kong Library; and Mr. Peter Wesley-Smith for helping a non-lawyer through some of the intricacies of international law.
(Reprinted with the kind permission of the Editors of the Hong Kong Law Journal.)

little known, transcended the necessarily limited significance of the histories of prisoner-of-war camps. The events during the 1941–5 occupation discussed in this article demonstrate the essential continuity of British rule of law over British civilian subjects in an internment camp, despite the ultimate authority of occupying armed forces. The background of these events was the disrepute into which the authority of the Colonial Government had been thrown, first by a number of scandals and controversies weakening the morale of the civilian population, both British and Chinese, in the immediate pre-invasion period; then by the refusal of H.M. Government to declare Hong Kong an open city to avoid the anticipated barbarities of the siege; and, finally, by the trauma of the demonstration of the superiority of Japanese arms. This political situation inevitably led to a challenge by British subjects resident in Hong Kong to the assertion of authority in the name of the Hong Kong Government. It would be going too far, in all the circumstances of British defeat, to describe this as a revolution by the internees against British colonial officials. Nevertheless, there was an acute conflict, which it is the purpose of this essay to describe and analyse.

It should be borne in mind that there was the strong possibility in 1945, when the atom bombs forced the surrender in due course of the Japanese occupiers of Hong Kong, that the Colony would no longer remain British. The history of those complicated diplomatic threats to British rule cannot form part of this analysis. However, both the United States Government, an Allied Power, and, apparently, the Japanese were in favour of the Chinese Government resuming occupation of Hong Kong. Two points have to be made which affect an understanding of the constitutional struggle to be described. First, the leading protagonist of constituted government, F.C. Gimson, Colonial Secretary, realized almost from the beginning that this threat was there and this braced his resistance to the demands for effective evacuation by the British through repatriation in 1942 and 1943. This, of course, provoked further opposition among the internees and raised acutely the question of loyalty to the Crown. Second, as was recognized by H.M. Government in Whitehall at the end of the war, the Colonial Secretary played a vital role, through his intransigence and foresight, in this period of conflict. It was a British officer, Vice-Admiral Harcourt, who as commander of an allied force re-entered Hong Kong on August 30 and who signed the formal deed of surrender from the Japanese Commander in Government House in Hong Kong on 16 September 1945, but Gimson had already set up a provisional British Administration and hoisted the Union Jack in place of the Rising Sun in advance of the arrival of the British fleet.[1]

It will be seen that although this episode presents the international lawyer with a nice problem of international law, there was much more at stake in practical terms – the continued future of Hong Kong as a British colony.

Occupation and internment

F. C. Gimson arrived to take up his appointment as Colonial Secretary in Hong Kong on 7 December 1941.[2] The following day Japanese troops of the 38th Division[3] crossed the New Territories

[1] The Imperial Rescript announcing Japan's surrender was dated 15 August 1945. As the Report of the Chief Civil Affairs Officer pointed out, 'The surrender of Japan had been virtually accepted by the Japanese Authorities in Hong Kong since 16 August, and within a few days they concurred in Mr. Gimson's suggestion that he should make preparations for an interim administration in order to facilitate the eventual re-establishment of British rule in the Colony' (*British Military Administration, Hong Kong, September 1945 to April 1946*, para. 2). 'Prior to 30 August an interim administration had been set up under the direction of the Colonial Secretary, Mr. F. C. Gimson, C.M.G., and former members of the Colony's Executive Council' (*ibid.*, para. 1). It was at this juncture, after some hesitation by Gimson, that the requisite oath of office as laid down by the Letters Patent was administered to the Acting Governor by the Chief Justice (see note 66 below). To resume the chronology of events, 'On 1 September the British Military Administration was established by a proclamation issued by Rear Admiral C. H. J. Harcourt, C.B., C.B.E., from H.M.S. *Indomitable*.' 'By further Proclamation (No. 2) [of the same date] certain executive and administrative powers were delegated to Mr. Gimson, who was appointed Lieutenant-Governor, pending the arrival in the Colony of the Chief Civil Affairs Officer.' After the arrival of this officer on 7 September, this Proclamation (the British Military Administration (Delegation of Powers) Proclamation 1945) was amended. The preamble to this Proclamation (No. 4, dated 13 September 1945) explains: 'Whereas His Excellency the Lieutenant-Governor, His Honour the Chief Justice and divers other officials and persons without whose assistance it is impossible to administer a civil government in the Colony or maintain the ordinary Courts, cannot in view of the privations they have suffered be expected to remain in the Colony . . . . ' now certain limited powers were delegated to the Chief Civil Affairs Officer. Full powers were delegated to the Civil Affairs Officer on 4 December 1945. Finally, since, as Proclamation No. 4 pointed out, it was not the intention of H.B.M.'s Government to restore civil government 'Until adequate and suitable personnel can be provided and the general conditions of the Colony permit', military government in Hong Kong did not come to an end until 30 April 1946: see F. S. V. Donnison, *British Military Administration in the Far East, 1943–46* (H.M.S.O., London, 1956), particularly Chap. XI.

[2] G. S. Hamilton, *Government Departments in Hong Kong 1841–1966* (Government Printer, Hong Kong, 1967), p. 18.

[3] S. W. Kirby, *The War against Japan: Official History of the Second World War* (H.M.S.O., London, 1957–61), Vol. I, Chaps. VII–IX, pp. 107–51, gives an account of the military campaign. Appendix 6 gives the Japanese order of battle.

border in force. In the following seventeen days the battle for Hong Kong, waged with fierce courage on both sides, thundered on to its apparently inevitable dénouement. Finally, on 25 December, the G.O.C., Major-General Maltby, reported to the Governor, Sir Mark Young, that the invaders had broken through the British lines on Hong Kong island and organized resistance would quickly cease.[4] The Governor and the Defence Committee, who had earlier rejected an ultimatum to surrender before the Japanese onslaught on the island itself, now had no alternative but to accept the Japanese G.O.C.'s demands for a British surrender. As is well known, this capitulation was made on Christmas Day, 1941, in the Peninsula Hotel, Kowloon. At Japanese insistence, the presence of the Governor was necessary to sign a deed of surrender.[5] He immediately entered into captivity; he was not allowed to leave the Peninsula Hotel, where he was kept for seven weeks before being eventually transferred to a camp for the other high-ranking commanders and administrators of the British Empire in South-East Asia in Manchuria.

The immediate concern of the Japanese forces was to stop the destruction of war material and of official documents and, possibly, to avoid the shedding of further blood. The purpose of a capitulation is, of necessity, limited to military objectives; that is, to formalize the cessation of hostilities. The political objectives of waging war have to be settled later by treaty. Moreover, the surrender terms need not make immediate provision for the hand-over of the civil machinery of government.[6]

Martial law had not been proclaimed in Hong Kong during the siege, nor had it been declared an open city as some of the internees of Stanley later thought it should have. The Colonial Secretary, who was now the nominal head of the Hong Kong Government, therefore summoned an emergency meeting of as many members of the Executive Council as could be gathered together immediately after the surrender and resolved, so far as was possible during the military occupation, to carry on the responsibility for civil government. Indeed, he and a group of senior officers, including the Chief Justice, were later removed from Government House to an office in the centre of Hong Kong

[4] Compton Mackenzie, *Eastern Epic, Vol. I* (*1939–43*) (Chatto & Windus, London, 1951), p. 213.

[5] The formal laying down of arms by the garrison took place at the Japanese Headquarters in Tai Hang at 6 p.m. on Christmas Day, 25 December 1941.

[6] R. Mayne, *The Recovery of Europe* (London, 1970). Admiral Dönitz's Government in Flensburg survived after the capitulation at Rheims until 23 May when the Admiral and his ministers were arrested.

in order to assist the hand-over of authority.[7] This was a crisis for which no civil servant was or could be prepared. As the Colonial Secretary later observed:

> There was no precedent for guidance as to the course of action to be pursued by an administration on the occasion of its surrender to a victorious and conquering army and no communication from the Japanese as to any future form of control had been received.[8]

The Japanese army, whilst *de facto* responsible for the maintenance of internal order, had an arbitrary and ineffective control over the citizens of Hong Kong. During the interval when the martial spirits of the *bushido* warrior had to be appeased with wholesale rape, plunder, and random slaughter of both combatants and civilians, British police officers desperately attempted to rally their demoralized forces of cowed and unwilling Indian police to stem some excesses among the Chinese population.[9] In any case, Hong Kong had not previously been designated as one of the captured territories to receive the benefits of the East Asian Co-prosperity Sphere. The only policy declared was for it to be treated as occupied territory.[10] The Japanese organization responsible for some semblance of government immediately following the surrender was the *Gunseiko* (Military Administrative Board).[11]

On 2 January 1942 was announced the first regular Japanese administration of the civil population of Hong Kong. This was the Civil Department of the Japanese Army under the command of Major-General Yazaki, an officer of the army of occupation.[12] Some public utilities such as water, electricity and gas were partially

[7] Sir Franklin Gimson, *Unofficial History of Hong Kong, 1941–5*. This is an unpublished MS. kindly lent to me by Sir Franklin. Hereafter it is cited simply as 'Gimson, *History*'.

[8] Sir Franklin Gimson, *Internment in Hong Kong, March 1942–August 1945* (Rhodes House Library, Ind. Ocn. MS. s. 222). Hereafter this is cited as 'Gimson, *Internment*'.

[9] See, for example, the diary of L. A. Searle, Asst. Supt. of Police, Hong Kong (Rhodes House Library, Ind. Ocn. MS. s. 76).

[10] International Military Tribunal, Tokyo War Crimes Tribunal, Exhibit 17937, Speech of Prime Minister Tojo in the National Diet. This was not given until 22 January 1942, but the policy perhaps was determined soon after the taking of Hong Kong.

[11] R. S. Ward, *Asia for the Asiatics? The Techniques of Japanese Occupation* (Chicago University Press, Chicago, 1945), pp. 38–45.

[12] *Hong Kong News*, 2 January 1942. All former government officials, unless British, were to resume their functions in the Civil Affairs Department. The newspaper also referred to rumours that Mr. Gimson, former Colonial Secretary, was to be the Governor-designate under the Japanese. This was discounted: 'There is not the least possibility of a British Official being appointed as Governor.'

restored. A Rehabilitation Committee of prominent Chinese citizens was set up[13] and the basic framework of Japanese administration was created at this time by the division of Hong Kong Island into twelve districts, and Kowloon into six. This was on 21 January 1942; shortly afterwards these administrative districts were sub-divided into wards.

On 20 February Lieutenant-General Rensuke Isogai took up office as Military Governor of Hong Kong.[14] The Civil Administration was dissolved and its functions were taken over by the office known as the Governor's Office, *tsung tu fu* (總督府). On 29 March 1942, administrative laws to control the lives and activities of those surviving in Hong Kong (but not those interned or prisoners of war) were promulgated.[15]

Meanwhile, on 5 January, all British, American and Dutch civilian residents of Hong Kong were mustered on the Murray Parade Ground, preparatory to being interned. After a sordid interval spent in former brothels and seedy boarding houses on the western waterfront, all those who had obeyed the Japanese orders or who had not claimed immunity on account of Irish citizenship or marriage to a Chinese husband, were taken by boat to Stanley, a relatively remote peninsula on the south side of the island. The question of their status as internees or as prisoners of war was to remain undetermined for a period of two years.

[13] On 2 January Lt.-Gen. Takashi Sakai, Supreme Commander in South China, gave a lunch for 133 Chinese former J.P.s and other distinguished leaders at the Peninsula Hotel.

[14] *Hong Kong News*, 21 January 1942, announcing Isogai's appointment as Governor, gives some biographical details: he was described as an expert in Chinese affairs and at some time previously had commanded a division in North China. A policy statement also announced: 'It [Hong Kong] will be run as a captured fortress through the military bureau .... The first use of Hong Kong is as a centre for supplies for the troops. But under the rule of the new governor it is hoped that Hong Kong will rapidly take its place as the heart of South China.'

[15] *Hong Kong News*, 29–30 March 1942. Governor's Office, Order No. 9. The legislation consisted of nine chapters, covering entry and departure from Hong Kong, the transport of goods, regulations concerning business and mercantile activities. Chap. 8 sets the penalties for infringement of the laws: 'All would be dealt with under military law.' The stated aim of these laws was to allow Hong Kong citizens to carry on their normal life without interference and with the protection of the Japanese authorities. The laws were to be enforced by the Gendarmerie. K. J. Heasman, 'Japanese Financial and Economic Measures in Hong Kong' (1957), *University of Hong Kong Economics Society Journal* 66, says some offences were tried under British law until October 1943, then a Civil Court was established to try criminal charges other than treason, espionage, or direct infringement of military regulations. Court proceedings were not open to the public.

Administrative developments in Stanley

Stanley Camp, from early 1942 until its disbandment in August 1945, was an isolated enclave in occupied territory. Its 2,800 men, women and children, who were predominantly British – especially after the repatriation of some of the old China hands back to Shanghai in 1942 and of Canadian and American nationals in that and the following year[16] – were thrown upon their own organizing abilities and precedents to devise the machinery of administration in order to deal with the mounting pressures of accommodation, food, health, commercial transactions,[17] law and order, and education – to name the most important.

The chief element of continuity and of conventional government in these administrative developments was, of course, Franklin Gimson, Colonial Secretary of the erstwhile unoccupied Colony. As Stericker, who acted as Administrative Secretary of the camp, remarked, Gimson 'passed through the phases of Colonial Secretary, Chairman of the (British Community) Council, Camp Commandant, Representative of Internees, back to Colonial Secretary and finally Lieutenant-Governor'.[18] And Gimson himself acknowledged the importance of his position, even if he would not have accepted this perspective of his 'unofficial' secretary, Stericker:

> I believe this period of continuity of office as prisoners' representative was unique in the Japanese prison camps. It certainly enabled me to establish a status not achieved elsewhere.[19]

He also realized that, more important than status, he was 'incredibly lucky . . . to survive the whole period of captivity', for his chief role as representative certainly carried with it the ever-present risk of arrest and execution for making complaints about the inhumanity of the Japanese.

Gimson's role in Stanley, regardless of official status, was certainly of crucial importance. However, after the immediate shocks and

16 Gimson, *Internment*.

17 Even in the tightest security gaols, trade in scarce commodities, such as cigarettes and canteen stores, plays an overwhelmingly important part in the lives of the prisoners. In Stanley Camp some internees received allowances and parcels of food and clothing from outside friends. In addition the Japanese allowed the sale of a desultory supply of 'luxuries' in a canteen. There eventually developed a rampant black market, often based on the issue of IOUs.

18 J. Stericker, 'History of Stanley Camp' (unpublished MS. in H.K.U. Library), Foreword; hereafter cited simply as 'Stericker'.

19 F. C. Gimson, 'Hong Kong Reclaimed' (unpublished MS., copy in Rhodes House Library and in possession of the author), p. 3.

demoralization of battle[20] and defeat, and the grim austerities of an unprepared and unorganized exodus to Stanley,[21] certain well-established traits of British character asserted themselves. Stericker wryly remarks in his account of these early days of crisis: 'When several are gathered together if they be Englishmen, one of the first things that enters their heads is to form a committee.'[22] Indeed, one of the most powerful impressions gained from reading the surviving records of camp administration – kept, it should be remembered, in secrecy and sometimes buried underground for fear of the consequences, is of the punctilious regard for protocol, democratic procedures documented in the minutes of meetings, painstaking memoranda and other quasi-official papers.

In the absence of the Colonial Secretary, and reflecting the first measure of independence from the apron-strings of the Hong Kong Government, on the day following the arrival in camp a temporary committee met. On 24 January executive officers were elected. They consisted of well-known merchants and businessmen: B. Wylie (*South China Morning Post*) who acted as Chairman, D. L. Newbigging (Jardine Matheson), L. R. Neilsen (a New Zealand businessman with interests in the U.S.A. and the Philippines), P. E. Williams (a representative of the Chungking Government), the Revd. C. Brown, D. N. Blake (solicitor), A. E. Nobbins (merchant), Drs. Uttley, Pope, and Herklots. There were two Hong Kong Government officers: J. A. Fraser (Defence Secretary) and H. R. Butters (Financial Secretary). Various functional officers, e.g. a Quartermaster and, realistically, a Treasurer, were appointed.[23] It is important to observe that the Colonial Secretary, who was not made a resident in the camp until 11 March 1942, was allowed by the Japanese authorities to visit Stanley and to attend this first meeting. Stericker states that subsequently it was reported that Gimson had expressed the wish that the camp should have 'a popularly elected representation'.[24] Also this organization was

[20] John Luff, *The Hidden Years* (S.C.M. Post, Hong Kong, 1967), comments upon the disintegration of government control of the civilian population. The failure of the military authorities to take over this responsibility is also noted by F.S.V. Donnison, op. cit., p. 6.

[21] Jean Gittins, *Eastern Windows Western Skies* (S.C.M. Post, Hong Kong, 1969), p. 139: 'Those early days were perhaps the most distressing.' She refers to the lack of furniture, inmates sleeping on the floor, low-grade food such as 'bad fish' or 'a few buffalo bones'. *Cf.* Stericker, chap. II, p. 9: 'The over-crowding and lack of any organization, apart from the absence of any persons of recognized authority to straighten things out, made one fear for the morrow.'

[22] Stericker, chap. IV, p. 1.

[23] Ibid., p. 2. The Chief Justice acted as accommodation officer.

[24] Loc. cit., insert.

recognized by the Japanese military inasmuch as copies of minutes of these meetings were sent to the officials in charge of the camp.[25]

This committee was short-lived. It was seen as a temporary expedient. It was a large body and possibly too unwieldy. First, a petition was drawn up, signed by 820 internees, calling for direct election of the chairman and vice-chairman. Also it seems there was a real crisis callingfor action which would have to have the backing of the Stanley constituents. In fact, the Japanese refused to supply further food without payment. It was therefore necessary to have a properly constituted body empowered to raise money for this purpose by withdrawing funds from private accounts. By the middle of February when the national and other groups (e.g. the police) of internees had settled themselves into different areas of the camp, a system of representation of these 'districts' (or blocks) was devised. Eight such representatives took up office as the result of an election on 18 February 1942. There was an almost complete turnover in personnel in the new British Communal Council. Only two members of the temporary committee survived this test, although Nielsen and Wylie were also included in a group of six general representatives. The Government representative was now J. P. Pennefather-Evans, Commissioner of Police. Stericker writes: 'It was obviously essential to have a senior member of the Government at Council meetings.'[26] This was, for the time being, J. A. Fraser. He regarded the Council as the permanent governing body of the camp which would act through an Executive Committee consisting of the chairman, Nielsen, Wylie, Newbigging and C. C. Roberts (Butterfield and Swire), and himself. In its work of co-ordinating the work of other functional committees (also, in Gimson's mind, acting as a board of review of the Japanese administration) it would operate almost as a cabinet, meeting nearly every other day.[27] The Chief Justice, Sir Atholl MacGregor, also attended the first meeting of this body by invitation of the chairman, in order to advise upon the establishment of a criminal judicial system. In the form of a legal committee and of a magistrates' court, this British machinery of justice operated, according to Stericker, for a year despite Japanese disapproval; it

[25] The Japanese administration was also a temporary arrangement. Gimson reports: 'Two Japanese residents of Hong Kong of no high standing were in immediate charge of the camp and resided in one of the bungalows': *Internment*, p. 6. One of these, one Yamashita, had outwardly been a barber at the Hong Kong Hotel.

[26] Stericker, chap. V, p. 1.

[27] Ibid., p. 7.

was then replaced by a Camp Disciplinary Tribunal.[28] It was resolved that the Colonial Secretary was to attend all meetings of this British Communal Council as of right and to continue as the negotiator for the internees with the Japanese.

Already, as a result of the ambivalence of these 'citizens' to the authority of H.M. Government in Hong Kong, it is clear that there was the desire to separate two functions: the responsibility for the internal administration of the British camp – the 'internal function' – and the responsibility for the British citizen *vis-à-vis* the Japanese – the 'Imperial function'. Here was the source of future conflict. Indeed, Gimson's own account of these early developments diverges in important details from this account. From the outset he had assured himself, through consultation with the Attorney-General before coming to take up residence in Stanley Camp in March, that 'the Colonial Government had not abrogated its authority over the British subjects of Hong Kong'.[29] In his testament he makes it clear that he joined the others in internment having adopted the legal position that he was the representative of the Government and of His Majesty. This distinction was evidently to meet the objections of those whom the Colonial Secretary soon encountered, who protested their loyalty to the British Crown but who were not willing to accord their allegiance to the now non-existent Hong Kong Government.

Gimson at first consented to co-operate with the Council and therefore, according to his testimony, for a period of three or four months operated in an ill-defined position 'as partner of the Chairman'. Then, responding to a petition from 'a large majority of internees', Gimson assumed office as chairman of the Council. Nevertheless, when the Executive Committee considered, on 28 March, the 'inter-relationship of the Government of Hong Kong and the British Communal Council', there resulted an agreement between these parties setting out their respective positions and functions.[30] This agreement, drawn up by the Colonial Secretary and his legal advisers, was based on two principles:

(1) In any matter including external affairs the Colonial Secretary would regard it as his duty to seek the advice of the Camp Communal Council and to give due consideration to any opinion which they might express

[28] Ibid., pp. 5–6. It was pointed out that punishments awarded by the court would have to be confirmed by the Japanese.

[29] Gimson, *History*.

[30] Stericker, Appendix No. II. No date is attached but from internal evidence it appears to have come into effect on 20 April 1942. This agreement is reproduced as Appendix 1 to this article.

with regard to relations which concern the British Community Council and the Japanese authorities.

(2) In domestic matters the principle of the self-government of the community within the camp is admitted, provided that the Colonial Secretary reserves to himself the right to ask for the reconsideration of any matters of vital importance to the community which affect the Imperial interests and their relations with the Japanese authorities.[31]

The agreement itself is significant, if only for the two explicit premises upon which it was based. The first was that Hong Kong was a British territory 'temporarily occupied by the Japanese' and as a logical consequence, therefore, 'as long as Britain claims, as she does, the right to re-occupy it, the British Government in Hong Kong is still in being and functioning except where prevented by the Japanese'.[32] The second premise was pregnant with far-reaching implications for the future: 'The maintenance of good government depends primarily on the good will of the governed but ultimately it is dependent on the enforcement by means of penal sanction of such laws as the Government promulgates for the benefit of good order and peace.' In Hong Kong, where the Government was deprived of the usual means of enforcing these sanctions, 'the Government must rely more than ever on the force of public opinion'. Thus the Colonial Secretary welcomed the appointment of the Council elected by the internees of Stanley to assist him in the maintenance and observance of the measures for order in the camp.[33]

In fact these arrangements again were destined not to endure. Psychologically it is understandable that these confined constituents should have welcomed changes in their drab lives. Stericker speaks of six months' terms for the camp parliament. However, as the internees moved quarters, and dissatisfaction with the camp officials mounted, there were temptations to amend this constitutional settlement. This gave Gimson the opportunity to prune the Council of its democratic trappings. In June 1942 the Colonial Secretary was drafting a new constitution in order 'to safeguard the privileges of the Crown',[34] and he was able to take the offensive and reduce the power of his opponents. 'I re-organized the Community Council,' Gimson reported later, 'maintaining its elected basis and appointed various senior and generally acceptable internees some of whom were members of the Colonial Service in

[31] Stericker, chap. V, pp. 19–20.

[32] Agreement between the Hong Kong Government and the British Communal Council, para. 3(a).

[33] Ibid., para. 3(b).

[34] Stericker, chap. VI, p. 12.

charge of the various camp services. They did not sit with the Council . . . but were present if required.'[35] Stericker reports that there was bitter resentment at this thrust of authority. Accusations were made that the petition had been engineered by the Colonial Secretary. Nevertheless Gimson rode out the storm and by August 1942, possibly taking advantage of the departure of American 'democrats' from the camp a month earlier, he was able to bring about the demise of the British Communal Council.[36]

In a letter to Consul (later Colonel) Hattori, who became Camp Commandant in January 1944, the Colonial Secretary gave his version of these constitutional developments. This patient attempt by the Japanese authorities to understand the constitutional niceties of the democratic rights of the internees is perhaps surprising and certainly is at variance with the assertion made by the Colonial Secretary that they would have no truck with elected bodies or representatives. 'It was decided,' wrote Gimson, reporting on discussions with the new Council, 'that a statement as to the functions of the members of the British Community Council and Camp Executive Officers might help define, clarify, and limit the degree and extent of personal responsibility of each member [of the Council].'[37] This is given in a schedule to the letter and reproduced as Appendix II to this article. Here it is made clear that the Council had been relegated to a purely advisory capacity. Moreover, Gimson pointed out:

> You will observe that the functions performed by the administrative officers, British Community Council and District and other Committees are limited to the housing, food, health, and welfare of internees, and in the maintenance of good order, and observance of the routine regulations made by the Camp Commandant . . .

Gimson further denied that this administration had within 'its competence to assume any responsibility involving matters of a political or military nature'.[38] To emphasize the responsibility of the Colonial Secretary the Executive Committee was dispensed with. At this time too there is mention of meetings of Executive and Legislative Councils in the camp. However, it seemed to Gimson that these two were recalcitrant bodies; moreover, they

[35] Gimson, *Internment*, p. 9.

[36] Stericker, chap. XII, p. 5: 'By his connivance in the downfall of the original council Mr. Gimson brought about a situation which many never forgave.'

[37] Stericker, Appendix VI. Letter from Gimson (no official capacity stated) to Hattori dated 8 December 1943.

[38] Nevertheless, when Gimson proposed to sign identity cards as 'Colonial Secretary', this was forbidden by the Japanese.

certainly incurred Japanese suspicion. By October 1943 Gimson was of the opinion that their existence was 'ill-advised'.[39]

The first British Community Council held its inaugural meeting on 18 August 1942,[40] and despite the conflict surrounding the Colonial Secretary's initiative which had brought it into being, the co-operation of members of the former communal council was on the whole secured. Several individuals served as administrative officers appointed by the Colonial Secretary. The change in the name of the council, moreover, was explicitly chosen to emphasize the distinction between this official body and the democratic 'communal' council. As Stericker says, this term had been 'tried to death in the camp and found wanting'.[41] Of course, if he referred to internal dissensions within the ranks of the internees – and there were hints of dissatisfaction with the privileged position of the 'taipans'[42] – this might seem to justify the Colonial Secretary's action. In fact, whilst there may have been some inevitable lack of interest in these political manoeuvres on the part of the internees, further elections were held at intervals of approximately six months in February and August/September 1943, to produce the second and third Community Councils. In 1944 the Japanese authorities made a gesture bringing these councils formally to an end on the ground that now, under the reorganized military administration of the camp, they could not recognize the right of the camp to be run by its own elected council. But apparently they were not very firm about this opposition. They were told that the system of elected District Chairmen was slightly different from the representative machinery for electing representatives to the Community Council. 'They accepted this without further enquiry.'[43]

The attitudes of Gimson's opponents and the most important issues upon which they flared up – over questions such as repatriation which were much more immediate to the interests of the internees, but also about Gimson's proposals for the reform of post-war Hong Kong – will be discussed later. It is evident, however, that the decisive change in the nature of the government of the camp

[39] Sir Franklin, in a private communication, confirms there was no other earlier diary written. He also mentions that in July 1944 when the alleged collaboration of a senior member of the Council with the Japanese was discussed at a meeting in the camp 'it was considered he should cease to be a member of the Executive Council'.

[40] The Council included ten elected representatives.

[41] Stericker, chap. VIII, p. 1.

[42] These commercial representatives were able to draw upon the banking accounts of their firms and receive allowances.

[43] Stericker, loc. cit. Gimson was appointed 'Representative of the Internees' and advised by a weekly meeting of a small group of five District Chairmen.

satisfied neither party. On occasion, before and after the change in emphasis in the stance of the Community Council, the Colonial Secretary was praying for the death of the Council.[44] As late as July 1945 when, despite signs of departure among the Japanese, there were, of course, no signs of the imminent end to the war, there were still disputes as to whether Gimson held his authority as 'representative of the internees' from the Japanese or the British authorities. This was a difficult month, with air raids increasing the mounting stress in Stanley. One could well sympathize with the exhausted and frayed administrator. 'So ended the month of July, a month which reflected more than ever the difficulties of administration especially as the result of the unstable mental conditions of the large majority of the internees.'[45] Indeed, in despair Gimson wrote about the internees: 'They are incapable of expressing any judgment on facts placed before them.' This incapacity, in Gimson's mind, rendered it quite impossible to form a democratic administration.

The issues

Whatever principles and issues might have been at stake, in the abrasive atmosphere of confinement it is understandable that, given the necessary intercourse between people of different temperaments and backgrounds, this would have brought dominant and sometimes incompatible traits of character to the surface, producing friction. Also the internees, having to accept, however unwillingly but *faut de mieux*, the authority of the military conqueror, would be the less likely to be willing to 'kow-tow' to another master too. Of course, in saner moments of reflection it might be realized that this assumption of authority by the Colonial Secretary was ultimately for their protection – against the enemy and sometimes against themselves. These reflections must, in the context, inevitably raise the question of loyalty and, one might add, the rights of the citizen to give or withhold his loyalty to the body of which he is a member.

Here again the matter was made more complex because the status of the internees was in doubt for two years after internment. The Japanese Government did not ratify the Geneva Convention of 1929 regarding the conduct of war and the treatment of prisoners. The enemy nationals were not regarded as prisoners of war, however: they were interned, according to the Japanese, 'for their own protection'. It is not proposed to give here a history of the changes in the Japanese administration of the camp which produced both

[44] F. C. Gimson, *Diary, June 1, 1943–August 15, 1944* (Rhodes House Library, Ind. Ocn. MSS. 222), entries for July 27 and November 1943. Hereafter this is cited as 'Gimson, *Diary*'.

[45] Ibid., entry for July 1945.

inconsistency in attitude and delays in arriving at a policy, but it was not until 1 January 1944, when the camp was put under the command of a Japanese official who was to assume military rank, that the internees had a definite status as prisoners of war in the eyes of the Japanese authorities. As a result of this delay the internees, particularly when it came to the question of rations, felt they had no rights. Moreover, it should not be forgotten that the inevitable episodes of attempted escape and unauthorized communication with the outside world[46] brought punishment to some unfortunates and, for a time, an atmosphere of terror in the camp.

According to Gimson, even at the beginning of internment demands were made for repatriation. Throughout the whole period, therefore, there were in confrontation two schools of thought not only about the possibility but, *a fortiori*, about the rightness of this understandable reaction to a grim present and a foreboding future. On the one hand there were the agonized pinings of those whom Gimson described as 'the birds of passage' who felt they had 'no association with Hong Kong of permanent or moral status'.[47] On the other hand, steadfastly opposed to any favourable consideration of these pleadings, was the Colonial Secretary. He explains his position: 'A colony was to me British territory as much as Britain itself. . . . British subjects resident in British territory would not be entitled to repatriation.'[48] Gimson had further arguments: first, that shipping would be in much greater demand elsewhere and, second, a reason which was not likely to appeal, that the numbers involved were only equivalent to the victims of an air-raid. In other words the Stanley inmates would be a 'write-off' so far as the British Government was concerned. But, these considerations apart, those who so keenly urged repatriation believed that Gimson had, in fact, a clandestine means of communication via the British Army Aid Group in Kwangtung and thence via Chungking to Whitehall, and that he was misusing the authority he was asserting in refusing to make this channel available for putting forward a case for repatriation.[49]

[46] On 19 October 1943, seven internees, including J. A. Fraser, the former Defence Secretary, were sentenced to death for operating a secret radio set. The executions were carried out on Stanley Beach and could be seen by the internees.

[47] Gimson, *Internment*, p. 17. [48] Loc. cit.

[49] It does appear that the Colonial Secretary was able to maintain contact with the outside world. However, after the tightening up of security by the Japanese, it became more difficult. Nevertheless, even before the hiatus between the Japanese surrender and coming out of Stanley to set up the provisional administration Gimson was able to make arrangements for a supply of banknotes to be ordered to meet the immediate needs of the new government. These

Gimson reported afterwards: 'I doubt if few accepted the force of my arguments and opinion hostile to me in the camp tried to jeopardize my influence and control by promoting antagonism.'[50] As Stericker comments on this issue, since these differences of opinion were taken to an extreme position, there was an open rift among the British internees over this question of loyalty and 'the camp as a whole was hurt at the implications that it was disloyal'.[51] This was no vague accusation; in October 1942 the Colonial Secretary announced to British subjects that those who signed a petition for repatriation should be prepared to face a charge of disloyalty to the British cause.[52]

From Gimson's diary for the year 1943 it is evident that, because of its support for repatriation and other issues, he regarded the British Community Council as a 'subversive organization'.[53] Four days later, Stericker, the Administrative Secretary who was closest to Gimson in the administrative work of Stanley and in the negotiations with the Japanese, and who writes with objectivity on these heated issues, was astounded at the Colonial Secretary's conviction that 'the British Community Council was a revolutionary body'.[54] Certainly Gimson was disquieted by the belief that a plot was hatching to depose him and to find a successor.

We do not have very much information about the occasions which produced conflict and provoked Gimson to confide bitter condemnations to his diary. In 1943 there was mounting concern over the inadequacy of the rations, over access to the representative of the Protecting Power (as provided for by the Geneva Convention), over favourable reports given by internees who had left the camp, and by the Red Cross representative in Hong Kong on the improved

arrived on 11 September 1945. He was not able to make contact with London via the British Consul in Macao until 27 August 1945. Authorization to set up the administration did not come until the 23rd.

[50] Gimson, *Internment*, p. 18.

[51] Stericker, chap. VIII, p. 5.

[52] Ibid. Another consideration present in Gimson's mind was that if British residents in Hong Kong were evacuated through repatriation, this would leave the door wide open for China to resume possession of the Colony. The Japanese had announced in the *Hong Kong News*, which was allowed into the camp, that the return of Hong Kong to China was a possibility for the future. Subsequent research in Japanese sources by J. H. Boyle, *China and Japan at War, 1937–45* (Stanford U.P., Stanford, 1972), has revealed that in 1945 proposals were put to a representative of the Chungking Government as part of a deal to forestall the Allied Powers' plans. Gimson's part in thwarting the designs of both Roosevelt and Chiang Kai-shek, which ensured the re-possession of Hong Kong by Britain, deserves separate description.

[53] Gimson, *Diary*, entry for 21 June 1943.

[54] Ibid., entry for 25 June 1943.

conditions in the camp – of course hotly denied by those remaining in Stanley! All these issues, and the tightening of discipline by the Japanese, put extra worries on Gimson who inevitably was later criticized for, if not actually accused of, being too diplomatic in his representations to the Japanese authorities.

There were differences of outlook and opinion, too, over the discussions, which must have been secret to many in the camp, concerning contingency plans for an emergency government when the Japanese should surrender, coupled with the wider problems of post-war construction. It was here again that the fundamentally different backgrounds of the protagonists showed up. B.J. Wylie, who thought that the Colonial Secretary had taken advantage of a temporary yielding of the chair at the early meetings, was picked out as a leading opponent by Gimson. The Colonial Secretary's authority was formally asserted. 'Hong Kong was still a British Colony. As a British subject he was still responsible to me for his dealings with enemy subjects.'[55] But there were others also who were lumped together as short-sighted businessmen. 'They cannot appear to consider any other world than that in which they can make money and retire.' The bankers pursued an independent line. 'Events in Hong Kong were merely a matter of report from them to their Head Offices in London,' Gimson comments, 'and they did not concern the Hong Kong Government. . . . With this view I disagree.'[56] Other businessmen refused to discuss even the commercial future of Hong Kong from fear of disclosing trade secrets. If Gimson was seen by these non-government men as 'academic', old-fashioned, rigid, autocratic, then he, too, had some justification for condemning them as narrow-minded. 'It is impossible for businessmen,' he averred, 'to discuss political questions. . . . [This] must be borne in mind in considering any proposals for the future of Hong Kong.'[57]

In fact Gimson, although a stranger to Hong Kong and its conventions, did have a long experience of working as a Colonial Officer and latterly as Colonial Secretary in Ceylon, where there was a greater acceptance of the political and social roles of the indigenous population. He therefore saw the need for reform in Hong Kong.[58] Stericker believed, indeed, that Gimson had been

[55] Ibid., entry for 14 June 1943.
[56] Ibid., comment written in January 1944.
[57] Ibid., entry for 23 June 1944.
[58] On the reforms ushered in by the Donoughmore Commission of 1927–8 see Lennox A. Mills, *Ceylon under British Rule* (Cass reprint, London, 1964), p. 167 *et seq.* and E. F. C. Ludowyk, *The Modern History of Ceylon* (Weidenfeld & Nicholson, London, 1966).

chosen for the Hong Kong appointment because of this experience; yet, ironically, through his intransigence, the Colonial Secretary now 'found himself opposed by those who advocated reform'.[59] It would, of course, be unfair to characterize a person's opinion on this complex problem with one quotation; nevertheless Gimson's views about the business community's own idea of the role of Colonial Government in Hong Kong were surely expressed in the following statement taken from his considered summary of these events:

> Hong Kong, still a British Colony, was in 1941 regarded by its European residents as little different from the many 'Treaty Ports' in China where they had special privileges for the pursuit of their personal and commercial activities. The representatives of the British Government, Consular or Colonial, existed to prevent infringements of any transactions likely to hamper European trade, and to safeguard their special status. The welfare of the local population did not come within, in any way, the sphere of concern of these foreign merchants. . . . These considered they had the traditional claim to control the policy of the Colony either directly through the Legislative Council or through influence in Whitehall. The officers of the Colonial Government were regarded as instruments in the pursuit of trade.[60]

Gimson's ideas of political reform in Hong Kong were focused upon the problem of securing 'adequate representation of the Chinese in Hong Kong'. At the same time he was aware, as other Governors had been, of the difficulty of ensuring that the Chinese Government should not be allowed to interfere 'in any matters which might concern the [H.K.] Government and the people of the Chinese race who were considered to be the responsibility of that Government'. Nevertheless, he was in favour of the election of a Chinese representative to the Legislative Council by popular franchise.[61] Stericker's explanation of the Colonial Secretary's conservatism over constitutional relations in the camp, therefore, that Gimson allowed himself to be too much influenced by 'advisors who represented the bad old days', does not seem to be confirmed.

Finally, as Stericker himself recognized, the discussion of future constitutional arrangements for Hong Kong itself seemed academic in the tense, grim atmosphere of Stanley. And, even allowing for the fact that the chief representative of Government might have been a man with a different personality, it was an open question which would have been the more appropriate policy to pursue: to

[59] Stericker, chap. XII, p. 2.

[60] Gimson, *History*. He does point out to me in a letter that some opinions expressed in the *Diary* he does not hold now. Nevertheless, the task of the historian is to discover what people said and thought at the time.

[61] Gimson, *Diary*, entry for July 1944.

assume the democratic, or at least communal, leadership of this group of loyal but displaced British citizens, or to take a stand on the legal interpretation of the situation, as Gimson did.

Gimson, in fact, as has been pointed out, was to play a vital part in securing Hong Kong again as British territory, thus confirming the premise upon which he acted throughout, namely, that the Japanese occupation was but a temporary situation in which the civilian government should continue to operate as closely to the pre-war norm as the military occupation would allow.

Questions of international law

The occupation of Hong Kong by the Japanese forces brought a number of cases, apart from war crimes and charges of collaboration with the enemy, before the Hong Kong courts in the post-war period. These raised the problems of the effects of this occupation in international law. As O'Connell explains,[62] the unprecedented circumstances where British territory had been occupied by the enemy and a system of Japanese government had been set up introduced a novel and important element to the concept of the alien enemy. Had residence in Hong Kong, voluntary or enforced, during the period of hostilities, transformed former British subjects into this category of persons who were, for the purposes of the law of personal jurisdiction and the prevention of intercourse between belligerent nationals, to be regarded as aliens and, further, through enemy occupation, as alien enemies? As O'Connell points out, the question of allegiance in this context is irrelevant.[63]

Under English common law all residents of enemy-occupied territory are probably to be regarded in English courts as alien enemies, irrespective of whether the residence is voluntary or not. However, in the Colony's courts Hong Kong residents during the war have not been so considered.[64]

[62] D. P. O'Connell, *International Law* (Stevens, London, 1965), vol. II, pp. 786–7.

[63] O'Connell, op. cit., p. 773.

[64] The case of *Li Tsz-chiu* v. *Lo Kar-yam* (1948) 32 H.K.L.R. 121 was heard before the Supreme Court of Hong Kong. It concerned two members of a partnership who escaped to China while the other partners remained behind in Hong Kong and carried on business. It was pointed out that counsel, in order to prove the dissolution of the partnership, had to demonstrate that under the existing law of Hong Kong (a) residents in Hong Kong became enemies during the Japanese occupation of Hong Kong, and (b) residents in Free China were therefore unable to communicate with them or remain in contractual relations with them. The Chief Justice, Sir Leslie Gibson, was not able to accept this argument: 'The law of England regards occupied Hong Kong as enemy territory, but it seems impossible to contemplate that the law of Hong Kong itself . . . could operate to turn all of the residents of the colony into enemies. Could it, for example, by turning them into enemies

Nevertheless, to the historian if not to the lawyer, this situation does appear to raise the issue of allegiance to the British Crown. More specifically, were Hong Kong residents bound to obey the lawful commands of British Government officers given after the surrender? One civil servant, although not arraigned before the courts, was in January 1948 charged before a Committee of Inquiry constituted under Colonial Regulations with disloyalty to the Crown, as well as disloyalty to the Colonial Service, apparently for agreeing to work in the Japanese civilian administration and for refusing to obey an order given by the Colonial Secretary to desist.[65]

---

preclude them from suing in their own courts? It might be that under some law of the Japanese administration . . . the principle was applied in reverse on the basis that Free China became the enemy, but in that case the result would flow from the Japanese law and not from the common law in force in Hong Kong.'

In a second case, *Hangkam Kwingtong-woo* v. *Liu Lan-fong* [1951] A.C. 707, it was argued on appeal to the Privy Council that the ruling of the Hong Kong Supreme Court given above was in error. At common law, it was unsuccessfully contended, the residents of Hong Kong became enemies of His Majesty and his allies during the occupation. Lord Simonds, giving the opinion of the Privy Council, said there was no authority of any real assistance to answer the question which was implicit in this case, namely, what would have been the common law of England if England itself became enemy-occupied territory? It was necessary to examine the principles on which trading with the enemy is held to be illegal and to apply the practical consideration whether a man's legal relations in an occupied territory were severed upon his escape. If they were, the loyal subject would hesitate to escape, and the King would lose a potential supporter. It was affirmed that the courts of occupied British territory may not regard either persons who left the country during the occupation or those who stayed behind as alien enemies. Both these cases are cited by O'Connell, op. cit. pp. 786–7.

[65] *Kennedy-Skipton* v. *The Attorney-General* (1950) 34 H.K.L.R. 234 (Gould J.); (1951) 35 H.K.L.R. 55 (F. Ct.). The plaintiff, an administrative officer of the Colonial Service in Hong Kong, was suspended by the Colonial Secretary in February 1942. On 24 April 1943, at Chungking, by a letter signed by one P.C.M. Sedgwick and purporting to be under the direction of H.M. Ambassador at Chungking, the plaintiff was informed that the Secretary of State had confirmed the suspension until such time as sufficient evidence was available to advise His Majesty in the matter. Subsequently, after the war, in 1948, the plaintiff was charged with improper behaviour and disloyalty before a Committee of Inquiry. The Inquiry found him not guilty of disloyalty to the Crown but guilty of disloyalty to the service of which he was a member. The plaintiff now denied the authority of Gimson to suspend him and the validity of the subsequent confirmation, and thus sought to recover arrears of salary owed to him by the Crown. Though not put to the court to adjudicate upon, Mr. Kennedy-Skipton's reason for not recognizing the authority of the Colonial Secretary, as he has told me in a private communication, was: 'I was his equal.' Kennedy-Skipton did not go into Stanley, his freedom being based on a claim to Irish citizenship. The Full Court dismissed his claim for wrongful dismissal on the ground that all government servants hold their offices at the pleasure of the Crown and no action lies for arrears of salary (but see now *Kodeeswaran* v.

After March 1942 residents who were not interned in Stanley were denied contact with any British officer who might have acted in the capacity of Representative of the Crown. Internees who were not British subjects owed no duty of allegiance to Britain or Hong Kong, but British or Hong Kong-born Chinese internees, not possessing the status of alien enemies in Hong Kong law, were in direct communication with a senior official of the Hong Kong Government asserting full colonial authority in respect of matters not dealt with by the Japanese administration. Were these latter internees under a legal obligation to support Gimson's own administrative arrangements? The question, if academic, is nonetheless intriguing, especially in the light of the Colonial Secretary's views of threatened revolution.

Another series of questions logically follows: did Gimson have the capacity in law which he claimed? It seems likely that not until the surrender in 1945 did he take the oath required under the Letters Patent for him to become Acting Governor.[66] Thus, in the absence of a Governor, can it be said that the Hong Kong Government continued to exist? If that is answered affirmatively, what form is necessary before the orders of the Colonial Secretary are to be regarded as legal commands? Was the superior officer of Government possessed of prerogative or emergency powers which could be exercised at his discretion? If not, and since the Colonial Secretary could not issue anything approximating to an Order-in-Council, proclamation, or official notification, in what sense can it be said that the internees, under a duty of allegiance to the Crown, were required to take notice of Gimson's informal pronouncements? Finally, what is the legal meaning of the concept of 'disloyalty to the Crown'? Could the British internees who refused to co-operate in Gimson's plans and day-to-day administration be considered guilty of some offence, despite the informality of the 'government structure' and the informality of the orders of the superior colonial officer?

Attorney-General of Ceylon [1970] A.C. 111 and the note by John Rear (1972) 2 H.K.L.J. 84). Since this was decided as a preliminary point, the validity of the suspension was not in fact considered by the court.

[66] The Letters Patent for the Colony of Hong Kong (dated 14 February 1917), constituting the office of Governor and Commander-in-Chief of the Colony of Hong Kong and its Dependencies, provided in Article XVII: 'Whenever the office of Governor is vacant, or the governor . . . is from any cause prevented from . . . acting in duties of his office . . . then the person lawfully discharging the functions of Colonial Secretary . . . shall administer the government of the Colony. . . .' However, it is uncertain whether in the desperate hours before the British surrender the oath of office was taken by Gimson.

If precise answers to these legal and constitutional questions are possible, the historian cannot give them. However, the historian can and should point out that Gimson, in maintaining the stance he took up over the Stanley internees and in relation to the Japanese authorities, provided a physical presence and symbol of the continuity of constituted British authority in Hong Kong. Thereby he strengthened the British hold on the Colony when he organized the setting up of a British Provisional Administration in Hong Kong before the formal surrender by the Japanese forces to Admiral Harcourt, representing the Allied Powers. Regardless of the legality of Gimson's position in Stanley, its effect was considerable and even crucial to the future of Hong Kong.

APPENDIX 1

Agreement between the British Hong Kong Government and the British Communal Council

1. When the British civilians of Hong Kong were interned in Stanley the leading representatives of this community at once organized themselves into a committee for the administration of the affairs of the camp. The Colonial Secretary on his periodic visits to the camp welcomed the establishment of this organization and was only too pleased to allow the officers of the British Hong Kong Government to co-operate with the activities of the temporary committee so formed. As more and more civilians arrived in the camp the committee so elected lost its representative character and early measures were taken in order to arrange for properly conducted elections and to establish a council truly representative of public opinion.

2. The Colonial Secretary on his arrival at the Camp immediately in the absence of His Excellency the Governor assumed such functions as his office demanded in the eyes of the British Imperial authorities and of the British community of which he is rightfully the head and so represented the authority to which all British subjects must look as the person acting on behalf of His Britannic Majesty. The earliest possible steps were then taken for the Council and the Colonial Secretary to act in association and to place the relationship of the two on a constitutional basis.

3. Accordingly the following statement was drawn up:

(a) Hong Kong is British territory temporarily occupied by the Japanese. As long as Britain claims, as she does, the right to re-occupy it, the British Government in Hong Kong is still in being and functioning except where prevented by the Japanese. The officials of the British Hong Kong Government will continue to perform such duties as lie in their power and as they may be directed by the Colonial Secretary, who must be regarded by British subjects in Hong Kong as the authority to whom they should look as representing His Majesty the King.

(b) The maintenance of good government depends primarily on the good will of the governed but ultimately it is dependent on the enforcement by means of penal sanctions of such laws as the Government promulgates for the benefit of good order and peace. In the absence of the usual means of enforcing these sanctions the Government must rely more than ever on the force of public opinion to secure the observance of any measures designed to benefit the health and general amenities of its nationals. In light of these considerations the Government, of which, in the absence of the Governor, the Colonial Secretary is the head, welcomes the appointment of a committee elected by the internees of Stanley Camp to assist him in the maintenance and observance of the measures mentioned above.

(c) The appointment of such a committee cannot be regarded as in any way lessening the authority or the responsibility which the Colonial Secretary and his constitutionally appointed advisers and officers have to discharge in virtue of their appointments and their oaths and duty to His Majesty the King.

(d) It is natural and right, therefore, in relation to any outside authority, and in particular to the Japanese, that the Colonial Secretary as chief representative of His Majesty should conduct the foreign policy of the Government and function and be regarded (as, indeed, he is regarded by the Japanese Authorities themselves) as the sole channel of communication between the British community and the Japanese Authorities. The Colonial Secretary, however, in any matter on which representations have to be made to the Japanese, would regard it as his duty to seek the advice of the Camp Communal Council and to give the fullest consideration to any opinions which it might express with regard to the relations which concern the British community and the Japanese Authorities.

(e) In domestic matters the Colonial Secretary will generally leave the administration of the camp to a council composed of the representatives of the British community, but in virtue of the authority entrusted to the Government by the Crown the Colonial Secretary must reserve to himself the right to request reconsideration by the Council of any matters reconsideration of which he deems to be of importance to the wellbeing or morale of the community or which affect the Imperial or Colonial interests in their relations with the Japanese Authorities. Request for such reconsideration is to be regarded as an intimation that the British Hong Kong Government cannot accept the decision of the Camp Council in the matter under reference; but it will depend, of course, on the nature of the decision whether it would or would not be acceptable if suitably modified. It follows from the foregoing that any individual in the community who feels himself aggrieved by a decision of any Government or Camp Official or council may appeal to the Colonial Secretary.

(f) The Colonial Secretary will appoint officers in charge of any functions which affect the amenity of the whole Camp. In the discharge of these functions the officers so appointed will be responsible to the Colonial Secretary but the former must keep in touch with such representatives as are appointed by the various communities to watch over these functions and must give due consideration to any representations that these communities may make in this connection.

(g) Government servants are directed to observe any requirements which the Camp Council may consider necessary in the interests of the good administration of the camp, and may offer themselves as representatives on the said council if they think fit. Their first duty is to the British Hong Kong Government and if they are elected to the Council there is no reason to suppose any clash of loyalties should arise. The officers concerned, however, should be free to consult the Colonial Secretary on any matter on which he fears his obligations to the Government and to the Council may conflict. In case of any embarrassment the officer must resign his position on the Council.

APPENDIX 2

Administrative Organization of the Camp

The Camp is organized for administrative purposes in the following manner:

1. The Camp Commandant is in general control of the administration.

2. He is assisted in his work by the following officers and bodies, who are directly responsible to him:

(a) Administrative Officer, appointed by the Camp Commandant personally, in charge respectively of Accommodation, Electricity, Health, Labour, Medical Affairs and Hospital, Works and Supplies: the Camp Quartermaster: and also the Administrative Secretary attached to the British Community Council.

(b) The Welfare Committee.

(c) The Board of Management of the Canteen.

(d) The Camp Relief Fund.

(e) The Disciplinary Tribunal.

3. The British Community Council, under the ex-officio chairmanship of the Camp Commandant and elected by the adult population of the Camp,

(a) acts in an advisory capacity to the Camp Commandant in respect of all matters which he may bring before it,

(b) receives reports from the Camp Commandant, the Administrative Officers and Bodies, as indicated in paragraph 2, and considers and votes upon any questions placed before it for decision,

(c) introduces subjects relative to the internal administration of the camp for consideration by the Council and resolves what attitude should be taken in regard to them,

(d) acts as intermediary between the Camp Commandant and his Administrative Officers on the one hand and District Committees on the other hand, and in this capacity

(i) it ensures uniformity of practice in essential matters throughout the camp.

(ii) its members act as a vehicle for the transmission of instructions and information to the District Committees from the Camp Administration in respect of decisions taken by the latter, which have been brought to the cognisance of its members,

(iii) its members, as representatives of the District Committees, bring to the cognizance of the Council as a whole and of the Administrative Officers such local problems as District Committees are not able to handle without reference to them,

(e) controls the local regulations issued by District Committees for the maintenance of discipline in the areas under their control,

(f) supervises the activities of the Committee appointed to organize sports and entertainment.

The functions of the Council are in all respects subject to the over-riding vote of the Camp Commandant.

Members of the Council are elected by the Districts into which the Camp is divided and are members 'ex-officio' of their respective District Committees.

4. District Committees, elected by the adult population of the respective districts, control and manage the local affairs of the Districts, into which the Camp is divided. Their principal duties are:

(a) to assist the Camp Accommodation Office in matters, arising out of billetting in their district, and to execute orders given by him,

(b) to provide for the proper handling of food and supplies, made available to their Districts, and for their equitable distribution,

(c) to assist the Administrative Officers, appointed by, and responsible to, the Camp Commandant, to carry out the duties assigned to them,

(d) to provide for the proper upkeep of their respective districts,

(e) to maintain discipline by enforcing, with such means as are at their disposal, the regulations promulgated for observance in each district.

5. Religious and cultural activities throughout the Camp are entrusted to the care of Committees constituted of persons recognized as leaders in such activities.

6. *JAPANESE ARMY OPERATIONS IN CHINA DECEMBER 1941 HONG KONG OPERATION*
U.S. Monograph No. 71

GENERAL SITUATION PRIOR TO THE OPERATION

When fighting broke out in Hong Kong, there was a land force of approximately 10,000 British and Indian troops combined and about 10 airplanes stationed in the area. The main defense line of Kowloon Peninsula consisted of several lines of pill-box positions running from Hakwaichung southwest of the Jubilee Reservoir to Hill 225, through Tate's Cairn to the vicinity of Hebe Hill. On Hong Kong Island there were guns of various caliber mounted to cover the shoreline which, in turn, was heavily protected with trenches and obstacles. Furthermore, in the highlands overlooking the city of Hong Kong, lines of pill-box positions had been constructed in depth.

Up to the time of the outbreak of the Pacific War no great changes had been discernible in the general conduct of the British concessions or their military installations. However, field maneuvers in the frontier regions were carried out fairly frequently and reconnaissance parties operated along the British-China boundary. About early December, most of the British-Indian troops which had been stationed on the plains of Sheungshui were withdrawn to the main defense positions. When hostilities broke out in Hong Kong, therefore, it appeared as though the fortress was ready to meet the challenge.

Further, the Chinese 4th War Sector Army with a force of approximately 10 divisions confronted at close quarters the northern battleline of the Japanese 23d Army.

Prior to the Pacific War, the 23d Army, commanded by Lt Gen Takashi Sakai, had occupied the area surrounding Canton with the 18th, 104th and 38th Divisions, the vicinity of Swatow with the 19th Independent Mixed Brigade, the vicinity of Shanwei, Tanshui and Shenchuanhsu with the Army Artillery Unit and the northern part of Hainan Island with one infantry regiment of the 48th Division. In the fall of 1941, when the 51st Division was incorporated into the 23d Army, some changes were made in the disposition of troops. The 18th Division was relieved of its garrison mission by the 51st Division and moved its main force to the vicinity of the Canton-Kowloon railway. The 38th Division, after transferring the responsibility for the security of the areas north of Chiuchiang to part of the 104th Division, moved closer to Nanhai and Sanshui. The Araki Detachment (three infantry battalions and one field artillery battalion) of the 51st Division was placed under the direct command of the Army and assigned the duty of garrisoning Shanwei and Tanshui. In mid-November, one battalion of the 19th Independent Mixed Brigade was assigned garrison duty in north Hainan Island, replacing the infantry regiment of the 48th Division, which then returned to its parent organization.

OPERATIONAL COMMAND

On 6 November 1941, Imperial General Headquarters ordered the Commander in Chief of the China Expeditionary Army, in cooperation with the Navy, to prepare to attack Hong Kong with a force of which the 38th Division of the 23d Army would form the core. Details of the operation together with the main points of the Central Agreement reached between the Army and Navy setting the time of completion of preparations as the end of November were communicated to him. He was ordered to carry out all preparations in the strictest secrecy.

This plan did not imperil the security of the area occupied by the 23d Army. An attack unit was to be used to strike Hong Kong while part of the Army's force was to check the Chinese troops from interfering from the north.

The main points of the plan were:

Objective:

The main objective of the Hong Kong Operation is to capture Hong Kong by destroying the enemy forces.

Policy:

In cooperation with the Navy, an element of the 23d Army will attack Kowloon Peninsula and Hong Kong Island from the mainland.

Strength:

Refer to attached Standard Table of Strength. (Chart No. 1.)

In strict secrecy, the 23d Army will assemble powerful units of its attack force in the vicinity of Shenchuanhsu while its main force will assemble in the vicinity of Humen, Shihlung and Canton.

The operation will commence immediately after the operation in Malaya is definitely known to have started.

As soon as the battle has begun, Army and Navy air units will strike Hong Kong and its environs. Enemy air power will be neutralized and all important military installations, as well as all vessels in the harbor, will be destroyed.

The invasion force, timing the action with the progress of the air attack, will break across the boundary near Shenchuanhsu, occupy Mt Taimaoshan and press forward to a line running east to west of the Hill.

At this line the invasion force will prepare for a major attack. It will advance and destroy enemy positions aligned east to west near Jubilee Reservoir and drive down to the southern tip of Kowloon Peninsula. To support the advance of the main invasion force, a small sea advance unit will operate near Tsingi Isle. Then, depending upon the battle situation, troops may be landed to the west of Mt Maonshan in order to attack the enemy's right flank.

Immediately after the capture of Kowloon Peninsula, troops will prepare to attack Hong Kong. Enemy military installations on such small islands as Tsingi, Stonecutter and others must be destroyed before the major operation is launched.

In attacking Hong Kong, troops will first land on its northern beach and from there enlarge their gains. To facilitate this operation, as large a demonstration movement as possible will be staged on the southern beach of Hong Kong to lead the enemy to believe forces will land there.

The invasion will be carried out in close cooperation with the Navy.

If battle exigencies demand, part of the Army and Navy air units already in action in other areas, may be called upon to support the Hong Kong Operation.

Movement after the Capture of Hong Kong:

The 23d Army will resume the mission of maintaining the security of the already occupied zones as well as the vicinity of Hong Kong.

The Army will assemble the 38th Division and other troops in the vicinity of Hong Kong and prepare them for new missions in other zones.

Chart No 1

STANDARD TABLE OF STRENGTH ASSIGNED TO THE CAPTURE OF HONG KONG

Combatant Units		
The 38th Div		
Inf Regt reinforced		1
Indep Anti-tank Gun Bns		2
Indep Mt Arty Regt		1
Heavy Fld Arty Regt		1
Heavy Fld Arty Bn		1
Mortar Bn		1
Arty Intell Regt		1
Indep Eng Regts	a. General Purpose	2
	b. Landing & Shipping	1
Air Units Air Sqrns	a. Recon	1
	b. Fighter	1
Air Regt (light bomber)		1
Airfield Bn		1
Signal Unit Comm Regt		Main Force
Indep Comm Co		1
Indep Radio Comm Plat		1
River Crossing Material Co		
Logistical Units		

Motor Trans Cos	4
Indep Trans Regt (horses)	Part
Fld Ord Depot	Part
Fld Motor Depot	Part
Fld Freight Depot	Part
Casualty Clearing Sec	1
Veterinary Depot	Part
Siege Unit	
Arty Hq	1
Hv Arty Regt 24cm howitzer	1
Indep Hv Arty Bn 15cm cannon	1
Indep Mortar Bn	1
Special Units	
Railway Trans Regt	Part
Duty Units Land duty units	3
Surface duty units	2
Const Units	2
Water Supply and Pur Depots	2
Vet Quarantine Depot	Part

The Central Agreement between the Army and Navy may be broken down into seven important clauses, namely: the objective of the operation; its policy; the time to launch the operation; the main points of the operation; the strength of the troops; the system of command and the division of security responsibilities. As the first three clauses are described in the foregoing paragraphs, there are described below only those points of operation which called for the coordination of the Army and Navy forces.

In strict secrecy, the Army will assemble part of its invasion force in the vicinity of Shenchuanhsu and its main force close to Humen, Shihlung and Canton.

In the meantime, the Navy will tighten the blockade in the waters around Hong Kong and prevent vessels from escaping from Hong Kong or coming to the rescue of the forces there.

At the outset of the operation, Army and Navy air units will attack Hong Kong. They will neutralize enemy air power and destroy enemy vessels in the harbor as well as important military installations.

The Army, timing its action with the progress of the air attack will, at an opportune moment, launch its attack first against Kowloon and then against Hong Kong Island.

The Navy will provide the Army with the necessary escort force to protect the transportation of Army troops and to support their landing operations. Should the situation demand, the Navy will assist the Army by shelling enemy positions.

If the battle situation demands, part of the Army and Navy air units in action in other zones will be transferred to the Hong Kong Operation.

In addition, it was stipulated that one division and one infantry regiment of the 23d Army and the main force of the Second China Expeditionary Fleet would form the main fighting body and that the operation would be carried out under the command system of cooperation between the Army and Navy.

The China Expeditionary Army placed three independent air squadrons, three reconnaissance planes and the 45th Light Bomber Regiment of the 1st Air Brigade under the command of the 23d Army and ordered the commander of the 23d Army to draw up an operational plan for the invasion of Hong Kong based on the Imperial General Headquarters' plan.

The objective, policy and time of the operation were the same as those described above. The planned action of the operational plan stated:

During the Hong Kong Operation, the Army will maintain those zones which it is already occupying.

As the time for the Hong Kong Operation approaches, the Army will make the necessary rearrangement of garrison forces in order to build up the invasion force which will then be drawn up secretly near the British-China boundary lines. All troops of this invasion force will prepare for action immediately in order that a powerful force may be ready to break through the borderline at the moment these tactics are called for.

The tactical organization of the forces to be used for the capture of Hong Kong are as shown on Chart No. 2.

Actions of Invasion Unit:

Simultaneously with the first attack by the air units, a powerful unit of the invading force will break across the border and attack and destroy the enemy advance units. Then, denying them the chance to regroup, the unit will advance immediately to the strategic line running from east to west of Mt Taimaoshan.

Upon completion of preparations to attack the enemy's main positions aligned east to west of the Jubilee Reservoir, the attack will be launched. The main point of the attack will be the high land east to west of the Jubilee Reservoir. At the same time, the enemy in the Taiwai sector will be attacked and destroyed.

If the battle situation demands, a small advance sea unit will support the action of the main force from the Tsingi Isle sector.

To facilitate the advance of the main force, another unit will cross Tide Cove and aim its drive from the southwestern part of Mt Maonshan toward the northeastern section of Kowloon city.

Should the enemy defenses on the peninsula east of Tide Cove prove weak, the spearhead of the main force may be turned toward that point.

On Hong Kong Island itself, an attack in force will be made on the northern beach. From this point, gains will be enlarged.

If the situation requires, the objective may be attained by blockading Hong Kong without attacking it.

Chart No. 2

AN OUTLINE OF THE TACTICAL ORGANIZATION OF FORCES OF THE 23D ARMY FOR THE HONG KONG OPERATION

		Units previously incorporated	Units newly assigned						
			A.T. Gun	*Arty*	*Eng & Bridging Materials*	*Signal*	*Medical*	*Transport*	*Others*
Attack Unit	Sano Group	38th Div	2 bns	3 mt arty bns, 1 mortar bn	2 indep engr regts 2 bridging material co's	1 radio plat	1/3 of medical unit	6 trans co's 1 motor trans plat	Medical Unit
	Army Air Unit	1 fighter regt & 2 small formations 3 hq recon planes 1 recon unit							1 airfield bn, 1 airfield co
	Kitajima Unit	1st Arty Unit		14th Hv Fld Arty Regt (less 1 bn) 1 mortar bn	1 co (less one plat)	1 radio plat	Part of water supply pur. unit	1 trans co	
	Kitazawa Unit	Part of the South China Anchorage Inspectorate			1 engr co				
	Army Signal Unit					2 radio plats 1 wire sig plat			

Chart No. 2

AN OUTLINE OF THE TACTICAL ORGANIZATION OF FORCES OF THE 23D ARMY FOR THE HONG KONG OPERATION (CONT'D)

		Units previously incorporated	Units newly assigned						
			A.T. Gun	*Arty*	*Eng & Bridging Materials*	*Signal*	*Medical*	*Transport*	*Others*
Support Unit	Araki Det	66th Inf Regt (less 1 co)		1 arty bn	1 engr co (less 2 plats)	2 radio plats	1/3 medical unit 1 fld hosp Part of water sup & pur. unit Part of vet depot	1 trans co (less 1 plat) 1 motor trans plat	Part of each sup depot and 1 fld ware-house
	Kobayashi Unit				1 ry bn			3 motor trans cos	
Logistical Unit	Sato Unit	Part of 5th L of C Sector Unit					Shenchuanhsu Br Hosp 1 casualty clearing plat Part of Vet Depot		1 inf co Part of Land Duty Co Part of each sup depot and 1 fld ware-house

During this operation, the Araki Detachment will withdraw its troops from Shanwei and Pinghai and mass them near Tanshui, where they will prepare to meet any action by the Chinese forces.

The 104th Division will assemble all its mobile forces and remain on the alert against any Chinese attack.

Supplies:

Paoan will be the debarkation base for munitions, which will be assembled as near as possible to Paoan and Shenchuanhsu before the operation. If the situation demands, munitions may be debarked temporarily at Humen.

The collection of war supplies will be completed by the early part of December.

The Army will be held responsible for the transportation of supplies by vessels and motor vehicles. Field supply points will be placed as far forward as possible.

Transportation south of the borderline will be as near as possible to the Canton-Kowloon railway.

The amount of ammunition to be stored at Paoan and Shenchuanhsu prior to the launching of the operation together with that carried by units, must be sufficient for one engagement.

Bridging materials (wood) must be sufficient to build a wooden bridge of about 1,000 meters in length. Bridging materials (pontoon Type B) will be the amount required by one bridging material company as well as 100 collapsible boats Model 95. The materials needed for advancing the operations of the siege artillery must be sufficient to fill the requirements of the Kitajima Unit.

Provisions: Rations sufficient for 90 days for a division. Forage sufficient for 60 days for a division.

Rations and forage must be sufficient to sustain the operational units for a period of 60 days. Consideration must be given to the supply of rations by sea route for the units that will operate from Tanshui.

As soon as Hong Kong is captured the 38th Division will promptly assemble on Kowloon Peninsula and prepare for action in new zones. An element of the 51st Division will garrison Hong Kong.

On the basis of the above operational plan, the 38th Division's operation was divided into three phases: first, to break across the border and advance to the front of the main enemy positions; secondly, to break through these main positions and occupy Kowloon Peninsula and thirdly, to capture Hong Kong.

It was planned that in the first phase the main strength of the advance unit, composed of two infantry regiments and three mountain artillery battalions, commanded by an Infantry Group commander, would break through the enemy's frontier positions from the eastern sector of Shenchuanhsu while part of force, which would embark in landing craft near Paoan, would land at Shataukok and advance into the Yuenlongkauhsi Plain. Another part of the force would start its action from Kaupingfong and advance via

Shataukok to the area west of Taipo. The main body of the advance unit, as promptly as possible, would drive toward the line of Yaukamtau, Mt Pakshakiu, Mt Taimaoshan, Grassy Hill and Cove Hill confronting the main enemy positions. At this line, they would prepare for an attack against the enemy lines.

The 229th Infantry Regiment was ordered to advance its main force from the sector east of Mt Taimaoshan to Grassy Hill and there await the main force of the Division. The regiment would then assemble in the vicinity of Taipo.

During the second phase, troops that had arrived at the line of Mt Taimaoshan and Grassy Hill would gradually press forward, at the same time preparing themselves to strike the enemy facing them. The main attack would be directed toward the eastern side of the Jubilee Reservoir and then to Golden Hill. After breaking through these points, they would aim their drive toward the southwestern tip of Kowloon Peninsula and occupy Kowloon city. The 229th Infantry Regiment would proceed by landing craft to the northwestern side of Mt Maonshan and, after breaking through the enemy positions in the neighborhood of Tate's Cairn, would advance into the eastern area of Kowloon city.

In the third phase, after Kowloon Peninsula was captured, they would prepare to attack Hong Kong.

The attack against Hong Kong would open with a powerful assault and, after landing on the northern beach, gains would gradually be enlarged.

On 1 December, 1941, after Japan had decided to declare war on the United States and Britain, Imperial General Headquarters issued the following order to the commander of the China Expeditionary Army:

> The Army, in cooperation with the Navy, will attack and capture Hong Kong. The 38th Division of the 23d Army will be used as the core of this force. The operation will begin immediately after it is confirmed that the Southern Army has achieved a landing or made air attacks on Malaya.
>
> After Hong Kong is captured, the Army will set up a military government on the island.

CONCENTRATION OF JAPANESE FORCES

Immediately upon receipt of this order, the 23d Army set the invasion troops in motion but, in order to keep the maneuver secret, the troops were forbidden to move in the daytime.

On the night of 1 December, the advance elements of the 38th Division, composed of the 229th Infantry Regiment and the 230th Infantry Regiment which were assembled in the Sanshui-Nanhai area began to advance to the area north of Shenchuanhsu.

Advancing only at night, they reached Shenchuanhsu on the night of 6 December.

The Kitajima Unit, the army artillery unit that had been guarding the vicinity of Shenchuanhsu, moved up to Paoan, while part of the Siege Artillery Unit and the Heavy Artillery Unit, which had been alerted at Canton, marching at night, also moved to Paoan. Upon arrival, these units were placed under the command of the Kitajima Unit.

The Araki Detachment left Shanwei and assembled close to Tanshui.

On 5 December, the main force of the 38th Division, together with other units left the Sanshui-Nanhai area, and on the night of the 6th assembled near Humen and Tungkuan.

PROGRESS OF OPERATION

At 0400 of 8 December, the Army ordered its troops to start the operation. The battle began with bombings by the air units aimed at the destruction of enemy planes and the Kaitak airfield.

The advance elements of the land forces broke across the border and, without meeting much resistance from the enemy, reached Yuenlongkauhsi [Yuen Long] and Taipo on the same day.

Assuming that the enemy would resist strongly at their main defensive positions, at 1000 on the 9th, the Army ordered the troops to prepare to attack these positions. It was estimated that preparations would be completed within a week. The main attack was to be directed against the high land southwest of Jubilee Reservoir.

The Sano Group was ordered to prepare to launch an attack against the main enemy positions from a line stretching from east to west of Mt Taimaoshan. Part of the invasion force was to strike and capture Tsingi Isle, while another force was to land on the peninsula at a point to the east of Tide Cove where it was to prepare for subsequent battle. The Kitajima Unit was to deploy its main force in the vicinity of Taipo with a partial force in the vicinity of Yuenlongkauhsi. The mission of these forces was the destruction of those strong points against which the spearhead of the attack was to be directed, as well as the overcoming of enemy artillery on Stonecutter Island.

The operation progressed much faster than anticipated. On 9 December, while a reconnaissance party headed by the reconnaissance officer of the 228th Infantry Regiment was surveying enemy positions on the high land of Hill 255, which was one of the strong points of the enemy main defense line south of the Jubilee Reservoir, they discovered loopholes in the deployment of the defenders and using these loopholes were able to capture the positions. This unexpected success spurred the first-line units on to launch an attack against the main enemy positions prior to the designated zero hour and, on the 11th, they broke through these positions without much opposition. The troops assigned to the capture of Tsingi Island made a detour far to the west and, on the 11th, struck and captured the island. Other troops, composed of the core of the 229th Infantry Regiment, maneuvering as a detachment to cover the left flank of the attack forces, crossed Tide Cove on the 10th and, the next day, destroyed the enemy positions near Tate's Cairn. On the 12th, Japanese troops had reached the line linking Kowloon city, Kaitak airfield and Tsenglanshu and, by the 14th, had mopped up the enemy on the entire peninsula.

Encouraged by the unexpectedly rapid capture of Kowloon peninsula, the Army decided to follow this up with an immediate attack against Hong Kong, thus denying the enemy an opportunity to regroup. It ordered the invasion troops to land and, without giving the enemy a breathing space, to storm the whole island of Hong Kong. The main points of the plan for the disposition of forces and preparation for attack were:

The Navy will support the landing. On a day predetermined for landing the Navy will stage a demonstration movement along the southern coast of Hong Kong Island in order to deceive the enemy into thinking that the landing will be carried out there.

The Siege Heavy Artillery Unit will take up its positions on the highland in the northern part of Kowloon city. Air units and the Siege Heavy Artillery Unit will support the movement of the landing troops by overcoming the fire of the enemy artillery and destroying their beach defense installations.

The movement of the landing forces will be carried out with the utmost secrecy. The main body will start from Kowloon and Taiwantsun and land at Braemar Hill. Elements will start from the vicinity of Kungtongtsai and land near Sauki Wan [Sha Kei Wan].

Disposition of the troops participating in the attack on Hong Kong will be as shown on Chart No. 3.

Preparations for the landing assaults were accomplished successfully, though not without many difficulties incurred in the transportation of bulky loads of landing equipment and materials. Zero hour for the landing was set for the night of 18 December and this information was communicated to all landing troops and to the Navy.

At dusk on 18 December, the Navy began to maneuver as though they intended to land on the southwestern coast of Hong Kong. The Siege Artillery Units opened fire and smashed the defense installations along the coast to the east of North Point, which was

Chart No. 3

DISPOSITION OF TROOPS FOR INVASION OF HONG KONG

	Infantry	*Artillery*	*Engineer & Bridging Material*	*Note*
Right Flank Unit	Inf Group Hq 228th Inf Regt-less 3d Bn 230th Inf Regt-less 3d Bn	5th Indep A.T. Gun Bn 1st Bn of 38th Mt Arty Regt	38th Eng Regt less 1 co	After landing at Braemar, break through the enemy positions on the beach & turn to the right. Adv westward over the northern half of Hong Kong & occupy the island.
Left Flank Unit	229th Inf Regt-less 1st Bn	2nd Indep A.T. Gun Bn (less 1 co) 1 co of 10th Indep Mt Arty Regt	1 co of 38th Eng Regt	After landing at Sahkeiwan, break through the enemy positions, turn to the right with the main force and adv westward over the southern half of Hong Kong. Part of the force will attack and capture Taitam Peninsula.
Right Arty Unit		38th Mt Arty Regt (less 1st Bn)		
Left Arty Unit	1 pltn of 229th Inf Regt	10th Indep Mt Arty Regt (less 1 co) 20th Indep Mt Arty Regt 21st Light Tr Mortar Unit 1 co of 2d Indep A.T. Gun Bn		
Landing Engr Unit			20th Indep Eng Regt 1st & 2d Bridging Mtl Cos of 9th Div	
Landing Support Unit			1 co of 14th Indep Engr Regt	
Reserve Unit	1st Bn (less 1 Pltn) of 229th Inf Regt			

Note: Two infantry battalions will remain in Kowloon City and guard the city.

to be the landing beach for the Japanese troops. They continued firing to hold down the remaining enemy artillery.

In the meantime, at 2100 on the same day, the 38th Division successfully landed its assault troops and these troops immediately proceeded to drive the enemy out of the eastern sector of the island. The main force of the enemy defenders retreated toward the southern sector beyond Mt Nicholson, where they offered determined resistance. The advance of the assault troops met with many setbacks. The following day, the first assault wave of troops to the right of the right flank came upon a powerful enemy group in sheltered positions with emplacements built into the eastern foot of Mt Nicholson. The enemy fire from these positions was so heavy that not only was the advance stopped but the Japanese troops were thrown into confusion. The left flank units also faced heavy enemy fire from the defenders occupying a hotel on the southern side of Violet Hill and their advance was slowed down. Furthermore, the terrain in this area was so rugged and separated by interlocking ravines that contact with the advance unit was, at one time, entirely broken.

On the 20th, the artillery units of the invasion force landed on Hong Kong and, on the 21st, the first combat line began to recover from the initial confusion.

In the subsequent stages of the battle, the main force successfully overcame the stubborn resistance of the enemy, gradually enlarged its gains and invaded the western sector. Part of the advance began to weaken and, on the 25th, they laid down their weapons.

Japanese casualties during this operation were 675 killed and 2,079 wounded, making a total of 2,754 casualties.

MOVEMENT OF CHINESE FORCES DURING THE HONG KONG OPERATION

Prior to the Hong Kong Operation, the Chinese 4th War Sector Army had more than 10 divisions facing the first line of the 23d Army but after the Hong Kong Operation had begun they maneuvered seven or eight divisions to the east of Canton. One army from Kwangsi Province and the 4th and 74th Armies of the 9th War Sector Army also assembled in the Canton area.

The Araki Detachment (composed mainly of three infantry battalions and one field artillery battalion) assembled its main force in the vicinity of Tanshui. It occupied the mountain areas to the north with part of its force and prepared to beat back any enemy offensives. Although during the Hong Kong Operation the Chinese moved about one and a half divisions closer to the Araki Detachment there was no active fighting.

ADMINISTRATION

Because of the specific problems involved in the jurisdiction of the occupied zone of Hong Kong, it was deemed necessary to carry out its administration on a basis entirely distinct from that of other occupied zones in China. For this reason, Imperial General Headquarters favored the idea of setting up a Governor-General in Hong Kong, under its direct command, who would direct the defense and military government of Hong Kong.

On 19 January 1942, the Department of the Governor-General of Hong Kong was created. The Governor-General, however, was placed under the delegated command of the China Expeditionary Army in regard to the collection of intelligence, lines of communication and maintenance of the blockade of southern China.

7. *SYSTEM OF GOVERNMENT ADOPTED BY THE JAPANESE IN HONG KONG, 1942*

(FO 371 (1942), 31671/9628)

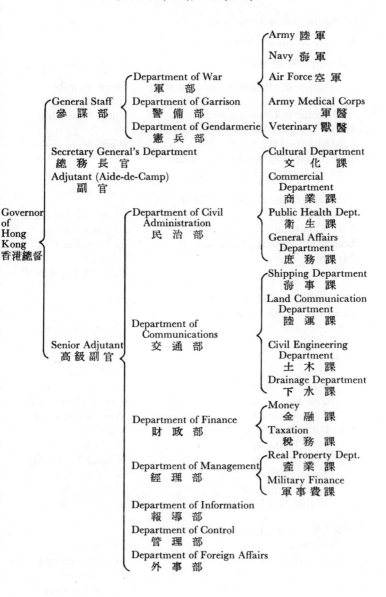

- Governor of Hong Kong 香港總督
  - General Staff 參謀部
    - Department of War 軍部
      - Army 陸軍
      - Navy 海軍
      - Air Force 空軍
      - Army Medical Corps 軍醫
      - Veterinary 獸醫
    - Department of Garrison 警備部
    - Department of Gendarmerie 憲兵部
  - Secretary General's Department 總務長官
  - Adjutant (Aide-de-Camp) 副官
  - Senior Adjutant 高級副官
    - Department of Civil Administration 民治部
      - Cultural Department 文化課
      - Commercial Department 商業課
      - Public Health Dept. 衛生課
      - General Affairs Department 庶務課
    - Department of Communications 交通部
      - Shipping Department 海事課
      - Land Communication Department 陸運課
      - Civil Engineering Department 土木課
      - Drainage Department 下水課
    - Department of Finance 財政部
      - Money 金融課
      - Taxation 稅務課
    - Department of Management 經理部
      - Real Property Dept. 産業課
      - Military Finance 軍事費課
    - Department of Information 報導部
    - Department of Control 管理部
    - Department of Foreign Affairs 外事部

8. *HONG KONG ADMINISTRATION, 1945*
(OFFICE OF STRATEGIC SERVICES)

Civil Administration Department

Chinese Section Chiefs

Controller of Fuel:	Lia Kia-fan
Director of District Affairs Bureau:	Hsien Ping-hsi (Peter H. Sin)
Director of Census Bureau:	Yung Ngai-sung
Hong Kong Construction Department	
Member of the Staff:	Wang Yung-nien
Hong Kong Opium Commission	
Chief (under a Japanese)	Liu Ch'uo-pak

Chinese Co-operative Council (1942–)

Chairman:	Chow, Sir Shouson
Vice-Chairman:	Li Kuan-ch'un
Education Representative:	Li King-hong
Members:	Lo, M.K.
	Tam, William N.T.

Chinese Representatives' Association

Council of the Association

Chairman:	Chow, Sir Shouson
Vice-Chairman:	Li Kuan-ch'un
Members:	
Wang T'ung-ming	Lu Ai-yün
Tung Chung-wei	Kuo Tsan
Yeh Lan-chuan	Chang Shu-ch'un
Teng Chao-chien	Yen Ch'eng-k'un
Chou Yao-nien	Wu Rua
Ling K'ang-fa	Li Chiu
Lin Chien-yin	K'uang Ch'i-tung
Feng Tzu-yin	Lo Wen-chin
Tan Ya-shih	Li Chung-fu
Wang Te(h)-kuang	Lee Jee-chor

The Office of the Association

President:	Lo Hsü-ho
Office Holders:	Liu Tieh-ch'eng
	Li Tzu-fang
	Ch'an Lim-pak

Chinese Representative Council (1942–)

Members:	Lo Kuk-wo
	(Sir Robert Kotewall)
	Ch'an Lim-pak
	Lau Tit-shing
	Li Tzu Fang
	Chou Yao-nien

The Asiatic Affairs Bureau

East Asia Cultural Association

President:	Chang Ku-shan
(Chairman – 1942):	Yeung Tsin-lei
Vice-Chairman:	Ma Kiam
Permanent Officers:	Cheung Koo-shan
	Kong Po-tin
	Luk Tan-lam
	Tseng Kwong-kung

Laborers' Association

President:	Lin Chien-yin

The Control Wards

Hong Kong Wards Control Officers:

Central Ward	Hsien Ping-hsi
	(Peter H. Sin)
Shang Huan Ward [Chung Wan]	Shao Wei-ming
Hsi Ying Pan Ward [Sai Ying Poon]	Li Ch'i-hsin
Shih Tang Chu Ward [Shek Tong Tsui]	Sun Nuang-ch'üan
Shan Wang Tai Ward [Hai Wan Tai]	Chien Wen
Wan Tzu Ward [Wan Chai]	Ho Jib-ju
E Ching Ward [?]	Ho Te(h)-kuang
Tung Lo Wan Ward	Kuo Hsien-hung
Race Course Ward [Happy Valley]	Wu Wen-tse
Yuan Hsiang Kang Ward [Aberdeen?]	Wang T'ai
Chih Chu Ward [Stanley]	Li Sung-ch'ing
Shao Chi Wan Ward [Shaukeiwan]	Tseng Shou-ch'ao

Kowloon Wards Control Officers:

Kowloon City Ward	Tai Jo-lan
Shen Shui Ward [Shamshuipo]	Huang Po-ch'in
Wang Chueh Ward [Mong Kok?]	Tseng Jung
Yaumati Ward	Feng Hao
Chien Sha Chu Ward [Tsimshatsui]	Liang Chi
Hung Kan Ward [Hung Hom?]	Li Shou-shan
Kowloon Tong Special Ward	Kuan Hsin-yen

Hsin Chieh Wards Control Officers:	
Ta Pu Ward [Taipo]	Ch'en T'iao-ch'in
Yuan Lang Ward [Yuenlong]	Peng
Eastern District Bureau	
Assistant Director:	Lo Chai-sing
General Affairs Bureau for Kowloon Districts Member of the Political Division:	Huang Chung
Banks and Banking Associations	
Bank of Communications	
Manager:	Lau Tit-shing
Overseas Chinese Bank	
Representative:	Tang Yat-yan
Hong Kong Bankers' Association	
Chairman:	Lau Tit-shing
Vice-Chairman:	Li Tsu Fang
Members of the Executive Committee:	Cheung Suk-shun
	Poon Shunt-um
	Yeung Yun-tak
Hong Kong Financier:	Ho Tung, Sir Robert
Hong Kong Propaganda and Press	
Central News Agency (Hong Kong Branch)	
Chief:	Wu Pei-yüan
Representatives:	Lo Ching-kwang
	Wei Kuo-lun
Hsiang Tao Jih Pao	
Proprietor:	Aw Boon Haw
Hua Chiao Jih Pao	
Editor:	Lu Meng-shu
Managing Editor:	Tsen Hsi-yung
News Editor:	Lu Mun-hsi
Hong Kong Jih Pao	
Editor in Chief:	Huang Pao-shu
Nan Hua Jih Pao	
Publisher:	K'uang Ch'i-tung
Editor:	Liu Hsien-t'ang
Journalists and Writers	Chang Kuang-yen
	Wong, Peter M.
Press Official in Hong Kong	Kong Kai-tung

Hong Kong Organizations and Associations

People's Food Association	
Chairman:	Aw Boon Haw
Hong Kong General Relief Association	
Chairman:	Ch'an Lim Pak
Chairman, General Affairs Committee:	Li Tzu Fang
Vice-Chairman, General Affairs Committee:	(Wong Yat-chung)
Secretary for Relief and Culture Exhibition:	Wang Te(h)-feng
Chinese Relief Association	
Chief of the Executive Department:	Lau Tit-s-ing
Chief of the General Affairs Department:	Lo Kuk-wo (Sir Robert Kotewall)
Trading Union of Hong Kong	
Director:	Kiu Kuk
Hong Kong Commercial Institute	
Director:	Yeh Lan-Ch'üan
Chamber of Commerce	
Representative for Foreign Goods:	Kwok, Chuen
Representatives of Commercial Associations	
Firewood Merchants:	Lai Kong-sun
Rice Importers Association:	Ma Ying
Nam Pak Hong Merchant Houses:	Tong Ping-tat
Hong Kong and Kowloon General Labor Association	
Chief Executive:	Ling Hong Fat
Kowloon Markets Bureau	
Chief:	Tong Ching Kan
Chinese Language Society	
Hong Kong Representatives:	Chan Pai-li Chu Sen
Hong Kong Race Course	
Chairman of Stewards:	Ho Kom Tong
Hong Kong Jockey Club	
Members of the Racing Committee:	Yip Kui-ying Pan, S.H. Pih, C.C. Wei, Peter
South China Athletic Association	
Chairman:	Luke Oi-wan

BIBLIOGRAPHY

I. OFFICIAL SOURCES AND PUBLISHED HISTORIES OF THE WAR

GREAT BRITAIN

Cabinet Papers, General Correspondence: Foreign Office (FO371), Colonial Office(CO129), Public Records Office.

London Gazette: Supplement, 29 January 1948.
Maltby, Major-General C. M., 'Operations in Hong Kong from 8th to 25th December, 1941'.

British Military Administration, 1945–6
Reports by Chief Civil Affairs Officer, General Officer Commanding, Commodore in Charge, Hong Kong, 1946.
'Colony Quarterly Review, December, 1945'.

Imperial War Museum
Official photographs, captured Japanese film, 'The Fall of Hong Kong', translations of Japanese army records.

Foreign Office
Documents on British Foreign Policy, 1919–39; (edited by E. L. Woodward and Rohan Butler).
3rd series, 1938–9, Vols. VIII and IX. London, 1946–

Official War Histories (Military, Naval, Civil and Medical Series):
DONNISON, F. S. V., *British Military Administration in the Far East*, London, 1956.
HOWARD, M., *Grand Strategy*, Vol. IV, History of the Second World War, August 1942–September 1943, London, 1956.
KIRBY, S. WOODBURN *The War against Japan*, History of the Second World War, Campaigns, 5 vols., London, 1957.
MEDLICOTT, W. N., *The Economic Blockade*, Vol. I, London, 1952.
ROSKILL, S., *Naval Policy between the Wars*, Vol. I (1919–29), London, 1968.
SELWYN-CLARKE S., *Report on the Medical and Health Conditions in Hong Kong, 1 January 1942–31 August 1945*. London, 1946. (Includes report by Macleod, N. C., 'Report of the Deputy Director of Health Services, Hong Kong.)

SMITH, DEAN A., AND WOODRUFF, MICHAEL F.A., *Deficiency Diseases in Japanese Prison Camps*, London, 1951.

Regimental Histories

KEMP, P. K., *The Middlesex Regiment (Duke of Cambridge's Own) 1919–52*, Aldershot, 1952.

MUIR, AUGUSTUS, *First of Foot: The History of the Royal Scots, the Royal Regiment*, Edinburgh, 1961.

YOUNG, D., *Forty-five, the story of the 45 Commando, Royal Marines, 1943–7*, London, 1972.

AUSTRALIA

WIGMORE, L., *The Japanese Thrust* (Vol. VI in the series Australia in the War of 1939–45, Series I, Army), Canberra, 1957.

CANADA

DUFF, SIR LYMAN P., *Report on the Canadian Expeditionary Force to the Crown Colony of Hong Kong*, Ottawa, 1942.

STACEY, C. P., *Six Years of War* (Official History of the Canadian Army in Second World War, Vol. I), Ottawa, 1953.

HONG KONG

A Record of the Actions of the Hong Kong Volunteer Defence Corps in the Battle for Hong Kong, December, 1941, Hong Kong, [1956?].

INDIA

BHARGAVA, K. D. AND SASTRI, K. N. V., *Campaigns in South-East Asia, 1941–2* (Official History of the Indian Armed Forces in the Second World War 1939–45, ed. Bishewar Prasad), Combined Inter-services Historical Section, India & Pakistan, 1960.

HAIG, B., *Fourteenth Punjab Regiment: a short history 1939–45*, London, 1950.

UNITED STATES

U.S. Army Forces in the Far East (Office of Chief of Military History, Dept. of Army, Washington, 1956).

South China Operations Record, 1937–41 (Japanese Monograph).

DEPT. OF STATE, *Foreign Relations of the United States*, Diplomatic Papers.

——— *The Far East, 1937–44*, Washington, 1954–65.

——— *Foreign Relations of the United States*, Diplomatic Papers, China 1944; Conference volumes: Cairo, Yalta, Potsdam, Washington, 1943–5, 1955–61.

OFFICE OF STRATEGIC SERVICES, *Structure and personnel of the Nanking Puppet Government and Hong Kong Administration*, Washington, 1945.

CHINA

HSU LONG-HSUEN AND CHANG MING-KAI (compilers), translated by Wen Ha-siung, *History of the Sino-Japanese War, 1937–45*, Taiwan, 1972.

JAPAN

HATTORI TAKUSHIRO, *Dai Toa Senso-shi Tenshi*, (A completed History of the War in Greater East Asia), Tokyo, 1st imp., 1965.

Gendaishi Shiryō (Documents on Contemporary History), *Nit-Chū Sensō* (The Sino-Japanese War), Misuzo Shobo, Tokyo, 1964–6.

IKE NOBUTAKA (ed.), *Japan's Decision for War records of the 1941 Police Conferences*, Stanford, 1967.

International Military Tribunal for the Far East, 1946–8, Prosecution documents and exhibits.

DULL, PAUL S., AND M. TAKAKI UMEMARA, *The Tokyo Trials*: a functional index . . . Ann Arbor, 1957.

SAITO, KOJI, *Hong Kong under military administration* (in Japanese) Hong Kong, 1944.

HONG KONG GOVERNMENT—OFFICIAL PAPERS AND REPORTS

Public Records Office:

H.K.R.S. 42/1/1–16, Registrar-General, Medical Records of Stanley Camp.

——— 56/5/1–159, Registrar-General, Japanese Memorials (162 vols.)

——— 57/61–16124, Registrar-General, Japanese Title-Deeds.

——— 112/1/1, Provisional lists of British and Foreign (other than Japanese) casualties, prisoners of war, and internees in Hong Kong, 1942.

HAMILTON, G. S., *Government Departments in Hong Kong 1841–1966*, Hong Kong, 1967.

HONG KONG GOVERNMENT, *Administration Reports*, 1937–9.
——— Administrator of Japanese Property, *Annual departmental reports*, 1953/4 – 64/5.
——— *Annual Departmental Reports* of the Custodian of Enemy Property, 1946/7 – 64/5.
——— *Annual Reports*, 1946–9.
——— *Colonial Secretariat, Civil and Miscellaneous Lists*, Hong Kong, 1969–74.
——— *Gazette*, 1939–41, 1945–9. (also *Special Supplement* to the *H.K. Govt.*)
——— *Gazette*, Vol. XC (2 July 1948) Sir Mark Young, 'Events in Hong Kong on 25 December, 1941'.
——— *Law Reports*, 1946–9.
——— Legislative Council, *Proceedings (Hansard)*, 1938–40, 1946–49.
——— *Report of the Re-constituted War Revenue Committee*, 1941.
——— *Report of the Hong Kong and Kowloon Magistrates*, 1 May 1946–31 March 1947.
——— *Sessional Papers*, 1938–40, 1946–9.
——— *Staff List*, 1938–41, 1946–9.

II. GENERAL SECONDARY WORKS (MAINLY DEALING WITH WORLD WAR II IN THE FAR EAST)

BOOKS

ASAHI SHIMBUN, *The Pacific Rivals*, Tokyo and New York, 1970.
BENDA, H. J., *The Crescent and Rising Sun*, The Hague, 1958.
BERGAMINI, D. *Japan's Imperial Conspiracy*, New York, 1971.
BUHITE, RUSSELL D., *Patrick J. Hurley and American Foreign Policy*, Ithaca and London, 1973.
BUSH, LEWIS W., *Land of the Dragonfly*, London, 1959.
CALVOCORESSI, PETER and WINT, GUY, *Total War: causes and courses of the Second World War*, London, 1972.
CHURCHILL, WINSTON, *The Second World War*, 6 vols., London, 1950.
CLIFFORD, N. R., *Retreat from China: British Policy in the Far East*, London, 1967.
COLLIER, BASIL, *The War and the Far East 1941–5*, London, 1969.

CROWLEY, J.B., *Japan's Quest for Autonomy: National Security and Foreign Policy, 1930–38*, Princeton, 1968.

ELSBREE, W.H., *Japan's Role in South East Asian Nationalist Movements*, Harvard, Cambridge, 1953.

ELLIOTT-BATEMAN, M., *Defeat in the East*, London, 1967.

FEIS, H., *The China Tangle*, New York, 1965.

——— *The Road to Pearl Harbour*, New York, 1962.

IRIYE, A., *Across the Pacific*, New York, 1967.

ISHIMARU TOTA, LT.-CDR. I. J. N., *Japan must fight Britain*; trans. G.V. Rayment. New York, 1936.

JONES, F. C., *Japan's New Order in East Asia: its Rise and Fall, 1937–45*, London, 1954.

KAJIMA MORINOSUKI, *Modern Japan's Foreign Policy*, Tokyo, 1969.

KUBEK, A., *How the Far East was lost: American Policy and the creation of Communist China, 1941–1949*, Chicago, 1963.

LEE, BRADFORD A., *Britain and the Sino-Japanese War 1937–9*, Stanford, 1973.

LOUIS, W. R., *British Strategy in the Far East*, London, 1971.

MACKENZIE, COMPTON, *Eastern Epic*, vol. 1, London, 1951.

MAMORU SHIGEMITSU, *Japan and her destiny*, New York, 1958.

MASAO MARUYAMA, *Thought and Behavior in Modern Japanese Politics* (expanded edition edited by Ivan Morris), London, 1969.

MAXON, Y. C., *Control of Japanese Foreign Policy: a study of civil-military rivalry, 1930–45*, Stanford, 1957.

MEDLICOTT, W. N., *British Foreign Policy since Versailles 1919–63*, 2nd rev. ed., London, 1968.

MILLS, LENNOX A., *British Rule in East Asia: a study in contemporary government and economic development in British Malaya and Hong Kong*, London, 1942.

MINEAR, R. H., *Victors' Justice: the Tokyo war crimes trials*, Princeton, 1971.

MORLEY, J. W. (ed.), *Dilemmas of Growth in Pre-War Japan*, Princeton, 1971.

RUSSELL, E. F. (Baron Russell), *The Knights of the Bushido: a short history of Japanese War Crimes*, London, 1958.

STRATEGICUS (O'Neill, H. C.), *The War Moves East*, London, 1942.

THORNE, C., *The Limits of Foreign Policy*, London, 1972.

TOLAND, J., *The Rising Sun: The Decline and Fall of the Japanese Empire, 1936–45.* New York, 1970.

TOYNBEE, A. (ed.), *Survey of International Affairs*, vol. 7, *The Far East 1942–46* (by F. C. Jones, H. Borton and B. R. Pearn), London, 1955.

TUCHMAN, B. W., *Stillwell and the American Experience in China 1911–45*, New York, 1971.

WARD, ROBERT E. (ed.), *Political Development in Modern Japan*, Princeton, 1968.

WHEELER-BENNETT, J. W., and NICHOLLS, A., *The Semblance of Peace: the political settlement after the Second World War*, London, 1972.

WOODCOCK, GEORGE, *The British in the Far East*, London, 1969.

YOUNG, A. N., *China and the helping hand*, Harvard, Cambridge, 1963.

ZIEGLER, J., *World War II: Books in English, 1945–65* (Hoover Institution Bibliographical Series 45), Stanford, 1972.

ARTICLES

IRIYE, A., 'Japan's Foreign Policies between the Wars – sources and interpretations', *Journal of Asian Studies,* vol. XXVI (1967), pp. 677–82.

YOJI AKASHI, 'Japanese Policy towards the Malayan Chinese, 1941–45', *Journal of South East Asian History*, Vol. I (2), pp. 61–89.

MATERIAL RELATING TO HONG KONG

III. PERSONAL ACCOUNTS OF INDIVIDUAL EXPERIENCES

(a) UNPUBLISHED PAPERS

ANDERSON, K. M., 'Stanley Internment Camp' (Rhodes House Library, Ind. Ocn. MSS. 110).

BARNES, Dr. R. J., 'Drawings and sketches done in Shamshuipo Prisoner-of-War Camp' (in possession of the artist).

BOURKE, Revd. Fr. S. J., 'Steering neutral in troubled waters, Hong Kong, 1941–45' (Endacott MSS.).

DUDLEY, MARION, 'Hong Kong Prison Camp' (typescript, New York Public Library, 1942?).

FORSTER, LANCELOT, 'Stanley Internment Camp' (Rhodes House Library, Ind. Ocn. MSS. 177).

GIMSON, F. C., 'Diary, 1 June, 1943–15 August, 1945, (Rhodes House Library, Ind. Ocn. MSS. 222).

——— 'Hong Kong Re-claimed' (Rhodes House Library, Ind. Ocn. MSS. 177).

——— 'Internment in Hong Kong, March 1942–August, 1945'. (Rhodes House Library, Ind. Ocn. MSS. 177).

——— 'An unpublished history of Hong Kong during the Japanese Occupation' (MS. in possession of the author).

HILL, A., 'Stanley Internment Camp' (Rhodes House Library, Ind. Ocn. MSS. 73).

HURLEY, PATRICK J., 'Western History Collections', University of Oklahoma Library.

LUKE, J. R., 'Personal Notes on Stanley Camp' (Endacott MSS. H.K.U.).

MURRAY, CONSTANCE B., 'Stanley civilian internment camp' (Rhodes House Library, Ind. Ocn. MSS. 185).

PUDNEY, E. W., 'Stanley Camp' (Rhodes House Library, Ind. Ocn. MSS. 51).

SALMON, A., 'An account of war experiences' (Endacott MSS. H.K.U.).

SEARLE, L. A., 'Diary, Hong Kong 1941–44' (Ind. Ocn. MSS. 76).

SIMPSON, R. K. W., 'These Defenceless Doors: a memoir of personal experiences in the battle of Hong Kong and after'. (H.K.U. Library).

SMALLEY, Dr. J. T., 'Diary of work at Kowloon Hospital' (Endacott MSS. H.K.U.).

STERICKER, J., 'Captive Colony: the story of Stanley Internment Camp' (H.K.U. Library).

SKVORZOV, A. V., 'Chinese ink and brush sketches of prisoner-of-war camp life in Hong Kong' (Urban Council Library, City Hall, Hong Kong).

BOOKS

ANDREA (as told to Trish Sheppard), *Darlings, I've had a Ball!* Sydney, 1975.

BAXTER, GEORGE E., *Personal experiences during the siege of Hong Kong; internment to June 1942*, Pamphlet issued by East Asian Residents' Association, Sydney, 1942.

BERTRAM, JAMES, *The Shadow of a War*, London, 1947.

BOWDEN, JEAN, *Grey touched with Scarlet*, London, 1959.

BROWN, WENZELL, *Hong Kong Aftermath*, New York, 1943.

BUSH, LEWIS, *Clutch of Circumstance*, Tokyo, 1956.

CASEY, REVD. GERARD, S.J., *A Priest in a Japanese Jail*, Dublin, 1948.

DEW, GWEN, *Prisoner of the Japanese*, New York, 1943.

DUFF, J. A., *Escape to Free China*, Hong Kong n.d. [1958].

FIELD, ELLEN, *Twilight in Hong Kong*, London, 1960.

FORD, JAMES ALLAN, *Brave White Flag*, London, 1961.

——— *Season of Escape*, London, 1963.

GILMOUR, ANDREW, *My Role in the Rehabilitation of Singapore 1946–1953*, Oral History Pilot Study No. 2, April 1973 (Institute of South-East Asian Studies, Singapore).

GITTINS, JEAN, *Eastern Windows – Western Skies*, Hong Kong, 1969.

——— *I was at Stanley*, Hong Kong, 1946.

GOODWIN, RALPH, *Hong Kong Escape*, London, 1953.

——— *Passport to Eternity*, London, 1956.

GUEST, FREDDIE, *Escape from the Bloodied Sun*, London, 1956.

HAN, EMILY, *China to Me*, Philadelphia, 1949.

——— *Hong Kong Holiday*, New York, 1946.

HAMILTON, G. C., *The Sinking of the* Lisbon Maru, Hong Kong, 1966.

HARROP, PHYLLIS R., *Hong Kong Incident*, London, 1943.

KEY, M. F., *Hong Kong: before, during and after the War*, Kapunda, 1945.

LAN, ALICE, and HU, BETTY, *We flee from Hong Kong*, New York, 1944.

LI SHU-FAN, *Hong Kong Surgeon*, New York, 1964.

LIANG YEN (Briggs, Mrs. Walter), *The House of the Golden Dragon*, London, 1961.

MARSMAN, J. H., *I escaped from Hong Kong*, New York, 1942.

MARTIN, G. P. DE, *Told in the Dark*, Hong Kong, 1946.

Nolan, Liam, *Small Man of Nanataki*, London, 1966.

Norman, J., *How to cure drug addicts*, London, 1971.

Priestwood, Gwen, *Through Japanese Barbed Wire*, London, 1943.

Proulx, B. A., *Underground from Hong Kong*, New York, 1943.

Ryan, Revd. Fr. T. F., *Jesuits under Fire in the Siege of Hong Kong, 1941*, London, 1944.

Sewell, W. G., *Strange Harmony*, London, 1948.

Smedley, A., *Battle Hymn of China*, London, 1944.

Stokes Gwenneth, *Queen's College, 1862–1962*, Hong Kong, 1962.

The Taipo Rural Home and Orphanage, *Report for 1945 (1941–6)*, Hong Kong, 1945.

Ward, R. S., *Asia for the Asiatics? The Techniques of Japanese Occupation*, Chicago, 1945.

——— *Hong Kong under Japanese Occupation*, Washington, 1943.

Zia, I. D., *The Unforgettable Epoch 1937–1945*, Hong Kong, 1969.

RECORDED INTERVIEWS

Bishop Hall, Dr. J. R. Jones, Dr. B. M. Kotewall, Professor W. G. Sewell, Revd. George She (Zimmern), Dept. of History (H.K.U. Oral History Collection.)

Radio Hong Kong – 'Time to Remember', Series conducted by Miss Wendy Barnes.

Letters, completed questionnaires and statements: Endacott MSS. file – 'Personal Statements'.

ARTICLES

Education Dept., Hong Kong 'The Effects of the War Years on School Children in Hong Kong'. *Oversea Education*, vol. 19, no. 3, pp. 692–4.

Forster, L., 'Education in the Hong Kong Internment Camp', *Oversea Education*, vol. 17, no. 2 (1946), pp. 252–4.

Harcourt, Sir Cecil, 'The Military Administration of

Harcourt, Sir Cecil, 'The Military Administration of Hong Kong', *Royal Central Asian Journal*, vol. 34 (1947), pp. 7–18.

HEASMAN, K. J., 'Japanese Financial and Economic Measures in Hong Kong', *Hong Kong University Journal of the Economics Society*, 1967, pp. 65–92.

LEIPER, G. A. (Nijuhachi), 'Some recollections of Duress Banking', *Curry and Rice* (Chartered Bank Staff Magazine), vol. 17, nos. 3 & 4 – vol. 18 (nos. 1–4), 1964–8.

McDOUALL, J. C., 'Impressions of Social Services in Hong Kong, Aug. 1945–May 1946', *Oversea Education*, vol. 18, no. 3 (1947), pp. 510–17.

SHEARER, G. P., 'Stanley, Hong Kong, the first three years', *Royal Engineers' Journal*, vol. 52 (1938), pp. 161–74.

South China Morning Post, 'Extracts from the Diary of a Hong Kong Volunteer', 1962 –

South China Morning Post, 30 May 1966 – 20 March 1967, 'Time to Remember', Series II (a series of 43 articles by a special correspondent).

IV. CONTEMPORARY NEWSPAPERS AND PERIODICALS (ENGLISH AND CHINESE)

China Weekly Review, 1937–41.

Hongkong News, 31 December 1941–17 August 1945.

Hua Shang Pao, issue for 19 February 1946.
'Statistics of allied personnel saved by the East River Section.'

Keesing's Contemporary Archives, 1937–40.

North China Herald, 1937–41.

South China Morning Post, 1 January 1939–25 December 1941, 31 August 1945–31 December 1948.

The Volunteer, Journal of the Hong Kong Regiment (The Volunteers), 1950–

Wah Kiu Yat Pao, June 1942–August 1945.

Collection of newspaper cuttings, 1945–7 relating to the 'Japanese Occupation of Hong Kong', compiled by G. A. Leiper.

AVEN, MARC, 'Stand to the East', *Asia*, January-December 1939, pp. 15–17.

Babcock, C.S., 'Hong Kong Campaigns. The conquest of Hong Kong from the Japanese point of view', *Cavalry Journal*, vol. LII, no. 4 (1943), pp. 26–31.

'British Humour Indomitable in Adversity', *Illustrated London News*, 24 November 1945, pp. 568–9.

'The Canton-Hongkong Guerrillas and Allied Strategy in the Pacific', *Amerasia*, vol. 8, pt. 14, (July, 1944), pp. 215–20.

'Food and War in Hong Kong', *Nature*, vol. 157, 16 March 1946, pp. 343–4.

'Hong Kong's Heroic Resistance in the face of Heavy Odds', *I.L.N.*, 3 January 1942.

Chen, J., 'A new Hong Kong', *Fortnightly Review*, n.s. No. 967, July 1947, pp. 9–15.

Hauser, Ernest O., 'Hong Kong is still alive', *Asia*, January–December 1939, pp. 384–6.

Simich, F., '1940: Paradox in Hong Kong', *National Geographical Magazine*, April 1940, pp. 531–8.

Sinimite, 'The Future of Hong Kong', *National Review*, vol. 128, no. 768, February 1948, pp. 148–56.

Woddis, H. C. K., 'Hong Kong and the East River Company', *Eastern World*, vol. 3, no. 7 (July, 1949), pp. 10–11.

V. SECONDARY WORKS ON HONG KONG

BOOKS

Carew, Tim (J. M.), *The Fall of Hong Kong*, London, 1960.

——— *Hostages to Fortune*, London, 1971.

Chiu, T. N. *The Port of Hong Kong*, Hong Kong, 1974.

Collins, Sir Charles, *Public administration in Hong Kong*, London, 1949.

Collis, M., *Wayfoong: The Hongkong and Shanghai Banking Corporation*, London, 1965.

Endacott, G. B., *Government and the People in Hong Kong 1841–1962; a constitutional history*, Hong Kong, 1964.

——— *A History of Hong Kong*, rev. ed., Hong Kong, 1973.

Harrison, B. (ed.), *The First Fifty Years*, Hong Kong, 1962.

Kenrick, D. M., *Price Control and its Practice in Hong Kong*, Hong Kong, 1954.

Luff, J., *The Hidden Years*, Hong Kong, 1967.
——— *Hong Kong Cavalcade*, Hong Kong, 1968.
McKay, R., *John Leonard Wilson: confessor for the faith*, London, 1973.
Morgan, W. P., *Triad Societies in Hong Kong*, Hong Kong, 1960.
Pope-Hennessy, J., *Half-crown Colony*, London, 1969.
Vaid, K., *The Overseas Indian Community in Hong Kong*, Hong Kong, 1972.

ARTICLES

'A presentation on the Fall of Hong Kong', C.B.F. Study Day, 22 October 1964.
Birch, A., 'Confinement and Constitutional Conflict in Occupied Hong Kong 1941–45', *Hong Kong Law Journal*, vol. 3, no. 3, September 1973, pp. 293–318.
——— 'Control of Prices and Commodities in Hong Kong', *H.K.L.J.*, vol. 4, no. 2, May 1974, pp. 133–50.
Chan, Kit-ching, 'The Hong Kong Question during the Pacific War, 1941–5', *Journal of Imperial and Commonwealth History*, vol. 2, no. 1 (1973), pp. 56–78.
Harris, P., 'Why Churchill swopped Hong Kong for Poland', *Hongkong Standard*, 24 February 1974.
Hayes, J. W., 'The Japanese Occupation and the New Territories', *S.C.M.P.*, 15 December 1967.
Lethbridge, H. J. 'Hong Kong under Japanese Occupation', in Agassi, J., and Jarvie, I. C., *A Society in Transition*, London, 1969.
Macrae, Kate, 'Hong Kong remembers Liberation', *Hongkong Standard*, 27 August 1973.

VI. JAPANESE ACCOUNTS (in Chinese)

GOVERNOR'S OFFICE

香港新生一週年紀念日總督告全港民衆
(The Governor's announcement to the people of Hong Kong on the first anniversary of new life in Hong Kong)

Hsin-tung-ya Journal 新東亞
2:1 (January 1943), p. 11.

INFORMATION DEPARTMENT OF THE GOVERNOR'S OFFICE OF THE OCCUPIED TERRITORY OF HONG KONG
新香港的建設
(The construction of new Hong Kong)
Hsin Hsiang-kang ti chien-she
(Hong Kong, 1942.)

FUJI KONGO 籐井金吾
LAO YU 魯愚 Tr.
香港邊境衝破記
(Breaking through the border of Hong Kong)
Hsin-tung-ya Journal 新東亞
1:1 (August 1942), p. 58.

HOTTO YOSHI AKI 掘田吉明
CH'EN T'IEN-FU 陳添富 Tr.
香港攻略經過
(An account of the invasion of Hong Kong)
Hsin-tung-ya Journal 新東亞
1:5 (December 1942), pp. 22–5.

ISHITA ICHIRO 石田一郎
HO PING-JAN 何秉仁 Tr.
香港攻略戰
(The strategy of the invasion of Hong Kong)
Hsin-tung-ya Journal 新東亞
1:1 (August 1942), pp. 86–90.

MATSUNAMI KOZABURO 松波幸三郎
HUNG HUNG 洪虹 Tr.
在九龍
(At Kowloon)
Hsin-tung-ya Journal 新東亞
1:1 (August 1942), pp. 91–2.

MISHIMA BUNPEI 三島文平
HSIN JIH-SU 沈逸需 tr.
赤柱幽居記
(My retired life at Stanley)

Hsin-tung-ya Journal 新東亞
1:1 (August 1942), pp. 93–4, 100.

OZAWA SOICHI 大宅壯一
LU FANG 呂芳
諜都香港之行
(My trip to the spy city – Hong Kong)

Shih-chieh Chien-wang 世界展望
No. 1 (March 1938), pp. 30–2.

鮫島盛隆 (SAMEJIMA, MORITAKA, 1897–)
香港回想記

Hong Kong reminiscençes
香港基督敎文藝出版社 1971

CHINESE ACCOUNTS

ANONYMOUS
半年來的香港
'Pan-nien-lai ti Hsiang-chiang'

Hsin-tung-ya Yüeh-k'an 新東亞月刋
Hong Kong, 1942.

ANONYMOUS
勝利之初在香港
(Hong Kong immediately after the victory, i.e. Japanese surrender)

Ta-jen Journal 大人 No. 16
(August 1971), pp. 23–4.

CH'EN T'SE 陳策 (Chan Chak, Sir Andrew)
協助香港抗戰及卒英軍突圍經過總報告
(A report on Chinese aid to the British armies during the Japanese War).

Chang-ku Yüeh-k'an, No. 4, December 1971, pp. 14–21.
掌故月刊 第四期 1971 年 12 月 頁 14–21.

CHANG-KU YÜEH-K'AN
see Journal of Historical Records
掌故月刊

CH'EN CHI-T'ANG 陳濟棠
香港脫險記
(The great escape from Hong Kong)

Kuang-tung Wen-hsien Chi-k'an
廣東文獻季刊第一卷第三期
1971 年 10 月 頁 60–65

CHIEN YU-WEN 簡又文
策叔突圍詳記
The great escape of Chan Chak

Chang-ku Yüeh-k'an 掌故月刊,
No. 4, December 1971, pp. 22–7.

CH'IU CHIANG-HAI 邱江海
戰火下的香港和我
(Hong Kong and I during the Japanese occupation)
The Seventies 七十年代月刊 第九期 1970 年 10 月 頁 4–7

FAN CHI-PING 范基平
香港之戰回憶錄
(A reminiscence of the Japanese invasion)

Ta-jen Journal 大人, No. 8,
December 1970, pp. 2–10.

FANG TS'AO 芳草
香港戰後景象瑣憶
(A reminiscence of Hong Kong after the War)
Hsin-tung-ya Journal 新東亞
1:5 (December 1942).

HSÜ PO-WEN 徐波文
香港新生一週年大東亞戰爭週年本港紀念過程特寫
(A special feature on the account of the celebration of the first anniversary of new life in Hong Kong)
Hsin-tung-ya Journal 新東亞
2:1 (January 1943), pp. 4–10.

HUANG CHU-KO 黃竹歌
大東亞建設與香港之地位
(The development of new East Asia and the role of Hong Kong)
Hsin-tung-ya Journal 新東亞
1:5 (December 1942), pp. 26–33.

HUANG LIEN 黃連
新香港的透視
(A perspective of new Hong Kong)
Hsin-tung-ya Journal 新東亞
1:1 (August 1942), pp. 64–70.

I CHI 一知
徐亨吉人天相
(Heavenly-blessed Hsü-heng)
Chang-ku Yüeh-k'an 掌故月刊
No. 4 (December 1971), pp. 28–9.

I MING 以明
新香港市政的檢閱
(A review of the urban policy of new Hong Kong)
Hsin-tung-ya Journal 新東亞
1:5 (December 1942), pp. 35–8.

JOURNAL OF HISTORICAL RECORDS (Special number).
掌故月刊編輯
No. 4 (December 1971), pp. 2–13:

ANONYMOUS
香港戰役始末
(The war in Hong Kong – from beginning to end)
Chang-ku Yüeh-k'an 掌故月刊
第四期 1971 年 12 月 頁 2–8

ANONYMOUS
[香港之戰]大事日誌
(A daily record of important events during the war in Hong Kong)
Chang-ku Yüeh-k'an 掌故月刊
第四期 1971 年 12 月 頁 8–10

ANONYMOUS
日據時代香港總督磯谷廉介
(The Governor of Hong Kong during the Japanese occupation – chi-ku nien-chieh [Rensuke Isogai])
Chang-ku Yüeh-k'an 掌故月刊
第四期 1971 年12 月 頁 11–12

ANONYMOUS
日軍香港攻略作戰經過圖
(The chart on Japanese strategy during the invasion of Hong Kong)
Chang-ku Yüeh-k'an 掌故月刊
第四期 1971 年 12 月 頁 13.

K'O JEN 戈仁
香港戰時生活回味錄
(A reminiscence of life during the Japanese occupation in Hong Kong)
Hsin-tung-ya Journal 新東亞
1:5 (December 1942), pp. 89–95.

CHUNG-KUO KUO-MIN TANG CHU KANG AO TSUNG CHIH PU
中國國民黨駐港澳總支部
(Kuomintang – Hong Kong & Macao Branch)
(An album commemorating the patriots of Hong Kong and Macao)
港澳抗戰殉國烈士紀念冊 Hong Kong 1946.

LAI CHUN KIT (LI, CHIN-WEI)
A Centenary History of Hong Kong (in Chinese)
香港百年史 *Hsiang-kang pai-nien shih.*
Hong Kong, 1948.

LO SSU-WEI 羅四維
新香港之觀感
(My impression of new Hong Kong)
Hsin-tung-ya Journal 新東亞
1:5 (December 1942), p. 34.

LO YÜAN-YU 羅玄囿
香港戰時生活回憶
(A reminiscence of life during the Japanese occupation in Hong Kong)
Hsin-tung-ya Journal 新東亞
1:5 (December 1942), pp. 79–83.

LU KAN-CHIH 盧幹之
(Hong Kong's painful past)
香港的沉痛往事
Chang-ku Yüeh-k'an, No. 6 (February 1972), pp. 56–7.
掌故月刊 第六期 1972 年 2 月 頁 56–57.

MA KUO-LIANG 馬國亮
八一三在香港
(Hong Kong on 13th August 1937)
Ta-feng Journal (大風)
No. 2 (March 1938), pp. 48–9.

PU-PING SHAN-JEN 不平山人
香港淪陷回憶錄
(A reminiscence of Hong Kong during the Japanese occupation)
Hsiang-kang lun hsien hui i lu
Hong Kong, 1971.

TANG HAI 唐海
香港淪陷記一十八天的戰爭
(The fall of Hong Kong – eighteen days' war)
Hsiang-kang lun hsien chi
Shanghai, 1946.

T'AO HSI-SHENG 陶希聖
九龍歷險記
(My adventure in Kowloon)
潮流與點滴
An excerpt from Ch'ao-liu yü Tien-ti
Chang-ku Yüeh-k'an 掌故月刊
No. 4 (December 1971), pp. 66–72.

T'AO WEI 陶惠
去年今日 香港攻略戰身歷記
(My personal experience of the invasion)
Hsin-tung-ya Journal
1:5 (December 1942), pp. 58–68. 新東亞

TI CH'EN 滌塵
回憶中的一年
(A year in my memory)
Hsin-tung-ya Journal 新東亞
1:5 (December 1942), pp. 69–76.

YAU KANG HOI 邱江海
艱苦的行程
(A Tough Journey)
Hong Kong, 1971.

Yu Shu-heng 喻叔衡

胎死腹中的香港市政府一記淪陷期中一秘聞
(A secret during the occupation – the abortive urban administration)

Ta-hua Journal 大華
No. 2 (March 1966), pp. 3–4.

Yun Yen 雲烟

日本侵攻香港時之忠義慈善會
(The loyal and benevolent society during the Japanese occupation)

Chang-ku Yüeh-k'an 掌故月刊
第十一期 1972 年 7 月 頁 50–51.

INDEX

G. B. Endacott